RAPE

RAPE

Edited by

Sylvana Tomaselli
and Roy Porter

Basil Blackwell

First published 1986

Basil Blackwell Ltd
108 Cowley Road, Oxford OX4 1JF, UK

Basil Blackwell Inc.
432 Park Avenue South, Suite 1503
New York, NY 10016, USA

British Library Cataloguing in Publication Data

Rape.
  1. Rape
  I. Tomaselli, Sylvana   II. Porter, Roy, *1946—*
  364.1'532   HV6558

  ISBN 0-631-13748-3

Library of Congress Cataloging in Publication Data
Rape.

  Bibliography: p.
  1. Rape. I. Tomaselli, Sylvana II Porter, Roy, 1946—
  HV6558.R3 1986   364.1'532   86—6148
  ISBN 0-631-13748-3

Typeset by Pioneer, Perthshire
Printed in Great Britain by
Page Bros (Norwich), Ltd

Contents

Contents

The Contributors

NORMAN BRYSON is a Fellow of King's College, Cambridge. He is the author of three books on painting — *Word and Image: French Painting of the Ancien Régime, Vision and Painting: the Logic of the Gaze,* and *Tradition and Desire: from David to Delacroix* — and is General Editor of *Cambridge Essays in New Art History and Criticism.*

GERARD A. DIZINNO is currently Assistant Professor of Psychology at the University of Albuquerque, and Visiting Professor of Psychology at the University of New Mexico, Albuquerque, New Mexico. He has carried out research on animal communications and human sociobiology, in particular chemical and auditory communication in rodents, and evolutionary factors which may help to explain human male homosexual behaviour and the behaviour of rapists and rape victims.

JOHN FORRESTER is Lecturer in the History and Philosophy of Science at the University of Cambridge. He is the author of *Language and the Origins of Psychoanalysis* (1980), and numerous articles on the history and philosophy of psychoanalysis. In collaboration with Sylvana Tomaselli, he has translated, prepared and annotated the English edition of Jacques Lacan, *Seminar I; Freud's Writings on Technique* and *Seminar II: The Ego in Freud's Theory and in Psychoanalytic Technique* (Cambridge University Press and Norton, 1987).

CHRISTOPHER FRAYLING read history at Cambridge University and wrote his PhD thesis on Jean-Jacques Rousseau. Since then he has published widely on aspects of modern popular culture, including books on 'The Vampyre' and 'Spaghetti Westerns'. He is Professor of Cultural History at the Royal College of Art.

ROSS HARRISON studied philosophy at the universities of Oxford and Cambridge before becoming first a Research Fellow of St John's College Cambridge and then a Lecturer at the University of Bristol. Since 1975 he has been a University Lecturer at Cambridge and a Fellow of King's College. His central interests are in metaphysics and political philosophy. He has written two books, *On What There Must Be* (Oxford University Press, 1974) and *Bentham* (Routledge & Kegan Paul, 1983) as well as editing the collection *Rational Action* (Cambridge University Press, 1979).

ROY PORTER read history at Christ's College, Cambridge. His PhD was published in revised form in 1977 as *The Making of Geology*. He has written articles on the history of geology and on eighteenth century science in its social locations. He has edited *Images of the Earth* (with L. Jordanova), *The Ferment of Knowledge: Studies in the Historiography of Eighteenth-Century Science* (with G. S. Rousseau), *A Dictionary of the History of Science* (with W. F. Bynum and E. J. Browne) and *The Enlightenment in National Context* (with M. Teich). He is now working on a history of psychiatry in Britain, and is also researching the history of quack doctors and the history of medicine from the point of view of the patient. He lectures on the social history of medicine at the Wellcome Institute for the History of Medicine, London.

PEGGY REEVES SANDAY is Professor of Anthropology at the University of Pennsylvania. She is the editor of *Anthropology and the Public Interest* (Academic Press, 1976) and the author of *Female Power and Male Dominance: On the Origins of Sexual Inequality* (Cambridge University Press, 1981). She is also author of *Divine Hunger: Cannibalism as a Cultural System* (Cambridge University Press, 1986). Her article 'The socio-cultural context of rape', which appeared in *Journal of Social Issues*, 37 (1981), was reprinted in *New Society* in September 1982. At present she is completing a book on sexual meanings and sexual expression on an American college campus. For the past several years she has been conducting a study of gender meanings and world view in West Sumatra, Indonesia.

JENNIFER TEMKIN is a graduate of the London School of Economics and a barrister. She is a Lecturer in Law at the LSE and has been a Visiting Professor of Law at the University of Toronto. She is also a member of the Society of Public Teachers of Law Criminal Law Reform Sub-Committee, the Editorial Advisory Group of the *Howard Journal of Criminal Justice* and the Editorial Board of the *Journal of Criminal Law*. Her work on sexual assault has been published in a number of legal journals.

NANCY WILMSEN THORNHILL is a PhD candidate in anthropology at the University of New Mexico. She received her BS and MS degrees in anthropology from the University of New Mexico. Her general research interests include the evolution of human social behaviour. Her dissertation addresses the evolution of cross-cultural variation in mating and marriage rules. She is the mother of two children.

RANDY THORNHILL is Associate Professor of Biology at the University of New Mexico. He received his BS and MS degrees in entomology from Auburn University and his PhD degree in zoology from the University of Michigan. His research interests include the evolution of animal mating systems and human social behaviour. This research has led to a number of articles dealing with insect and human behaviour and a book (co-authored with John Alcock), *The Evolution of Insect Mating Systems* (Harvard University Press, 1983).

SYLVANA TOMASELLI is a Research Fellow of Newnham College, Cambridge and an intellectual historian working predominantly on the seventeenth and eighteenth centuries. She has written on mind—body dualism and the history of women and is currently working on the Enlightenment's conception of personhood. She has translated Jacques Lacan's *Seminar II: The Ego in Freud's Theory and in Psychoanalytic Technique*, edited by Jacques-Alain Miller, prepared and annotated by John Forrester (Cambridge University Press and Norton, 1987).

FROMA I. ZEITLIN is Professor of Classics at Princeton University. She has published essays on Greek tragedy and comedy, ancient fiction, and myth and cult, and a book entitled *Under the Sign of the Shield; Semiotics and Aeschylus' Seven Against Thebes* (Ateneo, 1982). Her most recent piece, 'Playing the Other: Theater, Theatricality and the Feminine', appeared in *Representations*, ii (1985). She is currently working on a book about Greek notions of eros and sexuality.

Acknowledgements

The editors are grateful to the staff of Basil Blackwell for their efficiency and friendliness in the production of this volume. René Olivieri's initial enthusiasm, and the assistance later of Julia Mosse, Sue Banfield and Gillian Bromley, have been particularly appreciated. We are also grateful to Elaine J. Leek for her copy editing.

Preface

As we write this book, the rape crisis worsens all around us, almost by the day it seems. Is it not time for actions rather than words? For actions certainly, but also for words — if those words are going to help our understanding of this appalling crime and, by understanding it, help to end it.

Much has been said about rape already, of course, particularly in the past decade by feminist writers and activists. Susan Brownmiller's book, *Against Our Will: Men, Women and Rape,* proved a turning-point by focusing public attention upon rape, by demonstrating the seriousness of the problem and by demanding a rethink of the crime. After reading her book, and others like it, no one can continue to see rape as an isolated incident, simply as one man — a 'sex maniac' — sexually assaulting one woman.

But, over the past few years, as we read the relevant literature, we felt dissatisfied. In many books and articles we found outrage and anger, but no analysis of what was going so wrong with men in a man's world as to produce such abominations against women. Elsewhere, we found slogans: excellent for raising consciousness, but less effective at filling that consciousness with the facts, ideas, outlooks and arguments for doing something about it in a world all too ready to dismiss the voice of protest unheeded. Above all, so many questions are still unanswered; so many gaps remain in our basic knowledge. How does the law treat rape in different countries? Is rape more or less of a problem now than it was a hundred or five hundred years ago? What can scientists tell us about why rapes happen? What have anthropologists to say about why men rape in other societies? Did Freud and the psychoanalysts have any insights into it? All too often what other disciplines had to say about rape lay hidden in obscure periodicals, difficult to obtain.

Most of all, we found ourselves wanting to answer back, to pose searching questions to all those who offered sweeping theories about rape or who suggested neat and tidy solutions. Out of this desire to find out, to rethink, this book was born. It is our attempt to re-examine rape from a number of different viewpoints, and to put them all together, so that rape can be seen in the broadest perspective.

Each chapter considers rape from the vantage point of a specific discipline or school of thought: law, philosophy, psychoanalysis, biology, the study of classical myths, art criticism and history. Although each author has remained faithful to the methods and perspectives of his or her discipline and is contributing to his or her own field in such a way that each chapter can be read on its own, each has also been written with a wider readership in mind and with a view to future cross-fertilization. Indeed, the aim of the book, in so far as its structure is concerned, is to bring together a number of existing specialized debates on the subject (and this applies particularly to the disciplines of law, anthropology and biology) and to encourage others (especially those working on psychoanalysis, philosophy, classics and art criticism) to turn their attention to rape and open up new outlooks in their area.

The overall intent is not to produce any one or even a number of pronouncements on the nature of rape, but to provide the backdrop for further research and analysis. Not least amongst these would be a much-needed comprehensive history of rape. It was the absence of such a history that led us to think of editing the present collection. For in considering how such a history would best be written, we realized that history on its own could not answer many of the questions we would have liked to have addressed to it. It could not, for instance, speak on its own to the nature/nurture debate, so pervasive in contemporary assessments of the causes of rape. This issue called for anthropology and biology at the very least. Moreover, quite apart from the questions that history would have left unanswered, we recognized that such a project could not possibly run the risk of not benefiting from whatever insights other disciplines could offer. Finally, we had reason to believe that the need we felt as historians for the resources of other areas of scholarship might likewise be experienced in other academic quarters.

To have embarked on this projected 'total' history of rape without a preliminary assessment of the state of the debate would have been, at least as far as we were concerned, premature. This book therefore proposes to lay part of the foundation for such a wide-ranging cultural analysis. We say 'part' because a great deal remains to be done even at this initial stage before the implications of such an interdisciplinary outlook can be drawn out and put to use.

1

Introduction

SYLVANA TOMASELLI

Imagine a world in which women had no cause to fear rape, be it at home, on the way back from work or anywhere at all. Better still, imagine a world in which the word 'rape' no longer served any function, there being nothing for it to refer to; a world in which to speak of 'safe' areas or streets, towns or cities, was to speak in a mode comprehensible to none but a few historians. Imagine a world, then, in which to feel safe no longer made any sense to women, the very memory of any threat having faded away. What sort of world would this have to be? Could it, in fact, be not just idle fantasy, but a vision of a possible future for us?

A glance at a newspaper should convince anyone that these are questions we must attend to.[1] That they are difficult questions will require little persuasion, as a short reflection on our culture, past and present, cannot but reveal what very mixed and confused assistance it provides when we attempt to answer them. Apart from the all too many silences, responses to rape range from the ambiguous to the sardonic, from the sympathetic to the dispassionate. Moreover, when we come to take stock, as I shall try to do in this introduction, of the beliefs which are held about the nature of rape, these prove to be for the most part contradictory and bewildering. Unravelling the tangle of pronouncements on rape serves only to highlight the great complexity of the issue, as not only is the shape of a rapeless future difficult to make out from the vantage point of our present circumstances, but the very nature of the difficulty seems at times almost intangible.

To begin with there is the problem of determining at the outset whether we are engaged in something like science fiction or whether, in fact, we are embarking on a feasible, albeit undeniably formidable, project. There is as yet no final word on the possibility or impossibility of a world without rape. That rape is an inevitable feature of human social existence may be the tacit assumption, one which, like a refrain, will be repeatedly both challenged and returned to in this book, but we do not know it to be true. To be sure, social problems of this magnitude are never easily comprehended, much less resolved or even merely tackled. But while two millennia of theories of human nature and of social and political thought may leave us with conflicting views about the sort of world one without injustice or inequality or war would need to be, there are at least some well explored answers at hand, including, of course, the totally dismissive ones, which decry all hope as utopian. With rape, however, the question has been left open. Far from being torn, unable to choose, between competing visions of a world without rape, having to tinker with existing models or challenge pieties, we must think our own way to the end of rape, without a legacy, be it utopian or reformist, to draw from.

The absence of such a legacy is not the result of a more general silence on the relationship between the sexes within the history of Western thought. However unsatisfactorily from our present point of view, sexual mores, marriage, the family, the sexual division of labour, the question of the equality and of the difference between the sexes, have all received some attention in most political theories. Nor must rape, more specifically, be thought of as a subject no one dares to name. The fact that we have no history of rape, a fact discussed by Roy Porter in the final chapter of this volume, is more revealing of modern attitudes to rape than an indication of our forefathers' (and mothers') indifference to it. The reluctance to acknowledge the reality of rape, even to mention it, a reluctance which feminists[2] have done their utmost to combat and overcome in the past few decades, is only a relatively recent phenomenon, and one which we must, along with our other assumptions about rape, be wary of projecting back into time. For reasons which were, to be sure, fundamentally different, and more often than not diametrically opposed to those which motivate concern with the issue today, in the past rape was neither passed over in silence nor made light of. Think only of Helen, the Sabine women or Lucretia.

Of course, the significance for our culture of the existence of a great number of (maybe) myths or (maybe) stories about rape within it is not in itself a transparent or self-evident matter. What is one to make, after all, of the overwhelming presence of rape in the birthplace of our civilization, in Ancient Greece and Rome? Certainly we should hesitate before embracing what might be thought of as obvious, namely that telling, painting, or representing in any other manner a rape constitutes an unambiguous gesture of glorification or endorsement of the act.[3] Any doubt on this would be quickly dispelled by Froma Zeitlin and Norman Bryson in their respective contributions to this volume. But as they separate and interpret the many layers of meaning of some of these myths and stories, as well as of their repeated representations, be they literary or figurative, they no less demonstrate that, though not always easily decipherable, rape played a crucial role in accounts and explanations of the rise and demise of cities, of the causes of wars and of revolutions. However deplorable one might find the condition of women in those ancient times and places, and however remote these perhaps wholly symbolic treatments may have been from the real lives of men and women of that period, we need only contrast them with today's symbolic level to appreciate the importance of understanding what these myths and stories tell, and tell us now.[4]

Nor need we look so far back into our symbolic mythological or classical past to see rape considered as of such momentous consequence. For those writing with a concern for the stability and maintenance of power, rape remained a perceived threat at least until the sixteenth century. Machiavelli (1469–1527), for one, was at pains to emphasize the political danger it represented. Thus, in a chapter of *The Discourses* entitled 'How Women have brought about the Downfall of States' we find him giving the following lessons:

> First, we see how women have been the cause of many troubles, have done great harm to those who govern cities, and have caused in them many divisions . . . we read in Livy's history that the outrage done to Lucretia deprived the Tarquins of their rule, and that done to Virginia deprived the Decemviri of their power. Among the primary causes of the downfall of tyrants, Aristotle puts the injuries they do on account of women, whether by rape, violation or the breaking up of marriages . . . absolute princes and rulers of republics should not treat such matters as of small moment, but should bear in mind the disorders such events may occasion and look to the matter in good time, so that the remedy applied may not be accompanied by damage done to, or revolts against, their state or their republic.[5]

Here was advice which princes of the state and church seem to have heeded long before the Renaissance, for throughout the Middle Ages the suppression of rape and abduction constituted one of the pragmatic concerns of secular and ecclesiastical authorities as both sought to control the high level of violence within their society. As the French historian Georges Duby has remarked, rape is ubiquitous in the small number of ninth century texts that have come down to us.[6] *De la Répression du Rapt* [*Of the Suppression of Rape*] by Hincmar (*c*.806–82), the Archbishop of Rheims, is but one illustration of the attention the issue received in the early Middle Ages.

So, to return to our opening questions, whatever it is that makes for the difficulty of imagining a rapeless future cannot lie in the fact that our past has always been oblivious to rape; that it is a phenomenon, which for reasons engrained in the very fibre of our culture, we cannot, or cannot easily, deliberate on. Even the bare outline of a history of rape would suggest that such was not the case. Nor must a reading of history as the record and expression of a predominantly male outlook lead us to be dismissive. Once again we need only keep Machiavelli's recommendation in mind when reviewing twentieth century equivalents to see the very marked difference with which rape is considered. How many modern day politicians or their advisers make the suppression of rape part of their campaigning promises? And why, incidentally, is not the issue of rape one way of capturing women's votes?

We should furthermore refrain from hastily assuming, by blurring all historical distinctions, that the past was one homogeneous and unchanging tale, a long monotone of patriarchy and, as it has been argued, its henchman, rape.[7] Such reductive analyses of Western civilization presume that rape, no less than sex, is a constant, not a variable, in our culture and that attitudes towards both remained untouched by the passage of time and what amounted to total social transformations — a view seriously put to the test by Porter (chapter 10).[8] As he argues, we should not, in view of the evidence, regard rape as the theme that runs through our sexual history. This, it should be noted, by no means leads to an idealization of the past. To say that rape was not the norm in all Western history and that the subject was seriously addressed by some thinkers is neither to propose the past as model nor to forget that the nature of their interest in rape was likely to have been entirely different from what we would deem acceptable today.

Yet the nature of that interest is none the less worthy of notice today. Men may well have been concerned with preventing rape only in so far as they wished to protect their property — the chastity of their wives, the virginity of their daughters — quell feuds or reduce violence. But apart from the fact that these are in themselves differing reasons for acting — reflecting the difference between being subject to laws not of one's own making, and legislating them — they are, none the less, reasons for *acting*. It is essential, if we are to try to think about the nature of a rapeless future to distinguish between assessing social arrangements with regard to how far they do or do not foster, deter or eradicate rape, and assessing the motivation of the agents that are seen to sustain or create them. For as long as we maintain the notion that there are gender differences or, more minimally, for as long as we believe that some people — of either sex[9] — are vulnerable to being raped and others not, we will have to consider what motive or set of motives the latter do or could have to cooperate in a system that would ensure the protection of the former.[10] In other words, we cannot expect men and women, be they potential rapists, non-rapists, potential rape victims or legislators, whomsoever these turn out to be, to act except for their own, and quite obviously very different, reasons.

The feasibility of a society in which rape would be a thing of the past hangs on our finding motives for us all to bring about and maintain such a society. The more suspicious and distrustful one is about men or the masculine principle, the more one will have to discover what such motivation could prove to be in the future, unless, of course, one either is resigned to the fact of rape or has discovered and chosen to exercise the means to eliminate the masculine (or the feminine) from our culture.

Hence, in so far as we are committed to understanding the nature of the problem of rape and to tackling it as best we can in the here and now, or in a future which we can causally affect, such motivation and attitudes as prevailed in the past, and their history, are of no uncertain relevance to us. It may indeed be the case that in a world in which women are treated principally as means rather than ends, as objects rather than subjects, or in which they are primarily members of households deriving their status only through their membership of such social units rather than as individual political beings in their own right, men protected them from theft and violence, from abduction and rape for reasons of their own self interests. If this holds true we must be open to the possibility that such incentives might no longer hold good in a world in which the position of women is being radically changed.

The relative modern silence, or if you wish the relative modern 'male' silence, on rape may point in this direction. For having said that we must resist both the temptation of seeing ourselves, men and women, in the late twentieth century as emerging out of a timeless indifference to rape, and that of discarding the past as irrelevant, it remains none the less true that in the past few hundred years rape has faded from the political agenda. Coinciding with the swelling number of theories for either the gradual or revolutionary transformation of society is the relative disappearance of reflections on rape. The wealth of discussion about social, economic and even moral reform or revolution has not been matched by comparable proposals for the end of rape. Only recently has the issue been brought back into public debate, and this strictly owing to successful efforts by the feminism of the seventies and early eighties, a feminism which unlike its predecessors made rape the prime focus of its campaign. What accounts for this renewed (though still far from widespread) concern with rape is, in part, the increased incidence of the crime, particularly in the United States, and it may be, therefore, that the receding of rape from social and political discussion was in keeping with a relatively low incidence of rape in that period, as the evidence which Porter puts forward would suggest. To this we might also add the consideration that the more radical and reductive social theories since the Enlightenment have been, the more rape, and all issues pertaining to the relationship between the sexes, have been swallowed up, so to speak, within a wider critique, the solution to each problem being deferred to the post-revolutionary period. Moreover, the less committed such theories are to sexual difference, the less they can countenance the likelihood that rape has to be faced on its own.[11] But if radicalism has not favoured sustained consideration on rape, ameliorative theories have also contributed to the silence on rape, albeit in a rather distinct fashion.

Consider, for a moment, one of the few theories to give any thought to the end of rape and, more generally, the end of violence against women, that of the Scottish and French Enlightenment thinkers. These eighteenth century critics took it as given that the advent of society and the subsequent development of civilization gradually reversed what they conceived to be the unsurpassed brutality of the state of nature. Prior to what they called the gradual rise of manners and politeness, women had lived under the unmitigated tyranny of men, as these took every possible advantage of their superior physical strength. This was a picture of the state of nature which had already been made familiar in the seventeenth century, if only by Thomas Hobbes (1588—1679) in his *Leviathan*. He had deployed it, however, to describe the relations between men, not between the sexes, outside of civil society. In his account, the institution of government, and hence of a policing agent safeguarding the lives and liberties of individuals, was presented as the means of putting an end to violence and fear between men. When, a century later, there appeared theories that had women specifically in mind, it was the civilizing process itself which was considered to be the guarantor of their safety. What protected them was not, as in Hobbesian society, the fear that men lived under of institutional retribution, of the 'magistrate's sword', if they contemplated defying the law. Women's security lay instead in the fact that men were genuinely transformed, not to say metamorphosed, by socialization.

According to the Enlightenment's view of the history of the species, one woman had been as good as another for pre-social man, and her opinion of him a matter of complete indifference. There was no restraint, therefore, on the manner in which he treated her, no inducement to soften his ways with her. He simply took what he wanted. Civilized man, on the contrary, 'learnt' to single out the object of his desire; not any woman would do, he came to desire a very specific one. But, most importantly from the woman's point of view, and what distinguishes this theory of civilization from that caricatured by Susan Griffin, for instance, he sought to be no less specifically desired in his turn. He wanted his chosen woman to desire him and behaved accordingly. This, I hasten to add, never entailed the notion that what women want is to be raped. That fantasy is conspicuous by its absence in what was, after all, the age of the Marquis de Sade (1740—1814). No, what women wanted, on this view, was to be treated with decorum and politeness; they wanted to be wooed. It was an essential part of this account of the growth of culture that women came to be pleased where previously they had been forced. To please, men had had to become pleasing. Threat, therefore, gave way to plea, blows to language, rape to seduction. The history of civilization thus became the history of seduction.[12]

That a movement which effectively wrote rape out of history should be of no immediate use to us now is a point that scarcely needs to be made; but in helping us to isolate an aspect of the contradiction which we face today, the result of this foray into the eighteenth century theory of seduction will not have been wholly negative, nor purely academic. To Enlightenment thinkers, our age would have appeared anomalous, indeed even theoretically impossible, and our questions about the feasibility of a rapeless future no more conceivable given some of the salient facts of our circumstances. For whatever misgivings such thinkers had about the progress of civilization, they never doubted that the condition of women would gradually improve. In fact, the belief that the level of civility any nation had reached could best be gauged by the manner in which women were treated within it is the high-water mark of Enlightenment theories of civilization. This was a measure which they expected to yield an unequivocal reading and not, as when applied to our society, two radically opposed ones. Men and women were either living in a state of barbarism or they were not. The Hobbesian state of nature could not, by definition, subsist in civil society. Our current situation, i.e., one in which, despite all the real gains women have made in the past two centuries, culminating in their admission, however begrudgingly, into the body politic, they still live in fear and have increasingly more, rather than less, reason to do so, constitutes a phenomenon which an Enlightenment framework simply cannot accommodate. Whether any related or derivative theory of social progress can do so is of course what is partly at issue today.

Returning once again to our original questions, it would seem, therefore, that another reason for our difficulty in imagining the end of rape is that it does not suffice, as we are well placed to know, to imagine a world in which women have the vote, are coming into positions of authority and power and are increasingly recognized as the equal of men.

Still, before we dismiss the Enlightenment outlook on the history of the relations between the sexes as either overly confident, merely self-serving or grossly mistaken and irresponsible, it is noteworthy that we have here at least one example in the history of Western thought of the view that rape is not an unalterable characteristic of human societies, not even of Western societies. Neither human nature in general, nor masculine nature in particular, nor any other of the *a priori* reasons that may inform our present pessimism about rape, was evoked as a set and constant limitation to the trust women could place, if not in men themselves, then in the civilizing process. For however beastly man was by nature, women could have faith in culture as it took hold of this creature who indiscriminately grabs what he wants, and fashioned him into a being who seeks to be desired.

To be sure, this view was highly theoretical, and to the degree that it was inspired by any social practice at all, it was a reflection only of the lives of a very small and privileged minority of women, belonging mostly to the aristocracy of the *Ancien Régime*. Yet even if we regard it as mere idealization or as a utopia, rather than as history of any description, it must be stressed that women are not free from rape in every utopia, certainly not in Thomas More's original *Utopia* (1478–1535). Rape endures there. Though we are not told why it should persist in this ideal community, we must infer that it is beyond the reach of social and political reorganization, at least of the kind envisioned by More. The only solace women have in Utopia is that the crime, even if only attempted, is severely punished.

At this juncture the questions with which we began might be reformulated, and we might ask ourselves whether we are similarly committed to the view that rape will be present even in the best possible future for us or whether we share something of the Enlightenment's hopefulness in thinking that rape is not only a matter for the court rooms, something to be punished by the state, but rather something for civil society to attend to and to uproot.

Reading Jennifer Temkin's contribution, 'Women, Rape and Law Reform' (chapter 2), makes one realize at once, however, that posing the problem in this manner is misleading. It is not, in fact, as if the choice lay between thinking that there is some final solution to rape and undertaking it on the one hand, and, on the other, merely leaving the institutions of justice, such as they are, to handle rape on their own. As Temkin demonstrates, the law must itself become the concern of women (and one would like, as does Ross Harrison when he notes in his contribution that the law is something for all to reflect on, to be able to add 'men') in civil society, even if all else fails and rape is here to stay. Changing the law is in itself a very vital form of action. What Temkin's chapter makes no less clear, moreover, is that whatever answer we each give to the question of what can be done about rape will entail a scrutiny of the nature and definition of rape. No discourse, least of all legal discourse, can take the meaning of 'rape' as given.

So, what is rape? It will come as no surprise that there is no straightforward answer. If there were, we would not experience such difficulty in imagining the end of rape, nor would we have had to deplore the scarcity of treatments of the issue since the Enlightenment, for we would not have felt the need to hark back to them quite so acutely. Turning our attention from the past to the present, however, what we are struck by is no longer the paucity but rather the comparative abundance of material seeking to help us understand the problem of rape. There is a considerable literature on its incidence, with suggestions for its prevention, on the reporting of the crime and the various ensuing procedures and on the law of rape and its enforcement. Nor is this an instance of an abundance of theory uninformed by, or in the absence of, practice. There are rape crisis centres where girls and women who have been raped or sexually assaulted can find the support and assistance of other women. A growing number of publications are aimed at disclosing the facts of rape, while others try to provide women with some knowledge of self-defence. The media have focused attention on the manner in which the police and indeed the media themselves deal with rape cases. The law regarding sexual offences has been and continues to be the object of study throughout the Western world. In the past twenty years or so, rape has become a public issue again. Indeed we have reached the point when otherwise well-meaning individuals have dared give the topic that most damaging of labels, 'fashionable'.

Such flippancy must blush in the face of mounting statistics that cannot but underscore the importance of coming to terms with the nature of rape. That rape is heinous no one seems to deny. That we must press ahead in the direction already set out for us in the 1970s, providing greater protection, better care and treatment for the raped, improved police and trial procedures and tougher laws, is no less a matter of general agreement, at least amongst those who have given the issue some consideration. The problem in this respect lies only in extending consciousness further, lobbying and pressing for the kind of reforms that Temkin suggests. It is only when we look at what rape is taken to signify that the consensus really founders. A survey of the discussions of rape tends to leave one baffled, as rape assumes as many shapes as there are discourses about it, a point which prefaces, and is illustrated by, Norman Bryson's juxtaposition of modern and classical representations of rape. Few subjects exhibit the extent of the disjointedness of modern Western culture and, possibly, suffer more seriously from its consequences than does rape.

Open a science magazine or periodical and you will find rape discussed in terms of biology and the struggle to procreate. Enter feminist discourse and you will discover such a view decried as male mythology and an implicit endorsement of rape.[13] Trapped within the logic and sometimes illogicality of the nature—nurture debate, rape will, depending on the point of view, be presented as either crime, vice, sin, ritual, physical violence, perversion or just another word for sex. It will be treated by some as a particular act, a single instance, an individual's breach of the law, of morality and/or decency, devoid of any wider significance than the consequences it has for the victim. Others, however, will regard such an approach as myopic, if not deluded, and will instead argue for a sociological, economic, cultural or even cosmic perspective — the rape of the world.

Extended in its use to cover all heterosexual acts or all sexual advances initiated by men, as well as the latter's treatment of nature,[14] 'rape' will also be narrowed down to a very specific meaning when appearing within legal discourse as 'unlawful sexual intercourse with a woman who at the time of the intercourse does not consent to it' (s. 1 ((1)) ((a)) of the English 1976 Act) or in sociobiology as 'forcible copulation', i.e. 'when the victim shows obvious resistance, copulation being preceded by vigorous struggle and escape behavior, and without the precopulatory courtship displays characteristic of "normal" mating between members of an established pair'.[15] *The Concise Oxford Dictionary*, for its part, begins with the poetical meaning:

> *rape* v.t., & n.1.v.t. (poet.) Take by force. 2. Commit rape on (woman); hence *rap*ist (1)n. 3. n. (poet.) Carrying off by force. 4. Forcible or fraudulent sexual intercourse esp. imposed on woman; *statutory—, sexual intercourse with girl below the age of consent; (fig.) forcible interference with institution, country, etc., violation of. (ME,f. AF *rap(er)* f. L. *rapere* seize)

It would be self-defeating to try to discriminate between true and false senses of the word or to dispose of some as mere metaphor. Each usage of the term seems to capture some relevant aspect of the problem even if none encompasses them all. To favour any particular usage or usages would therefore foreclose insights into the question of rape and force us to come down on one side or the other of the issue before we have actually settled its nature. Yet this openness has itself very definite implications. While it might allow us to be truly historical, for instance, and not pre-empt our research by giving such definition of the word as would exclude abduction from being part of what in the past might have been considered rape, it also renders this historical project potentially amorphous as it might come to cover everything from kidnapping to unhappy or pre-arranged marriage to non-consensual sexual intercourse under the threat of violence. Or to use another kind of example, it might lead us to regard all violence against women as rape, and hence place Jack the Ripper and Peter Sutcliffe, the 'Yorkshire Ripper' with rapists who are convicted as such under the present criminal law.

Such are some of the complexities that constitute the problem of rape. True, several of these are not peculiar to rape. Problems of definition attend nearly all discussions of any consequence. What makes them more taxing in this case has to do with the fact that unlike say, injustice, the topic of rape, the discursive field around it, still needs to be constituted for reasons which have been sketched above. In other words, it is not just a definition that is wanting, it is a discipline, a language, a methodology or even simply a 'classic' around which we could articulate our thoughts about the subject. As a consequence, and given that we cannot privilege any discipline or discourse as having either authority on or exclusive access to the issue, for that would clearly beg the entire question of the nature of rape, this collection of essays lets each of a number of disciplines speak for itself, and this in its own voice, following its own procedures and style of approach. This book is, therefore, interdisciplinary, not by trying to amalgamate all voices into one, but by bringing divergent and scattered debates about rape together in one volume. Each chapter thus addresses the issue in a different way. Neither the methods nor the conclusions will, therefore, be always compatible or even directly comparable. Some of the contributors are, in fact, in complete disagreement with one another. Our purpose is not to fabricate what could only be a wholly artificial consensus. On the contrary, since the dissonances are inevitable, it is the editors' view that they must be faced head-on.

Rape is a form of violence, of physical violence. To say this, though, does little to explain the horror, anger and controversy it arouses, far more than any other crime of violence. The outrage which a rape case elicits would alone seem to indicate that we take the violation involved to go beyond that of the body alone. Is it because of its violation of the person of the victim that rape is considered so horrendous a crime? Rape does indeed depersonalize, and, since in our present culture our sexual identity is regarded as constituting such an essential part of our personal identity, the offensiveness of the act is multiplied. Thinking along these lines, some writers have sought to specify the character of the violation still further by defining rape as an extreme infringement of a right to sexual freedom.[16] But do we actually conceive of sexuality in the language of rights? And even if we do or should, is rape just the denial of individuals' rights to sexual freedom or choice?

There is a powerful case being made for the view that what is wrong about rape is not simply its specific, individual occurrence, but its wider social implication in terms of the fear it instils in all women at all times. On this view, what is threatened by the phenomenon of rape is not only individual sexual choice, therefore, but the general freedom of movement and being of women. In this context rape has been described as an institution, indeed even 'a Rawlsian kind of "practice": a "form of activity specified by a system of rules which defines offices, roles, moves, penalties, defences and so on, and which give the activity its structure"'.[17] Within this conception of rape, the act of rape is but the visible and most awesome aspect of an unspoken system which keeps women in their place.

Taking up some of these threads, Ross Harrison in his contribution 'Rape — a Case Study in Political Philosophy' (chapter 3), considers what light philosophy can cast on what makes rape the outrage it is. He examines a number of controversial positions, including the view that all sexuality between men and women is rape, as well as that which questions the authority each of us claims to have in determining the shape and content of our desires. Though taking us through a philosophical assessment of some of the ways in which rape has been or could be conceived of, he is insistent on the need to think of rape as it is experienced in the real world.

But the real world of desires and fears is, as Harrison himself has helped us to appreciate, a complex and elusive one. It is not simplified by the fact that those theories that present themselves as elucidatory of the nature and content of these desires and fears are the very theories that are castigated for the support they allegedly lend to male dominion, indeed to rape itself. Psychoanalysis, whose technique purports to give access to the unconscious, the seat of all our desires and fears, has especially been taken to task, and although Susan Brownmiller is by no means the only person to have done so, she has probably given the critique its most succinct and economical formulation: 'Men have always raped women, but it wasn't until the advent of Sigmund Freud and his followers that the male ideology of rape began to rely on the tenet that rape was something women desired.'[18]

The question of whether psychoanalysis provides a justification of a rather elaborate sort for rape is at least one of the issues which John Forrester addresses in chapter 4, 'Rape, Seduction and Psychoanalysis'. But he also contributes two other very important facets to our discussion in so far as he examines Freud's work on the sexual abuse of children and looks at the relationship between rape and seduction. Ultimately, however, psychoanalysis sends us back, no less than philosophy does, into the real world of interpersonal as opposed to analytical relations. For its own very good reasons, reasons which he very succinctly gives us, psychoanalysis cannot help us when it comes to rape, though it can help particular victims.

This leads us to approach the matter from a completely different angle, especially if we do not want to lose sight of our opening quest for a vision of a rapeless world. Could the question of why men rape hold the key to the nature of the act? If addressed to the psychologist, it would seem to elicit a clinical response, in that it focuses on each individual rapist and seeks, within his particular psychological make-up, the answer as to why he did it. His relation to his mother, to women, to sex and so forth will be presented as an explanation for his behaviour. While by no means devoid of interest, if one has the psychological endurance to hear rapists speak in their own voices, the overall difficulty such accounts tend to present is simply that, granting that an individual's past history is relevant to explaining an attitude or tendency to extreme forms of violence, why rape? Why not murder? Mutilation? Even abstinence? To put it another way, it is not infrequent to hear someone like the Yorkshire Ripper, Peter Sutcliffe, talked of as a rapist — a cultural stereotype which Christopher Frayling explores in his account of the rapist in popular culture (chapter 9). In fact, Sutcliffe did everything but rape. He murdered, and mutilated some of the bodies of his victims. This violation may certainly be likened to rape; none the less, he did not rape. Yet, had he done so, his background, his attitudes to women, to his mother, and so on, would not have been evoked any differently than they have been to explain, whether adequately or not, why he did it.

This is not to denigrate the study of rapists and of men who are violent towards women. Such work cannot but be therapeutically rewarding and may even have something to offer in terms of prevention, but it is unlikely to cast much light on the nature of rape. For when men rape, as opposed to murder or beat up women, they effectively help themselves to a pre-existing set of symbolisms. So the question as to what rape means in our culture is still left standing. Unless, of course, the question of why men rape is not to be answered in terms of the behaviour of individuals at all.

Two ways of dealing with rape share this particular response: evolutionary biology and, as we have already seen, some radical feminisms. What such an individualistic psychology misses, according to the evolutionary biologists Randy Thornhill, Nancy Wilmsen Thornhill and Gerard Dizinno (chapter 6), is, to use the title of their piece, 'The Biology of Rape'. What has, on their view, eluded psychiatrists and social scientists is that rape constitutes a form of reproductive strategy. Beginning with an analysis of rape in another species, they put forward a controversial hypothesis about human rape.

Though these authors take feminism and the social sciences to task for their inability to produce an adequate explanation for rape, one may still be reluctant to abandon these theoretical approaches, whatever their weaknesses, as rape is such a complex and many-sided phenomenon in humans. In the history of Western culture it has assumed different shapes, and the archetypal rapist has taken on many guises: the Greek god, the knight errant, the young nobleman, the madman, not to mention all the stereotypes discussed by Frayling. Yet, whatever one makes of the provocative conclusions reached in this volume by the evolutionary biologists, the task of putting an end to rape will not be advanced one step further by insisting, in spite of all the evidence to the contrary, that rape is a uniquely human phenomenon.[19] Yet, if some animals rape, not every species does; nor do men in every society.

That is what Peggy Reeves Sanday (chapter 5) makes clear to us, and in showing that rape is not universal she helps sustain some degree of optimism as to the feasibility of a world without rape. She also turns some of our assumptions upside down. Natural vulnerability, which many of us might think of as a distinctively female or feminine characteristic, is taken in her work as a male attribute, one which men endeavour to manipulate and transform. In this particular context, her perception of rape is surprisingly and most challengingly close to that of biologists, in that both see rape as a masculine way of coping with male deficiency, dependency or maladaptiveness. But it is in providing us with an insight into the overall and contrasting forms of what she terms 'rape-prone' and 'rape-free' societies that she lends fuel to our imagination for the project with which we set out. If she is right, however, the optimism which the news that rape is not ubiquitous the world over might give rise to will be seriously mitigated when we think of a rape-free future for ourselves. For it is not at all clear that we are moving towards the kind of world she describes in her study of rape-free societies. If anything, we seem to be moving away from it.

What we must hope is that some of the features she isolates in these societies are compatible with the life men and women lead in the post-industrial world, a world in which communities can no longer exercise a sufficient degree of control over the behaviour of their wayward sons, to use Roy Porter's phrase. As things stand, women have constantly to turn to the state for increased protection, not only against rape, but also to counter sexual harrassment. The piecemeal gains of legislation are important, but the way forward must also be by other means: the ongoing critique of the ideology of misogyny, the replacement of discredited cultural symbols with new ones which associate women with those things that are valued and respected in our culture, and the categorical expression at all levels of our society and our culture of the contempt we feel for those who do not take the desire of the other as the pre-condition for the satisfaction of their own.

Rape is too complex and too serious a matter for us to hope that this book can do more than help focus debate and show how different intellectual disciplines and traditions can be brought to bear on the issues. If it can succeed in doing that much, it will help bring us nearer to a rapeless future.

2

Women, Rape and Law Reform

JENNIFER TEMKIN

In the late 1960s, the rape debate was launched in the United States of America. It has since spread to every nation in the Western, industrialized world. In each place the law of rape and the handling by the criminal justice system of rape complaints have been subjected to scrutiny. Generally, both have been found wanting. In this chapter it is proposed first to discuss some of the problems which rape poses for the legal system and then to raise the question why some jurisdictions have proceeded further in resolving them than has been the case in Britain.

RAPE AND THE CRIMINAL JUSTICE SYSTEM

There are a number of interconnecting problems which rape currently presents for the criminal justice system. First, there is the victim, doubly traumatized by the event itself and its subsequent handling by police and courts. Secondly, and in part consequentially, there is the low reporting rate. Thirdly, there are the rapists, prosecuted infrequently and convicted rarely. Finally, there is the law of rape and the evidential rules which surround it.

The victim's experience

Individual accounts by victims of physical and mental suffering which they have endured as a result of rape have formed a vital ingredient of the discourse on the subject.[1] Their reports are borne out by studies which confirm the existence of a rape trauma syndrome. According to Burgess and Holstrom, 'This syndrome has two phases: the immediate or acute phase, in which the victim's lifestyle is completely disrupted by the rape crisis, and the long term process, in which the victim must reorganize this disrupted lifestyle.'[2] A recent study from New Zealand concluded:

> Rape is an experience which shakes the foundations of the lives of the victims. For many its effect is a long-term one, impairing their capacity for personal relationships, altering their behaviour and values and generating fear.[3]

In addition to the trauma of the rape itself, victims have been further mistreated by the legal system. Be it in England,[4] Scotland,[5] Australia,[6] Canada,[7] Scandinavia[8] or elsewhere,[9] the rough handling of complainants has been much the same. English television viewers may have been shocked at the verbal brutality of Thames Valley police officers who were filmed interrogating a rape victim,[10] but rape crisis centre workers pointed out at the time that such interrogations were run-of-the-mill. That the officers involved were well aware that the cameras were trained on them is itself of some interest. Some British policemen appear to consider that harsh questioning, far from being undesirable, is precisely what is required, as may be gauged from the following advice extended by a detective sergeant to fellow officers in the pages of *Police Review*:

> It should be borne in mind that except in the case of a very young child, the offence of rape is extremely unlikely to have been committed against a woman who does not immediately show signs of extreme violence. If a woman walks into a police station and complains of rape with no such signs of violence she must be closely interrogated. Allow her to make her statement to a policewoman and then drive a horse and cart through it. It is always advisable if there is any doubt of the truthfulness of her allegations to call her an outright liar . . . Watch out for the girl who is pregnant or late getting home one night; such persons are notorious for alleging rape or indecent assault. Do not give her sympathy. If she is not lying, after the interrogator has upset her by accusing her of it, then at least the truth is verified . . . The good interrogator is very rarely loved by his subject.[11]

In a study conducted by the Scottish Office Central Research Unit, 70 Scottish victims of sexual assault were interviewed. Forty were victims of rape, 28 of assault with intent to ravish. The views expressed by complainers on their interactions with CID officers and uniformed women police officers were mainly critical or negative: 'In the main the criticisms were concentrated . . . on the unsympathetic and tactless manner in which interviewing was often conducted'.[12] The researchers concluded that 'there is considerable scope for the development of police interviewing skills in relation to sexual assault complaints'.[13]

It would be wrong, however, to suggest that police are uniformly unpleasant to rape victims. Holmstrom and Burgess in the United States found that victim reactions to their encounters with the police were mainly favourable.[14] Similarly, Kelly, in 1980, interviewed 100 adult female rape victims from four jurisdictions in the Washington metropolitan area. These women for the most part expressed satisfaction with their treatment by the police. Yet Kelly found that the same women also complained, often bitterly, about police behaviour. Her explanation for this paradox is 'that victims rated police and prosecutors highly because they expected to be treated so poorly'. Many had seen the film *Cry Rape*, which had depicted rape victims being humiliated by the police. Thus, their satisfaction arose from receiving better treatment than they had expected.[15]

A major problem confronting the criminal justice system, therefore, is that of changing the attitudes or at least the behaviour of police who deal with sexual assaults.[16] In the United States, police practices in some states have been transformed.[17] In England, too, there have been recent indications that the police are beginning to query their present methods of handling such cases. Indeed, Deputy Assistant Commissioner Wyn Jones of Scotland Yard's Crime Department has publicly stated:

> There may have been shortcomings in the past. But our intention is to improve the lot of victims. We want to kill the myth that rape is sexually motivated — it is usually intended to inflict violence and humiliation. And we want people to report it every time.[18]

It has to be recognized, however, that there are limits to what can justifiably be expected of the police in this context. The victim of rape is often severely traumatized when she arrives at the police station and in need of a large measure of solace and support. Whilst police lose nothing and gain much by showing kindness and sympathy, the role of counsellor and friend should be shared or left entirely for others to perform.[19] In the United States[20] and elsewhere,[21] state-operated schemes to cater for the specific needs of sexual assault victims co-exist with rape crisis centres. In England, government support for rape crisis centres and victim support schemes[22] is vitally necessary since other appropriate counselling services do not appear to exist.

The victim in court If the police have behaved brutishly towards rape victims, it is the courts which may be said to have set the tone. Indeed, it is often claimed that in rape cases, the complainant rather than the defendant is on trial.[23] Certainly the focus of the court's attention is frequently upon her and rather less upon him. Yet the complainant generally has no legal assistance. In England, counsel for the prosecution represents the state and will not have met the complainant before the trial.

Much criticism of the treatment of rape victims in court has centred on the use of sexual history evidence to blacken their character. But other strategies commonly employed against them are equally oppressive and invidious. Newby identified three distinct tactics utilized by defence counsel in rape trials in Western Australia.[24] They are also in frequent use elsewhere.[25] The first is continual questioning as to details of the rape. The woman is required 'to re-iterate again and again the details of the rape incident . . . The purpose is to test her story for inconsistencies and to attempt to twist her interpretation of events so as to make them consistent with an assumption of consent'.[26] The second strategy relates to cases where the victim and accused were known to each other. In such cases, questioning will be particularly detailed and the most intimate aspects of any pre-existing sexual relationship will commonly be rehearsed in court. Finally, the defence may seek to challenge the general character of the witness. This may include but goes far beyond references to her sexual past. The idea is to suggest to the court 'that this sort of woman, who behaves in this kind of way, in these circumstances is quite reasonably to be taken to be consenting'.[27] Thus, attention will be drawn to behaviour such as hitch-hiking, excessive drinking or smoking, the wearing of 'seductive' clothing or the use of bad language.

The major question in all this is what are the judges doing during these cross-examinations? The law permits only relevant evidence to be included in criminal trials. What notion of relevance is it that permits prolonged questioning on matters of this kind? It is for judges to control the conduct of a trial. In rape cases they appear all too often to have given defence counsel free rein.

But it is not only for their omissions to act that the judges must be castigated. Throughout the years in England, a steady stream of judicial utterances on rape have caused amazement and consternation. In 1982 Judge Wild at the Cambridge Crown Court summed up to the jury thus:

Women who say no do not always mean no. It is not just a question of saying no, it is a question of how she says it, how she shows and makes it clear. If she doesn't want it she only has to keep her legs shut and she would not get it without force and there would be marks of force being used.

In the same vein, Sir Melford Stevenson has remarked:

It is the height of imprudence for any girl to hitch-hike at night. That is plain, it isn't really worth stating. She is in the true sense asking for it.[28]

It is of no surprise that victims have found rape trials a traumatic experience. Complainants interviewed in the New Zealand study found the experience of giving evidence in court 'negative and destructive'.[29] The report states: 'Three said that they considered the ordeal to be even worse than the rape itself, and one likened it to being crucified. Undoubtedly, the court proceedings added to and prolonged the psychological stress they had suffered as a result of the rape itself.'[30]

The conduct of rape trials is thus a second major problem confronting the criminal justice system. Undoubtedly, strict rules limiting the use of sexual history evidence can help to alleviate the victim's plight in court, but these alone are insufficient to protect her from needless distress and humiliation. Legal representation for complainants is one method of protecting their interest, and is currently provided as of right in Denmark and Norway.[31] But it would appear that a radical change in the attitude of defence counsel and judges to sexual assault is also required. Continuing education programmes for judges should include re-education about sexual assault. Changes in the substantive law might also be helpful in producing new ways of thinking about this type of crime.[32]

Reports, prosecutions and convictions

In England, there has been a fairly regular increase in the number of rape offences (i.e., rape and attempted rape) recorded by the police in the years immediately following the Second World War until the present time. A comparison between the years 1947, in which there were 240 cases, and 1954, in which there were 294, reveals a 22.5 per cent increase.[33] In 1976, there were 1,090 cases and in 1980, 1,225. These figures are, respectively, over four and five times that for 1947.[34] In 1983, 1,334 rapes were recorded.[35] In other countries, too, increases have taken place. In New Zealand, for example, the number of recorded rapes and attempted rapes rose from 268 in 1975 to 396 in 1981.[36] In the United States between 1970 and 1982, reports of forcible rape more than doubled from 37,860 to 77,763.[37]

It is universally recognized, however, that the number of offences recorded by the police is a small proportion of the number of rapes which actually take place. The United States National Crime Survey of 1979 estimated that only 50 per cent of forcible rapes were reported to the police.[38] Some researchers consider that the proportion of unreported rapes is far higher. Amir[39] and Dukes and Mattley[40] suggest respectively that two-thirds and three-quarters of rapes in the United States are unreported. In New Zealand it has been estimated, on the basis of victim studies conducted there and overseas, that four out of five rape offences are not reported.[41]

In Britain, it is only recently that attempts have been made to assess the level of unreported crime. Some 93 per cent of the sexual assaults uncovered in Scotland by the British Crime Survey were not reported to the police.[42] In England and Wales, the survey estimated that only 26 per cent of offences of rape and indecent assault were in fact recorded, although under-reporting was also found to be a feature of many offences.[43] The survey in England and Wales involved an interview in their homes with one person over 16 years of age in each of 11,000 households.[44] Only women were asked about their experience of sexual offences. No rapes and only one attempted rape were revealed.[45] However, it is most unlikely that this is an accurate reflection of the amount of unreported rape which in fact occurs. The rape trauma syndrome involves feelings of extreme degradation, humiliation and fear. A rape victim is likely to feel inhibited about discussing the matter with an interviewer, particularly one who is male. A survey of this kind is better placed to reveal unreported crimes such as burglary and theft which do not carry the same emotional load. Moreover, sexual assault victims are frequently anxious not to reveal the incident to their families, members of which may well have been present or nearby during the interview.

Figures from other English sources suggest a far higher level of unreported rape. Of the women who reported sexual assault to the London Rape Crisis Centre between 1976 and 1980, 75 per cent did not, it seems, go on to report the matter to the police.[46] A recent survey, conducted by Women against Rape (WAR), revealed an even higher level of unreported offences.[47] Unlike the British Crime Survey, this research was designed specifically to find out about rape and sexual assault. The methodology employed was quite different. A Women's Safety questionnaire was distributed to 2,000 women in London (mostly Inner London) during the summer of 1982. In order to ensure as broad a cross-section as possible, a variety of distribution points were selected, including high streets, bus queues, street markets, hospital wards, pensioners' clubs, colleges etc. Women were permitted to answer the survey in their own time and on their own. The questionnaire was on women's safety in general

— a matter of concern to most women — to ensure that it was not merely women with a specific interest in rape who answered it. A total of 1,236 women (62 per cent) responded. Of these, 214 had been raped (17 per cent), 60 by their husbands. A further 243 (20 per cent) had been the victims of attempted rape. Thus more than one in six of those who responded had been raped and one in five had been the victim of attempted rape.[48] However, out of 145 women who were raped (this figure excludes most but not all of those in the survey who were victims of marital rape), only 12 (8 per cent) reported the matter to the police.[49]

There are many reasons why rape victims do not report. Their perception of police attitudes seems to be a major factor. Thus, out of the aforementioned 145 raped women in the WAR study, 55 per cent of those who did not report thought the police might be unsympathetic and 79 per cent thought that the police would be either unhelpful or unsympathetic. Thirty-one per cent felt too traumatized to face the prospect of police interrogation.[50] In two Australian studies, fear of the reaction of family members was also revealed as significant.[51] Snare suggests on the basis of Swedish research that rape by a stranger is far more likely to be reported than rape by someone well known to the victim. Where there has been some initial voluntary contact, such as having a drink with the offender, she suggests that one in ten cases is likely to be reported.[52] The WAR study provides some confirmation of this. Out of the 145 victims, an estimated 60 were raped by a husband, boyfriend, family member or man in authority. None of these cases was reported. A further 50 victims were estimated to have been raped by a friend, acquaintance or workmate; only two of these cases were reported. The remaining 10 reported cases all involved strangers.[53] It may be that some victims believe that unless the assault conforms to the stereotypical idea of rape, i.e., by a stranger, their story is unlikely to be believed. Certainly 37 per cent of those who failed to report in the WAR study gave as a reason that 'they knew the man well or fairly well and did not think the police would take it seriously'.[54]

A second reason why the official statistics of rape tell only part of the story is that many women who do report rape do not have their complaints accepted by the police. Richard Wright, for example, found in his research into rapes and attempted rapes reported to the police between 1972 and 1976 in six English counties that in about 24 per cent of the 384 cases made available to him, the police decided that no crime had taken place. Of these he writes: 'A number of them were clearly false. But it seemed equally clear to me that a significant proportion represented true rape offences.'[55] Similarly, in the Scottish report, in 44 (25 per cent) out of a total of 196 cases of rape and assault with intent to ravish in the study sample, a no-crime classification was given to the crime report, thus ensuring that the incident did not enter into the official statistics of recorded crime.[56] In 24 of the no-crime cases, the complaint was registered as withdrawn. However, the report notes, 'It did not happen very often that complainers of their own accord and without encouragement withdrew their complaints'.[57]

The prosecution rate for rape also tends to be low. This is so even with respect to the proportion of cleared up offences of rape which are prosecuted. Thus, for example, in the Scottish study, the Procurator Fiscal decided not to initiate proceedings in 30 per cent of cases sent to him by the police with a view to prosecution. This was a much higher no-proceedings rate than research reveals for other crimes of violence in Scotland.[58] The study further illustrates the low conviction rate for rape. In all, a conviction was returned in 49 (25 per cent) of the 196 researched cases. In over one-third of these, however, the conviction was for a lesser offence or for one which was not the subject of the original police report.[59]

Wright's study presents a similar picture. Of the 255 rapes and attempted rapes carried out by solitary offenders which were investigated by the police as genuine in six counties of England between 1972 and 1976, 240 men were involved and 204 men were actually arrested. Of these, 39 never appeared before the courts.[60] Only 22 were found guilty of rape and 13 of attempted rape, making a total of 17 per cent of those arrested. Nine of these were not imprisoned. A further 65 were convicted of other offences in connection with the assault, 42 of a lesser offence, such as indecent assault. Out of the 65, 35 did not receive custodial sentences. Wright concludes:

> Given the attrition of rape cases at every stage from the attack onwards, the rapist who receives a stiff fine must consider himself extremely unlucky. And the rapist who goes to gaol must believe that he was doubly unfortunate — the odds weigh heavily against that happening.[61]

Wright claims that his findings should not be regarded as necessarily representative of the national picture, but other studies indicate the high attrition rate in rape cases elsewhere. Thus, the New Zealand report concluded, 'The chances that a rapist will actually be caught and convicted may be as low as 4 per cent, a figure which is probably much lower than that applying to most other serious offences'.[62]

For those who subscribe to the ideal of the rule of law, the reporting, prosecution and conviction rates for rape should be a cause of deep concern. Of course, low reporting in itself is not necessarily a serious matter. Where victims fail to report crime because their experience of it was not particularly disturbing, it might be said to be pedantic to manifest disquiet. In the context of rape, however, non-reporting would appear to be quite unrelated to reactions of this sort. If large numbers of victims, as the studies suggest, refrain from reporting out of fear that they will be treated without humanity or respect, this is indeed a grave indictment of the criminal justice system. Changes in police practices should produce both higher reporting and prosecution rates. The police, however, are unlikely to wish to expend undue time and energy prosecuting cases of this kind if convictions remain disproportionately hard to obtain. Higher conviction rates may demand alterations in court procedures, in rules of evidence and in the substantive law. They will certainly require changes in general attitudes and assumptions about sexual assault, which reforms within the criminal justice system may in themselves help to achieve.

The law

Rape laws have presented a series of problems for the criminal justice system. First, in many respects, their ambit has been too narrow. This has been a factor in low prosecution and conviction rates. In Michigan, for example, to prove rape it was formerly necessary to show that force was used by the defendant and that the victim did not consent. To establish non-consent, the victim was required to have resisted 'to the utmost' from 'the inception to the close' of the attack.[63] In England, as in many other jurisdictions, rape covers only penile penetration of the vagina. The objection here is that other sexual assaults, often considerably worse in character, are relegated to less important offence categories. Moreover, by confining the offence to women who are not married to the perpetrator, rape laws are discriminatory and deny equal protection to a class of persons on account of their status.

Use of the term 'rape' accounts in part for the narrow scope of the offence. Moreover, the word evokes images and associations which are not altogether helpful in a modern context. For rape, as the dictionary states, is a taking or carrying off by force, the ravishment or violation of a woman or of a country. Arguably today, the law should seek to protect the right of every woman to choose whether to have sexual intercourse or not and its language should reflect this objective.

It is, of course, true that the legal definition of rape in England is sexual intercourse without consent,[64] which, on the face of it, seems rather broad. Certainly it is an improvement on the position which prevailed until the nineteenth century when rape constituted an act against a woman's will so that violence or the threat or fear of it was required. However, whilst 'without her consent' may have a broader meaning than 'against her will', precisely what that meaning is remains a legal mystery. The likely result of this is that police and courts return to the word rape and ask themselves whether the deed really amounts to their own notion of it.

One solution to this difficulty would be the enactment of a comprehensive definition of consent; but such a reform begs a major question. It might be said that a crucial problem in the law of rape is precisely that it focuses unswervingly upon the non-consent of the complainant. Did she consent or did she not? That is the question. It is she who is the object of attention. The prosecution must prove beyond all reasonable doubt that she did not consent and the defence will be irresistibly tempted to raise that doubt by suggesting that she is the type of woman who might well have done. In England, moreover, the judge is obliged to administer the corroboration warning. He must warn the jury that it is dangerous to convict on the basis of the complainant's evidence unless it is corroborated. Perhaps the wonder should be that any convictions are returned at all!

There is nothing inevitable in this legal arrangement. Sexual intercourse without consent can be shifted from centre stage towards the wings even if it can never be removed from the set altogether. For other nefarious conduct will generally accompany the act of non-consensual sex. There may, for example, be violence, a variety of threats, the presence or participation of a gang, or the commission of another offence such as burglary immediately beforehand. There is no reason why the spotlight should not, in the first instance, be directed at the defendant and at acts such as these. Moreover, rather than letting the officials of the criminal justice system interpret rape as they choose, there is much to be said for spelling out in precise terms the circumstances in which a sexual offence is committed.

There may also be a case for a scale of penalties for rape rather than a single maximum of life imprisonment. Under the present system, most defendants plead not guilty to rape and indeed, given the high penalty and the low prospects of conviction, they would be foolish to do otherwise. The advantage of a scale is that it permits a defendant to decide where he fits on it and to plead guilty if he so chooses.

Rape law reform is both simple and hard. It is simple to abolish the marital rape exemption and the corroboration warning. Only atavism and sexism stand in the way. To move further is more complicated. The construction of a ladder of offences instead of the one offence of rape is a particularly complex matter. Whilst in England there is a reluctance to embark upon even the simple tasks, elsewhere the hard ones have been tackled and, it seems, with a measure of success.

THE RAPE DEBATE AND LAW REFORM IN THE 1970s AND 1980s

In most states of the United States, legislation has been passed to amend the legal framework relating to rape. In some states, radical change has been introduced.[65] In Canada[66] and Australia,[67] law reform in this area is advancing apace. In England, whilst certain amendments have been implemented, relatively little has been achieved and little more is on the present legislative agenda.

Why is it that England has proceeded so cautiously whilst elsewhere there has been a genuine willingness to contemplate and implement radical change? The answer to this question will require the research of political scientists and sociologists perhaps more than lawyers. In this chapter, it is intended merely to outline certain possible lines of inquiry.

It is proposed first of all to consider how legislation came to be achieved in two other jurisdictions, namely the American state of Michigan and in Canada. The Michigan statute, passed in 1974,[68] is regarded as a turning point in rape law reform and has been used as a model by other jurisdictions.[69] The Canadian provisions were enacted almost a decade later, in 1982,[70] and thus provide an example of more recent law reform in this area.

Michigan

In the early 1970s, the women's movement in the United States succeeded in bringing the issue of rape to the attention of the nation. During the same decade, rape crisis centres sprang up throughout the country and the Federal Government manifested its concern by making available between 1973 and 1981 an estimated $125 million for research into sexual assault.[71] This led, *inter alia*, to a nationwide study of rape conducted by the Law Enforcement Assistance Administration.[72] Other federal initiatives included the setting up of a National Center for the Prevention and Control of Rape within the Department of Health, Education and Welfare and the launching of prevention programmes and projects concerned with the care of victims and community education.[73] It is thus against a background of growing official concern about rape, prompted by both the dramatic rise in the reported incidence of the crime and the agitation of the women's movement, that the achievement of law reform in Michigan may be viewed.

The achievement of law reform in Michigan[74] The Michigan legislation was not enacted in response to the proposals of an official law reform committee, neither was it introduced by the State Government. On the contrary, it was very much the product of a grass-roots initiative resulting from the dissatisfaction felt by many women working in rape crisis centres at the criminal justice system's treatment of rape victims. The events leading up to the passage of the legislation may briefly be described as follows. In June 1973, a meeting of women working in some of Michigan's rape crisis projects was held at the home of Jan Ben Dor. Those assembled (with the exception of a few radical feminists) decided to take action to promote law reform. It was thus that the Michigan Women's Task Force on Rape came into being. It proceeded forthwith to commission Virginia Nordby, a lecturer at the University of Michigan Law School, to draft legislation. With the help of student researchers, she eventually produced a Bill. Armed with this, the Task Force arranged meetings with the Michigan House of Representatives Judiciary Committee, and it finally managed to persuade a white Republican Senator and a black Democratic Representative to sponsor the Bill. However, setbacks were soon to occur. A Senate Judiciary Committee lawyer produced an alternative draft bill which would have excluded the provisions on sexual history together with those abolishing the marital rape exemption. The Task Force was compelled to accept a compromise by which the sexual history provisions were retained but marital rape became a crime only in certain circumstances where the couple were living separately.[75] It was in this form that the Bill was passed.

The achievement of what was, despite these alterations, radical reforming legislation is attributable to a number of causes. First, the Women's Task Force on Rape proved to be a highly effective organization. Many of its members were veteran campaigners from the battles for abortion law reform. They published a newsletter, they liaised with women working in the media, they lobbied relentlessly — 95 out of 110 House Representatives were lobbied personally — and they made a point of courting conservative as well as radical politicians. Their recruitment of Virginia Nordby was particularly felicitous. She and her student team left no stone unturned in researching every aspect of the proposed legislation. One member of the House Judiciary Committee commented: 'Of all the issues that have come before the Committee recently, rape reform has been the best researched and best presented.'[76] Nordby was also astute enough to include in her team Elaine Milliken, the Governor of Michigan's daughter, and the Governor's decision to support the Bill was undoubtedly significant. Of further assistance was the showing on television of *Cry Rape*, a film drawing attention to the ordeal of rape victims[77] who report the offence. It was thus that eventually there existed considerable public support for the Bill. In an election year, this was a major advantage since politicians felt it was expedient to vote in its favour.

The reform Michigan's Criminal Sexual Conduct Act has four central features. First, instead of rape, it creates a ladder of offences, each of which is described as criminal sexual conduct.[78] The first degree offence carries a maximum penalty of life imprisonment, with 15 years maximum for the second and third degree offences, and two years for the fourth degree offence. Each degree covers a range of sexual assaults, so that, for example, the first degree offence covers any act of sexual penetration. The four degrees are differentiated according to the amount of coercion used, whether or not penetration has taken place, the extent of physical injury inflicted and the age and incapacitation of the victim. The law describes with great particularity precisely the conduct which is covered by each degree. In this way, it is hoped to encourage prosecutors to prosecute and defendants who are guilty to plead guilty. Moreover, juries saddled with a stereotypical notion of rape and confronted with a case that does not conform to it may well be prepared to convict of a crime called criminal sexual conduct in the third degree where they would baulk at the idea of a rape conviction.

The new Act also dispenses with the need for the prosecution to establish the victim's resistance.[79] The offences of criminal sexual conduct focus entirely on the conduct of the defendant and do not specifically include a non-consent requirement. On the other hand, the Act cannot in all circumstances prevent the defence from seeking to allege that the victim consented, particularly where no weapons were used and where little or no injury was sustained.

The third important feature of the Michigan legislation is its strict regulation of sexual history evidence,[80] which is totally prohibited save in two exceptional circumstances. These are where the past sexual conduct was with the defendant himself and where the evidence relates to the source or origin of semen, pregnancy or disease. Thus, for example, where the complainant alleges that the criminal sexual conduct in question led to her pregnancy, the defence could adduce evidence to show that the pregnancy was in fact caused by sexual activity with another on a particular occasion.

Finally, criminal sexual conduct may be committed by one spouse against another provided that they are living apart and one partner has filed for separate maintenance or divorce.[81] It is also gender-neutral, so that women may perpetrate it and men may be its victims.

Whilst the new law has in no sense eradicated all the problems which face the criminal justice system in dealing with sexual assault — it has, for example, had no appreciable effect so far on reporting rates[82] — its most solid achievement is to produce a clear increase in the number of arrests and convictions for conduct of this kind.[83] It has also improved the treatment of victims within the legal process.[84]

Canada

In Michigan, rape law reform appears to have been achieved mainly by the dedicated efforts of an *ad hoc* committee of women who adroitly handled the legislative process. In Canada, the legislation passed in 1982 was federal not provincial, but women, once again, played a powerful role in securing it.

The achievement of rape law reform in Canada Before outlining the course of events which would appear to have led up to the passage of the legislation, it is necessary briefly to consider certain aspects of the organization of women in Canada.[85]

Paul Rock has drawn attention to women's 'entrenched place in the institutional structure of Ottawa'.[86] This came about largely as a result of the Report of the Royal Commission on the Status of Women published in 1976 which recommended, *inter alia*, that a Status of Women Council should be created to assist in the improvement of the position of women. The Government responded by creating what is now referred to as Status of Women Canada. A cabinet minister was also given responsibility for coordinating government policy on women, and in 1972 it was reported that special advisers on the status of women were to be positioned in a number of key government departments. In 1976, after the Canadian Government's endorsement of the United Nations' 'Decade for Women', Status of Women Canada was enlarged and became an independent agency. Its brief was, *inter alia*, to advise, encourage and monitor the progress of government legislation, policies and programmes for women and to liaise between women's organizations and government.

At the same time as women were gaining a foothold in the federal institutions of government, developments were taking place at other levels, particularly in relation to the issue of violence against women. Largely influenced by initiatives taken in the United States and England, rape crisis centres began to appear. Whilst these were never to combine into anything resembling a movement or political lobby, their existence, together with the activities they organized, was of considerable influence in drawing attention to the problem of violence against women. Certainly they suggested to the coterie of women in Ottawa that women's issues were not confined to jobs and career opportunities.

Standing between Status of Women Canada and its off-shoots in government on the one hand, and feminist activity in the shape of rape crisis centres on the other, are a number of influential women's organizations, including the National Action Committee on the Status of Women (NAC), which is of particular interest in this context. NAC is a very large umbrella organization to which numerous others are affiliated. Their range is noteworthy and includes the YWCA, the Imperial Order of the Daughters of the Empire and church organizations as well as the rape crisis centres. NAC is active and meets regularly: it holds conferences, issues publications and lobbies Parliament.

It was at the end of the 1970s that activity at a number of levels on the issue of violence against women was to coalesce and accelerate. Of particular significance was the publication of a book by Lorenne Clark and Debra Lewis in 1977 which has since gained a worldwide readership. Avowedly feminist in its orientation, *Rape: The Price of Coercive Sexuality* was described as a 'break-through', providing 'the first solid data on rape in Canada'.[87] One Canadian reviewer, Eleanor Pelrine, commented:

> Clark and Lewis in their carefully documented, rational study of 117 rape complaints laid with the Metropolitan Toronto Police Department in 1970 have struck the first blow against the individual and collective misogyny responsible for perpetuating bad law, inadequate enforcement and injustice before the courts in Canada. The rest is up to us.[88]

The book was immediately influential. Moreover, Clark, who was Associate Professor both in the Department of Philosophy and the Centre of Criminology at the University of Toronto, and Lewis, who was a researcher at the Centre, were soon to demonstrate that their talents were not exclusively academic. Both embarked upon a course of entrepreneurial activity in the wake of the book's publication. Thus, Clark spoke at conferences; she was commissioned by the Solicitor-General to compile a bibliography of works on rape; and in 1978 she became Vice-President of NAC. It was she who introduced the issue of rape to that influential committee and it was she who drafted its position paper on the subject. Moreover, she was, it seems, 'always talking to one bureaucrat or another'.[89] Lewis, who had earned her feminist stripes in the Toronto Rape Crisis Centre, was equally prepared to lecture throughout Canada on the rape issue.

The strength and tenacity of these two women must surely earn them a place in the history of those who have laboured in the cause of women, but the extent of their influence has been called into question. Rock's research into the evolution of a policy for crime victims within the Department of the Solicitor-General has led him to conclude that in that particular field they had little direct influence on government. He suggests that government policy-makers retroactively 'bestowed luminosity'[90] upon them and upon feminist activity in this area. In other words, once it was decided that steps should be taken to assist the victims of crime, it was considered expedient to invoke the support of the women's movement. He argues: 'A political community of substance and permanence never really evolved around the social problem of violence to women. Neither did the campaign achieve direct effects.'[91] It will be suggested here that whilst this may indeed be true in relation to policies for victims which emerged from the Department of the Solicitor-General, in relation to sexual assault law reform Clark and Lewis, together with women operating in other ways, were directly, although not exclusively, influential in producing it.

In 1978, the Law Reform Commission of Canada published its Working Paper on Sexual Offences.[92] This has only to be compared with that of the English Criminal Law Revision Committee[93] to appreciate how much the thinking behind it, whether consciously or not, was influenced by feminist discourse. Thus, the approach of the Working Paper to rape victims is unashamedly sympathetic. There are none of the usual warning statements about false complaints of rape,[94] no suggestion that the concern about rape is out of place or indicative of a layman's misunderstanding. It speaks approvingly of the work of rape crisis centres. Moreover, unlike the Criminal Law Revision Committee, the Law Reform Commission recognized that the substantive law of rape is not to be considered in a vacuum but in the context of its operation in the criminal justice system as well as in society at large. Most significant of all, however, is its central proposition that

> rape is actually a form of assault and should therefore perhaps be treated as such under the law . . . The concept of sexual assault more appropriately characterizes the actual nature of the offence of rape because the primary focus is on the assault or the violation of the integrity of the person rather than the sexual intercourse.[95]

This statement may be compared with what Clark and Lewis had to say in their book, published the previous year. Under the heading 'The Female Perspective: Rape as an Assault', they state:

We are saying that our rape laws should reflect the perspective of women — the victims of rape. They experience rape as an *assault*, as an unprovoked attack on their physical person and as a trangression of their assumed right to the exclusive ownership and control of their own bodies . . . This act is experienced by the rape victim as a denial of her physical autonomy . . . This follows from her belief that she is a fully human person and entitled to all the protections given to persons under the law. Since she knows that the right to exclusive control over one's own body and to freedom from unprovoked physical interference by others, are two of the fundamental rights guaranteed to persons under the law, she quite justifiably expects redress when she is raped.[96]

The repetition must have been effective in bringing home the message to the Law Reform Commission. It singled out 'the protection of the integrity of the person' as a central policy issue.[97] It spoke of 'the right to be free from unwanted infringement of one's bodily integrity'[98] and 'the right to be free from physical assault'.[99] It was in this context that its proposal to abolish rape and introduce a new offence of sexual assault was made.

On the matter of the marital rape exemption, however, the Commissioners could not achieve a consensus. Some favoured its complete abolition, while others would go no further than to agree that the exemption should be lifted where the couple were living separately. Thus, the Law Reform Commission of Canada, in June 1978, had reached the position at which the English Criminal Law Revision Committee was to arrive in 1984:[100] it was prepared to recommend that non-cohabiting spouses should not be covered by the exemption, but it would go no further.[101]

In May 1978, one month before the official publication of the Working Paper, Bill C52 was introduced into the Canadian Parliament. It contained, *inter alia*, provisions designed to amend the law of rape. These were clearly influenced by the Working Paper's proposals. Rape was to be abolished in favour of a newly defined two-tier offence of indecent assault for which a spouse could be liable provided that he was living separately at the material time.[102]

The events that followed the presentation of the bill are noteworthy.[103] The Canadian Advisory Council on the Status of Women, the National Action Committee and the National Association of Women and the Law all publicly condemned the Bill's failure to abolish the marital rape exemption. Delegations were sent to lobby the Department of Justice, including one from NAC which was 40 women strong.

It seems clear that one of the reasons why Bill C52 died never to be revived was because of the lobbying by these groups about the marital rape exemption, as well as certain other aspects of the Bill. Rock himself states:

> What is significant about the campaign and the reverses of the Department of Justice is that officials of that Ministry were to become so rudely and abruptly acquainted with the sentiment which women felt about rape and sexual assault. Officials had been unprepared for what had happened. They had been discomfited. Ever afterwards, they were to be solicitous about the victimization of women and the political response of women's organizations.[104]

In November 1978, the Law Reform Commission of Canada produced its final Report on Sexual Offences.[105] This too recommended the abolition of the offence of rape and its substitution by two new offences, described as 'sexual interference' and 'sexual aggression'.[106] On the marital rape exemption, the Report commented as follows:

> The great majority of those consulted by the Commission on this question favoured total abolition of the spousal immunity. Difficulties of proof do not appear to be insurmountable and the danger of groundless accusations made from motives of revenge or as preliminaries to divorce or separation proceedings may be counter-balanced by stricter exercise of discretion in assessing the appropriateness of prosecutions. Furthermore, as experience has amply demonstrated, groundless or ill-founded prosecutions have little chance of passing through the filtering processes implicit in our legal system and present-day criminal procedure.[107]

The women's organizations had made their point and had won it. The introduction to the Report ends with an expression of thanks by the Commission to a number of groups and associations for their cooperation. First on the list are 'representatives of women's groups and associations and rape crisis centres'.[108]

In March 1979, the Minister of Justice announced that a new Bill was on its way 'following representations I have received from women's organisations and various other groups'. In an information paper published later, in December 1980, a subsequent Minister of Justice promised that the marital rape exemption would go:

> This spousal immunity from rape derives from the traditional belief that marriage meant irrevocable consent to sexual intercourse. If the new law is

to protect the integrity of the person . . . marriage should no longer mean forced sexual submission.

Bills C53 and C127, which eventually followed, proceeded through Parliament while women's groups continued to lobby. For, as Rock points out 'The more eminent women's organisations had acquired a stake in the campaign to change the law on spousal immunity, previous sexual history and consent.'[109] These issues were no longer matters of concern merely to a few radical feminists. In bringing the debate to a different level in the hierarchy of women's organizations, Clark and Lewis had clearly played a central role. The radicals were still active, however, indicating their continuing concern. Rock has described the marches and the 're-claim the night' demonstrations. He also mentions the use of 'charivari', as on one occasion when women stood outside the home of a man accused of rape chanting, 'We know what you did. We know who you are. We're watching you. We're going to fight back.'[110] The newspaper reports which Rock quotes regarding these events all refer to the period between 1977 and 1981 when legal reform was being debated at the highest levels.

Rock also points to the influence of young, feminist lawyers located in and about Ottawa. He quotes a legal adviser to Status of Women Canada:

Once the Bill was introduced it became clear that the Government was willing to act in this field so women's groups decided that they'd better act on this thing and not something else. We in Women and the Law group formed this Committee, starting in May 1978, as soon as the Bill came out. We met regularly, at least once a week, for an entire evening or a whole day, until October, to hash out a policy.[111]

Whether or not the legislation finally passed in August 1982 met with the approval of all those women who had actively participated in the law reform saga, the fact remains that the shape the law finally took is largely attributable to the argument put forward by women. In this instance, luminosity was not 'retroactively bestowed'. Women had exercised a direct and powerful influence on the legislation.

The reform The Canadian reform of 1982 bears a certain resemblance to the Michigan legislation looked at previously, although it is weaker in certain respects and stronger in others.

The crime of rape no longer exists in Canada. Instead, a gradation scheme has been introduced which creates three offences of sexual assault covering rape and certain allied crimes. The three grades are distinguished purely in terms of the level of violence involved and no distinction is drawn between penetration and other sexual acts. Simple sexual assault carries a maximum of ten years' imprisonment but may, at the prosecutor's discretion, be tried summarily, in which case the maximum penalty is six months' imprisonment or a fine of not more than $500.[112] Next on the ladder is an offence carrying a maximum of 14 years' imprisonment, which applies where the defendant, in committing a sexual assault, carries, uses or threatens to use a real or imitation weapon or threatens to cause bodily harm to a person other than the complainant or is a party to the offence with any other person.[113] Finally comes aggravated sexual assault, which is the most serious offence of the three and carries a maximum of life imprisonment. This offence is perpetrated where the defendant, in committing a sexual assault, wounds, maims, disfigures or endangers the life of the complainant.[114]

The new law entirely abolishes the marital rape exemption.[115] It also places firm restrictions on the use of sexual history evidence,[116] although the Michigan legislation is stronger in this respect. Thus, for example, under the Canadian provisions sexual incidents involving the defendant are not vetoed at all, neither is evidence of the complainant's sexual reputation where this is relevant to the issue of consent.[117] Exceptions to the rule prohibiting sexual history evidence exist where such evidence would tend to establish the identity of the person who had the alleged sexual contact with the complainant or where it relates to sexual activity on the same occasion as the offence if this is relevant to the defendant's plea of belief in consent, or, finally, to rebut sexual history evidence adduced by the prosecution.[118] As far as corroboration is concerned, the judge is no longer permitted to issue the corroboration warning, although he will still be able to comment on the evidence.[119]

The Canadian legislation is less radical in its approach to consent: assault is defined by s. 244 of the Canadian Criminal Code as an act committed without the victim's consent so that the prosecution will still be required to establish its absence. But a number of situations in which consent will not be deemed to exist are listed. These include circumstances in which the complainant submits 'by reason of' force used or threatened against her or a third party or through fear of the application of such force.[120]

It remains to be seen what effects this reform will have. Whether or not it encourages prosecutions and convictions as it is intended to do, there can be no doubt that its symbolic achievements are considerable. Abolition of the marital rape exemption and the corroboration warning are vitally significant in terms of the status of women in the eyes of the law.

England

When the rape debate reached these shores in the early 1970s, it met with a receptive and sympathetic response in many quarters. In the mid-1980s, however, radical law reform is as remote a prospect as ever. In considering the broad history of the English law of rape over the past decade and contrasting it with the achievement of reform in Michigan and Canada, two factors stand out for consideration. The first is the lack of academic interest in and commitment to rape law reform; the second is the absence of anything resembling a cohesive and powerful women's political lobby which might have taken up the issue, as well as a general absence of women in the 'corridors of power'.

Rape and academic inquiry In both Michigan and Canada academics liaised successfully with women's pressure groups and political organizations to play a major role in bringing about legislative change. In England, however, the law of rape never became an issue of great interest or concern to academic lawyers or criminologists and remains today an area in which there has been relatively little scholarly endeavour. The contrast with the United States in this respect is dramatic. There, a vast legal literature on rape laws has emerged. Moreover, whereas in England, there exists scant information about how the law of rape operates within the criminal justice system, in the United States, funds have been made available to produce valuable empirical research.[121] One reason for the dearth of English writing in this field may be that amongst academic lawyers there has been a continuing preoccupation with the mental element in crime, which has consumed much of their energy and creativity. Subjectivity, the idea that a defendant should be judged according to his individual mental state at the time of the crime, has been the watchword of academic thinking.[122] Given the predilections of some English judges, the perceived need to safeguard the interests of defendants is totally understandable; it may at times, however, have resulted in the eclipse of the victim from academic legal discourse.

It is against this background that the first crucial legal decision to be taken in this period may be viewed. *DPP* v. *Morgan*,[123] decided by the House of Lords in 1975, involved an issue of critical significance in the law of rape. The House of Lords was invited to decide whether a man who honestly believes in a woman's consent to sexual intercourse can be guilty of rape if his belief was based on unreasonable grounds. Their Lordships held by a majority that he could not. Academic orthodoxy perceived the case in one light only: it was seen to raise in stark form the issue of subjectivity and criminal liability. The House of Lords' decision was regarded as a triumph, as a turning point in the development of the criminal law. One writer commented that it was particularly remarkable that the House of Lords had responded to the academic call for subjectivity in an area such as rape where 'there might have been a strong temptation to take a line less favourable to the defendant'.[124] The truth of the matter was rather, perhaps, that in rape the judges felt more comfortable in pursuing the subjectivist line than they would have felt in many other areas of the criminal law.

It was left to the press and to diverse women's groups to protest at the decision in *Morgan*. Mr Jack Ashley, MP, a notable defender of women's rights, was given leave by an overwhelming majority of the House of Commons to introduce a Bill to overrule it.[125] The Government subsequently intervened and set up a committee under the chairmanship of Mrs Justice Heilbron to look into the matter.

In considering the arguments for and against *Morgan*, the committee was faced on the one hand with academic opinion[126] and that of the National Council for Civil Liberties,[127] which was solidly in support of the decision, and on the other with what must have seemed to be the far less informed voice of the press and the women's groups. The dissenting speeches of Lords Simon[128] and Edmund Davies[129] in *Morgan* did not sufficiently develop the arguments *contra*, and the reasoning of the Court of Appeal,[130] whose decision the House of Lords had overruled, was too technical and convoluted. The case against *Morgan* was never given adequate legal expression.[131] It is hardly surprising, therefore, that Heilbron came out eventually in its favour,[132] that Ashley and others who opposed it were dismissed as laymen who had misunderstood the case and that the decision was eventually ratified by Parliament in the Sexual Offences (Amendment) Act 1976.[133]

Women — an absent force In England there are certainly women who are prominent in public life or who can be wheeled into prominence when necessary. At a time when there was a public demand for action, Mrs Justice Heilbron was clearly a wise political choice to head a committee on rape. But the fate of the Heilbron Committee's proposals illustrates perhaps that the existence of a few prominent women is not sufficient to bring about effective reforms in areas of law which are crucial to women's status, welfare and progress.

The Heilbron Committee took the view that the popular clamour against *Morgan* was in part due to a general and justified lack of confidence in the way that rape cases were handled by the criminal justice system. It drew up radical proposals which would have severely restricted the use of sexual history evidence in rape trials[134] and would also have afforded anonymity to rape victims.[135] It is noteworthy that as well as being chaired by a woman, two out of four of the remaining members of the Committee were female, as was its secretary.

It was once again Jack Ashley, MP, who was the moving force in seeking to implement the Heilbron Committee's recommendations. He persuaded Robin Corbett, MP, to introduce a Private Member's Bill which was closely modelled on the Heilbron Report. From the outset, however, it became apparent that the clauses dealing with sexual history evidence were likely to founder because of poor drafting. It was plain that if Heilbron's radical approach was to be preserved, re-drafting was necessary. This did not happen and the clauses moved unamended to the House of Lords where they were duly savaged by the Law Lords. The Government returned with a substitute provision which, while excluding sexual history evidence in principle, gave discretion to the judges to admit it where they considered that its exclusion would be unfair to the defendant. This provision proved, unsurprisingly, to be quite acceptable to their Lordships and it was acordingly enacted into law.[136] Thus, the judges were put in charge of regulating the use of sexual history evidence even though it was largely due to their inactivity that its use had become widespread in the first place. The anonymity proposals were also implemented in a different form from that which was intended by Heilbron. An amendment was introduced to the Bill which gave anonymity not merely to the victim, but to the defendant as well.[137]

This debacle may be contrasted with the course of events surrounding the introduction of rape law reform in the two jurisdictions previously considered. Particularly noticeable was the apparent absence in England of a well-organized, well-briefed and powerful women's lobby. Had there been one, the law might have taken a different course.

Rape and the Criminal Law Revision Committee Both the lack of strong academic support for rape law reform and the absence of a powerful women's voice in its favour, may be said to have contributed to the negative approach to the matter manifested by the Criminal Law Revision Committee (CLRC) in its final Report on Sexual Offences published in 1984.[138]

Academic writing is not infrequently a powerfully persuasive influence upon the law reform bodies of England. In the absence of much legal scholarship to provide guidance, the CLRC was left to form its own views on the legal aspects of sexual assault. It is not therefore entirely without relevance that 15 out of 17 members of the CLRC at that time were male, as was its secretary and deputy secretary.[139]

In its report the CLRC proposed that the law of rape should continue to cover only penile penetration of the vagina.[140] It was not prepared to recommend abolition of the marital rape exemption, only that it should cease to operate where the couple were living separately.[141] On the issue of consent, the Committee's approach was similarly restrictive. It recommended that legislation be introduced to ensure that threats other than of immediate force be precluded from the scope of rape.[142] The effect of this requirement of immediacy would be to place a fresh limitation on the scope of the offence.

The CLRC's recommendations will ensure that rape remains a crime with a narrow ambit. Since the Committee considered the law of rape entirely in isolation from its operation within the criminal justice system and within society, its proposals are not entirely surprising. Although it received representations from a considerable number of women's organizations and groups, their views often appear to have been rejected.[143] Thus, for example, in connection with s. 2 of the Sexual Offences (Amendment) Act, which regulates the use of sexual history evidence, the Report states:

> It seems that some people, and in particular some women's organisations, think that these statutory provisions are proving ineffective for the protection of complainants because many judges, so it is alleged, grant leave to cross-examine about a complainant's previous experience upon being asked to do so. Critics do not seem to appreciate that a complainant's previous sexual experience may be relevant to the issue of consent.[144]

The Committee decided to ask the Recorder of London to ask the judges at the Old Bailey (the central criminal courts) whether, in their view, the criticism of them was justified. The reply came back that it was not.[145] The Committee therefore reported that all was well and that the law with respect to sexual history should remain as it stood save for certain minor amendments.[146]

The Criminal Law Revision Committee has thus set its face against radical reform of the law of rape. The Law Commission is most unlikely to take the matter on board. In England, we have, for the time being it seems, reached the end of the road so far as legislative change at the instigation of the law reform bodies is concerned.

CONCLUSION

In Michigan and Canada women played a major role in the accomplishment of radical rape law reform. In countries as diverse as Australia, Israel, Denmark and Sweden women have actively and successfully campaigned against antiquated rape laws and retrogressive proposals for reform.[147] In England, by contrast, traditional women's organizations and those of the radical fringe have, for the most part, shown a marked disinclination to do battle for legal change.[148] It is no coincidence that little progress in this area has been achieved. Thus, rape, it seems, is a women's issue in every sense: not merely does it vitally affect women, but without their active political intervention, it appears that few initiatives to combat it are likely to be pursued.

Acknowledgement

I am indebted to Dr Paul Rock for his assistance.

3

Rape — a Case Study in Political Philosophy

ROSS HARRISON

Rape is obviously a bad, indeed a horrific, thing. It belongs to the real world in which people are hurt, humiliated and abused. Philosophy, on the other hand, displays an image of rational, unemotional lack of involvement or concern. It might well be thought, therefore, that any attempt to apply such rational thought to the subject matter of rape in itself merely reveals insensitivity to its evil or horror. The disparity between the grim facts and the calm reflection of a philosophical book or seminar seems too great. Violation of the body is also violation of rational understanding; and philosophy itself would be violated by any attempt to come to terms with the folly and the mire.

Although it is unproblematic that rape is a bad thing, however, there is a problem about why precisely it is bad and, related to this, about how bad it is. Theft is a bad thing and so is attempted murder; but which of them is rape more akin to? It does not seem to me that the answer to these questions is totally obvious and so, at the risk of charges of insensitivity, I would like to explore how, if at all, some current philosophical resources could be used to provide an answer.

We should remember, after all, that rape, horrible as it may be, provides a problem not only for the victims, or even for the much larger number of women whose actions are constrained by fear of rape, but also for society as a whole. The law of a society is a fit object of reflection for anyone in that society, and on this basis rape may be thought about and analysed by victim and bystander, male and female, participant and theorist alike. There has to be law about rape, education about rape and a general social attitude to rape; and it may well be that these would benefit from dispassionate or impartial consideration.

PHILOSOPHICAL THEORIES

If the problem of the badness of rape is considered as a philosophical issue, then it becomes a problem in applied ethics, or value theory. To find a solution we would seem to need some general criterion about how to make such value judgements, a criterion that we can then apply to the specific case. One natural, or at least normal, constraint on value judgements is that it ought to be possible to make them from many different points of view. That is to say, they are not held simply because of the special or peculiar circumstances that happen to apply to someone at the time at which they make the judgement. It is this consideration that lies behind many people's view that moral judgement ought to be impartial, itself an application of the feeling that philosophy (or theoretical thought in general) ought to be impartial.

Now, suppose we consider all positions or points of view impartially, that is, in some sense we give them all equal consideration. This could still be understood or interpreted in two quite different ways. Giving all positions equal consideration might be understood to mean that we should support those moral judgements which are acceptable from most of the positions, or it might be understood to mean that we should support those judgements which are acceptable from all positions. On both understandings all positions are treated equally, but in the former case, this means that they are given equal weighting, and hence the majority wins out, while in the latter case we treat each position as having an equal veto.

Another way of considering this difference is by trying to think about how we would feel if we were in other people's positions. By imagining what something looks like from other people's points of view, we do something to give these other points of view equal consideration with our own. With such imaginative access, we clearly gain extra information, but there still remains the question, of how to treat this extra information.

Again, we have the two cases. We can think that it gives us a basic input of data about how something affects people, weight the effects on everyone equally, achieve impartiality by considering ourselves no more or no less than anyone else, and then sum up the different outcomes of different courses of action. This amounts to the first case treated above, where (for equally strong feelings) treating people equally involves following the majority. It is also very like the moral position known as utilitarianism, in which actions are assessed as good or bad in accordance with the effects they have upon people, and these effects are then summed up giving equal weight to all the affected parties so that, for equally severe effects, what affects the majority therefore becomes more important in value. If something is done which pleases the majority on this view, then everyone is treated impartially or equally by this action even if it harms the minority. We can realize that it harms the minority by using our imagination to see how we would feel in that position; nevertheless, we can also see or imagine what it feels like to be one of the majority, and summing up all these feelings equally means that the majority wins out.

There is, however, another way in which we can treat the information we gain by such imaginative access; our understanding of the harm done to a minority, for example. In this way, once we have thought ourselves into such a position we feel that it would be intolerable for our interests or desires to be sacrificed for the sake of someone else. This approach is like the second case above, in which treating people equally is to give a veto to everyone. For we would now think that, however many other people there are, and however pleased it may make them, this is something which should not be done to us. Instead of our distaste being treated as an input into a calculation in which everyone's desires are weighed up and ours happens to be outweighed, we now think of it as something that cannot be traded off against any amount of happiness to others. It is non-negotiable and we have, or would like to possess, a veto.

This latter position is similar to rights-based theories of evaluation in which rights form a sort of trumps in that something which affects an individual's rights is always considered to be more important than anything else. On this view sacrificing the basic rights of a single individual would never be justified however much good might come to others from such a sacrifice.

APPLICATION

The discussion above has sketched the outlines of two general approaches to evaluation and gives a framework within which to consider how the particular case of rape would fare under the two general approaches. In fact, whichever approach we adopt, the evil of rape is revealed in a relatively unproblematic manner.

On the first approach, the question is resolved by considering, and as far as possible adding up, the happiness and unhappiness caused by the action on all affected parties. In most cases of rape there are only two parties immediately involved. So, since numbers are equal on each side, it becomes a matter of comparing the intensity and duration of the happiness produced in the man with the intensity and duration of the unhappiness produced in the woman. Although these questions can, of course, only be answered by empirical facts, which cannot be produced by mere thought, the facts nevertheless certainly are that, in the overwhelming majority of cases of rape, both the intensity and also the duration of the suffering far outweigh the intensity and duration of the pleasure. So, as a general rule (and it is only general rules that we are concerned with here) rape comes out as a bad thing. How bad it is, on a utilitarian account, will again depend upon the actual effects; but the facts seem to be such that in general, rape causes prolonged and severe upset to the victim. Rape, therefore, comes out as pretty bad, much nearer attempted murder than theft.

The significance of this from a utilitarian point of view, at least if it is meant to be the basis of prescriptions for public policy, is that rape would naturally therefore merit a high level of punishment. The utilitarian theory of punishment is that punishment, a pain in itself, is justified if this pain is offset by the beneficial consequences of deterring harmful activities. Assuming that potential rapists can be deterred by the threat of punishment, a heavy punishment would therefore be justified for rape because, even though a considerable harm in itself, it would be more than offset by the serious harms it prevented.

Notice here that the calculations involved in considering punishment depend on the indirect benefits caused by immediate harms. Once indirect effects are considered, however, it can be seen that the harms of rape have so far been underestimated. For, as well as the direct harm to the victim, there is the much more prevalent indirect harm of the fear caused by cases of rape in large sections of the population. Even if many rapes are committed in domestic contexts between people who already know each other, many are not. There is an anonymity about rape such that women never know when they might be a victim. A woman is much more likely to be raped than murdered by someone with whom she has no previous acquaintance; and this in turn constrains, sometimes severely, the things that she thinks it safe to do. This is a massive harmful consequence of rape; for even if the inconvenience of such constraint in particular cases may be small, so many people are involved that the total cannot but be large. So, as well as the high level of seriousness of rape, and so punishment, which even consideration of the direct consequences would imply, there is also a greatly raised level of seriousness implied by the indirect consequences.

Consideration of these further, or indirect, consequences brings out an analogy between rape and punishment. On the utilitarian view the punishment is a harm in itself which is only justified by its overall social consequences: if it is calculated correctly, people's actions will be constrained in particular ways so that they will not (normally) do such things as murdering and stealing. But this is exactly how it is possible to look at rape: particular unpleasant things which happen to a few people constrain the actions of the female half of society. Freedom to travel, to dress, to conduct sexual and other relationships, may all be constrained by the threat of rape if someone happens to be a woman. So rape could be seen as a sort of punishment of women by men which, applied in a few cases, has the effect of moulding general patterns of social behaviour.

From this point of view it might seem that the sovereign male exerts his power by the exemplary punishment of the few subject women who step out of line; this is reinforced by court proceedings in which the woman rather than the man seems to be on trial. Yet although there is an interesting analogy between this use (or abuse) of power and justified punishment, the disanalogy is more important. With justified punishment, the indirect effects are beneficial, yet here the indirect effects are, taken as a whole, harmful. The constraint on the liberty of half the members of society forms a sizeable disutility which could not plausibly be offset by the supposed gain to the other half. Once the indirect effects are properly considered, this breaks the analogy with justified punishment and strengthens the utilitarian case for the badness of rape.

Some sort of answer is possible therefore from a utilitarian perspective to the question of the badness of rape and this could be used to assess either its harm as a general rule (for example as a basis for legal or social policy) or its harm in a particular instance (for example as the basis for the punishment of an individual or other moral assessment of an individual's actions). The fact that it does provide answers is supposed to be one of utilitarianism's strengths. On the other hand, a frequent objection to utilitarianism is that the definite answers which it does provide can clearly be seen to be wrong; that is, it would only take a moment's thought by any right-minded person to see that we should not do what utilitarianism prescribes.

As was seen above, utilitarianism allows the sacrifice of a minority to be outweighed by the greater happiness of a majority. However much a general rule can be formulated which establishes the badness of a particular course of action, it is nearly always possible to construct individual cases in which the particular benefits that follow from the action more than outweigh its harms. This applies also to rape: gang rape, or multiple rape by, for example, the soldiers of a victorious army is probably even more horrific for the victim than single rape. However, the numbers are no longer balanced evenly and so it becomes conceivable (if these things can be weighed or calculated at all) that the happiness of the majority of rapists might outweigh the unhappiness of the single victim. Even if this never holds, there could be additional side effects of a particular case of rape (such as, for example, the birth of a child who would not have been born if the rape had not occurred) which produced more happiness in the long run than the unhappiness to the victim (even if having such a child might not give pleasure to the mother, the child is normally glad to have been born). Even if this is excluded by a decision not to include the effects on currently non-existing people, or to exclude unpredictable effects, there could be other cases where a rape is undertaken as a piece of intentional political or public policy so that the happiness of the many is an explicit part of the act. The rape of the Sabine women might be such an example, or an act in which the rape of a symbolic political figure or priestess was an essential part of an attempt to destroy her power (an action somewhat similar to tyrannicide). These are only rough sketches of possible examples, but it does seem fairly certain that if we work by utilitarian criteria, even if they unproblematically make the normal case of rape an unjustified harm, there are still a few actual or possible cases of rape which these criteria would not condemn.

This will be unsurprising to the standard opponent of utilitarianism who has no difficulty (as the case of tyrannicide suggests) in showing how utilitarianism also justifies murder, breaking of promises, execution of the innocent, or any other activity that is supposed to be wrong. For all these unpleasant activities it is similarly possible to construct particular actual or possible circumstances in which they would be justified from a utilitarian point of view. So it would seem that the only viable moral theory to have must be a theory of rights in which no one is justified in doing anything to anyone which violates any one of his or her rights. With such a theory it would no longer be permissible to kill a tyrant or to execute an innocent man, however good the results. Similarly (at least on the plausible assumption that control of one's own body and freedom from attack or violation is a basic right), however good the consequences, no one would ever be justified in raping anyone else. So it seems that the natural or expected result emerges easily from such a theory. Even more simply than in utilitarianism, the normal case of rape is unjustified and, unlike utilitarianism, all the abnormal or special cases are also unjustified.

This apparent gain, however, is not as impressive as it looks. For I started by saying that it is unproblematic that rape is a bad thing and that the problems come more with deciding why it is bad and how bad it is. Even though a theory of rights might provide some answer to the first of these problems, even if rather too short an answer, it cannot, at least on present showing, provide any sort of answer to the second. The whole problem about rights being trumps is that once we have two trumps there is no way with these trumps (unlike a normal suit of trumps) to decide how the different trumps should be ranked. Talking of rights has the virtue of making certain courses of action impossible or unthinkable. It makes it impossible (legitimately) to rape someone or to execute an innocent man. However, once we are stuck with a choice between two such impossible things, we have no guidance about what to do; whatever we do will be impossible or wrong, and one thing will be no worse than another.

We could, of course, change our view of rights in order to meet this objection so that we now held that rights were ordered in accordance with their importance. This would indeed dispose of some of the examples that many people would feel to be difficult on the original view. If, for example, we assume that people have a right not to have their property invaded without permission, then, however great the benefit, or whatever other rights might be preserved, on the original view, someone would not be legitimately entitled to invade someone else's property. So, faced with a choice between rape or death on the one hand, and a minor trespass in order to hide from an aggressor on the other, the original view would not permit such a trespass. If, however, the view is revised so that some rights are now held to be more important than others, then the trespass now becomes permitted. It would be possible to rank these two rights so that the right not to have one's property invaded counted less than the right not to be killed, and the invasion (infringing a lesser right to preserve a greater) would now be justified.

Unfortunately, however, such an attempt to preserve a theory of rights runs into the obvious problem of how such a ranking might be achieved. The natural way to rank rights is in terms of the damage (the harm, or pain and suffering) caused to the victims. Doing it in this way, however, is to do it very much as utilitarianism does: something that causes more suffering comes out as worse, and rape becomes a more important violation of rights than trespassing on to someone's land just because it causes more suffering to the victim. So, it seems, the same result is reached in the same way. Furthermore, the chief point of moving to rights from utilitarianism was that the rights approach prevented the kind of trade off between different advantages or harms which utilitarianism permits, and which therefore allowed the suffering of one person if this was compensated by the greater good of someone else.

Once we come back to allowing the comparison of different rights, sacrifice of the lesser for the greater reappears and trade offs again become permissible. In the trespass example, the rights of an innocent third party, the landholder, are sacrificed in order to preserve the greater right of someone else, the person who would be otherwise raped or murdered. But if I may enter your land to stop myself being murdered or raped, may I then also rape you to stop myself being murdered? The circumstances in which such a choice could occur would be extremely rare, but this is also true of some of the strange examples which are thought up to produce apparently strange results from utilitarianism. Once it becomes possible to compare and trade off one rights violation with another, violation not just of rights but also of people again becomes possible. Just as in utilitarianism, such a theory of rights would mean that rape was not permitted in all normal cases, but it would be allowed under certain exceptional circumstances.

One way in which this objection could be met would be to continue to allow that certain rights were more important than others but to forbid comparing the violation of one person's rights with the violation of someone else's. In this way it could be agreed that there was a greater violation of my rights if I was raped than if there had been trespass on to my land, but not so great as if I had been murdered. (This would not be a vacuous assessment as it might have an important bearing on punishment.) However, it would not be permitted to infringe one of your rights, however relatively unimportant, in order to prevent the infringement of one of my rights, however important. This, however, merely returns us to the original problem of forbidding trespass on an innocent third party's land in order to prevent rape or murder; for such trespass would now once again not be permitted. This is a logically consistent view, but a difficult one to maintain with conviction. Once it is agreed that some rights are more important than others, then it seems more natural (even if it is not logically compelled) to compare the less important right of one party with the more important right of another. The impartiality mentioned at the beginning again leads off in a direction similar to utilitarianism in which the harms to people are looked at equally and hence the greater harms are prevented at the cost of permitting the lesser ones.

It might be thought that the problems here are created by the original example, in which it seems (to most people) absurd to forbid the trespass on someone's land in order to prevent a rape or murder. The example makes the point because it compares what would normally be regarded as a less important rights violation with a more important one. However, another way of getting rid of the example would be to hold that it was not an example of rights violation at all; that is, that no one had a right not to have his land trespassed upon. The counter-examples, and the general argument based upon them would be met by shrinking the area of rights to a small central area. These few remaining rights could all be looked at as being of equal importance so that for them the problem of trade off would not arise. This, of course, would work, but would still leave the question of which of the many things normally regarded as rights should be privileged to occupy the small area. If the area was too large, the pressure would become too strong to treat some of them as being of more importance than others. On the other hand, if the area was too small, then the theory of rights would have little impact upon problems arising out of the moral or social assessment of action, and these issues would all have to be handled by another means, such as utilitarianism.

It seems, therefore, as if the answer to our original problem will be provided by assessing the relative harms and benefits to victim and aggressor. Either these harms and benefits will be directly compared with each other and traded off, as in utilitarianism, or else they will be used as the basis of a theory of rights in which they are used to rank rights so that rights violation (or the violation of more important rights) is a worse thing than anything else. This, however, still leaves us with the problem of how these harms are to be assessed and compared one with another.

COMPARISON OF HARMS

When assessing the results of rape, either directly or indirectly, we have to be able to compare the harm to the victim with the benefit to the aggressor. In traditional utilitarianism this was done by considering the happiness or unhappiness (the pleasure or pain) which each experienced. Yet the measurement of happiness, or even deciding what happiness is, let alone comparing such apparently dissimilar things as pleasure and pain, are all fraught with difficulty.

This is familiar and difficult terrain for anyone thinking about utilitarianism. A tempting short cut is to see whether we might not be able to move more directly to the answer by working backwards from the facts of choice to the reasons for them rather than forwards from the supposed reasons to the choices. In other words, whatever happiness (or pleasure and pain) are, people do seem to be able to choose between different courses of action. So, the attempted short cut is to count something as being of greater happiness (and so, by extension, of more benefit) if it is something which people would choose. So, for example, if people normally choose to experience a passing pleasure rather than a passing pain, this shows that the pleasure brings more happiness than the pain. Because people can choose, we assume that some basis of choice must exist; that is to say, the apparently dissimilar things are, after all, comparable.

These comparisons are, of course, only made by a particular individual and different individuals may prefer different things. Many of the answers that we wish to reach in this area, however, are merely generalizations. We want to know whether, in general, one thing is better or worse than another as a guide to our legal or social policy. In this context it seems quite reasonable to say, as was said above, that the harms suffered by the victim of rape outweigh the benefits to the rapist. This is a generalization. Nevertheless, in that it is not the same person who is both victim and rapist, it might seem that in this case not even a general comparison can be made. The short cut attempted to avoid any direct measure of happiness, or comparisons of pleasure and pain, by looking instead at what people choose. There is no one person, however, in any normal example of rape, who can choose whether to be victim or rapist. We cannot, therefore, use the choice of such a person to compare the suffering of the victim with the pleasure of the aggressor in the way that we might be able to decide whether or not, for example, the pain of visiting the dentist was compensated for by the future benefits. In that circumstance the same person both suffers and benefits from the experience and so can choose whether the one is worth the other. This is not the case with rape, and so it seems that not even generalizations are possible.

Solving this problem depends upon returning to the idea of imaginative access to the positions of people other than ourselves. Even if there is no direct choice, we can still consider what it might be like to be the people involved. This demands imagination but, in so far as we can have some idea what it would be like to behave in a way different to that in which we do behave, or experience things different from those which we do in fact experience, we can have some idea about which experience or course of action we would choose in hypothetical circumstances. So, we might be able to ask ourselves as a thought experiment whether we would be prepared to undergo two experiences, in one of which we were raped by someone and in the second of which we raped someone. The question we ask ourselves is whether we would prefer to have both experiences or neither, on analogy with the question of whether we would prefer to go to the dentist (and have both the drilling and also the ultimate relief) or not to go (and have neither experience). If this sort of imaginative assessment or choice is possible at all, then we should be able in this way to measure whether the pain experienced in the one incident would be outweighed by the pleasure experienced in the other.

With the particular case of rape in mind, however, it may reasonably be claimed that it is exactly this kind of thought experiment which it is senseless to suppose can be undertaken. Here the strains between a thought experiment engaged in in the calm of philosophical study and the realities of what actually happens become only too apparent. In everyday sorts of cases it might plausibly be supposed that a third party could assess the relative benefits and harms of some action on other people. A mother, for example, may be able to decide on the relative pleasures and disappointments that giving a treat to one of her two children at the expense of the other would cause, relying in doing so on her understanding (her ability to grasp in imagination) of the feelings produced in her children by the alternative courses of action. She could even ask herself whether she would prefer to be like (both of) John pleased and Henry disappointed or like (both of) Henry pleased and John disappointed.

This example, however, is an everyday comparison between everyday objects of experience. In abnormal kinds of behaviour, such as rape, people may very well feel that they lack this kind of imaginative access. There is no problem imagining what it is like to be a victim, but imagining what it is like to be a rapist is peculiarly difficult, for to understand him from his own point of view involves understanding the pleasure that he gets from the activity. However, since this is an activity which most people do not, and would not, choose to undertake, it is difficult for the majority of people to understand the attraction.

If a position is imaginatively inaccessible, however, then there is no way of comparing the benefits and the harms. In one way this might be thought to be a useful result, because, assessed from the standpoint of the supposed normal person, there are no obvious benefits in rape to set off against the understandable harms. On the other hand, just because the normal person might not feel any particular benefit does not seem to be a good reason for supposing that no one might; after all, the original utilitarian idea proceeded on the assumption that all were to be treated alike or equally. The person, that is, with abnormal tastes and pleasures should be treated in just the same way (given neither more nor less weight) than someone with normal tastes and pleasures. If this abnormal person is imaginatively inaccessible, then it does not seem that he can be given any weight at all and so the utilitarian calculation would seem to be impossible.

INTENTION AND CHOICE

We have looked at only part of a general problem regarding the whole method of assessing comparative pleasures and pains (happiness) by means of people's preferences. For such assessment, even if we do have the kind of imaginative access just described, also depends on the assumption that people understand fully the courses of action between which they are choosing; and that, if they get what they want, they like what they get. Yet such a supposition is at best artificial and at worst false. Again it is the case that assumptions that might work elsewhere, at least for practical purposes, become exposed as intolerably artificial in the special case of rape. There is no reason to suppose that a rapist driven by desire is necessarily satisfied at all, even if he gets what he wants.

The particular bearing of this on rape is because the concepts of intention and desire play a crucial part not just in our understanding or assessment of rape, but also in its very identification. What principally distinguishes rape from normal sexual activity is the consent of the raped woman. Of course, in law, the intention of the man is also very important. However, what the man's intention is, and hence what action the man takes himself to be undertaking, depends upon what he understands the intention of the woman to be. So the central feature here again is what the woman is intending to do, even if reflected through the man's perception of this intention rather than what the intention actually is in itself.

This involvement of intention with the very identification of rape is not merely a semantic matter; that would be less important, and we could in the end decide to define 'rape' as we wished. The important point is that the identification of rape is bound up with its evaluation. Rape is distinguished from other forms of sexual activity precisely because it is normally evaluated in a different way, and, at least in the normal liberal approach to questions of evaluation, what crucially makes it different is that with rape someone is forced to engage in an action that they do not wish to engage in. The lack of intention to do what was done both identifies what was done as an example of rape and also, on the same basis, displays what was wrong with it.

From this normal perspective, the central point about rape is that it is something which a woman is made to undertake against her will. If she had willed it, it would not be wrong. This is in line with the reasonable and frequently accepted legal maxim *volenti non fit iniuria*, that is, that when someone wishes something there is no (legal) injury or harm (even though this maxim is not one that is universally followed in English law). So, it would seem that if only the apparent victim willed the action, this would make all the difference. Physical hurt or pain is not the point but the attitude of the person so hurt: if that person really wants what happens, then although people might find what happened distasteful, it would not be positively wrong.

This could be tested out by comparing cases in which a woman is hurt but consents with one in which the power relations are reversed, such as a man employing a prostitute to beat or humiliate him. If the man, who can be assumed to be in a position of considerably greater financial power, purchases such a service, particularly if he has done so before and so it is clear to him at the time of purchase what it involves, then it is reasonable to say that he is getting what he wants. Yet what he is getting is hurt and suffering; indeed that is precisely what he has paid for. Just like playing rugby or boxing, the actual or possible suffering was envisaged and chosen, and because of this it is something which, although we may not understand it, we are reluctant to forbid unless it leads to positive harm to others (even though it is just in this kind of area that English law is reluctant to follow the *volenti non fit iniuria* principle). So: if wanted, then no harm; if harm, then not wanted. What is important here is not the normality of the sexual activity, nor even whether it causes pain, but whether it is freely desired by the parties involved.

This frequent, or normal, evaluation of the importance of choice and the utilitarian assessment of benefit and harm march hand in hand; indeed they come from the same stable. If people are the complete authorities about what they want (or what gives them satisfaction), then following their free choices is the way of providing most benefit to them. Correspondingly, there is no reason to impede someone's getting something that they want unless it leads to the greater harm of someone else. It is on these assumptions that this chapter started: rape was taken to be fairly unproblematically harmful on balance because it was supposed that it was nearly always the case that any pleasure that the rapist gains is more than outweighed by the pain of the victim, and it was presumed that the one party gained pleasure and the other pain because the one party chose the action while the other did not. However, once it is supposed that the choices that people make may not adequately represent their real desires, then the comparisons which form the basis for the utilitarian assessment are no longer available. Correspondingly, we may no longer have the basis for making an evaluative distinction between rape and normal sex, for if people are no longer authoritative about their desires, then the apparent or expressed desire of the apparent victim may no longer be the appropriate thing on which to base the distinction.

If we lack the possibility of assessing relative harms and benefits because of the great variety of human desires (including pathological ones, as in the case of rape), and if we cannot find out even generalizations about relative harms and benefits by observation of the actions of possibly self-deceived people, then it seems that the only possible way to proceed would be by some *a priori* model of what people desire or of what really makes them happy. It is tempting to use such a language of 'real desires' or of 'real happiness' because what such a model aims to reveal is that people may think they want those things they are trying to get, but what they really want is something quite different; it appears to them as if something will satisfy them, but it is only something else which really will. The rapist's pleasures might then be taken to be ephemeral or fundamentally unreal, not even bringing any (real) pleasure to the rapist himself as compared with the only too real pain and violation of the victim. Hence, in any comparison there would be no problem and no contest and rape would come out as unproblematically bad as it was before this discussion started.

A PRIORI MODELS

The idea of the *a priori* model seems to solve our problem — or would do — except that any such handy model of the (real) nature of man and hence of what (really) makes him happy is liable to be purely stipulative and hence unpersuasive. We might, for example, say that man was the son of God and so what really made him happy was approach to God. We then could disallow all apparent attempts to seek or choose other things as not bringing real happiness and set aside apparent miseries or difficulties in the pursuit of God. Or we might hold that the real essence or nature of man was to live as an unalienated being and so hold that this is what he really wanted, or what would really make him happy, even if all or nearly all the actually observed men did not seem in the least to desire to be unalienated. Powerful tool though this is, however, it only works for the converts; and, in general, there is not enough widespread acceptance of, or agreement about, any underlying metaphysics which might deliver such results.

The same is true if we consider what sort of analogous general views about the nature of man (or man and woman) would deliver similar conclusions about what people really want, or what really makes them happy in sexual relations. Again we can find powerful models. Once again, however, it seems that they are too stipulative to work as an adequate foundation for a policy, an argument, or even a discussion. In fact they are so powerful that they can very easily deliver the converse, but equally apparently absurd, results that all cases of sexual activity are really cases of rape or that no cases of sexual activity are. To achieve the latter we merely need the view that the real nature of women is that they all really want it, to make all the normal cases of male—female rape concealed cases of benefit to the apparent victim. The cries of protest or apparent evidence of lack of desire are taken to be no better evidence of what someone really wants in this case than the apparent disinclination of people to put themselves closer to God or to join the true and unalienated party.

On the other hand, if this wiping out of the whole of rape at a stroke is thought to rest upon a deficient (sexist, patriarchal) model of woman, restoring it with a model of man as the inveterate aggressor and woman as natural victim is liable to tilt the balance the other way. All cases of normal heterosexual sexual activity become examples of the exercise of inegalitarian male power. In other words, they all become cases of rape in which the male abuses his position of power in order to pleasure himself at the cost of his female victim. The fact that many women seem to enjoy this sex would again be quite irrelevant, as irrelevant as the fact that many people seem to whore after false gods or to enjoy living in the highly alienated surroundings of capitalist society. The only good sex would be lesbian sex among the sisterhood itself.

Such models, then, seem too powerful and immediate in their results and so, even if suitably qualified and controlled, we seem forced back on some form of utilitarian assessment if we want to measure the harm, particularly the amount of harm, involved in rape. For this to be possible, in turn, depends upon out being able to meet, or allay, some of the scepticism expressed above about whether we could understand choice (and so assess amounts of benefit or harm) in these psychologically unusual or pathological cases. Here, even if imaginative appreciation fails, observation of what actually happens may work. We need to be able to tell, as a sheer observable matter of fact, whether the pleasure gained by the rapist is real or lasting and whether the harm experienced by the victim is real or lasting. Because of the problem raised above about people being deceived about their desires, this would involve more than just observing what people choose to do. However, more than observation of the initial choices seems to be available to us. It is also possible, at least to some extent, to observe whether or not people are satisfied or disappointed with the choices they initially make. This involves, in part, observing subsequent choices which they make, such as choices about whether to repeat an experience or to stay in a situation.

Of course, all this involves actual observation, and so, as an actual empirical question, the answer to how long the delights of rape or the horrors of rape endure is not one that can be answered philosophically. All that can be done philosophically is to outline what things are observed in observing this, that is, what things should be observed in order to observe this. It does seem, however, that such observations can be made, even if it can not be dictated *a priori* what the results are.

If we allow that people can make mistakes, then we allow that, although a man wants to rape, and chooses to rape, this might not bring him the satisfaction he thought it would and also that, conversely, although a woman may not want to have sex with a man and is forced into doing so, in fact this might bring her ultimate satisfaction or liberation. This would be settled empirically, but the difficult questions for evaluation which such empirical investigations might throw up are again questions to which philosophy can be applied. If we did find, for example, that a course of action (stopping someone raping, being raped) made someone happier in the long run even though it was not what they had wanted at the time, would this, in itself, be a reason for doing such a thing? The answer to this is liable to depend upon the original split in value theory with which this chapter started: from a utilitarian point of view, doing something to someone for their own good is exactly that, for their own good, and so not in itself to be condemned; conversely, an upholder of fundamental rights might hold that it was a fundamental right of people that they should be free to damn themselves if they chose. Forcing ecstacy on others is merely an interference with human liberty.

The empirical investigations lead to philosophical questions which, in turn, suggest further empirical questions. So even though this short case study returns to the empirical, that is to the folly and the mire of the real world, philosophical questions remain. What starts as questions posed in the real world must in the end return to questions answered in the real world. In the interim, however, it is possible, without complete lack of sympathy or relevance, to consider them as questions posed and partially answered by political philosophy.

Acknowledgements

The approaches and problems presented in this chapter are fairly standard in current political philosophy, but I am particularly indebted to the work of Amartya Sen, who uses an example similar to the trespass example used above. The metaphor whereby rights are considered as a kind of trumps derives from Ronald Dworkin.

4

Rape, Seduction and Psychoanalysis

JOHN FORRESTER

INTRODUCTION

In the 1890s, Sigmund Freud proposed a theory of the aetiology of the neuroses which he called the seduction theory: the claim that neuroses were caused by the after-effects of the sexual abuse and seduction of children. Some five years ago, I began to ask myself the question: why did he call this theory the seduction theory rather than the rape theory?

In reading feminist writers on rape, I was driven to recognize that many of them regard psychoanalytic writings as being profoundly iniquitous. At a cursory glance, it seemed as if these writers assumed that *any* psychoanalytic account of rape would paint the rape victim as *wanting* to be raped, so that *any* psychoanalytic account became synonymous with *excusing* the rapist, by portraying him as a seducer, rather than a rapist.

In this, the feminist writers were in part reflecting the practice of rape defence trials, in which the victim is often imputed to have tacitly consented to intercourse. Such defences often revolve around the folklore wisdom that 'No' sometimes means 'Yes'.

So I was led to consider the difference between rape and seduction. In particular, I found myself concerned with psychoanalytic writings (in which rape is never mentioned, despite Freud's early concern with sexual assault as the original trauma in the neuroses), with feminist writings on rape (which assume that psychoanalysis excuses rape and vilifies rape victims, by giving a cast-iron defence case to each and every man suspected of rape) and with legal writings, in which heterogeneous views of intention, motive and sexual behaviour are woven together around the basic concept of consent. This chapter attempts to unravel the issues raised and confused by many of these writings, drawn from these three heterogeneous discourses.

The axis of my argument hinges around the distinction between rape and seduction, so important in legal practice. Yet I examine this primarily from the perspective of psychoanalysis, in which the distinction between rape and seduction is seemingly ignored, in favour of the interminable ambiguities of seduction. It is precisely this preoccupation with the ambiguous and the ambivalent that seems to be recognized by feminist writers on rape as antithetic to their certainties, which embody a hasty temptation to regard seduction as just rape under another name. In psychoanalysis, on the other hand, the tendency is the opposite: an inability to recognize rape as falling within the field of the analyst's operation and action. Both tendencies elide the distinction between rape and seduction. It is this elision that the chapter explores.

RAPE AND PSYCHOANALYSIS

We may thank the legacy of Freudian psychology for fostering a totally inaccurate popular conception of rape . . . the serious failure of the Freudians stemmed from their rigid unwillingness to make a moral judgment.

Susan Brownmiller puts her finger on the problems raised by linking rape with psychoanalysis, as she does with so many other questions relating to rape in her influential work, *Against Our Will.*[1] Yet, within her discussion of rape and psychoanalysis there is an interesting contradiction that this chapter will aim to explore. Brownmiller recognizes the paucity of material on rape produced by Freud and the Freudians, and yet claims that their legacy fostered 'a totally inaccurate popular conception of rape'. How can both these claims be true?

Perhaps we should first inquire whether it is true that the great modern authority on sexuality said nothing about rape and rapists. *The Concordance to the Standard Edition of the Complete Psychological Works of Sigmund Freud* records only one usage of the word 'rape' — and that is an 'attempted rape'. There is certainly no case history of a rapist, nor of a rape victim, in the fifty or so cases listed in the Index of Cases. Rather, it is through the psychology of women propounded by Freudians that an influentially misleading conception of rape is said to have arisen, and in particular, for Brownmiller and others, from the work of Freud's close disciple, Helene Deutsch.[2]

Men have always raped women, but it wasn't until the advent of Sigmund
Freud and his followers that the male ideology of rape began to rely on the
tenet that rape was something women desired.[3]

Brownmiller reconstructs a chain of arguments stemming from Freud's
work, elaborated upon brilliantly by Deutsch as her 'dictum of the hysterical,
masochistic female',[4] and finding their way into the dominant Freudian
school of criminology of the 1950s, which essentially *does away* with the
crime of rape by proving that there are no victims. In Brownmiller's portrayal
of the argument, Freudian psychology provided a scientific carte blanche for
anyone wishing to doubt the word of a rape victim. Feminine sexuality was
by nature masochistic, hence rape could not take place since it encountered
female masochistic nature and was immediately accepted by it.[5] It is this
argument that feeds into the four 'deadly male myths of rape', in particular
the belief that 'ALL WOMEN WANT TO BE RAPED'.[6]

But, of course, there is also the other side of the coin — the rapist. How
has Freudian theory presented him? Certainly, there are very few accounts of
the psychoanalysis of a rapist, but there are a number of psychologically
orientated studies of the rapist-in-prison (no doubt a different creature from
the rapist-at-large). It is these studies that Brownmiller castigates for their
moral neutrality. She quotes without comment — as if the preposterous and
demeaning character of the argument were obvious for all to see — from a
study of the *wives* of rapists, which aimed to show that the sexual frustration
these wives induced in their husbands was one of the factors motivating rape,
since they elicited from their husbands 'a displaced attempt to force a
seductive but rejecting mother into submission'.[7] With a rhetorical flourish,
Brownmiller abandons, with relief, the individual-orientated, clinical,
psychopathological studies of rapists, for the more modern sociological
studies, which give us, 'above all, hard, cold statistical facts about crime'.[8]

Such treatment of the Freudian criminological literature, by no means
restricted to Brownmiller, is designed to head off argument concerning her
major contention, that the act of rape is committed by ordinary men on
ordinary women. The profile of the rapist is not to be cordoned off into the
specialist field of the psychiatrist since the 'typical American perpetrator of
forcible rape is little more than an aggressive, hostile youth who chooses to
do violence to women'.[9] Brownmiller, and many other feminist writers since,
are concerned to demonstrate that the rapist is not capable of being
distinguished from ordinary men by his character structure, or his early
development, or his relations with women, in the same way that the rape
victim is not to be distinguished from ordinary women by her disposition to

hysteria, to masochistic fantasy and to telling lies. The argument aims to render void both strands of a psychological account of the rapist, the one pertaining to him, the other pertaining to his victim. Freudian theory is seen to be the main support for both these psychological accounts. Indeed, the implication of this argument is that *any* psychological account of the facts of rape, whether it be Freudian or any other, is potentially dangerous and misleading, since it will obscure the conclusion, that:

> police-blotter rapists are dreary and banal . . . Rape is a dull, blunt, ugly act committed by punk kids . . . , not by charming, witty, unscrupulous, heroic, sensual rakes, or by timid souls deprived of 'normal' sexual outlet, or by *supermenschen* possessed of uncontrollable lust.[10]

These dreary punks have as their 'historic mission the perpetuation of male domination over women by force'.

There are a number of responses one could make to this line of argument. The first, and least fertile, is to defend the psychoanalytic concept of masochism from certain misunderstandings.[11] It is possible to retrieve psychoanalytic accounts from these criticisms without disputing the detrimental effects psychological and psychopathological theories have had upon discussion of rape. Brownmiller herself, like many other feminists, has complex reactions to Deutsch's 'sombre' view of sex and feminine sexuality, and to Freud's version of the feminine psyche. The feminists sense a truth which they usually repudiate in the form: this applies to what happens now, in patriarchal society. One can also show how Brownmiller misreads both Freud and Deutsch — where Brownmiller simply states that Freud put forward the 'dogma that women are masochistic by nature and crave the "lust for pain"',[12] one could easily show that she is misunderstanding Freud, whose discussion of feminine masochism is entirely based, as he, perhaps ironically, notes, on work with male patients. He found that fantasies (and sexual acts) of a feminine masochistic character are those that 'place the subject in a characteristically female situation; they signify, that is, being castrated [i.e. 'the wish to have a passive (feminine) sexual relation with the father'], or copulated with, or giving birth to a baby'.[13]

The overall details, however, are not what is at issue. Brownmiller's has been the strongest, but by no means the only, voice taking issue with any intrusion of psychoanalytic ideas into discussion of rape. There is a sense of a real threat here, even though psychoanalysis does not talk of rape. Why?

UNCONSCIOUS MOTIVATION

There is one, seemingly insignificant, passage in Freud which deals with sexual attacks on women. It appears as a footnote in *The Psychopathology of Everyday Life* (1901), in the chapter on 'Bungled Actions'. Freud is discussing whether 'half-intentional self-injury' exists, and proposes a model in which an unconscious intention to self-injury or self-destruction may make skilful use of a threat to life in order to manifest itself. He then turns to suicide:

> Even a *conscious* intention of committing suicide chooses its time, means and opportunity; and it is quite in keeping with this that an *unconscious* intention should wait for a precipitating occasion which can take over a part of the causation and, by engaging the subject's defensive forces, can liberate the intention from their pressure.

There then follows a footnote:

> After all, the case is no different from that of a sexual assault upon a woman, where the man's attack cannot be repelled by her full muscular strength because a portion of her unconscious impulses meets the attack with encouragement. It is said, as we know, that a situation of this kind *paralyses* a woman's strength; all we need do is to add the reasons for this paralysis. To that extent the ingenious judgement delivered by Sancho Panza as governor of his island is psychologically unjust (*Don Quixote*, part 2, chapter 45). A woman dragged a man before the judge alleging he had robbed her of her honour by violence. In compensation Sancho gave her a full purse of money which he took from the accused; but after the woman's departure he gave him permission to pursue her and snatch the purse back again from her. The two returned struggling, the woman priding herself on the fact that the villain had not been able to take the purse from her. Thereupon Sancho declared: 'If you had defended your honour with half the determination with which you have defended this purse, the man could not have robbed you of it.'[14]

The complexity and allusiveness of the argument here should not prevent us from extracting the important point from it. Freud is proposing a model whereby a conscious desire to repel a man's assault is subverted by an unconscious impulse to meet it with encouragement: hence the well-known paralysis of women when sexually attacked.[15] But the point in quoting the story from *Don Quixote* is to show that discovering such an unconscious impulse at work in a given case of *successful* sexual assault is *not* a reason for declaring that the woman had not been raped. The presence (or, for that matter, the *absence*) of an unconscious desire for sexual relations is not relevant to the question of whether the assault was against the woman's will or not. One might add: how could the question of consent be resolved by the existence of such an unconscious desire, since, in the Freudian universe, everybody has such unconscious desires? As Freud had argued on the penultimate pages of *The Interpretation of Dreams*, despite declaring himself unqualified to answer the question as to the ethical significance of suppressed wishes, 'would it not be right to bear in mind Plato's dictum that the virtuous man is content to *dream* what a wicked man really *does*? . . . we shall have to conclude, no doubt, that *psychical* reality is a particular form of existence not to be confused with *material* reality'.[16] Similarly, one does not hold a woman responsible for the unconscious desire for sexual contact made manifest in the paralysis she evinces when assaulted.

It should be noted that the force of this argument does not depend upon whether or not one believes that women, or some women, or any women, have such unconscious desires. The argument applies to all cases in which unconscious desires that are different from conscious desires exist, and manifest themselves on specific, stressful occasions. There is also an immediate corollary to the argument: whatever unconscious desires a subject may possess should play no role whatsoever in evaluating whether they did or did not consciously wish such and such an event to take place. Or, to put it another way, the domain of the unconscious is entirely separate from the domain of the will. And, it should be noted, from the nineteenth century onwards, the will, or consent, has been taken to be the crucial touchstone by which the existence of the act of rape has been judged.

So, the sole and unique passage in which Freud discussed the question of the adjudication of a case of sexual assault allows one to construct a clear argument as to why psychoanalysis is *irrelevant* to the class of questions raised by juridical investigations into rape. We also gain a sense of the differences between Freud and those of his followers who did enter into discussions of the motivations of rape victims: for Freud, such investigations were flawed since they did not take into account the difference between a conscious and an unconscious motive or impulse. As he put it:

> the pathogenic conflict in neurotics between mental impulses is not to be confused with a normal struggle between mental impulses both of which are on the same psychological footing . . . the disputants can no more come

to grips than, in the familiar simile, a polar bear and a whale. A true decision can only be reached when they both meet on common ground.[17]

Many of his followers, however, regarded the discovery of unconscious impulses, and the demonstration of their effects in symptoms, character traits etc., as giving an imperialistic licence for according them a privilege *over and above* conscious motives. For them, there was only one 'common ground' that counted, which might just as well be a court room as a couch. For Freud, psychoanalysis is the study of where conscious and unconscious motives fail to meet: he could give an account of the paralysis of victims of assault, but this would not lead him to commit the *injustice* (the word is his) of weighing such motives in the scales of justice. However, for many of his followers, psychoanalysis vouchsafed a *disregard* of conscious motives, since they subscribed to a view of unconscious motives as being the 'real' motives behind any and every act.

This distinction aids us in considering another question that has bedevilled discussions of rape: the relevance of women's rape fantasies. Many feminists have written as if the very *existence* of rape fantasies were an embarrassment, a collective shame of women, as if admitting their existence might give hostile men, or even simple sceptics, cause for returning to one of the male myths that all women (or, more moderately, those women who have rape fantasies) want to be raped. On this point, Brownmiller astutely keeps the arguments concerning unconscious and conscious rape fantasies entirely separate. With respect to conscious rape fantasies, she has little in the way of argument besides the statement:

> *The rape fantasy exists in women as a man-made iceberg. It can be destroyed — by feminism.*[18]

This statement seems to me only to repeat the disowning of responsibility that lies at the heart of the rape fantasy itself. It perpetuates, rather than examines, the common fantasy that sexuality is introduced into the woman from the 'outside', by an external force ('man-made'). (That is, it refuses the paradox of masochism, how can pain be pleasurable?, by regarding as a ridiculous imposition the question, how can something against my will be something I desire?)

The resolution of the problem for feminists anxious to keep the seemingly incriminating fact of rape fantasies at a distance seems to me to be the following: taking responsibility for one's fantasies is not the same sort of mental act as taking responsibilities for one's actions. It is much more like taking responsibility for one's memories, or for the conditions of one's early childhood, than for one's projects and conscious aims. If it is objected that psychoanalysis, as I have discussed it above, does not legitimate taking a rape victim's unconscious rape fantasies into account in considerations of rape as it actually happens — indeed quite the opposite — and now I seem to be arguing that one can reduce the conceptual tension associated with rape fantasies by taking responsibility for them, the objection allows me to point out the difference between the third party (police, court, friends, family) imputing 'responsibility' for a rape to a rape victim simply because they infer that she was prey to fantasies of violation or of 'irresponsible' sexuality, and the case I am considering here, in which the subject 'recognizes as his or her own' a fantasy, desire or memory. To be sure, the act of taking responsibility for one's memories affects one's projects and aims — that, after all, is precisely the goal of psychoanalytic therapy — but these projects and aims will not be faithful reproductions or blind repetitions of the past. Turning a rape fantasy to good use is no more likely to result in a project of being raped than turning a vengeful fantasy of suicide to good use will result in one's death.

Glanville Williams addressed these questions in his classic textbook, *Criminal Law. The General Part* (1953). In a section on unconscious motives, he recognized that the discovery of unconscious motives (and he here cites the chapter of Freud's *Psychopathology of Everyday Life* that the Don Quixote story comes from) presents difficult problems for legal thinking about intention. It must be said that the various arguments he employs do not sit well together. Williams is inclined to set aside unconscious motivations '(1) because it is difficult to prove satisfactorily, (2) because we have little knowledge of how far the threat of a sanction can influence the unconscious'.[19] However, he goes on to give an example of a neurotic symptom, arguing that

> it is not brought about by conscious intention, it is concealed from awareness; and it is therefore regarded as involuntary . . . a man is not criminally responsible for what he does in a *dream*. This would be so even if the dream happened to coincide with a conscious desire. The *mens rea* of a dream is not a *mens rea* for which a man is punishable; it is only the waking consciousness that involves criminal culpability.[20]

The argument is very close to that advanced by Freud. However, something goes amiss when Williams comes to address the question of proving the absence of consent in rape cases, in his *Textbook of Criminal Law* (1978).

Having recognized that 'the facts of life make consent to sexual intercourse a hazy concept', he argues, first, that: 'Many complaints of rape are false, since the woman in fact consented'. Secondly, he raises the question of the peculiar character of female sexuality:

> That some women enjoy fantasies of being raped is well authenticated, and they may welcome a masterful advance while putting up a token resistance . . . [He cites Deutsch at this point] This possibility needs consideration where the man was well known to the woman and where it is clear that she was not intimidated. If in these circumstances the woman failed to use all means open to her to repel the man, including shouting for help, the jury may well think it unsafe to convict him. Obviously the argument has no force where the man made an express threat or used *real* violence, for these are inconsistent with a *merely pretended* rape . . . One woman faced with a rapist intruder reported that her limbs seemed to go like jelly — though in the particular case she put up a resistance. Another confessed that her abhorrence of violence was so great that she preferred to submit than to attack. There is no evidence that juries are unduly prone to take the woman's non-resistance in such circumstances either as consent or as giving the man a credible defence of belief in consent.[21]

This passage pays careful attention to considerations of unconscious interference with a woman's capacity to resist (exactly Freud's point about paralysis due to unconscious interference), but it slides from recognizing the existence of rape *fantasies* to inferring from their existence a woman's conscious consent. It is beside the point whether a woman enjoyed the masterly advance or not; what is at issue is whether she consented — and in the final quoted sentence, Williams recognizes that assent is not the same as the absence of dissent, and it is the absence of assent which the law regards as sufficient to lead to conviction.

The scenario evoked is one in which both man and woman are play-acting at rape. Williams is evoking a seduction masquerading as rape. Yet if the seduction misfires, if the woman does not consent, then there is no reason for attenuating the degree of her non-consent (in any case, a legally impossible procedure), simply because it started off as play. Horseplay may well always end in tears, but a seduction that ends in rape is still rape.

We thus see that Williams is sensitive to the limits of psychoanalytic arguments about the significance of unconscious states of mind (including here unconscious consent, if needs be, although there are good grounds for believing that the unconscious is beneath the age of consent, since Freud maintained that in the unconscious there is no negation — and hence no affirmation of the sort required in law). However, Williams does not maintain this conceptual vigilance when the question of rape fantasies is at issue. There are parallel arguments in the law of assault, where consent to bodily harm is not taken to be legally viable. The analogy may be extended, since it is clear that certain forms of violence can be consented to: in boxing, for instance. But these are highly ritualized and controlled forms of assent to assault, corresponding to the play-acting account of the masterly advance and the token resistance. The question is, what are the limits of this game, and if one of the parties stops playing, can the other validly claim that the signal to end the game is a part of the game itself? As we shall see, psychoanalysis does venture on to this territory, but Freud was clear that invoking unconscious fantasies to remove responsibility from the assailant is not sanctioned by his concept of the unconscious.

THE CONCEPT OF CONFLICT

One can, however, go one step further. Not only does psychoanalysis in Freud's version specifically exclude itself from weighing the impact of unconscious desire on conscious states of mind, there is also an immiscibility of the topics of rape and psychoanalysis of a more fundamental character. Put simply, I want to argue that psychoanalytic discourse and legal discourse are entirely antipathetic.

In his study of the use of the insanity defence in nineteenth century murder trials, Roger Smith describes the conceptual confusions of doctors and lawyers alike in their attempt to integrate a psychiatric conception of mental states with a legal conception.[22] Psychiatrists often conceived of psychiatric descriptions as replacing traditional legal categories, such as *mens rea* (the legal term for the guilty state of mind). To enlightened positivistic psychiatrists, it seemed that the simple and crude, all-or-nothing categories required by law were anachronistic and inhumane.

The conflict between the two modes of discourse still exists, and has recently re-emerged in the context of notorious sexual murders, specifically the cases of the Boston Strangler and the Yorkshire Ripper. The function of court cases as public spectacle, reaffirming, or affirming with special emphasis, the guilty man as morally abhorrent, has once again become of special importance. This is also the sense in which, as we have seen, Freudians are reproached for their unwillingness to make a moral judgement. The argument always seems to be, either mad or bad. Yet, as our discussion above made clear, Freud was careful to distinguish moral judgements according to whether they were based on conscious or unconscious contents. For him, 'mad' and 'bad' work on entirely different axes. Yet it is, of course, true that if one looks to Freudian theory for moral support, one is sure to be disappointed, and with reason: its claim to avoid moral positions one way or the other is a jealously guarded privilege through which it offers asylum to its clients.

However, rape has become the site for a social and ethical crisis, associated with the women's liberation movement. Disappointment with liberalism, with live-and-let-live attitudes to ethics, with radical politics and with the defence of liberties (especially those of the rape defendant) at all costs, has included disillusionment with any institution that fails to offer an ethical or indeed spiritual lead. In this area, psychoanalysis is doubly offensive, since its very existence stems from an a-moralism, a refusal of ethical positions. (This refusal stems, as I will show later, from the discovery of the 'transference'.) What is more, the ethical crisis is often couched in terms of a struggle for the recognition of absolute and inviolable rights. For some, what is offensive is the imagined condoning of rape, by psychoanalysis or other discourses, through invoking the universal presence of rape fantasies or the naturally masochistic nature of feminine sexuality. But for others, the issue of rape symbolizes any restriction of the right of women to sexual self-determination. Rape is the principal violation and the principal challenge to this right: it is the strategic site for the battle that will determine the course of the war.

Psychoanalysis turns its back on social conflict; or, more accurately, it brackets off social conflict, conflict *between* individuals, to highlight the conflict *within* individuals. If the iconography of rape is ideally suited for an allegorical portrayal of social conflict, and of sexual conflict, psychoanalysis can find no or little use for rape as metaphor, model or theme. In the ceramics that Froma Zeitlin discusses in chapter 7,[23] the conflict is between *demand* (on the part of the god, usually male) and *resistance*. Similarly, as Norman Bryson demonstrates (chapter 8), rape provides a code for developing founding myths, although the 'privatization' or internalization of the experience of rape leads away from this function, sexualizing rape and bringing it closer to a seductive, fantasy-rich representation. Psychoanalysis, however, both as theory and practice, avoids conflict between parties, replacing it with a two-fold strategy. First, the theme of intra-psychic conflict, e.g. between the ego and the id, in which the id might well 'rape' the ego (Freud's term, in an early draft was 'overwhelm', a term that also crops up in the much criticised psychoanalytically influenced Benjamin Karpman, *The Sexual Offender and his Offenses*, New York: Julian Press, 1954). Secondly, any conflict that is seen to exist between analyst and patient is interpreted as a repetition of a past conflict, or a present unconscious conflict.

The exclusively intra-psychic conflict model of psychoanalysis has no place for rape, because it is solely concerned with the intra-subjective. Equally important, however, is the fact that rape cannot permit any hint of intra-subjective conflict to be admitted. If there is evidence that the victim was in a state of inner conflict, not attributable to the threat of force or duress exerted by the assailant, the prima facie case for rape is considerably attenuated. If it is thought the woman sets a 'price' on her consent,[24] if it is consent that can be measured against some other good, if it is a consent that can be argued with, or around, the case may well be set aside.[25] For instance, the police marked as 'unfounded' a case in which a woman consented to various sexual acts, believing that the man had agreed to stop short of vaginal intercourse: 'I did not want to have intercourse with him as the word is out that he has something wrong with him.'[26] In this case, the fact that she experienced orgasm, both before and during intercourse, probably had some influence on the police assessment of the immutability and intransigency of her lack of consent, despite this factor being strictly beside the point.

This latter case might well be seen to illustrate the psychoanalytic category of ambivalence: this woman both had good reasons for withholding consent, and did in fact withhold her verbal consent, while having an inclination to engage in the act. It is this perception of ambivalence, of competing and conflicting motivations, that seems to deprive the category of 'without her consent' of its necessarily absolute character. Note, however, that this is not an instance of *psychoanalytic* ambivalence, since there is no recourse to the notion of an unconscious impulse. Moreover, as we have seen, such a recourse is an illegitimate application of the psychoanalytic hypothesis of the unconscious, or of ambivalence. But it is exactly this sort of case that has earned psychoanalysis a bad reputation in the rape literature: its categories are seen to encourage the perception of mitigated or less than whole-hearted lack of consent. The crucial point is that, legally speaking, the concept of consent is an all-or-nothing one. To secure a rape conviction, the only psychological (if it is properly described as psychological rather than legal) state of the victim's mind that bears examination is her state either of consent or non-consent.

Such a presupposition about mental states parallels the controversial considerations of *mens rea* in murder cases (though many other crimes involve complex consideration of *mens rea*; in particular the notorious 1975 *Morgan* rape case, described by Temkin in chapter 2, was very important within 'subjectivist' legal thinking in general[27]). But such presuppositions are incompatible with those of psychoanalysis. To take one example: Freud noted in his Dora case history that the inner consistency of the life history the patient recounts is a means for differential diagnosis. Where there are inner inconsistencies, or manifest gaps, the diagnosis is probably hysteria. Where there are no such inconsistencies, the physician should look for an organic nervous disease. The assumption of psychoanalysis is that inner states of conflict manifest themselves in neurosis, and that these manifestations will always appear as faults, breaks, jumps in the life story recounted. But if there are any breaks in the narrative of a rape, if there is a gap in which the question of consent remains unsettled, one way or the other, the police and/or the court are liable to regard the rape as unfounded.

THE SEDUCTION THEORY

It may be true that the word 'rape' does not figure in Freud's vocabulary, but he did give prominence to sexual assault as a widespread trauma in the aetiology of the neuroses, especially in his early work. In this respect, he has been regarded as an early precursor — and traitor — of the recent spate of researches, conducted very much in parallel with detailed work on rape, on the sexual abuse of children.[28] If we were to follow the recent accounts of Florence Rush and Jeffrey Masson,[29] we would regard Freud as one of the earliest discoverers of the widespread sexual abuse of children, an early pioneer of understanding the extent of the permanent damage this caused to their psyches, but also one of those responsible, through failure of nerve, cowardice and self-deception, for engineering a cover-up on behalf of the perpetrators, taken to be male, of this crime.

In the 1890s, Freud slowly worked his way towards a full-blown theory of neurosis as resulting from the after effects of sexual abuse in childhood.[30] Beginning in May 1893, when he notes the absence in one specific case of memories of sexual abuse combined with things seen or heard and only half-understood, by November 1895 he was actively searching for 'infantile abuse' in his patients, both male and female — excitedly, he writes to his friend Fliess that one of his 'male hysterics . . . has given me what I was waiting for'.[31] In 1896 he went into print with his theory, in an article entitled 'The aetiology of hysteria'. In January 1897, he writes that the period when 'sexual abuse' in childhood brings about neuroses in later life covers the first three years of life.[32] In June 1897, he hypothesizes that, as children grow older, the father treats them with more circumspection, so that the 'seducers' in such instances are older brothers and sisters.

But, on his return from his summer holidays in 1897, Freud confesses the great secret that had been dawning on him for some months, namely that he no longer believes in this theory: he implies that he had never had an explicit case of sexual assault in childhood that adequately accounted for the structure and character of the adult neurosis his patient presented him with. None the less, though abandoning this theory, he retained much of the language: in July 1898, he is still referring to the 'seducer', when giving his interpretation of a work of the novelist Ferdinand Meyer, *Die Richterin*, and in his own analysis, in October 1897, he refers to his childhood nurse as his 'instructress in sexual matters'.

In place of the theory that every neurosis can be traced back to the effects of infantile sexual abuse, Freud argued that the infantile scenes still had a causative function, but that it did not matter whether they were real or imagined scenes. This discovery of the importance of fantasy opened up the way to the recognition that infantile sexual fantasy includes elements that are not usually present in adult sexual activity, involving the anus and the mouth. Beyond that, Freud recognized that the great theme of childhood fantasy is the fantasized relations to the parents — what he was later to call 'the Oedipus complex'. Most historians of psychoanalysis thus regard the abandonment of what Freud had called his 'seduction theory' as opening up the possibility of the discovery of two fundamental elements of Freud's later theory: infantile sexuality and the centrality of the Oedipus complex.

Yet a number of writers, including Jeffrey Masson and Alice Miller,[33] have regretted this action of abandoning the early seduction theory. They think that the turning away from the reality of sexual abuse both entailed by and a consequence of this abandoning was really a turning away from an unpalatable reality that Freud did not *want* to recognize. They, together with others who are less interested in psychoanalytic theory and more interested in determining the reality of infantile sexual abuse, claim that the extent of such abuse is enormously underestimated, as are its long-term effects. Such claims are often linked with the recent concern with rape, sometimes seen as a modern epidemic, or alternatively as an age-old consequence of a patriarchal, or male-dominated, social system. What I now want to examine is this seeming contradiction: Freud is said both to have ignored rape in a quite remarkable fashion, given his extensive concern for sexuality, while others have claimed him as a precursor, albeit a cowardly one, of the present concern with the widespread damage caused by rape and infantile sexual abuse.

A THEORY OF RAPE

As we have seen, Freud did not call his theory the 'rape theory'; nor did he use the word 'rape'. Instead, his name for it was 'the seduction theory'. The incidents this theory referred to were sometimes called 'abuse' (*Missbrauch*) or 'passive sexual experience'; but the most frequent term was 'seduction' (*Verfuhrung*) or, just as frequently, the verb form, and often the term 'seducer'. Why did Freud employ this term?

It is not straining the historical or textual evidence to claim that the reason Freud employed the term 'seduction' instead of 'rape' was because the traumatic effects of the event *when remembered* arose from the events not being experienced as rape. Instead, the subject's reactions to the memory were ones that implied his or her implication in the event: they might feel shame, guilt or tenderness. By 1895, Freud's cases had convinced him that it was always *sexual* fright that characterized the key trauma in the neuroses. The original trauma consisted in an adult performing sexual acts with a child. What distinguished Freud's theory from Charcot's and others', however, was his claim that the trauma only became *effective* in causing a neurosis by acting as a memory: the fright only occurred later, on the occasion of the second, seemingly innocuous scene. It was not the trauma that was 'traumatic', but rather the *memory* of the trauma, the trauma as memory.[34]

The idea that a distinctive process of remembering was a crucial part of the pathological process predated both the sexual thesis and the infantile thesis. This importance of remembering was bound up with the process of discovering the trauma: tracing a set of memories, conceived of as a chain or sequence, back through the past, in search of an experience that would be judged appropriate to count as an original trauma. At first, this process led to events at the age of puberty. At this point Freud raised an objection to regarding these memories as being the efficaciously 'traumatic' ones:

> In some cases, no doubt, we are concerned with experiences which must be regarded as severe traumas — an attempted rape, perhaps, which reveals to the immature girl at a blow all the brutality of sexual desire, or the involuntary witnessing of sexual acts between parents, which at one and the same time uncovers unsuspected ugliness and wounds childish and moral sensibilities alike, and so on. But in other cases the experiences are astonishingly trivial . . . For [one] young lady, simply hearing a riddle which suggested an obscene answer had been enough to provoke the first anxiety attack and with it to start the illness.[35]

What is more, he noted that in some cases the experiences were 'actually innocent': hence he was driven to look for the appropriate memories further back than puberty. He was quite explicit that a necessary condition of these experiences being traumatic was that they be bodily, or organic in some respect — 'sexual experiences affecting the subject's own body — of *sexual intercourse* (in the wider sense)'.

However, pushing back towards the period of childhood, 'a period before the development of sexual life',[36] only confirmed the centrality of memory:

> And since infantile experiences with a sexual content could after all only exert a psychical effect through their *memory-traces*, would not this view be a welcome amplification of the finding of psychoanalysis *that hysterical symptoms can only arise with the co-operation of memories?*[37]

Freud highlights this specific feature later, when he reflects:

> . . . we are not accustomed to the notion of powers emanating from a mnemic image which were absent from the real impression.[38]

In dealing with the vigorous objections he anticipated to this hypothesis, Freud recounted how venturing back into infancy had obliged him to reflect on the murky conditions of belief, lack of conviction and the grounds for verisimilitude of memories. Yet his response was already a sophisticated, some might say sophistical, one:

> While they are recalling these infantile experiences to consciousness, they suffer under the most violent sensations, of which they are ashamed and which they try to conceal; and, even after they have gone through them once more in such a convincing manner, they still attempt to withhold belief from them, by emphasizing the fact that, unlike what happens in the case of other forgotten material, they have no feeling of remembering the scenes.
>
> This latter piece of behaviour seems to provide conclusive proof. Why should patients assure me so emphatically of their unbelief, if what they want to discredit is something which — from whatever motive — they themselves have invented?[39]

Freud outlined other sources of confirmation or support for his claim as to the reality of the scene of sexual assault: the uniformity of the scenes described, the inclusion of details in the scenes whose significance the patient could not have known otherwise, the fact that the case history suddenly acquires a clear-cut, logically structured and self-evident character once the details of the scene are placed at the centre. The one 'really unassailable' proof would be the corroboration of the reality of the event by a third party, who had participated in it. He cites two such cases.

Having disposed of the twin objections that childhood seduction is either too frequent or too infrequent an event to be the cause of neurosis,[40] Freud then proceeds to give an account of the material at his disposal, asserting that 'it seems to me certain that our children are far more often exposed to sexual assaults than the few precautions taken by parents in this connection would lead us to expect'.[41] He divides his cases into three groups, according to the character of the other person providing the stimulation. The first category was assault by strangers, who engaged in isolated acts of abuse. 'In these assaults, there was no question of the child's consent, and the first effect of the experience was preponderantly one of fright.'[42] The third category was seductions of children by children: he lays down the rule that this can only occur if one of them has previously been seduced by an adult, the scene being an exact repetition of the original seduction. The most important class, however, is the second, much more frequent than abuse by strangers, in which an adult looking after the child 'has initiated the child into sexual intercourse and has maintained a regular love relationship with it — a love relationship, moreover, with its mental side developed — which has often lasted for years'.[43]

It is at this point that a different tone enters Freud's paper. Until this point he might well have been thought to have been sustaining the moral tone and engaging in the moral judgement that Brownmiller found so singularly and regrettably lacking in the writings of the Freudians. Freud does say:

> For the idea of these infantile sexual scenes is very repellent to the feelings of a sexually normal individual; they include all the abuses known to debauched and impotent persons, among whom the buccal cavity and the rectum are misused for sexual purposes.[44]

But, in the next sentence, he puts himself at a distance from this position of moral distaste:

> For physicians, astonishment at this soon gives way to a complete understanding.

Replacing amazement and repulsion by understanding, rather than indignation, allows Freud to describe the sexual abuse as an important and complex *relationship* between the adult and the child (or between the two children):

> All the singular conditions under which the ill-matched pair conduct their love-relations — on the one hand the adult, who cannot escape his share in the mutual dependence necessarily entailed by a sexual relationship, and who is yet armed with complete authority and the right to punish, and can exchange the one role for the other to the uninhibited satisfaction of his moods, and on the other hand the child, who in his helplessness is at the mercy of this arbitrary will, who is prematurely aroused to every kind of sensibility and exposed to every sort of disappointment, and whose performance of the sexual activities assigned to him is often interrupted by his imperfect control of his natural needs — all these grotesque and yet tragic incongruities reveal themselves as stamped upon the later development of the individual and of his neurosis . . .[45]

Here, Freud was specifically pointing to a class of cases in which the question of the child's consent did not arise; here, the predominant immediate effect or affect was not fright. In most of his cases of 'sexual abuse', the relationship is of the sort described above, in which (as recent commentators on child abuse have hastened to point out) the question of the child's consent is beside the point.[46] In Freud's cases, the relationship is as complex as one between adults: right from the start, before he had developed the concept of infantile sexuality, Freud was writing as if the child is as capable as an adult of complex relations involving sexual intercourse, 'with its mental side developed'.

Let us pause at this point and take stock. Freud may well have been an early discoverer of the surprising prevalence of childhood abuse, but what he focused on was the fact that it was *memories* of these events that were of significance to him as a neurologist-psychotherapist. What is more, the sexual abuses frequently, and most importantly for their later effects, included a complex relationship between child and adult. Consent is beside the point here. To be sure, Freud recognizes the absolute authority which the adult exerts over the child. Yet it is the dialectic of authority and servitude, of power and helplessness, of mutual dependence, of expectation and disappointment, of shame and embarrassment, which characterizes the relationship *and which leaves its mark on the child.*

It is clearer now why Freud called his theory of neurosis the seduction theory rather than the rape theory. In his account, it is not so much the presexual sexual shock (his phrase) or the fright induced in the child that is aetiologically significant. Rather, it is the implication of the child in a world that is foreign to it, a world which it is none the less destined, come puberty, to be obliged to make its own. 'Seduction' is etymologically a 'leading away'; Freud's theory is close to this sense — with a difference: the child is more properly being 'led towards'. What children flee from through repression is what the fleeing runners on the Greek vases described by Zeitlin (pp. 134—43) may be fleeing from — the loss of childhood.

So Freud's theory was never a simple cause—effect model of traumatic sexual abuse followed by neurotic effects. Three features of his seduction theory already point to psychological complexity well before he discarded the seduction theory; well before he ceased to attach importance to the reality of the infantile scenes. First, neurosis only arises when an infantile scene gives rise to an unconscious memory that is defended against in puberty; if the memory is not unconscious, defence has no pathological effect. Secondly, he was emphasizing that the coherence and inner consistency of the patient's life story (present symptoms leading back to early adolescent memories and traumata, which themselves lead back to the unconscious infantile scenes) was an important proof of the reality of the infantile scene.

With hindsight, we can see that this argument has little force: it proves the necessity of invoking a scene in early childhood, with such and such characteristic detail, but the reality of the scene is incidental to the criterion of consistency and coherence. What Freud's argument actually proves is that the patients did not *arbitrarily* invent the scenes: the detail of the scene has a logical or associative connection with later memories and symptoms. Its reality was first and foremost psychic, and only secondarily real in the sense of 'having occurred *out there*'.

Thirdly, he was as interested in the inter-subjective dialectic of adult and child as he was in the effects on the child of a sexual experience he or she was unprepared for. Fright might well have been an immediate effect, but for Freud the necessary condition was that the scene become unconscious, and fright was not closely connected with that process. More to the point, the interest in the dialectic of adult and child pointed somewhat imprecisely, but with far-reaching implications, towards focusing less on what the adult did to the child than on what elements in the child's complex response to the adult left traces. In Freud's account, the child is not a passive *tabula rasa* whose surface an adult violently breaches. Freud diverges from the original, Greek sense of trauma, meaning the breaching of the skin by external violence, by reconceptualizing it as a trace, a mark, like a tattoo, a lasting memorial of a communication. Precisely because memory was from the beginning of his work so central, the child's desires, fears, shames and guilts are Freud's focus.

The psychological complexity of Freud's account, even before he decides to regard the distinction between reality and fantasy as not applicable to memories of early childhood, entails that the shift from reality to fantasy was not such a marked break as it has seemed to many commentators (amongst whom Freud sometimes included himself). Indeed, the formulation I have been employing — *disregarding* the distinction between fantasy and reality, which is by no means the same as taking reality to be fantasy — indicates why. Freud's technique was from then on to place the utmost *trust* in what his patients told him, but *without deciding* whether the stories they recounted described a real event. The event was now bracketed off, with its reality-sign (*Realitätszeichen*) regarded as an added feature, rather like quotation marks in the written reporting of speech.

Here we see how psychoanalytic discourse differs so radically from legal discourses about rape. In practice, rape cases centre on two questions, conveniently grouped by lawyers under the headings external and internal evidence. The external evidence pertains to the act itself, whether it took place, and who were the parties involved in the act. The internal evidence pertains to the reality of the state of mind, *as remembered*. Note that memory is crucial here, since implicit in the crime of rape is the notion that the victim was capable of consenting and of maintaining that state.[47] Moreover it is crucial that the memory pertain to a real event at the time (and not to a before or an after).

Freud's seduction theory, then, was never a theory of the consequences of the rape of children: it was a theory of the pathogenic effects of memories of sexual relationships in childhood. In this sense, it was akin to those studies of the long-term effects of rape on victims which have emphasized that the victim often has the feeling of being implicated in the attack.

> She wonders if she resisted actively enough, if she used every possible avenue of escape, or if she cried out loudly enough. In these cases, the victim harbors doubts about the appropriateness of her behavior. She wonders if, perhaps, her behavior was tantamount to consent even though she refused the encounter.[48]

Freud was more concerned with the effects on the general psychic economy of guilt and doubt than whether the victim had, in effect, consented. Whether or not, in actual fact, the victim had consented was a matter for the law courts, not the psychoanalyst. Inevitably, however, we will be obliged to return to the contentious question of consent.

Freud's lack of interest in the adult 'assailant' and the general issue of assigning moral blame would necessarily seem to follow from the fact that his professional interest lay in the patient who was recounting these stories, under severe internal pressure, with help and 'pressure' from the analyst. By its very nature, Freud's contract with the patient did not lead him to an interest in the adult of those early years, the 'seducer'. The three factors mentioned above, together with the professional fact that his client (as opposed, say, to a lawyer's) was the patient reporting the facts of sexual abuse, entailed that discarding the seduction theory and shifting the emphasis to fantasy was not such a major step.

TRANSFERENCE AND SEDUCTION

I will now turn to another sphere of Freud's work that is crucial to understanding why his seduction theory, which seemed so close to being a study of the effects of the 'rape' of children, was in fact something entirely different — this new factor is the transference. Thinking ahistorically for one moment, the problem I wish to address can be simply stated. The major feature of psychoanalytic practice as distinctively conceived of and organized by Freud is the development of the transference: a powerful emotionally charged relationship between patient and analyst. The analyst's task is to analyse the transference: to demonstrate to the patient, with the patient, how the patient's feelings towards and perception of the analyst are structured like a symptom: derived from past experience, often in the form of a repetition of a past relationship. But it should be emphasized that both parties experience the relationship as a *real* relationship: there is a good case for arguing that the burden of reality in psychoanalysis shifted on to the present relationship between patient and analyst once Freud had consigned to the limbo of 'non-proven' the question of the reality of the patient's *memories* (of past sexual abuse, seduction, etc.).

> We have no right to dispute that the state of being in love which makes its appearance in the course of analytic treatment has the character of a genuine love. If it seems so lacking in normality, this is sufficiently explained by the fact that being in love in ordinary life, outside analysis, is also more similar to abnormal than to normal mental phenomena.[49]

Some sense of the *reality* of the relationship founded on the state of being in love can be gained from the following passage, in which Freud makes it clear that the analyst experiences the patient's transference-love as presenting him with a temptation — in short, it is experienced as being a seduction:

> . . . when a woman sues for love, to reject and refuse it is a distressing part for a man to play; and, in spite of neurosis and resistance, an incomparable magic emanates from a woman of high principles who confesses her passion. It is not a patient's crudely sensual desires which constitute the temptation. These are more likely to repel, and it will call for all the doctor's tolerance if he is to regard them as a natural phenomenon. It is rather, perhaps, a woman's subtler and aim-inhibited wishes which bring with them the danger of making a man forget his technique and his medical task for the sake of a fine experience.[50]

Transference can only be conceptualized if the analyst withdraws from an engagement with the patient on his — or her — terms. Yet, as Octave Mannoni notes,[51] it could only be 'discovered' by the physician accepting the relationship as exactly that — a relationship, whose components were real — and not dismissing it as an 'illusion', a 'fantasy' or a 'lie'. The analytic position is one which accepts the patient's feelings, beliefs, perceptions as genuine, but which does not *engage* with them.

The experience of the analyst is thus an exceedingly uncomfortable one: the seduction must be declined; but it must not be rejected.[52] Even if the transference takes the form of a hostile attack, or a condescending undermining of the analyst's usefulness, his kindness, or his belief in himself, the analyst will be *tempted* to step out of the position of neutrality and react to the patient's hostility with sarcasm, or a *tu quoque*, to his condescending undermining with self-justification (even if unvoiced to the patient). At every step, then, the analyst experiences temptation to react 'normally', and to step out of the analytic position. Of course, as soon as he were to react 'normally', the transference would disappear. Instead, he would be engaged in 'the pursuit of a fine experience', or a slanging-match, or a contest to see who can treat the other with a more refined and self-flattering *hauteur*.

The discovery of the position to adopt in analysis was made on the terrain of sexual advances and retreats. Freud, writing in 1895, outlined a series of obstacles centring on the erotic attachment the patient develops for the analyst.[53] The case he discussed at greatest length occurred when the physician became the object (or 'subject') of an erotic train of thought. The instance he gave was of a patient who was horrified when she realized she wished the analyst 'to take the initiative and give her a kiss'.[54] Such transference-thoughts are to be interpreted, not responded to. Yet they must not be dissipated, Freud finally came to recognize, since psychoanalysis depends upon them for its continued existence: 'the patient's need and longing should be allowed to persist in her, in order that they serve as forces impelling her to do work and to make changes'.[55]

Harnessing the force of the transference becomes the sole aim of psychoanalysis: 'We are no longer concerned with the patient's earlier illness but with a newly created and transformed neurosis which has taken the former's place'[56] — the transference *is* that neurosis. In this process, the aim of the analyst is always double: to entice or attract, and then to decline and evade, to defer and delay. He or she must avoid the charge of suggestion — of inserting foreign material into the patient's mind (and here, the patient's consent is immaterial for the charge to be seen to be serious) — while making use of the forces that make such an intrusion possible in the form of a genuine emotional tie. Whether the bond is affectionate or hostile is neither here nor there.[57] Thus seduction in psychoanalysis appears both as affection and hostility. True, the transference was discovered on the more obvious terrain of the erotic, but whatever its 'sign', plus or minus, the analyst, seemingly surprised by being the object of a seduction, now behaves as if he or she were seducing the patient on to his or her own terrain. To comprehend this sequence of seductions, a theory of seduction is needed.[58]

A THEORY OF SEDUCTION

I have emphasized that, right from the start, Freud's descriptions of seduction recognized that an inter-subjective relationship existed between adult and child. Even though the adult's authority and will were absolute, the relationship was still one of mutual dependence — it is not a case of the blind alley of tyranny, but of something much more dialectical, like Hegel's master—slave dialectic. Even though one is truly in thrall to the other, there is a future to the relationship. This is the possibility inherent in seduction, which rape excludes.[59]

For Freud, the seduction theory opened out on to the dialectic of fantasy and memory.[60] Recognizing the relation as dialectical immediately forecloses the possibility of calling it rape. Yet others have gone beyond this implicit contrast between the dialectical inter-subjectivity of seduction and the brutal annihilation of the other aimed at in rape.[61] In *De la Séduction*, Jean Baudrillard advances a philosophy of seduction whose main themes are as follows.[62] Seduction is a play on the appearances of things — but it does not try to dispel appearance for the sake of a reality beyond. Instead, it dwells in and on appearances, flaunting its mockery of the idea of a reality beyond appearances. Seduction is a mastery of signs, in contrast with power, which is mastery of the real. In gender terms, the masculine is certain of itself, sovereign and phallic, sure in its sexual identity, whereas the feminine dissembles and undercuts the direct sexuality of the male (Freud's phallic stage, in which both boy and girl believe there to be only one sex, only one sexual pleasure). Seduction is play, a challenge, a strategy of appearances. Seduction is ritualistic, in contrast to the naturalism of modern sexuality.[63] Baudrillard argues that 'naked' sexual desire appears at the expense of seduction. Hence, there are two primary senses of seduction: first, its opposition to naturalized sexuality and, secondly, its undermining of all discourses aimed at truth, aimed at piercing through the veil of illusion and dissemblance to appropriate the truth (identified with what is real).

Seduction, however, does not play only with truth; it is a challenge to our ideals of freedom. Our ideal of love is one that requires perfect freedom, a free choice, and yet it would not be thought of as love without the blindness of the hold of desire, the enslavement that we sense as the consequence of passion. When viewed from outside, free choice is the salient feature of love. Yet, if love were experienced as a 'free choice' from the inside, it would not have the quality of being taken over by the object that is its hallmark, making it so longed for and dreaded. Seduction is thus the mediation of freedom and slavery in the sphere of love.

Is love or seduction primary?[64] However we resolve that question, we recognize that love cannot but be refracted through the prism of seduction, and that the prism of seduction can darken and become the wedge of rape. Seduction is the art of love, and, for Baudrillard, it is more, it is what saves humans from the normalizing discourse of truth and the objectifying pornography and instrumentalization of sexuality of our epoch.[65] Yet seduction is also first cousin to rape, and it is rape whose representation we see haunting many discourses on male—female relations. Seduction, unlike rape, has a positive and a negative face, as even *The Concise Oxford Dictionary* is careful to point out:

> *Seduction*, n. Seducing or being seduced; thing that tends to seduce, tempting or attractive quality *of* (often with merely playful or no imputation of blame).

In law, seduction was originally an action that a father or guardian brought against a man for loss of services of a servant (hence the need to demonstrate that daughters who were seduced had performed services for their parent). Breach of promise actions performed this function for the middle classes.[66] However, even the crime of seduction, where it existed, had or has this two-edged quality to it: the recently reformed State law of Nevada defines statutory seduction as 'ordinary sexual intercourse, and intercourse, cunnilingus, or fellatio committed by a person 18 years or older with a consenting person under the age of 16 years'.[67] This reform is very much in the same spirit as other states' reforms, in which statutory sexual offences depend upon the age of *both* parties involved. As Feild and Bienen note, 'feminists generally wanted to legalize consenting or nonforcible relations between teenagers while protecting children of both genders from being preyed upon sexually by adults'.[68] Similarly, in English law, there is the 'young man's defence': if a man under 24 believes the girl to have been over 16, he may be acquitted — though this defence can only be offered once.[69]

So this area of law, regarded as covering the field of seduction, continues to be couched in terms of innocence and authority (or 'supervisory power'[70]). Age and consent are juggled together, so that the law enters into territory that it recognizes as being that of seduction (without calling it such). Logically, and inter-subjectively, law recognizes that the 'consent' of a 14-year-old (male or female) has a different legal status depending upon to whom her 'yes' is addressed.

The area of consent has provided the most anguishing experiences for the principal witness in rape trials, and the most leeway for the sexual imaginations of commentators on rape. Rape defences focus either on the question of consent or on the question of the identity of the assailant (in these cases, the fact of rape is usually not denied). If consent is the defence, the defendant is portrayed as a seducer, and the 'victim' as a woman who says 'no' and means 'yes', or says 'yes' at one time and then claims that it was really a 'no'.[71] If the rapist often masquerades as a seducer, by casting the victim's 'yes' or 'no' in doubt, what of the seducer?

> Most men enjoy a young girl as they do a glass of champagne in a single, frothing moment . . . This momentary enjoyment is, if not in a physical yet in a spiritual sense, a rape, and a rape is only an imagined enjoyment; it is like a stolen kiss, a thing which requires no art.[72]

Rape is seen here, by Kierkegaard, to lie on the borderline of seduction — the seducer sets himself at a distance from it, in a twofold manner: in the distinction between physical and spiritual rape, and in his emphasis on the time of seduction. Seduction takes time, but how much time? In theory, seduction is endless. It is only spiritual rapists who take the achieving of intercourse, or orgasm, or marriage (as in the Jamesian or Balzacian parables of fortune-hunters) to be the end of seduction.

So we can see one form of defence, by which the seducer puts him or herself at a distance from rape. Rape is punctual, instantaneous, involving not only physical violence, but temporal violence. Seduction is interminable, and even the spiritual rapists may imitate this interminability through their endless repetition (as in Leporello's list). Other strategies of seduction may affront the charge of rape. The seducer may turn him- or herself into the seduced, by introducing into the other a passion which then overwhelms him. Kierkegaard portrays Don Giovanni as such a seducer: he embodies the 'exuberant joy of life', which communicates itself infectiously to all.

> Nor are they disappointed, for he has enough for them all. Flattery, sighs, daring glances, soft handclasps, secret whispers, dangerous proximity, alluring withdrawal — and yet these are only the lesser mysteries . . . the gifts before the wedding.[73]

This account places seduction at the level of desire, not that of judgement, where questions of consent intrude. The seducer counts on introducing desire into the other, he casts himself as midwife to desire, so that a reversal of roles takes place. He is the one who can then cry rape, feel overwhelmed.

Wherever there is desire, there will be doubts as to rape — even though we have shown that the question of desire and the question of consent are entirely separate. (Cf. the example of the woman who consented to sexual acts other than intercourse, experienced orgasm during the rape/intercourse, but had quite clear *other* reasons for not consenting to intercourse.)

We now see a further reason why psychoanalysis speaks to seduction and love rather than rape: in the Freudian universe there is no zero state of desire, there is always *some* desire (even if it manifests itself as horror).[74] Even if there is a nothing at the heart of the experience, an absence, something will be read back into it afterwards, and this is the kernel of the traumatic reaction, the kernel of what will later be repudiated. Rape victims experience this crisis, when they torment themselves with asking why did they not resist more, asking themselves whether they perhaps gave a sign that was misread as consent. A rape victim might well wish to take the chance offered by psychoanalysis of thinking her way into the unthinkable — a theoretical and clinical preoccupation of the later work of Wilfred Bion. But the risk will always be that the rape will turn into seduction, as she discovers that, to quote one rape victim trying to come to terms with the experience, 'it's not *that* different from ordinary sex'. The domestication of rape, like the domestication of mourning, may well lead to a healing in which the moment of non-consent is filled in, in a reassertion of omnipotence: the victim implicates herself, retrospectively, in the experience.

To be asked to do so in a court of law, however, is not only conceptually confused, it goes against the ethics of psychoanalysis, and against those, one would hope, of the court. None the less, there is one feature of the court room experience of rape victims which has a structure that may well give rise to feelings of extreme distress. To the court, the rape victim is simply a witness for the prosecution: she has to give evidence of the acts of the defendant; she is cast as a *witness* to his act. Yet she is recounting the violation of her own capacity to act as a subject.[75] In being asked to be a *witness* to this violation, she is being asked to *repeat* the experience of being deprived of this capacity. In the nature of the legal functions of 'witness' and 'complainant', she is being asked either to *repeat* the rape by alienating herself from the experience of being raped, or to *identify* with the position of the raped victim (herself). Either way, she is 'raped' again. No wonder that the victims, when acting as witnesses or as complainants, adopt evasive action. And, as I have tried to demonstrate, any evasive action will be perceived as her having been engaged in seduction, not rape. Psychoanalysis is the mapping out for a subject of her or his evasive actions — no wonder that it is caught up in seduction.

Acknowledgements

I would like to thank Sylvana Tomaselli for her aid in writing this paper, from the preliminary draft prepared in April 1981, as a paper read to the New York Conference on 'Sex and Language', to this final version; at every step she has contributed enormously both in discussions and in formal criticisms of the style and argument — she has been my best, because toughest, critic. I would also like to thank Roy Porter, Jennifer Temkin and Ross Harrison for incisive criticisms of earlier drafts which made me aware that I still had much more thinking to do.

5

Rape and the Silencing of the Feminine

PEGGY REEVES SANDAY

Cross-culturally the incidence of rape varies considerably. Some societies can be classified as rape-free, others as rape-prone. In West Sumatra, for example, a man who rapes demeans himself and everyone he is associated with. His masculinity is ridiculed and he faces assault, perhaps death, or he might be driven from his village, never to return. By rape-free I do not mean to imply that rape is entirely absent. In West Sumatra, for example, during the year 1981–2 police reports noted 28 rapes for a population of three million. This figure can be compared with the more than 82,000 'founded' cases of rape reported in the 1980 US Uniform Crime Reports.[1] Fieldwork in both societies confirms the classification of West Sumatra as rape-free relative to the United States, which is rape-prone.[2]

One of the most important lessons of twentieth century anthropology concerns the enormous variability in the ways humans have found to channel basic drives. This finding applies to the sex drive as much as to any other. In order to understand sexual behaviour in any society, we must turn to the social and cultural forces that programme its expression. As Malinowski put it: 'Sex, in its widest meaning . . . is rather a sociological and cultural force than a mere bodily relation of two individuals.'[3] More recently, anthropologists studying sexuality and sex roles have convincingly demonstrated that 'male and female, sex and reproduction, are cultural or symbolic constructs, whatever may be the 'natural' bases of gender differences and human reproduction'.[4]

This proposition is supported by my study of the cross-cultural incidence and socio-cultural context of rape. I found that approximately one-half (47 per cent) of a sample of 95 band and tribal societies are relatively free of sexual assault, while 18 per cent are unambiguously rape-prone. To explain such variation in the incidence of rape we cannot fall back on ethnocentric assumptions about the 'animal' or rape-prone nature of men. Innate tendencies do not explain the incidence of rape. Whatever the biological basis for sexuality may be (and I do not deny a biological component), the variation in the incidence of rape cross-culturally demonstrates that culture is a powerful force in channelling the human sex drive. For example, when I questioned informants in West Sumatra on the reason for the relative absence of rape there compared with the United States, they replied that rape was impossible in their society because custom, law and religion forbade rape and punished it severely.

In previous work I have shown that rape is an expression of a social ideology of male dominance.[5] Female power and authority is lower in rape-prone societies; women do not participate in public decision-making and males express contempt for women as decision-makers. The correlates of rape that I present suggest that rape is the playing out of a socio-cultural script in which the expression of personhood for males is directed by interpersonal violence and an ideology of toughness. On the other hand, in rape-free societies women are respected and influential members of the community. The maternal features of nurturance and child-bearing provide models guiding the nature of human interaction. The attitude towards nature is one of reverence as opposed to dominance and exploitation and the relationship between the sexes tends to be symmetrical and equal.[6]

The data of cross-cultural research are too thin to provide more than an outline of the parameters associated with rape. In the following I turn to ethnographic studies of sexuality and gender that have been published in the past few years and to ethnographic research of my own in West Sumatra in order to examine in more depth the social, cultural and psychological dynamics evident in rape-prone as compared with rape-free societies. Analysing these dynamics in the light of Susan Griffin's insightful discussion of the 'silencing' or repressing effect of pornography, I suggest that rape can also be understood as a form of silencing or concealing male vulnerability and maternal dependency.

MALE VULNERABILITY AND RECREATING THE FEMININE
IN A MALE IMAGE

Susan Griffin suggests that pornography in America is a cultural mode for silencing vulnerability, and rape is a mode for expressing rage. The vulnerability stems from the boy child's early dependence on maternal physical and psychological nurturing. If male vulnerability and dependence are culturally rejected and male superiority and power rewarded, the maturing male must reject a part of himself that developed as a natural consequence of maternal nurturing. In doing so, he suppresses his own vulnerability and the knowledge of his body experienced while suckling at his mother's breasts.[7]

The images of pornography recreate the feminine in the image of males who are frightened of natural physiologically based feelings and the emotions these feelings generate. These images place men in control of the feelings of the body, enabling them to live autonomously without vulnerability or dependence. In rejecting the knowledge of the body derived from early experience and by replacing this knowledge with control of bodily forces, men communicate with other men through fantasized images of the feminine. The bond males forge with one another through pornographic images reinforces their sense of autonomy and independence. The prostitute and pornographic images remake the feminine in a safe image by placing knowledge of the body beyond a man's emotional reach at the same time that experience of the objectified female body satisfies sexual desire.[8] In this murder of the natural feminine, Griffin says 'feeling is sacrificed to an image of the self as invulnerable'.[9] The male punishes 'that which he imagines holds him and entraps him: he punishes the female body'.[10]

Griffin's remarks, which are applied primarily to the meaning of pornography, are relevant for understanding two very common forms of rape in tribal societies: the rape of women who accidentally observe male ritual secrets and the rape of boys who are being initiated into the world of adult males. These two forms of rape are frequently found in the same society. In these cases male vulnerability is evidenced in the sense of inferiority that men display *vis-à-vis* female reproductive functions. This inferiority is culturally displayed and resolved in a ritual complex that recreates the maternal body in masculine fetishes symbolizing the maternal womb and nurturing breast. Any woman who sees these fetishes risks gang rape, an act that defiles the female body in order to sacralize its man-made counterpart.

In tropical forest societies of South America and in Highland New Guinea it is fairly frequent to find the threat of rape used to keep women from the men's houses or from viewing male sacred objects. A well-known example are the Mundurucu of South America among whom the symbolic dominance of women motivates the real dominance enforced by men. Mundurucu men believe that there was a time when women ruled and sex roles were reversed, with the exception that women could not hunt. During that time, it is said, women were the sexual aggressors and men were sexually submissive and did women's work. Women controlled the sacred trumpets (the symbols of power) and the men's houses. The trumpets are believed to contain the spirits of the ancestors who demand ritual offerings of meat. Since women did not hunt and could not make these offerings, men were able to take the trumpets from them, thereby establishing male dominance.[11]

There are three major structures in which the Mundurucu live their lives. The men's house, Nadelson says,[12] is the key institution structuring Mundurucu life in general. Its totally male character and the fact that it is the primary residence for men reinforces the extreme separation of the sexes. The second structure for living is the dwelling, which has a decidedly heterosexual character. This dwelling is where the wife lives and where men go to have sex with their wives. The area of Mundurucu life which balances the homosocial nature of the men's house is the '"farinha shed", a village structure where women collectively process the bitter manioc, extract its poisonous acid and turn it into flour'.[12] This balance, however, is offset by the fact that the most important items of ritual, believed to be the source of reproductive power, are guarded in the inner sanctuary of the men's house.

The men's house consists of an open lean-to where the men hang their hammocks. Sequestered in a concealed, closed chamber attached to the men's house are the sacred trumpets that women may not see under penalty of gang rape. Such a threat is necessary because men believe that women will attempt to seize from the men the power they once had. The trumpets must be properly played and 'fed' with meat from the hunt to please the ancestor spirits that dwell within the trumpets and to ensure the fertility of humans and animals. Thus, the playing and feeding of the trumpets constitutes a fertility rite, the only ceremonial activity in this society.

The symbolism of the trumpets suggests that they are like reproductive cavities, the source of all fertility. The trumpet complex involves men in the emulation of female reproductive functions. The uterine—phallic nature of the trumpets (they are long and hollow, yet contain spirits within them) and the idea that animal and human fertility depends on their being properly fed, suggests that the trumpets symbolize the wellspring of life. Ownership of the trumpets, then, makes men both like women and in control of female fertility.

Thus, the symbolic apparatus supporting Mundurucu maleness is modelled on female reproduction and hunting. Men's fear that women will steal the trumpets to reclaim what was originally theirs suggests that the male gender identity is constituted by the symbolic usurpation of female reproductive functions. Women are victims of phallic sadism because men are victims of uterine dependency. This is much more than womb envy. It is male dependency on the feminine reproductive model for their masculine sense of self, power and control. Men rape women when they are threatened with the loss of their culturally constructed maleness.[13]

I suggest that the silencing effect of pornography in the United States is also seen in the Mundurucu trumpet complex: both pornography and the trumpet complex recreate the feminine in a male image, establishing for men a means for escaping from and taking their revenge against an entrapping nature, which they perceive as dominating them. As Nadelson says about the Mundurucu,

> the assertion of male homosexual reproductive capacity, protected as it is by ritual secrecy, equalizes the capacities of men and women. If men and women both reproduce, each in their own way, there is nothing of *importance* that a woman can do that a man cannot.[14]

The sexual segregation, secrecy attached to male ceremonial functions and violence against women in societies like the Mundurucu conceals a hidden dimension of the male gender identity — homosexuality. In his study of the bullroarer, an object employed in the same manner as the Mundurucu trumpets, Dundes suggests that through ritual masturbation and ritual homosexuality men reject heterosexual intercourse temporarily in favour of homosexual intercourse. Boys are torn from the domain of women to act as passive agents in homosexual intercourse in the context of their initiation into the world of men. The rationale for such behaviour is usually that it makes boys grow. The penis is likened to the breast, semen to mothers' milk; or, the anal cavity is the male womb. Sodomy makes the boy's penis grow strong and large. Fellatio inseminates a barren boy with semen, which produces semen in him. Usually, sodomy is associated with the bullroarer and fellatio with the trumpet. In one case marked by sodomy the boys are forced to eat lime so as not to become pregnant as a result of serving as objects of anal intercourse. It is thought that were a man to succeed in delivering a child, sodomy would be revealed, a revelation which, according to the ethnographer, 'would cause extreme shame to every man'.[15]

The would-be superiority of men would be revealed as a sham if women knew what they did in their secret ceremonies. 'The secrecy', Dundes says, 'permits the males the luxury of thinking they are superior to women or at least of not being dependent upon them or possibly just of enjoying the culturally sanctioned pretence of trying to fool women.'[16] In either case, the conclusion is the same: male dominance is acquired, female submission is enforced. When rape is the threat that guards male secrets, phallic sadism subordinates women to male reproductive functions, a subordination that hides men's reliance on the feminine reproductive model. Men become men by becoming masculinized women.

Gilbert Herdt's study of male initiation in a Highland New Guinea society reinforces these observations of male inferiority *vis-à-vis* women's reproductive functions. Sambia initiation is a time when young boys are torn from their mothers and, in the context of forcible fellatio with older bachelor men and other initiation rites, learn to give up their dependence on the female world for the hardened masculine qualities of young men ready for war. Fellatio is introduced with the ritual playing of flutes by female impersonators of female hamlet spirits who at first force the boys to suck the flutes as a preliminary to homosexual fellatio. Herdt hypothesizes that the female hamlet spirits are mother surrogates for the boys and the impersonating flute players become mother substitutes whose penis is equated with the breast.[17]

Herdt suggests that the equation of the breast with the penis in initiation is a necessary component of transforming the Sambia's boy's identity with women to that of being a man. In interviews with the initiates, Herdt learned that their earliest reaction to being initiated involved feelings of longing for their mothers. The initiation experience involves considerable coercion on the part of the initiators and death threats are necessary for men to accomplish their task for, as Herdt says, 'maternal separation and ritualized masculinization are not actions that boys would themselves initiate'.[18] The homosexual behaviour that is at first forced upon the boys and which may later turn into significant liaisons between the boys and bachelors, Herdt suggests, has the quality of substitute maternal attachment as the boys begin to identify consciously (including literal introjection) with the masculinity of the bachelors.[19]

The coercion of Sambia initiation, the rape of the boys, and the dominating acts of the initiators reduce the boys to a helpless state and engenders in them an inescapable 'awareness that personal choice (e.g., in gender behavior) is being utterly withdrawn, perhaps forever'.[20] The ritual forges in the initiate a gender identity, which according to Herdt, 'makes men erotically excited first by boys and then by women; and not just any sexual excitement, but a kind built around rigid, untender rules'.[21] Thus, boys who begin life too closely identified with their mothers are ritually transformed by means that include sadism and rape into men moulded according to a cultural image. All of this, Herdt suggests in conclusion, creates the constant hostility that is needed 'to create *enough* of a distance, separateness, and dehumanization of women to allow there to occur the *ritually structured* sexual excitement necessary for culturally tempered heterosexuality and the "reproduction" of society'.[22]

The various cultural transformations of the theme of male vulnerability and fear of the feminine so far discussed suggest that a logical question to ask of both rape-prone and rape-free societies concerns the cultural mechanisms for resolving male vulnerability and alleviating what may be a generically human potentiality for fearing entrapment by the maternal.

Before proceeding to ask these questions of a rape-free society, I want to introduce an example of the sociological analysis of rape in the anthropological discourse. Within the anthropological study of sex and gender two broad approaches have been identified. The culturalist approach, illustrated by the above analysis of the Mundurucu trumpet complex and Sambia initiation rituals, examines systems of symbols and their motivating effect on behaviour. Within the terms of the culturalist approach, Ortner and Whitehead point out, we cannot stop at discovering the meaning of gender and sexuality in a given culture, we must also seek to understand the meaning of male, female, sex and reproduction within the larger context of inter-related meanings. 'The emphasis', these authors say, must be on '"making sense" of sex and gender symbols in terms of other cultural beliefs, conceptions, classifications and assumptions'.[23] The second broad approach discussed by these authors is called the 'sociological approach'. Whereas the culturalist approach examines the motivating effect of symbols on the system of sex and gender, the second approach considers 'how certain types of social orders tend to generate, through the logic of their workings, certain types of cultural perceptions of gender and sexuality'.[24] An example of the sociological approach is found in Ortner's analysis of hierarchy, sexual politics and rape in Polynesia.

SEXUAL POLITICS IN POLYNESIA: THE PROBLEM OF JUNIOR MALES IN A
HIERARCHICAL SOCIETY

In Polynesian societies women as wives and lovers are degraded and defiled by male sexuality, while women as sisters are exalted, a position that grants to kinswomen considerable power. Ortner argues that this state of affairs can be understood as part of the workings of the 'prestige system', which in Polynesia is a system of hereditary ranking. People are born into their status position which is theoretically unchangeable for life and is passed on to offspring. The cross-sex bonds of most significance are not those forged between husband and wife, but between siblings. Among male siblings relative position within a sibling set determines individual status. Sisters are very important for building up descent lines for purposes of status advancement, whereas wives do not enhance a man's status. Thus, sisters dominate the category of female. In a small society where everyone is related, all women, even wives and lovers, may be seen as sisters. Because sisters are respected, all women get the respect of sisters. But, Shore suggests that this tendency to see all women as sisters may account for the high incidence of rape as men turn to aggression in order to transform a brother—sister relationship into a sexual relationship.[25]

Polynesia is an area where sexuality is encouraged for junior males and commoner girls. Elite girls are carefully guarded and preserved for elite men, while commoner girls may be involved in extensive sexual relations. There is some indication that elite senior males are also removed from the adolescent sexual playground, leaving junior males open access to the available women.

Ortner says that the sexual activities of junior males solidify the sibling bond and reinforce the prestige structure in which junior males play the field while the senior elite males accede to the titles. The freeness of sexuality granted to junior males, and the definition of their masculinity in terms of their sexual conquests, creates a pattern of low emotional involvement between members of the opposite sex. The effect of this detachment, Ortner says, is not only to leave the sibling bond relatively unthreatened by competing attachments during adolescence, but it possibly also establishes (or reinforces) a pattern that will continue after marriage as well. The delay of marriage and the encouragement of non-involvement supports the cohesiveness of the sibling bond and of kin relations in general.[26] Ortner argues that adolescent male sexual and sports activity functions 'socially and psychologically, as a cathartic mechanism for potentially disruptive junior siblings'.[27] In both sex and sports these young men 'get to play at power and status in ways that have few real-world effects, but yet presumably satisfy desires for prestige felt by all in these status-conscious societies'.[28]

Fathers are in control of their children and their wives. Children are the source of greater personal status for a man as children constitute a man's (but not a woman's) social and political base. A chief is as strong as the social unit he heads. Fathers have a vested interest in not only having legitimate children, but in seeing to it that they remain loyal members of his kin group.[29]

Women, on the other hand, have little political interest in their children because women are not directly involved in the processes of maintaining or building descent lines. Women gain no personal status from motherhood and the mother role carries no special prestige. In some cases a mother is as much a commoner to her children as a wife is to her husband.[30] It is as kinswomen — daughters, sisters, aunts — that women have high status. A girl is valuable to her descent line because she can bring in a husband, his land and their children.[31] In her role as sister a woman is of value to a man's status hopes and expectations. In her role as wife, however, a woman may thwart these hopes as she acquires prestige for her descent line. Thus, a woman may be both attractive to a man but potentially disruptive to his status ambitions. The contradiction between the status of sister and wife or lover is also seen in presenting sisters as sexually attractive in order to draw in males, at the same time that a sister's value is enhanced if she is a virgin. These paradoxes are fuelled by the stress on the sexuality of junior males as a means for enhancing and defining masculinity.

In light of this information, Ortner sees rape as a logical consequence of the dual status of women. She says:

> Rape presupposes the resistance of the girl (or woman), and it seems reasonable to suggest that girls accept the symbolic value placed by their kin on their virginity, their sexuality, and indeed their persons. They would tend to consider themselves sought-after and valuable objects who may voluntarily withold sex altogether, and who always at least retain the right to pick and choose their lovers. Because girls and women are in fact genuinely valued by their kin, and in some sense 'by society', their stance is consistent with their status, but to men it may appear 'stuck-up' and haughty. Hence the 'taming' aspects of rape motivation. But a girl's haughty stance might not in itself provoke sexual assault, were it not for the other message the girl is transmitting, a message *also* consistent with her self-perception as encouraged by her treatment in her kin group: enhanced sexual attractiveness. I suggest that it is the combined and contradictory message transmitted by the girl — 'come hither/go away' — that is so provoking to the men. The permissive cultural attitude toward rape would moreover seem to recognize the 'legitimacy', as it were, of this sort of reaction to this sort of bind.[32]

Ortner presents an interesting sociological analysis of gender status and its relationship to the prestige structure. Because it is external to the motivational aetiology of rape, her reasoning as to why young men rape remains unclear. For example, one wonders why rape is necessary for transforming a perception of women as sisters into a perception of women as sex objects; or, why does rape help to resolve contradictory signals occasioned by using women to attract men while at the same time virginity is valued?

Because it is couched within the terms of the sociological analysis, Ortner's hypothesis that adolescent male sexuality gives subordinate males an opportunity to seek status in a game that does not threaten the cohesiveness of the sibling bond and of kin relations in general is more convincing. The only source of status for subordinate junior males in this hierarchical society seems to be in the realm of sexual politics, where the sexual conquest confers prestige and bolsters the young man's position in the hierarchy of junior males.

Ortner's argument can be profitably compared with Porter's discussion in this volume (chapter 10) of the incidence of rape in certain male youth subcultures at the periphery of the social status system. A similar argument illuminates the incidence of acquaintance rape among American college males. I suggest at the end of this chapter that here, too, the sexual conquest confirms a young man's masculine identity and grants prestige to an individual whose source of prestige is dependent on his status in a group of junior males who, although they will one day replace their fathers in a hierarchical social structure, are temporarily peripheral to this structure.

RESPECT FOR NATURE AND THE PROTECTION OF THE VULNERABLE

There is considerable difference in the character of heterosexual interaction in societies classified as rape-prone as compared with those classified as rape-free. In rape-free societies women are treated with respect, and prestige is attached to female reproductive and productive roles. Interpersonal violence is minimized, and the people's attitude regarding the natural environment is one of reverence rather than one of exploitation. Rape-free societies are characterized by sexual equality and complementarity.[33] Although the sexes may not perform the same duties or have the same rights or privileges, each is indispensable to the activities of the other. Sex role separation may be as extreme in rape-free as in rape-prone societies. Of importance is not whether sex roles are similar or different, but whether the sexes have access to balanced power spheres.

To give a specific example of interpersonal relations in a rape-free society I will draw on my own fieldwork in West Sumatra. Following publication of my work on the socio-cultural context of rape in 1981, I decided to conduct fieldwork in a rape-free society in order to gain a more thorough understanding of the philosophical underpinnings of peaceful heterosexual relations. I chose the Minangkabau of West Sumatra because of the cultural importance of women in stories, legends, the system of descent and the economic system.

The Minangkabau of West Sumatra are the largest and most modern matrilineal society in the world today. One of the prominent Indonesian ethnic groups, the Minangkabau constitute three per cent of the entire

Indonesian population and 25 per cent of the Sumatran population. The
Minangkabau pride themselves on their matrilineal social system, believing
this to provide the core of their customary law and the basis for their social
identity.

The centre of the Minangkabau world is located in the highlands of West
Sumatra. Expanding outwardly from this centre, referred to as the heartland
of the Minangkabau world, is the *rantau* (migration area) where some one-
half of the Minangkabau people live. The *rantau* is found in the western
coastal lowlands of West Sumatra and in all the adjacent Sumatran states. A
substantial number of Minangkabau have also made their home in other
parts of Indonesia as well as in Malaysia, where the state of Negri Sembilan
was formed from groups tracing their origin to the Minangkabau heartland.

The significance of the *rantau* for this discussion is that migration together
with matriliny constitute two crucial axes in the social life of the sexes.
Traditionally, men were expected to leave their homes and villages as young
men *in order to prove their worth and leave their sisters and mothers
securely in charge of the matrilineal property.* While away from their villages
men were expected to provide economic support to their mothers and wives.
Although separated from the matrilineal household during their years in the
rantau, upon returning men play a crucial role along with their kinswomen
in the ceremonial and social activities of the matrilineage.

Thus, like the Mundurucu and Sambia cases, maturation of the
Minangkabau male involves physical and emotional separation from the
maternal; however, unlike these cases, there are no rituals that either display
male dominance of the maternal or the recreation of the feminine in a male
image. Silencing the feminine is not necessary for becoming a proud and
independent male in Minangkabau society.

Minangkabau women live in matrilineal extended households with their
kinswomen. These households form a structurally central core which upholds
the lineage and customary law. As one woman said to me: 'Women cannot
leave their home to go somewhere like men do. A woman stays in the place
where she was born and upholds Minangkabau custom [*adat*]. The way a
woman behaves is part of custom; she keeps *adat* going through her
behaviour'.

The co-resident structural core of kinswomen is reinforced by the practice
of matrilocality, and by the fact that a man's responsibilities are divided
between his matrilineal household and that of his wife or wives.[34]
Matrilocality in extended family households means that a woman is
surrounded by her relatives who have both an emotional and an economic
investment in her well-being. A man who abuses or rapes his wife must

answer to his wife's extended family. A wife can prevent her husband from returning to the household by simply shutting the door and thus denying him entrance. Any male who abuses or rapes an unmarried woman faces severe punishment and public ridicule.

The importance of the structural core of related kinswomen does not mean that men, too, are not essential in the perpetuation of *adat*. The male contribution is seen in their knowledge of *adat* words and speeches so essential to the proper performance of *adat* ceremonies, which, in turn, are framed by the equally indispensable contribution by women of ceremonial food. Thus, although male and female roles are played out separately, these roles form the interconnected strands of the rope of *adat* that upholds and perpetuates the Minangkabau world.

In the literature of the past and even today it is not uncommon to read that the Minangkabau are matriarchal. Matriarchy, in this case, should not be taken to mean political dominance by women. In West Sumatra, men occupy the main leadership roles. As noted above, however, the authority of women is clearly evident in all major ceremonies and in the running of the domestic and economic activities of the household. Today, the Minangkabau would best be considered a society in which feminine symbolism dominates the domain of culture, and males play key political roles. Both men and women manipulate political and cultural symbolism in the perpetuation of Minangkabau customary law and practice.

The Minangkabau exhibit some of the psychological traits Bachofen associates with matriarchy. For example, like the Lycian common law emphasizing matriliny, the Minangkabau common law stressing matriliny is unwritten and is believed to have been handed down by the godhead itself. What Bachofen refers to as the feminine principle, by which he means passivity, is characteristic of Minangkabau interaction. All human behaviour should be non-aggressive and polite, thinking first about the feelings of others. Lessons for living are taken from observing the surrounding nature: one of the most frequently cited proverbs is 'Let Nature be your teacher'. There is an air of graciousness that suffuses all human interaction, an air Bachofen says is characteristic of the second stage of primitive matriarchy.[35]

The passivity and kindheartedness characterizing interpersonal behaviour as well as the expectations regarding the roles of men and women are mentioned in the statement quoted below made to me by one of the foremost leaders of customary law (*adat*) in West Sumatra. This man has devoted his life to upholding Minangkabau traditional ways in the face of Westernization. He is a member of the West Sumatran provincial parliament and is known throughout West Sumatra and surrounding states for his wisdom and knowledge. In the interview he speaks about the importance of women *vis-à-vis* men, a relationship that other informants said makes rape impossible.

The main core of *adat* philosophy is good deeds and kindheartedness. Democracy and thoughtfulness for the feelings of others is very important. *Adat* teaching is orientated to human morals, the principle of which is kindheartedness. You do not accuse someone directly. You do not criticize directly. You do so with proverbs. It is very rude to point out mistakes directly. There should be no force in decision-making. There should be mutual understanding. In Minangkabau democracy there is no room for rivalries. Differences of opinion are regarded as normal — consensus is arrived at through discussion. About differences of opinion there is a proverb: Crossing wood in the hearth makes the fire glow.

One of the mottos of *adat* says that you have to like what other people like. You have to practise what others like. You may not practise what would hurt others. For example, if I want to do something in this house, I have to think of how each person in the house will be affected. In other words, you have to think of others before you act. If you feel it is painful to be pinched, don't pinch others. The practices of *adat* go together with the practices of Islam. Many are overlapping and the same. The reason that *adat* is quite strong in our villages is because it is supported by religion. In *adat* the possessions go to women. In Islam possessions go to men and women. But actually the two things are not contradictory. In *adat* there are two kinds of possessions — clan and individual. Clan possessions go to women, from one woman to another. Individual possessions — the things a husband gets together with his wife — go to their children.

Women and men are the same, but women are more respected and given more privileges. All ancestral property goes to women. The house goes to women. Women keep the key to the rice house because women are more economical. Young boys sleep in other houses (usually prayer houses) to show their sisters that they do not own the house. Men feel proud because they don't take anything from their mother's house. Men who take from another's house are accused of being weak or robbers.

Women are given more privileges because people think that women determine the continuation of the generations. Whether the next generation is bad or good depends on women. Women's role will determine future generations, because children stay most of the time with their mother and mothers are primarily responsible for teaching children. In the home *adat* is taught by the oldest sister who is called *Bundo Kanduang* [real mother].

Why was Adam sent into the world by God? To accompany Eve. So Eve is just as important as Adam. Women play a very important role. Without women life would be impossible. So for these reasons women are given more privileges.

If women don't have the same rights as they do in Minangkabau they will be doing negative things. For example, when the house goes to men, women have to go out. Because she is weak she will be molested or treated badly by men on the outside. Because she stays at home she is more protected. She will not wander here and there. Fights and disagreements are settled quicker and more effectively when women take part. When two men fight and their wives ask them not to, emotionally the fight won't happen. When one country fights another if women take part the war will end quicker because women will talk about the safety of the children. When it comes to children women are very emotional. Women have more human feeling, they are more humanitarian. They think more about people's feelings and because of this they should be given rights to speak. Women understand emotions. Wars in the world would have stopped earlier if women were given more roles to play. In reverse, when a man is chicken hearted, women can inspire men to fight. A man will fight very bravely when he is insulted by his wife. No one can insult a man more than his wife.

This interview demonstrates that the cultural importance of women derives from their roles as mother, educator, guardian of the emotions, keeper of the rice house, holder of matrilineal property, all of which puts women in control of the future and makes them regulator of the present. The mother's brother (the uncle) also plays a pivotal role, as the clan leader and senior male of the matrilineage. The activities of both sexes can be interpreted as controlling, but in different ways.

The definition of truth in terms of behaviour that will not violate human feeling and the emphasis on protecting women in the matrilineal household suggests that vulnerability and sensitivity to others are qualities the Minangkabau respect and uphold. These qualities are evident in the emphasis on nature reflected in their proverbs and traditional designs. For example, one informant said to me:

We study everything around us; human life, animals, plants, mountains, hills and rivers. Nature surrounds us in all the events of our lives. The rules of *adat* are based on nature. Like nature, *adat* surrounds us.

Motifs drawn from nature are applied in weaving, the carving of traditional houses and in the proverbs spoken at *adat* ceremonials.[36] One of the most common motifs is the fern leaf tendril. The fern leaf tendril is a metaphor for Minangkabau interpersonal and social life. There is a proverb that suggests that like the fern leaf tendril one should be fair and tactful in social relations in order to preserve *adat*. This motif symbolizes the Minangkabau character, which is supposed to be gentle, humble and easily adjustable. The inward curve of the tendril suggests that people should think first of their own family, while the outward curve reminds people that they should also involve themselves with the larger problems in the village outside the family.

> Fern leaf tendril, balmbing nuts
> Shake the shell of a coconut
> Plant pepper with the roots
> Seat your child and guide your nephew
> Think about your village people
> Prevent your village from destruction
> And keep up the tradition

   The Minangkabau emphasis on and protection of the vulnerable in nature and in life is the key for understanding why their society is rape-free. If vulnerability is valued culturally, then it need not be hidden or silenced. Minangkabau men are separated from the domain of the feminine as part of the masculinization process but they do not kill vulnerability in themselves by flexing their muscles *vis-à-vis* women. There is no symbol system by which males define their gender identity as the antithesis of the feminine. Male and female alike define their gender identity according to the rules of nature taken up in *adat*, which emphasizes corporate behaviour and makes the family a major predicating metaphor.

CONCLUSION

Contrary to popular American belief, men are not human versions of predatory jungle beasts. Although powerful, the sex drive does not channel behaviour in the absence of social encoding. Men whose masculine identity and sense of self is predicated on exerting dominance and control over others will undoubtedly at some times express these characteristics in sexual interaction. In societies like that of the United States, where sexual success is integral to the profile of the 'successful man', it is not surprising that some men rape women. Speaking of his motives for raping, one rapist said:

> It gave me a sense of power, a sense of accomplishing something that I felt I didn't have the ability to get. You see something or somebody that you want, and you know that under normal circumstances you wouldn't be able to attract this person, so you take her.[37]

Sexual arousal for another rapist was channelled by the desire to destroy a woman's attractiveness. This rapist, a sadistic killer, was sexually stimulated by films such as *A Clockwork Orange*: 'You know they'd go around with clubs, billy clubs and raping, all that stuff,' he said. 'I like it so much I went back to see it again.'[38]

The sexual encoding of male power and prestige, evident in the degradation and objectification of the feminine projected on to cinema screens and enacted in 'porno parlours', helps explain the high incidence of acquaintance rape reported by researchers on American college campuses.[39] Cultural theory in anthropology, which posits an interconnection between *models of and for behaviour*, suggests the hypothesis that the sexual expression of male power such as projected in pornography and actual sexual behaviour will be related. Such an interconnection was admitted by a college fraternity brother, who said about his participation in an alleged incident of gang rape that took place in a fraternity on my own college campus, that the sexual activities of that night did not seem odd because of the films he had seen on television.

> We have this Select TV in the house, and there's soft porn on every midnight. All the guys watch it and talk about it and stuff, and it didn't seem that odd because it's something that you see and hear about all the time. I've heard stories from other fraternities about group sex and trains and stuff like that. It was just like, you know, so this is what I've heard about, this is what it's like, what I've heard about. That's what it seemed like, you know.[40]

Group sex that turns into rape, we are now discovering, is quite common (and may always have been) on American college campuses. Young men whose masculinity is dependent on the feeling of success are not very different from the peripheral males of American street gangs discussed by Amir, or the Polynesian youths discussed by Ortner. In a sense, American college males are also peripheral while they are learning the skills they will eventually use to usurp their fathers' places in the corporate world.

The images projected by the media in the United States teach men to silence the vulnerable in themselves by objectifying and possessing the bodies of women. Interviews with male students indicate that frequently their sexuality is stimulated (or at least discussed in terms of) images drawn from pornography or the media. Male tenderness or the display of vulnerability is anathema. Male students claim that a man who shows tenderness or who cries is either homosexual or bisexual. One student who fell from a third storey window said that as he lay broken on the ground he could not let himself cry because of the women students who were present. Surely a man whose sexuality and sense of self is dependent on repressing deeply human feelings is sadly oppressed. A society that produces men like this denies them a precious possession, the ability to feel the full range of human emotions.

In the United States the satisfaction of lust is now being placed on a par with freedom of speech. Whereas in West Sumatra lust is channelled in strictly regulated social forms, in the United States lust receives instant gratification. Striking examples of the current mentality can be found in arguments for pornography. A man who owns a pornographic magazine in Philadelphia said to a woman arguing against pornography in a recent television talk show: 'What right have you to deny me my satisfaction? I should have the right to go into a porno movie, masturbate, and relieve my sexual needs.' On my own college campus the argument for pornography was phrased in similar terms. The profit motive and pious remarks about censorship provided student leaders with the rationale for bringing pornographic movies on to the campus. This action, which occurred after the alleged gang rape incident mentioned above, ignored references by dissenting students to the role pornography played in that incident. The almost complete absence of a concern for propriety and respect for women by those debating in favour of pornography is discouraging for many young women. In the absence of strong and well-articulated moral leadership which respects feminine dignity, these women become depressed and begin to blame themselves for the incidents of sexual coercion they experience.

The popular view that man (i.e. the male) is basically an animal who evolved by virtue of his dominance over others rationalizes the pornographic mentality. The picture of early human social life that emerges from the work of anthropologist Nancy Tanner paints a quite different picture. She argues that male tenderness and female bonding led to the evolution of *Homo sapiens*. It was not hunting that brought about early human society but gathering plant food. Mothers who gathered plant food in groups with other women and who learned to walk upright and carry implements were those most likely to have children who survived to contribute to the gene pool. Natural selection favoured those with the intelligence to gather and the sociability to share with offspring. The men who belonged to these groups were those who, like women, were intelligent and sociable, adept with their hands and able to cooperate. The scenario of the violent male who roamed around beating and raping women is extremely unlikely given the need for cooperation in the gathering of plant food, which probably comprised the majority of the diet. Tanner's analysis suggests that it was male tenderness along with female sociability that produced human beings.[41] We can conclude that while male violence will almost certainly end the world, it was heterosexual cooperation that began the long path to humanity.

6

The Biology of Rape

RANDY THORNHILL, NANCY WILMSEN THORNHILL
and GERARD DIZINNO

INTRODUCTION

The study of behaviours from a biological perspective has often been
construed to be the study of various physiological or genetic causes. While
these areas certainly fall within the spectrum of biology, they are not an
inclusive list of all biological approaches to the study of behaviour. For
example, as part of a long historical and philosophical tradition, the field of
ethology has emphasized the study of behaviours from an adaptive or, in
many cases, an instinctive point of view. However, because of its reliance on
such concepts as instinct, and its relative de-emphasis of the variability of
behaviour, we feel that a traditional ethological approach to the study of
animal behaviour needs to be supplemented by a more accurate evolutionary
approach.

Evolution by selection is the unifying theory of life. As first stated in detail
by Charles Darwin and Alfred R. Wallace, independently at approximately
the same time, the theory of evolution by selection has come to attain nearly
unanimous acceptance by biologists in its general form. However, there
appears to be considerable misunderstanding outside biology — in the social
sciences, for example — about the nature and validity of the evolutionary
approach, especially as applied to human behaviour. The value of the theory
of evolution by selection in the study of all living things is beyond question.
This theory has achieved eminence because of its logical structure, testability
and power of explanation. The scientific method used productively by
evolutionists and other scientists is the hypothetico-deductive model, which
we will outline below before going on to discuss how we have used
evolutionary theory to direct our investigation of human rape.

Human rape is an aspect of our behaviour that seems contrary to the theory of evolution by selection. We feel, however, that an evolutionary approach promises a perspective of rape and related behaviour different from any other view, and as such may significantly improve our understanding of this behaviour. It is our view that human rape may be an evolved, facultative behaviour that is condition-dependent. In this view, rape may be engaged in by men who are relatively unsuccessful in competition for the resources and status necessary to attract and reproduce successfully with desirable mates.[1] We will show how this hypothesis is derived from evolutionary theory so as to clarify its utility for future studies of human rape. We point out an additional alternative evolutionary hypothesis which may apply: human rape may be a maladaptive effect of the general adaptive male mating strategy, which includes persistence in copulation attempts.[2] It is our feeling that neglect of an evolutionary explanation for human rape will produce insufficient understanding of this behaviour.

Proximate and ultimate cause

Before one is able to appreciate fully an evolutionary approach, a distinction must be made between two quite different ways of viewing causation — the proximate and ultimate. By making this distinction, futile arguments about causation can be avoided. These two perspectives are not alternatives; they complement one another to produce a more complete understanding of causation.

Explanations for biological traits that deal with genetic, biochemical, physiological, developmental (including learning) and social factors are referred to as proximate causes. Proximate causes are best viewed as ontogenetic events and other immediate causes that lead to the expression of any characteristic. On the other hand, ultimate causes are evolutionary explanations, which address factors that operated during evolutionary history and result in various biological traits, including behaviour. An ultimate causation approach seeks to provide explanations for the relationship between biological characteristics and the selective forces in the environment that affected them. In this view, we seek to understand how any trait contributed to the differential reproduction of individuals over generations. An ultimate approach to the expression of traits can account for the existence of the various proximate causes of these same traits. In this sense, the two forms of causation are not alternatives. Evolution by selection is *the* unifying theory for studying living things, and thus an understanding of ultimate causation provides the most important perspective for studying any aspect of living things.

It is important to note that understanding proximate causation is also important, but that a complete description and understanding of any trait includes proximate and ultimate explanations. We feel that the theory of evolution by selection is the most profitable way to investigate proximate causation. This has been shown repeatedly in investigation of non-human organisms and is more frequently being used to explain human traits. For example, evolutionary theory can be used quite well to predict and analyse mechanisms of learning associated with kin recognition.[3]

Selection has acted continuously on all living things throughout the history of life and continues to do so today. Thus the features of living things are what they are because of selection in the past. In this sense, these features should ultimately affect reproduction or genetic propagation of individuals in evolutionarily relevant environments. This approach then generates tests via experiment, observation and comparative analysis.

An adaptation is a feature of a living organism that is the product of the direct action of selection. These features, however, may or may not be presently adaptive. That is, the definition of adaptive must include a consideration of the relevant environmental conditions. If the relevant environmental features change, then it is possible that previously adaptive traits may be rendered maladaptive.[4] Care must be taken, in this regard, not to view erroneously an incidental effect of an adaptation as an adaptation. For example, human rape may not be an adaptation, but instead a maladaptive effect of an adaptation.[5] This is not our view of rape, but it should be examined empirically. If this view of human rape is better supported by the evidence than our view, which suggests that rape is itself an adaptive trait, then the best understanding of rape will result from an analysis of the nature of selection that has led to the adaptation that causes rape to occur as an incidental consequence.

It may be claimed that our emphasis on viewing evolution primarily as a function of selection prematurely dismisses the roles of other evolutionary agents such as genetic drift and mutation.[6] These factors also cause changes in gene frequencies from generation to generation (evolution). However, mutation and drift are relatively impotent evolutionary forces, compared to selection, because of their random action with regard to fitness. Thus, they cannot bring about directional change, i.e., significant cumulative change.[7] Since complex traits would require directional change, it appears quite unlikely that random forces such as drift and mutation can yield complex traits.

Selection is non-random differential reproduction of individuals. It should not, however, be defined in terms of genetic variation because this confuses selection, which occurs at the level of the phenotype, with evolution, a genetic change in populations over generations. Although selection can only affect evolution if there is relevant genetic variation, an investigator may still fruitfully study the causes and effects of selection without any knowledge of whether there is underlying genetic variation. In studying selection, evolutionists initially form hypotheses about the nature of selection maintaining a biological trait or about the history of selection that has produced a trait, and then test predictions which follow from these hypotheses. It is our belief that investigators interested in any aspect of life who ignore selection theory are unlikely to arrive at a complete understanding of the phenomena they are studying. The futility of scientific investigation without a general theory is beyond question,[8] yet only recently have the social sciences begun to use modern evolutionary theory. We feel that it will revolutionize the study of human behaviour.

The theory of evolution by selection applies universally to all organisms. By testing this theory with anything and everything biological, any limitations the theory may have are more likely to be identified. Thus there is value in identifying features of life that seem contrary to evolutionary theory. For example, some apparent exceptions to theory seen in non-human organisms are abortion of fetuses in mammals and embryos and fruits in plants, sterility in certain social insects, infanticide of own offspring, highly female-biased sex ratios in certain insects which inbreed, and adoption of unrelated offspring in certain birds, mammals and fish. Since these traits are directly linked to reproduction, it appears unlikely that these are merely side effects of adaptive characteristics. These apparent exceptions and others are being studied vigorously, and everything known about them at present indicates that they may be legitimately regarded as adaptations rather than exceptions to evolutionary theory. Human rape could be added to this list of apparent exceptions to theory because rape is apparently a behaviour of high risk (injury, imprisonment etc.), with little or no apparent return benefit. Additionally, reports in the popular media imply that rapists do not discriminate victims on the basis of age, that rapists derive equally from all walks of life, that rapists frequently kill victims etc. Thus, on this level, it appears that human rape and its consequences are in conflict with expectations from evolutionary theory, regardless of whether rape is viewed as an adaptation or an incidental effect of adaptive male sexual behaviour.

Before discussion of the application of evolutionary theory to human rape, we feel it is necessary to address the scientific method in general, since many misconceptions about the relevance of applying evolutionary theory to human behaviour often are misconceptions concerning the scientific method.

The method of science

The scientific method consists of the following interactive stages: observation, hypothesis formation, identification of predictions from hypotheses and testing predictions. One can do science by generation and testing hypotheses and/or by testing the assumptions of the hypotheses. These endeavours often include locating errors in the observations, hypotheses and tests of others, and for this reason science is often defined in terms of its repeatability and self-correcting nature.[9]

The hypothetico-deductive model may be applied in a number of ways. These methods are very different in terms of their underlying assumptions, and all are equally valid for examining cause and effect.[10]

An ad hoc hypothesis, that is, one that is only applied to a particular phenomenon and question without sufficient generality to allow testing, is not useful in a scientific sense. It has been argued that many evolutionary hypotheses are ad hoc.[11] In this view evolutionary hypotheses are similar to 'just-so stories', in the same way that Rudyard Kipling explained the leopard's spots, the camel's hump, etc. While speculation is an important and necessary part of the scientific endeavour, ad hoc arguments are not appropriate. Rather, the proper speculations of the evolutionist and other scientists are post hoc. Post hoc explanations represent an inevitable first step in any observational science.

A scientific hypothesis is a testable hypothesis. In this sense it must predict and be empirically falsifiable. The predictions must be logically derived from the hypothesis and, most importantly, must be statements about unknown events, relationships etc. The predictions of evolutionary theory often focus on historical causes rather than on future events.[12] Prediction of future events is not a requirement of a scientific theory; prediction of the unknown, whether past, present or future, is the important issue. The theory of evolution has been criticized because it is perceived as a non-falsifiable theory,[13] but any thorough reading of Darwin's work reveals his care in identifying observations that would falsify his theory.[14] The importance of falsifiability, or the criterion of demarcation as it has been referred to, was emphasized by Popper,[15] who is usually given credit for recognizing its importance, even though, as we have noted, the significance of this criterion was apparent to Darwin.

By using the criterion of demarcation, a scientist will avoid the fallacy of affirming the consequent. For example, if the predictions derived logically from a hypothesis are found to be true, it may be tempting to argue that if the predictions are true, the hypothesis is true. This conclusion is invalid. If the predictions of a hypothesis are confirmed, it is not valid to conclude that the hypothesis is correct, because one or more other hypotheses might yield the same predictions. However it is logical to conclude that a hypothesis is false when its predictions are false.

The major value of the criterion of demarcation, however, is that it forces scientists to formulate predictions that if found to be correct would eliminate a given hypothesis from consideration. Otherwise, time may be devoted to evaluating predictions that will support a particular hypothesis regardless of whether they are true or false. The importance of falsification of hypotheses in the advance of science was eloquently stated by Darwin:[16] '. . . false views, if supported by some evidence do little harm, for every one takes a salutary pleasure in proving their falseness; and when this is done, one path towards error is closed and the road to truth is often at the same time opened.'

Whilst advocating the importance of prediction and the criterion of demarcation, however, we would also suggest that an overly strict application of Popperian philosophy may be inappropriate because this would deny the significance of positive results in the achievement of understanding and promote the erroneous view that knowledge is an illusion, a notion that stems from the Popperian philosophy of science.[17] A strict Popperian accepts only negative results, because, so runs the claim, in accepting positive evidence one commits the fallacy of affirming the consequent.

In actual practice, although one cannot prove a hypothesis to be true in the sense of *logical proof*, science can lead to proof of a hypothesis in the sense of meaningful understanding, even certainty, about natural phenomena. For example, we certainly know that insulin is produced in the islets of Langerhans, that bacteria and viruses can cause disease, that natural selection acts incessantly and that chromosomes house genes, all facts that were once hypotheses. The list of what we know assuredly is long and is growing.

In our view, the strongest test of a hypothesis involves identification of competing hypotheses that predict mutually exclusive and empirically falsifiable outcomes. Such a test in its strongest form supports one hypothesis and falsifies the alternative hypotheses.[18] Another aspect of strong scientific testing is that the predictions be precise, which increases the likelihood of falsifying the hypothesis generating the predictions. A hypothesis that has passed many such crucial tests can be said to be corroborated, and it is not the number but the severity of the tests that determines confidence in the hypothesis.

AN EVOLUTIONARY HYPOTHESIS FOR RAPE

Human rape can be considered an evolved facultative behaviour that is condition-dependent. That is, it is engaged in by men who are less able to compete for the resources and/or the status which are important in attracting desirable mates and reproducing.[19] This hypothesis is based on the comparative biology of forced copulation, the evolution of intra-specific phenotypic variation, and the general sex difference across organisms in reproductive strategy.

Long-term and detailed research on the biology and behaviour of scorpionflies of the genus *Panorpa* has helped clarify the way in which selection has acted in the evolution of forced copulation.[20] We feel that a description of this research will help to clarify our hypothesis regarding human rape.

Male *Panorpa* exhibit three alternative forms of mating behaviour which are present within the behavioural repertoire of each individual male. Two alternatives employed by males to obtain copulations involve nuptial feeding, i.e., the male presents a food item to the female during courtship and the female feeds on it throughout copulation. The third behaviour employed by males is forced copulation. A forced copulation attempt involves a male without a nuptial food offering rushing towards a passing female and lashing out his mobile abdomen at her. If such a male successfully grasps a leg or wing of the female with his genital claspers, he then attempts to reposition her so as to secure the anterior edge of the female's right forewing in his dorsal clamp. When the female's wing is secured, the male attempts to grasp the genitalia of the female with his genital claspers. The male retains hold of the female's wing with the dorsal clamp throughout copulation. Forced copulation in *Panorpa* is in no way an abnormal or 'aberrant' behaviour; it is an aspect of the evolved behavioural repertoire of individual males that is widespread among species of the genus *Panorpa*.

The behaviour of females towards males with and without a nuptial offering is distinctly different. Females flee from males that approach them without a nuptial offering; however, females approach males with nuptial offerings and exhibit coy behaviour towards them. Also, females struggle to escape from the grasp of forceful males, but females do not resist copulation with resource-providing males.

It has been shown in studies involving several species of *Panorpa* that the extent of use of each of the three behavioural alternatives by males is related to the availability of food items (dead arthropods) in the habitat, which is determined by absolute abundance of arthropods and by male—male competition for the arthropods. Individual males prefer to adopt the three alternatives in the following sequence: Alternative I (presentation of a dead arthropod) > Alternative II (a salivary secretion used as a nuptial gift) > Alternative III (forced copulation). That is, when males are excluded from dead arthropods via male—male competition, they attempt to secrete saliva (a male's ability to secrete saliva is determined by his recent history of obtaining food), with which to entice a female, and males only adopt forced copulation when the other two alternatives cannot be adopted. A male's body size influences his ability in male—male competition and thus which alternatives are adopted most frequently. Large males tend to adopt the use of dead arthropods as nuptial gifts; medium-sized males most frequently use saliva; forced copulation is adopted most frequently by small males.

The behavioural alternatives contribute differently to male fitness. First, the preference of alternatives employed by males is consistent with female choice and thus male mating success. Females prefer males with arthropods over males with salivary secretions and actively attempt to avoid force copulating males. Second, the alternatives appear to be associated with different male mortality probabilities. Relative to large and medium-sized males, small males tend to lose in the competition for food, and thus are forced to feed on dead arthropods in the webs of web-building spiders, which results in high mortality. Third, force copulators have relatively low fitness compared with resource-providing males because females lay few eggs following forced copulation. Finally, whereas resource-providing males always transfer full ejaculates to females, force copulators only transfer sperm in 50 per cent of forced matings.

Forced copulation in *Panorpa* clearly circumvents female choice. In terms of the fitness interests of female *Panorpa*, it is disadvantageous for them to engage in forced copulation relative to unforced copulations. Females experiencing forced copulation lay few eggs and apparently experience higher mortality as a result of the need to feed on their own. As mentioned above, feeding is a risky endeavour in these insects because of exposure to web-building spiders. Selection has operated on female *Panorpa* resulting in their ability to: (*a*) often escape forced copulation attempts (females successfully escape about 85 per cent of the time); (*b*) avoid insemination in 50 per cent of forced copulations; and (*c*) resume sexual receptivity quicker after forced compared to unforced copulation, thus enabling females to solicit food from males rather than scavenging from dangerous spider webs.

Conflict between the sexes (in terms of each sex's evolved reproductive interests) in *Panorpa* is extreme in the context of forced copulation. Forced copulation is detrimental to the female because it circumvents female choice, a major route to fitness maximization for female organisms in general (see below). Moreover, when a male is dominated socially, forced copulation may represent his only route to successful reproduction despite the low fitness pay-offs associated with forced compared to unforced copulation.

Based on understanding the selection that has operated on male *Panorpa* in the context of sexual competition for females, it can be hypothesized that forced copulation as an alternative male behaviour frequently will have evolved in resource-based polygynous mating systems (see below). When female mate choice is based importantly on resources and male striving for resources produces losers and winners, forced copulation may be a viable alternative for losers. There is increasing evidence outside humans that forced copulation often has evolved in resource-based polygynous systems.[21]

Is it valid to apply this hypothesis to humans? For this to be appropriate, certain aspects of human biology must be described, and found to be consistent with the assumptions of this approach.

It should be emphasized that our work on human rape *is not an extrapolation* from non-human to human animals. Extrapolation means to infer (i.e., logically deduce and conclude) the unknown by extending or projecting known information. We are not saying that since males of certain non-human animals engage in forced copulations for certain reasons so must humans. Nor are we saying that since the selection has been identified that apparently led to forced copulation behaviour in *Panorpa*, the same selection has acted in human evolutionary history. The study of *Panorpa* mating systems in itself says nothing definitive about humans. Any insight gained from the study of a particular biological system must be tested elsewhere in order to determine its value outside that system. Furthermore, our approach does not involve an 'animal model' as some social scientists have suggested to us. Instead, we use an evolutionary model based on an interpretation of how selection should act in the context of sexual competition among males in polygynous systems.

Polygyny is a breeding system in which fewer males than females contribute genetically to each generation. Said differently, polygyny is characterized by greater variance in the reproductive success of males than of females, which stems from greater competition among males than among females for resources and/or status attractive to the opposite sex. As the degree of polygyny increases, it becomes increasingly more difficult for individual males to reproduce because fewer and fewer males obtain all the mating opportunities.[22]

Humans have the morphological, developmental, sex ratio, mortality, senescence, parental and general behavioural correlates of an evolutionary history of polygyny shown by other polygynous mammals.[23] Furthermore, most human societies investigated show sanctioned or permitted harem polygyny.[24] In harem polygynous human societies some men have more than one mate, most men have one mate at a time and there is a pool of bachelors. Studies of harem polygynous pre-industrial societies have demonstrated that variance in numbers of offspring attributable to men is much higher than variance in numbers born to women.[25] The same pattern is suggested by studies of pre-industrial harem polygynous societies generally.[26] As expected from mating systems theory, the important factor explaining the degree of polygyny in pre-industrial societies appears to be variation among men in resource holdings and status;[27] there appears to be a positive relationship between the amount of a male's resource holdings and/or status and the number of wives and offspring he has.[28]

In the relatively few human societies in which polygynous marriages are not permitted, variances in male and female reproduction are more similar than under harem polygyny, but that of males is still greater.[29] Thus, it appears that all human societies investigated exhibit some degree of polygyny, even those in which monogamous marriage is socially imposed. Human polygyny creates a situation of greater competition among men directly for women or indirectly via competition for the resources or status which are attractive to women than vice versa. Since the evolutionary history of humans was apparently one of polygyny and modern humans exhibit polygynous mating systems, we feel that it is appropriate to proceed with an investigation of our hypothesis for rape as applied to humans.

Some social scientists might point out here that humans are 'cultural animals' and this implies that we cannot examine human behaviour in light of evolutionary theory. In this regard it should be noted that humans are not the only animal species to exhibit cultural behaviour.[30] Second, and most importantly, cultural behaviour occurs via learning processes, which are themselves products of selection. In order to connect evolutionary theory with cultural behaviour we must first discuss the evolution of behavioural variation in general.

Biology has provided a foundation for understanding intra-population variation in behaviour. Intra-populational behavioural alternatives are of three general types.[31] First, individuals may have different pure alternative strategies as a result of an evolutionarily stable polymorphism in the population. In this case, the different alternative strategies stem from genetic differences that exist between individuals of each type. Secondly, individuals may have a single strategy which provides for two or more alternatives. They then would spend a fixed percentage of time in one alternative and then automatically adopt another. Here, all individuals carry the genes coding for all alternatives, each of which is adopted for a fixed portion of time. Lastly, a single conditional strategy consisting of two or more alternatives may exist within an individual, but adoption of alternatives is condition-dependent and the alternatives are associated with different reproductive returns. All individuals in the population carry genes for all alternatives comprising a conditional strategy.

Conditional strategies are likely to represent the most common form of intra-population variation in social behaviour of human and non-human animals. Selection should typically favour a condition-dependent switch from one alternative to another because a 'big-winner' alternative will usually exist that will be more reproductively profitable than other alternatives.[32]

The behavioural variants comprising a conditional strategy are best viewed as alternatives because reproductive effort (proportion of an organism's total resources devoted to reproduction) is finite. This is not to say that humans (or other organisms) cannot simultaneously employ multiple alternatives of a conditional strategy, but because reproductive effort is finite, any effort expended in pursuit of one alternative limits that which can be directed into other alternatives.

Conditions causing *Panorpa* males to shift from one alternative behaviour to another are understood (see above). Conditions causing people to shift from one alternative behavioural pattern to another have been recognized and are under investigation. Social class and correlated income appear to be important determinants of facultative shifts in aspects of sexual behaviour.[33] Patterns of wealth and other ecological factors influence the inheritance patterns adopted, the mating system and the nature and extent of nepotism and reciprocity.[34] Social factors influencing male reliability of parentage (i.e., probability that a putative offspring is a genetic offspring) cause shifts in the nature of male reproductive effort expenditure.[35] Social circumstances may be important conditions influencing the switch from other reproductive alternatives to forced copulation by men.[36]

Thus, in all likelihood it seems that differences in behaviour among human societies or among individuals within a society probably do not reflect underlying genetic differences, but instead reflect only a single general genetic programme very indirectly related to behavioural differences via the influence of differences in the developmental or general social environment. This means there need not be a fixed genetic programming for a given behaviour of humans (or scorpionflies) but only a general genetic programme whose influence on the phenotype depends on conditions encountered.

The interaction of genes and environmental influences determines eventual phenotypes, human and non-human. In the case of humans, these two components interact to produce a behavioural phenotype which has been selectively favoured because of its flexibility.[37]

Modern biology argues that the sexes differ in reproductive strategy because of a disparity of reproductive interests. This is not an incompletely thought out notion, but one that has proved valuable in its degree of explanation and prediction of sex differences in behaviour and other phenotypic traits in humans, non-human animals and plants.[38] A disparity in reproductive interests of the sexes stems from the evolution of the sexes themselves. This disparity leads to sexual conflict, as was seen in the *Panorpa* scorpionflies. Conflict between the sexes may occur in many contexts.[39] Sexual conflict includes those circumstances in which males reduce female ability to choose mates freely or choose the most adaptive schedule of maternal care. This male strategy may be detrimental to female fitness because it appears that control of reproduction, especially mate choice, is a major avenue for maximization of reproductive success by females.[40] Certain males, by preventing or limiting female interaction with other males, may reduce greatly the freedom of females to choose mates. Males may also circumvent female choice by engaging in forced copulations with an unwilling female — that is, rape.

Our definition of human rape incorporates components we feel to be important for an evolutionary view of rape. Rape is forced copulation of a female by a male. By forced copulation we mean copulation without the female's explicit or implicit consent; it need not involve physical force. Males will always strive to control female reproductive behaviour and, as mentioned above, this may result in a conflict of male and female reproductive interests. Any male activity which prevents a female from exercising choice as to copulatory partner or in any other way reduces a female's ability to control her own reproduction may adversely influence female fitness. Rape is a form of behaviour in the general behavioural category of sexual conflict involving males' reducing female ability to choose mates or choose mates optimally. From an evolutionary perspective, rape occurs when a male circumvents female choice by forced copulation. Thus, from the standpoint of the victim's evolutionary interests, rape entails two related factors: (*a*) the ability of the female to choose her sexual partner is circumvented, and (*b*) the female's option of exchanging sexual favours for social position or material gain is denied. Although we emphasize the relationship between rape and circumvention of female mate choice, rape may sometimes primarily circumvent a female's ability to time offspring production optimally.

By considering rape as a category of sexual conflict, we place the behaviour squarely in the field of comparative biology and evolutionary theory. All knowledge of sexual differences in reproductive strategy and associated conflict indicates that the view of human rape given above is reasonable.

Present understanding of general sexual differences in reproductive strategy in organisms also allows us to place the striving of human males in biological perspective. Human males compete with each other for relative status, including wealth and prestige, which by its nature is always limited.[41] Relative advantage brings with it the resources necessary to successfully rear offspring and thereby brings access to desirable females. Emerging from this competition are males graded by success. At the top of this continuum are the 'big winners' — those males who have achieved high rank (the wealthiest, most prestigious men). These males are represented by men with multiple wives in pre-industrial human societies and by the highest executives in large corporations, powerful politicians, leading scholars and outstanding athletes and entertainers in many industrial societies. Then there are those males who emerge from the competition with enough resources to enable them to rear offspring and gain access to a limited number of desirable females. These males are represented by most males on the face of the earth, i.e., most monogamous males in industrial and all monogamous males in pre-industrial societies. Then there are the 'big losers': those men who are excluded from a share in the wealth, prestige and resources, and thus access to desirable mates.

The hypothesis that human rape is an evolved mating tactic argues that it is those human males who have the greatest difficulty in climbing the social ladder who are most likely to rape. Such males are expected to employ rape as the only behavioural alternative, or, depending on their relative social status, they may incorporate rape into a repertoire of other behavioural patterns including pairbonding with little commitment to one or more females and/or investing any available resources towards sisters or offspring of sisters (the avunculate).

The avunculate is a cultural system in which brothers provide primary support to the offspring of their sisters, and it seems to be associated with social circumstances causing low reliability of paternity. Under the avunculate, the dispenser of resources is related to beneficiaries by at least ⅛ (if half-sibs are involved).[42] If reliability of paternity is low in general, a man's brothers are also likely to have reduced paternity reliability and therefore his brother's children are less appropriate recipients of potential reproductive benefits than his sister's children.

In humans the benefits to reproduction associated with rape are small because of the small probability of conception following a single copulation or brief episode of copulation; this is the case even in societies without modern methods of birth control and it probably was the case in human evolutionary history. However, we feel that the important factor influencing costs and benefits associated with human rape, and thus the factor that allows an exploration of this behaviour from an evolutionary perspective, is the likelihood of success via other alternatives.[43] Thus, when pairbonding is likely to be an unsuccessful male alternative because of paucity of resources needed successfully to acquire a fit mate and rear offspring and/or because of low reliability of male parentage, rape is more likely to be adopted by a man. Low parental resource levels and probably low reliability of paternity are associated closely with inability to climb the social ladder. Similarly, when the avunculate is unlikely to be successful, because of family composition and especially low reproductive value of sister or sisters' offspring, rape is more likely to be used as an alternative.[44] Thus the adaptiveness of rape must be viewed in relation to the adaptiveness of other, alternative strategies.

Human rape may currently represent a maladaptive expression of adaptation in the past; that is, rape occurs under conditions similar to those that account for its evolution but it is not currently adaptive since the costs to reproduction exceed the benefits when rape is employed. On the other hand, rape may currently be adaptive. This is an important distinction, but one beyond the scope of our present work. In order to obtain insight into the present adaptive significance of rape, a detailed analysis of costs and benefits to reproduction of rape behaviour is necessary. A complete analysis of costs and benefits of rape would be difficult in any human society, even in a pre-industrial society with relatively simple social structure and uniform punishment for rape and without widespread use of modern conception prophylaxis. Instead, in our work on human rape we have focused on testing predictions pertaining to whether or not societal rules regarding rape and the behaviour of rapists and rape victims reflect patterns indicative of an *evolutionary history* in which rape was contextually adaptive for men.

In considering this evolutionary view of rape, it is important to keep in mind that very small consistent differences in fitness among individuals may have large long-term effects. A small difference in fitness between men who raped when other avenues of reproduction were closed compared to men who did not rape in this context during human evolutionary history would be expected to lead to major evolutionary change.

SOCIAL SCIENCE HYPOTHESES PERTAINING TO RAPE

In our search of the social science literature dealing with human rape, we have only rarely encountered identifiable hypotheses with testable predictions. However, one can extract views from this literature in an attempt to test them scientifically. There are two general views of rape identifiable in the social science literature: first, that rape is a social pathology which stems from the complexity of modern industrial societies; and secondly, rape is an act used by men to dominate women. The first hypothesis stems from sociology and areas of psychiatry.[45] The second derives from feminist ideology.[46] These hypotheses only address possible proximate causation and *are not* alternatives to an evolutionary approach. However, if they are correct, an evolutionary approach to human rape would be questionable, because they are not derived from, or consistent with any biological view of behaviour. We can, however, derive consequences (predictions) that will be met if these hypotheses are applicable, and see whether these predictions are consistent with historical and present conditions of human groups and individuals.

The social pathology hypothesis primarily restricts rape to industrial societies. This prediction is false. Rape is probably cross-cultural and universal. Its prevalence varies across societies; this variation seems explicable only in terms of evolutionary theory.[47] The feminist hypothesis seems to predict that men will rape powerful, older women.[48] This is false. Rape is directed primarily at young, poor women.[49] The feminist view would also predict that rapists will derive equally from all walks of life and adult age categories. This appears to be false in all human societies for which there are data. Rapists primarily are young, poor men.[50] The existence of some wealthy rape offenders does not negate this general pattern. Wealthy men who rape are apparently the exception, not the rule.

We conclude that the social pathology and feminist hypotheses are not supported by anything other than an ideological fervour, and that they should be replaced by an evolutionary perspective on rape, or incorporated into that view.

EVOLUTIONARY ANALYSIS

Eighteen predictions were derived from the hypothesis that human rape is an evolved facultative behaviour.[51] The predictions that one derives from any hypothesis vary in strength in direct relation to their ability to address alternative hypotheses. This is the case with these 18 predictions. For example, one prediction states that fighting back will deter rape. This is consistent with the hypothesis as well as with any model of behaviour in which the currency is reduction of cost or maximization of pleasure to the individual. On the other hand, some of our predictions arise *de novo* from an evolutionary perspective on rape. One prediction states that rapists will find women of maximum fertility (high probability of successful present reproduction) most desirable as potential victims, whereas other men *and rapists* will find young women at maximum reproductive value (high future reproductive potential) most desirable for long-term pairbonding purposes. A female of maximal reproductive value has her whole reproductive life ahead, which her mate will be able to capitalize on. For purposes of successful immediate reproduction (e.g., rape events, casual affairs), however, males are expected to find females of peak fertility most attractive.

This prediction is also very useful because it is quantitative rather than qualitative. That is, it does not only say that young women will be over-represented in the rape victim population (a qualitative prediction), but it also says that rapists will primarily rape women of high fertility rather than high reproductive value (a quantitative prediction).

For clarity we will go through the derivation and analysis of this prediction.[52] According to evolutionary theory,[53] human male standards of beauty are expected to reflect correlates of high reproductive value and high fertility. Men who concentrated their reproductive effort towards females outside the age categories of high reproductive capability in human evolutionary history are no one's ancestors. Rapists and non-rapists alike are expected to prefer nubile women. Rapists in particular are expected to unconsciously prefer fertility of potential victims to a greater degree than reproductive value because fertility is most closely related to the probability that a copulation will lead to conception and a successful gestation and live birth. Female reproductive value peaks in the mid-teens and fertility in early twenties in American women.

In previous work, the ages of rape victims were compared with the ages of females in the general population of the United States.[54] Statistically, young women are greatly over-represented and older women are greatly under-represented in the data on victims of rape. The peak in rape victims in relation to age corresponded with ages of high reproductive capacity. All major data sets on ages of rape victims in the United States were also examined. The same pattern is revealed by all data sets: young females of high reproductive capacity are raped most often. This is not to say that men do not sometimes rape old women or young girls. Females in these age categories are represented in the rape victim statistics (see below for possible reasons for this and other exceptions). However, the undeniable pattern is one of young, reproductively capable women representing the majority of rape victims.

A possible factor contributing to this pattern might be a recent cultural change in attitudes in the United States about rape reporting due to wide publicity regarding the more sensitive treatment of victims. Any such change could have conceivably had more of an influence on younger than older women, but if such a report bias exists, which may be the case, it is unlikely to account for the magnitude of the age effect in rape victimization in America. Furthermore, some of the data we used were compiled in 1958 and 1960 prior to this possible shift in attitude.[55] Finally, data from industrial societies other than the United States reveal the same pattern as the American data.

The distribution of rape victims across age categories in relation to calculated values of reproductive value and fertility was also examined. These comparisons were made for each of the two largest sets of rape victim data from the United States. It is interesting that ages of rape victims seem to follow fertility distributions to a greater extent than reproductive value distributions.[56]

Clearly the prediction about female age in relation to rape victimization was supported, and there is evidence to suggest that fertility of females is more important than reproductive value in rape victimization. As far as present data allow comparisons of ages of rape victims with ages of female victims of other crimes, it appears that only rape is primarily directed at young females of high reproductive capacity.[57] We emphasize, however, that more testing is needed on the question of ages of rape victims, especially in relation to ages of female victims of other crimes and biases in age-related rape report data.

It has been suggested[58] that female fitness is negatively affected by rape. The observation that anxiety and other forms of emotional distress are common following rape led us to consider these responses as possible evolved adaptations to a fitness-reducing circumstance. In an evolutionary sense the negative effects of rape are greatest for females of high reproductive capacity. From this hypothesis, several predictions follow. One prediction is that females of high reproductive capability should experience greater anxiety and emotional distress than victims of low reproductive capability. This prediction was tested using a data set comprised of 790 rape victims.[59] The data were collected by McCahill, Meyer and Fischman of the Joseph Peters Institute in Philadelphia. The prediction was supported, suggesting that adjustment difficulty following rape (extent of anxiety and emotional distress) is related to reproductive capability. A related and more quantitative prediction is that rape victims of high fertility should have greater anxiety and emotional distress than rape victims of high reproductive value. This prediction was also supported.[60] Women of high fertility seem to experience greater difficulty in adjustment following rape than do women of high reproductive value.

A prediction from the hypothesis that rape is an evolved, facultative male mating alternative is that rapists, compared to non-rapists, will tend to lack reproductive sisters to serve as recipients of collateral investment (the avunculate, see above). The avunculate is less costly than rape and may represent a viable alternative to rape when men cannot compete successfully.[61] This prediction about the relationship between the avunculate and rape, like the previous predictions, is difficult to derive from views of human behaviour outside evolutionary theory and thus is of considerable value for examining the evolutionary perspective on human rape.

It was also predicted[62] that married women should have greater adjustment difficulty following rape than unmarried women, because rape lowers the paternity confidence of married men. This prediction was supported when tested by analysis of the Peters Institute data.[63]

Unlike the prediction regarding rapist family structure, the prediction regarding adjustment of married as against unmarried victims does not appear to be unique to an evolutionary perspective. A hypothesis regarding female socialization seems to yield the prediction as well;[64] that is, females are encouraged throughout development to please men, eventually to please their mates. Indication of displeasure by a mate (e.g. following rape) may cause a female to become anxious.

This hypothesis seems to predict that when mates of rape victims exhibit no displeasure (or are supportive) the victims should experience no adjustment difficulty. Conversely, when mates of rape victims are not supportive, major adjustment difficulty should be exhibited by the victim. This prediction from the socialization hypothesis was examined using the Peters Institute data and was not supported. There were no significant differences in adjustment between rape victims with as against without supportive mates.

Rape offenders generally state that their desire is not to 'hurt' (i.e. physically harm) their victims,[65] although sometimes they do anyway. It is our guess that severe injury or death caused by a rape offender, as well as much of the variance in offender behaviour unexplained by our evolutionary hypothesis (e.g. rape of pre- or post-reproductive women), can be attributed to accident or psychotic mentality.[66] The behaviour of psychotics is not expected to fit an evolutionary model. It is impossible to test with existing data the prediction that exceptionally deviant rape is the result of psychoses.

A further prediction generated by the hypothesis regarding adjustment difficulty following rape is that anxiety and emotional distress should not positively correlate with extent of physical trauma (other than the rape) experienced by a victim. Physical trauma is a reliable indicator that rape rather than consensual sexual intercourse has actually occurred. Unambiguous rape may cause fewer adjustment difficulties for a variety of reasons, including female ability to convince her mate, family or herself that she was not responsible for the act.

This prediction was tested with the Peters Institute data and was supported. Extent of adjustment difficulty does not increase with extent of physical trauma. Further, rape victims with physical trauma other than the rape had fewer adjustment difficulties than rape victims without physical trauma.[67]

The above prediction regarding physical trauma as well as the two predictions regarding adjustment difficulty with respect to rape victim ages and reproductive capability, seem to be unique to our hypothesis that adjustment difficulty following rape is an evolved response of females.

There is an evolutionary hypothesis for human rape behaviour that is an alternative to the view of rape we have emphasized in this paper. It is a possibility that human rape is an inevitable outcome of an evolutionary history in which males were selected to persist in their attempts to copulate and females were selected to discriminate among males and often refuse copulation. In this view, human rape is a maladaptive consequence of an adaptive general mating strategy of men.[68] This hypothesis is as evolutionary as the notion that human rape represents an evolved facultative behaviour. The maladaptive consequence hypothesis views rape as an incidental effect of an evolved adaptation whereas the other hypothesis views rape as moulded directly by selection. If the incidental effect hypothesis is correct, an understanding of the evolutionary history of the basic adaptive mating strategy of men should yield more understanding of rape and related topics than can be obtained in any other way.

We feel that the maladaptive consequence hypothesis is probably incorrect for two reasons. The first pertains to the costs that we envision to have been historically associated with human rape. At the point in human evolutionary history when retribution from society and/or the victim's kin or mate became a component of the cost/benefit in male decision-making about rape as an alternative, those who persisted in copulation attempts to the point of rape when costs exceeded benefits would have been outreproduced by males who adopted rape when benefits exceeded costs. Thus we envision selection acting on human males in evolutionary history in the context of their persistence and forcefulness in copulation attempts.[69] Secondly, the idea that rape is a maladaptive outcome of an adaptive male mating strategy lacks a foundation in comparative biology, which we feel is a major strength of the view that rape is an evolved facultative mating tactic of males. Yet the maladaptive consequence hypothesis remains viable, because available data on human rape do not rigorously discriminate between the two hypotheses. The prediction pertaining to avuncular behaviour, which is discussed above, appears to derive solely from the hypothesis that human rape is a facultative mating tactic, and thus if met may falsify the hypothesis that rape is an incidental consequence of adaptive male sexual behaviour.

More data are thus required to examine the two evolutionary hypotheses for rape behaviour. Our guess is that the notion that rape is an incidental effect will fail and that the view of rape as an evolved facultative behaviour will lead to significant understanding of rape and related topics. We stress that it does not matter which hypothesis is most successful, or whether they are both wrong. What does matter is that investigators identify the best hypothesis, i.e. the one that achieves the most understanding of rape. We have emphasized the hypothesis that rape is an evolved facultative mating behaviour in hopes of showing that it is a straightforward logical view from biology, and that it is worth further consideration and refinement.

We have sought to outline several predictions in an effort to elucidate the behaviour of rape offenders and rape victims. Further predictions and analyses are discussed in another publication.[70] All these analyses support an evolutionary view. Our conclusion is that an evolutionary view is particularly relevant to any attempt to understand rape and all related behaviour.[71] In fact, it appears that significant understanding of rape will derive primarily from such an evolutionary approach.[72]

Acknowledgements

We thank Larry Marshall, Heidi Struse and Peggy Totzke for help with data analysis in connection with our study of rape victims. The scorpionfly research has been supported by grants to Randy Thornhill from the National Science Foundation, USA (BNS—7912208, DEB—7910293, BSR—8219810). The Joseph J. Peters Institute provided the data on adjustment difficulties of victims.

7

Configurations of Rape in Greek Myth

FROMA ZEITLIN

What men or gods are these? What maidens loth?
What mad pursuit? What struggle to escape?

So Keats, in his 'Ode on a Grecian Urn', questions the identities of the figures on the first panel of the sculpted frieze that encircles this imagined Greek artefact. No reply to the questions is ever given in the course of the poem, whose interest lies elsewhere than in naming the 'leaf-fring'd legend' on the urn. Yet the refusal to name also implies no need to name. The scene itself suggests a signifying system already in place that instantly identifies the world of Greek myth by referring to a general setting of sexual pursuit and struggle to escape.

Keats may offer a choice of location as either Tempe or the dales of Arcady, two geographical sites that in later classical tradition stand in for the entire pastoral erotic realm, but any natural decor would serve equally well for his 'sylvan historian', whether woods, mountains, meadows, springs and rivers. The fact is that this motif is one of the most characteristic features of classical mythology, whose ensemble offers us a prodigious, at times, monotonous abundance of narratives that recount the violent appropriations (or attempts at appropriation) of females by males, especially in those landscapes that lie outside the city's boundaries. These assaults, as Keats's verses indicate, are typically those of gods on mortals or of mortals on other mortals, but they also run the gamut to include those of mortals upon gods (e.g., Ixion on Hera, consort of Zeus), of gods upon gods (e.g., Poseidon on Demeter, Hephaestus on Athena) as well as attacks of semi-divine hybrid personages such as satyrs and centaurs upon nymphs and maidens.

Whatever the outcome of the particular tale, and to whatever different uses it may be put, the repertory of Greek myth leaves us in no doubt that the female body is vulnerable to sexual assault. It takes as naturally given that starting from pursuit and flight, women may be overtaken and seized against their will unless they find some drastic way to defeat their pursuers. Death is one means, but the most dramatic solution is metamorphosis, a change at the last moment from one's human shape into some other aspect of nature, as when Daphne, fleeing Apollo, is transformed into a laurel tree. Fleeing sexual violence only entails another kind of forcible change to the body, while those who succumb, especially when gods are the desirers, become pregnant and produce a hero child.

The motif is so familiar in the narrative grammar of Greek myth, and its relation to nature so insistent, that we might be led to the idea that there is some 'natural', even biological basis to this model of relations between the sexes that is constituted on the domination of phallic power and female victimage. Or we might be tempted to construe more subtly and to displace the raw crudeness of physical sexual violence into a shorthand abbreviation of some 'natural' psychological pattern of male and female behaviour. Incorporated into the mystery of the sexual encounter and the enhancement of desire is the prescription that the male pursue and the female struggle against his embrace. Does Greek myth then support a general model of courtship in which the male is expected to take the initiative and the female coyly or modestly to resist? Does she say 'no' when she actually means 'yes', dissimulating desire behind a screen of feigned reluctance or taking refuge in fantasies of ravishment and forced possession?

'Nature' in this context has a double connotation: first, what Greek myth portrays as belonging to some dimension of nature and incontrovertible reality and secondly, the status of Greek myth within the Western tradition as a reservoir of powerful archetypal images which lay claim to some privileged kind of truth about human nature. As models for imitation and elaboration in art and literature, or as expressions of deeper psychic impulses or as conveyors of mental categories, Greek myths invoke the prestigious authority of their entire culture to try to persuade us of the way things are and have always been. Such is the system of thinking to which Keats subscribes when he addresses that Greek urn, that 'unravish'd bride of quietness and slow time', and on which he reads his mythic scene of 'mad pursuit' and 'struggle to escape' in order to arrive at his philosophical, Platonic, conclusion: 'beauty is truth: truth is beauty'. On a different plane, such is the power of that same system, for Freud, for example, that it leads him to 'discover' the unconscious and to derive universal patterns of psychological development from mythic scenarios.

We might simply think that the classical speaks directly to us — that which, as Gadamer says, 'is preserved precisely because it signifies and interprets itself'. Yet we must remember that its survival is also predicated on its capacity to reproduce the cultural values required for its survival.[1] Nature itself is a cultural construct, and never more difficult to perceive in that light than with respect to the categories of male and female, especially as sexual beings. What Greek myths have to say, therefore, on the topic of the abduction and rape of women is of particular interest to our own historical awareness.

Charting that influence is not, however, the main topic of this present essay, but rather how we should read these myths on their own territory of classical antiquity. Myths, in general, comprise a body of significant and memorable stories, which often address those problematic areas of human experience that resist rational explanation, and they explore and express the complexity of cultural norms, values and preoccupations. Through their use of story patterns, programmes of action and language that is 'charged with multiple meanings and symbolic values',[2] myths raise questions especially about nature, the universe and the gods, and probe the relations of the self to family, society and the 'human condition' in its biological life cycle. Hence myths often focus on that critical period of passage to adulthood which for Greek society, as for many others, is a moment of acute crisis that crystallizes the continuing social concern with defining (and maintaining) the boundaries between those all-inclusive categories of 'nature' and 'culture'. What happens around that transition exemplifies the kinds of tensions and ambiguities that mythic discourse is designed to confront, discourse which, as we have learned, serves not to resolve those dilemmas, but 'to obfuscate, circumvent, or mediate' them.[3]

Myths may be put to many uses and operate on a number of different levels. Thus the motif of rape may retain its primary reference to notions of sexuality and gender roles and tend to surface in the cultural context of prescribed (and proscribed) behaviour for male and female within and without the institution of marriage. The theme also operates, however, as a symbolic point of reference for expressing wider existential, theological and political issues. Taking account of Greek myth as a product of a male-dominated society, there is an ideological value to representing the aggressive exercise of phallic power as the physical and concrete sign of male supremacy and potency, best incarnated in the figure of Zeus, the chief divinity, 'father of gods and men'. Enthroned on Olympus, he augments his political and cosmic power, symbolized by his sceptre and thunderbolt, with a sexual energy of seemingly unlimited desire by which he pursues and mates unstintingly with both gods and mortals. At the same time, sexuality is a mode of relating two opposite entities, and the gods' predilection for seizing mortal women provides a way of crossing the boundary between gods and men. The single violent encounter bears political fruit when it produces offspring with impeccable pedigrees as founders of cities and other geographically defined areas; it also bears witness to a mode of intervention that affects religious notions of divinity on the one hand and, on the other, gives expression to human concerns about the identity and boundaries of the self. Greek thought situates man between beast and god, allied to both and to neither, and myths of gods raping mortals, sometimes in animal disguise, highlight this existential question in which sexuality (and mortality) plays so large a role.

These same two terms, sexuality and mortality, organize a still more complex scenario in that best-known Greek myth of abduction and rape, the myth of Persephone, in which the daughter of Demeter, goddess of grain, is stolen away by Hades, god of the underworld. It is a myth that interweaves the categories of marriage and agriculture, establishing an analogy between the maiden and the seed corn. It also suggests, on a sociological and psychological level, that marriage is a kind of death (i.e. a violent abduction from a former state) but also, on the religious level, that death may be assimilated to a mystic marriage. In fact, this myth, which recounts the rape of the maiden, the mother's grief and the daughter's eventual return, at least for part of the year, serves as the charter for the sacred rites of the Eleusinian mysteries. There those initiated into the sacred rites, both male and female, acquire some secret knowledge from re-enacting this myth of female experience that will promise them immortality after death.

As a set of preliminary observations, however, on the configurations of the theme of sexual violence in Greek myth, we might propose the following. The impulse to seize the female and take her against her will is an act profoundly linked to the conception of nature or anti-culture, whether in its positive life-giving aspects or under its negative sign. Although the refusal of sexuality constitutes a refusal to yield to the demands of culture, so that, like the hunter or militant virgin in Greek myth, one remains on the side of savagery and wild nature, the clearest sign of sexuality as a natural, if yet untamed, instinct is the propensity of the male towards rape.

Culture in these terms is, of course, Greek culture, and Greek myth, therefore, almost invariably projects its scenarios of sexual violence on to others than adult Greek males, others who in one way or another inhabit the peripheries of its cultural space. These actors may be either gods, whose sexual energy represents their natural fecundating force, or those demonic hybrids of mixed human and animal nature such as satyrs and centaurs. They may be barbarians whose despotic and sensuous nature puts them outside of

Greek rules, and they may be adolescent males who are still on the boundary between child and adult. It is this latter category most of all, however, that in aligning sexual violence with nature, links up with those questions raised at the beginning of this chapter about the 'natural' configuration of pursuit and struggle to escape as an underlying physical or psychological model for relations between the sexes.

What makes sexuality finally so conflicted an area for thinking and feeling is that it is associated with two contrary affects: love and tenderness, on the one hand, and aggressive violence, on the other. Male sexual desire is separated culturally from the hunt and war but these are also its metaphors. Hence the line of demarcation, so firmly erected, is also liable to slippage, especially in that first sexual act in which the bloody defloration of the virgin arouses such anxiety, and in a system in which males are expected to be active and females passive.

This outline is the backdrop against which the themes of sexual violence play. But what of their uses? We must remember that our most important confrontations with Greek myth come to us elaborated in higher cultural forms — both literature and art. Myths as a kind of naive story-telling or simple narrative are transformed through the society's poets and artists, the composers of epic, lyric and tragedy, sculptors, painters and architects, as well as its orators, historians and politicians. They are therefore always subject to differing considerations of genre and historical context as the tradition develops over time, reshaping and adapting mythic motifs, endowing them with new meaning as well as consolidating them, as in later antiquity, into conventional paradigms as well into an aesthetic code. We must also remember that Greek culture is one that already finds the mythic a problematic category when confronted with other modes of apprehending reality. After all, the status of mythic stories of abduction and rape of women as founding events in human culture (such as the abduction of Helen as the cause of the Trojan War) or as acts committed by the very gods who are worshipped as religious powers prove to puzzle, embarrass and scandalize the sensibilities of the Greeks themselves as soon as a sceptical or ethical eye is trained on these narratives. If Keats begins with a 'leaf-fring'd legend' of amorous pursuit and ends with the abstract 'truth and beauty', he is only replicating in miniature the trajectory from *mythos* to *logos* (reason) the Greeks themselves devised, especially the Athenians of the fifth and fourth centuries BC. Moreover, it is the Greeks too, in their self-conscious interrogation of myth, especially as confronted with history and philosophy, who have bequeathed to us the range of possible responses to myth, including modes of acceptance or denial as well as ways of reviving and reinvesting them with meaning through various strategies of 'reading otherwise'. The Hellenic influence upon us is therefore twofold: the awareness of myth as a complex and problematic form of discourse and, as posited earlier, a corpus of myths which have claimed from our tradition the 'right' to represent nature and reality.

As a way then of respecting the many modes of reading Greek myth, as well as of covering the different types of male actors involved in scenarios of sexual assault, I propose the following: to take that explosive period of cultural development in fifth century BC Athens so cherished to the Western tradition as its 'Golden Age', and to look at two kinds of documents it produced — art, both pictorial and monumental, and drama. For the first, we will consider three favourite mythological themes: 'amorous pursuits' by gods of mortals; the centaurs, those hybrid creatures, half-man, half-horse, who shamelessly attack Greek women; and, more incidentally, the case of the Amazons, who put Greek men in the position of combat with alien women. For drama, we will briefly examine Aeschylus's *Suppliants*, the play which opens his Danaid trilogy and treats of that band of 50 girls, descendants of Io, herself the target of Zeus's desire, who, in having been forced to marry against their will, slay their husbands, all but one, on their wedding night. In the last part of this chapter we will confront more directly again the obsessive concern of myth with the topic of sexual violence as it relates to the issue of eros itself and how it works. We will explore some significant Greek notions of sexuality in order to situate the physical assault upon the feminine body within a wider imaginative range that will prove to include the masculine as well as the feminine and will counter the facile ideology of active men and passive women.

ICONOGRAPHY

What Keats in his poem takes to be a timeless icon of amorous pursuit that extends throughout the long expanse of Greek antiquity, we know to be a development in art of a very particular period which begins in the late archaic period at the opening of the fifth century BC and reaches its climax some 70 years later around the time when the Parthenon was finished and Herodotus completed his histories of the Persian Wars. Art objects from antiquity may be described, catalogued and approximately dated, but since few other interpretative data are available, it is not easy to fix what these objects might have meant to the members of a society that engendered and represented itself through visual images. Conclusions must of necessity, therefore, remain tentative and incomplete. Yet the exploration of these images will suggest a general ideological context for myths of rape in the social and political imagination.

Amorous pursuits

The opening years of the fifth century BC are important dates in both political and art history. The fledgling democratic city of Athens had begun to consolidate its institutions while the red-figured technique of Attic vase painters, invented some decades earlier, now occupied the premier place in the ceramicists' art and ushered in a creative profusion of new themes and motifs. Suddenly, for the first time, we find representations of amorous assaults by gods upon mortals, a motif that will establish its characteristic conventions and persist with remarkable popularity to the end of the period. The god either pursues the girl with outstretched arm, his instrument of power in the other, or he has caught her and grasps her arm, shoulder or back. She, in turn, usually registers terror and shock (in the convention of the upraised arms) and resistance, thrusting forth one hand, sometimes in a gesture that may seem to supplicate or ward off her pursuer, and the movement of her feet and body often represent her attempt to flee. If female age-mates accompany her, they are often depicted as more agitated than she is, even rushing off to the girl's father seated upon his throne who seems to be uncomprehending or else helpless to intervene.[4]

How should we read these scenes in which one demands and the other resists? As 'a popular artistic convention for portraying action,'[5] or 'not as rape' but just 'as a symbol of sexual desire'?[6] Unlike those 'amatory pursuits', represented at times in the archaic period as encounters between heroes and their women or in playful scenes between satyrs and maenads on numerous Dionysiac vases, these new scenes depicting the sexual moment between male and female also involve contact between mortal and immortal domains. In earlier black-figured vase painting, the gods are remote spectators of rather than participants in the human drama. Now we see these divinities taking part in mythic narratives and displayed as erotic beings. Satyrs may provide the model for these actively pursuing gods, but we cannot compare those buffoonish earthbound creatures with the elevated Olympian gods.

Here are some proposals for interpretation of these scenes:

1 Disparagement of the gods for their lechery or, on the contrary, enhancement of their dignity by giving them this show of force.

2   The motif signals some new tragic tension between gods and mortals or inversely, attests to some new intimacy, a mark of divine election.
3   If the latter, it may be a sign of divine intervention in the life of human affairs, or ravishment by the gods may suggest some new hope for immortality after death.[7]

All these suggestions immediately displace this show of sexual energy to the metaphorical plane as exemplifying the profound cultural energy of this momentous historical period. But representing the erotic impulses of anthropomorphic gods may also covertly address some new concern with human sexuality. There is no way to read with certainty these vivid scenes that symbolize both a threat and a promise and hesitate between public and private motives.

On the political level, it can be argued that this unprecedented meeting of human and divine arises out of the dynamics of the democratic city whose confidence is vindicated in the unexpected triumph over its external enemy, the Persians, who threatened the very existence of Athens and indeed of all Greece, and by that threat, sharpened the sense of a local and national identity. The gods and buried heroes were on their side in this moment of crisis. The god Pan, the very embodiment of sexual power, was hitherto a stranger to Athens, but materialized, according to Herodotus, just before the battle of Marathon to the Athenian messenger, Pheidippides, the runner who first travelled this famous course (6:105—106). Aigina, the nymph we often see on the vases as Zeus's target of desire, personifies the island that lies between Athens and Salamis, while Boreas's choice of Oreithyia, an Attic maiden, may well recall the aid of this blustering north wind that wrecked the Persian fleet once at Mt Athos in 492 and again more decisively near Artemision not long before the battle of Salamis in 480 (Herodotus 7:189).

On the erotic level, however, the new motif of gods' amatory advances joins up with other artistic developments in representing amorous scenes. For example, our theme of 'pursuit and struggle to escape' coincides with another innovation of the same period (500—570 BC) that for the first time shows active resistance of maenads to satyrs in the Dionysiac milieu when before their relations were more lusty and affectionate. To explain this shift, once again we are faced with a number of competing hypotheses: the influence of the theatre, a sign of general social tensions, or of a new antagonism between the sexes. It has even been proposed that hostility between maenad and satyr may represent some cognitive split for the individual, who, under the pressures of the new intellectual movements of the day, struggles between the imperatives of passion (eros) and reason (logos).[8]

The matter becomes more interesting still if we consider the problem of both types of amorous pursuit (gods/mortals, satyrs/maenads) within the larger context of the erotic iconography of the period, which from about 530 onwards takes a secular turn in its depiction of ordinary men and women (probably courtesans) engaged in more or less realistic amorous behaviour in the convivial atmosphere of the banquet. We cannot discuss here the revolutionary aspects for the history of art of this more explicit eroticism,[9] but it is perhaps significant that, around 470 BC, changes in public taste phase out both the openly sexual scenes in private symposia as well as the theme of resistant maenads. Henceforth, the secular erotic art, much reduced in quantity, tends towards a gentler and more private depiction as an intimate act between individuals, while the open sexual contact between satyr and maenad, whether amicable or hostile, generally gives way to mere adjacency, and shows the maenad aloof in thoughtful contemplation. There is a certain chiasmus here between a private sexuality that is more romantic and a maenadic version that is no longer interested in the satyr as partner. Different considerations, to be sure, may also be at work in each case that distinguishes developments in the private sphere from the ritual Dionysiac milieu, but both stress a more inward form of desire. Although gods continue to pursue mortals (albeit with a diminishing violence), this motif, whatever its allegorical or political value, must also be included in the larger erotic corpus.

In broadest terms, the history of Greek vase painting may be viewed as modulating gradually from a combative and assertive mode to a more pacified, more domestic and more interiorized style. The almost wholly masculine world of black figure with its emphasis on battle scenes and combats with monsters, for example, shifts thematically to one less austere. There is greater interest in the world of the young, including a trend towards representing several gods as younger, unbearded figures. Above all, we find a radically new interest in depicting women and their milieu.[10] The major motifs that retain their interest undergo a softening, which by the last quarter of the fifth century tends toward the sensuous and sentimental.[11] The erotic repertory itself follows the trend: the shift in pederastic courting with animal gifts to a tamer version, as well as the private erotics of the banquets and the more spiritual maenads to which we have referred, while scenes of Menelaus pursuing Helen, weapon in hand, now adopt the motif of the 'falling sword', as he confronts in amazement the beauty of his errant wife. Pursuits of mortals by gods are similarly tranquilized, and in general, the presence of the pretty winged figures of Eros fluttering here and in other scenes might be taken as a symbolic point of reference for this entire development.[12]

Viewed along a spectrum that leads roughly from war to eros, from militancy to more peaceable attitudes, the combativeness of the erotic style that enjoys a certain limited run may perhaps be seen as a transitional point between a more unfettered sexuality to one that stresses love over lust. But most significantly, the existence of this varied dynamic repertory may in turn be linked with a growing cultural preoccupation as to the nature and expression of the erotic. This has its solid roots in the sixth century, especially in lyric poetry, but now fully becomes a problematic topic for debate and reflection, most particularly in the dramas enacted on the tragic stage and in treatises on eros by the sophists that culminate in the next century in Plato's great work, the *Symposium*.

It is impossible, therefore, to fix a single meaning for this sexual encounter between gods and mortal women upon which political, spiritual and erotic motives converge, and this demonstration alerts us to the more general ambiguities that attend the reading of the mythic theme. But let us note with regard to vase paintings that sexual aggression in its unambiguous form as pursuit is mainly attributed to those who are not human actors — gods and satyrs. If these supernatural beings act out masculine fantasies of phallic power and desire, whether seriously or in play, other myths that are favourite iconographical themes of the period show Greek heroes mainly in another light. Either these defend their women against rape in their struggles with the lustful centaurs, who embody an uncontrolled animal sexuality, or, when Greek heroes exercise force against women, the sexual motive is masked by or mingles with the military, as they confront those barbarian warrior women, the Amazons, who, in every detail of their behaviour and way of life, threaten Greek political and social ideology.

The two most important Greek heroes, Heracles and the Athenian Theseus, confront both centaurs and Amazons and always, of course, defeat them in public battles of retaliatory violence.

Centaurs and Amazons

The iconographical history of centaurs and Amazons is far more extensive than the theme of gods engaged in amatory pursuits. Amazons, especially, are beloved by vase painters of both black- and red-figured types, appearing with astonishing frequency (more than 1,100 examples) and in a wide variety of scenes, poses and attitudes. Centaurs also continue to be represented, sometimes in fact paired with Amazon battles on the same vases.[13] We will focus here mainly on the myth of the centaurs and its representation, not in vase painting, but as recurrent coded elements in the monumental art of the great temples that were constructed after the triumph in the Persian Wars. These hybrid beings embody the essence of rape as unequivocal and unacceptable violence which may be interpreted allegorically in political terms and may be situated firmly in a canonical system of values pertaining to legitimate relations between the sexes.

These fantastic creatures are themselves the product of a delusive fantasy, as we shall see. Their begetter was a man named Ixion whose transgressive career falls into three acts — two offences and punishment. In the first, the human domain, Ixion promised bride-gifts to his intended father-in-law, but reneged on his obligations. When in retaliation the other seized Ixion's herd of mares, Ixion, pretending reconciliation, invited him to a banquet but in reality prepared a treacherous pit in the middle of the road that concealed a bed of glowing coals into which the poor father fell and met a fiery end. Ixion's deed, which contravened all the rules of proper marriage exchange, represented an even graver innovation in human history, marking the first deed of bloodshed involving a kinsman. The crime required purification, but there was no one, god or mortal, who was prepared to relieve the suppliant except for Zeus himself. Accordingly, in act two Ixion is invited now as a guest to the table of Zeus but repays this generous hospitality with a more serious outrage. He attempts to rape Hera, the consort of the Olympian 'father of men and gods', but finds in place of the real object of his desire a deceptive phantom named Nephele (Cloud), who exactly resembles Hera. Of this extraordinary union, the first centaur was born and he, in turn, mated with a mare, thus producing the race of centaurs.

In the last act, Ixion takes his place among the ranks of the proverbial sinners who offended against the gods — Sisyphus, Tantalus, Prometheus, or Tityus, another would-be rapist who attacks Leto, the mother of Apollo and Artemis. Each receives an eternal punishment whose unifying feature is its tedious and painful renewal. Ixion is assigned to be bound forever in spread-eagled fashion to a fiery wheel that turns him in perpetual motion. The vertigo of the circulating wheel expresses his failure to stabilize a proper system of exchange in which there is a just circulation of gifts and countergifts. Bound to the wheel, Ixion also embodies the whirling of an illicit love charm called the *iunx* that is used as an instrument of coercive magical seduction and as such, also stands outside the normal exchange of eros between sexual partners.[14]

The sexual violence that caps Ixion's series of offences and escalates at the same time into an act of unparalleled hubris against the gods leaves no doubt as to the ideological significance of the myth which reports not one, but two violations of the rules of marriage. These, in turn, although focused on the shock of the physical assault, are reinforced by the other elements of the story: material greed, bloodshed, fraudulent exchange, gross ingratitude, and finally, sacrilege of the highest degree. The general Oedipal quality of Ixion's behaviour, that each time directs its insult against a paternal figure, underlines the gravity of the offence. Its specific quality as an assault upon the Olympian family system registers the special horror of its monstrosity and, as such, logically produces monsters. Zeus may be noted for his own generous sexual appetites, that extend from those females of his own kind down to innocent mortal maidens, often incurring Hera's jealousy and revenge along the way, but it is part of the paradox of this system that it confirms masculine sovereignty with its imperious phallic expression and yet, when it situates Zeus in conjunction with his legal spouse, it makes one or the other or both those who oversee and guarantee the sacred dictates of the social order. Ixion's union with the cloud instead of Hera thwarts his success in crossing the threshold of this forbidden zone into the domain of the gods, attesting to the union's insubstantial status as seductive but hollow delusion. Yet the outcome also reveals how potent is this fantasy of a forbidden sexual possession. The spilling of the bad seed expresses the generative power of a desire that bodies forth in the figure of the centaur, who himself stands on the strange imaginative boundary between vivid dream and fantastic reality.

There are several different myths associated with these centaurs who make their mountain homes in various localities and remain close to the landscapes of a wild nature that resembles their own. The myth that concerns us here takes place in Thessaly at the wedding of Pirithous, Theseus's frequent companion, to a Lapith princess named Hippodameia. The centaurs, as invited guests to the celebration, tasted the wine at the banquet, and unable to tolerate the fermented liquid of civilized conviviality, ran amok and tried to carry off the Lapith women, including the bride herself. A struggle between the Lapiths and centaurs ensued with Theseus and Pirithous demonstrating their heroic prowess. The centaurs were soundly defeated.[15]

An interesting detail of this battle concerns a casualty on the side of the Lapiths, a figure named Caineus who has a rather remarkable history. Caineus was originally a girl named Cainis who was raped by Poseidon. In compensation, the god considerately granted her wish to change her sex into that of a male so that she might never again undergo the experience of a woman. Caineus became an outstanding warrior, not only invulnerable to the thrust of any man-made weapon, but one who hubristically elevated the sword to his sole object of worship, thereby scorning the gods and their authority. The centaurs, who fought with tree trunks and boulders, discovered the means to Caineus's destruction by beating him into the ground with their stones,[16] thus unwittingly removing from the Greek scene an internal threat to its social concept of marriage. Who, on the one hand, might better defend women against rape than one who owes his present identity to the revulsion inspired by the forcible penetration of his once female body? Yet this hybrid/hybristes whose figure is a response to the exaggerated outrage of the obdurate virgin incarnates a hypermasculinity on the side of a warrior violence. This male refuses any activity but that of armed combat, rejects any relations between the sexes and confirms the danger such a caricature represents by the blasphemy additionally (or necessarily) attributed to him. As an emblem of the most extreme form of feminine resistance to male sexuality, the end of Caineus suggests that this subversive presence is also out of place at a wedding feast. He sets a bad example, as it were, for the new bride. The misbehaviour of the alien centaurs which conforms to their genetic origins, establishes a reassuring line of demarcation between the drunken bestial sexuality of untamed instincts and the structures of marriage exchange. Marriages are contracts made between father and bridegroom and made acceptable to the bride through the latter's proper comportment that blocks from her consciousness any alternative version, like that of Cainis, to mar the experience she soon will undergo.

The myth of Caineus is an unwanted fantasy element hovering about the edges of the sexual encounter. In its sequence of violation, transformation and counterviolation, it is a lesson to the male. On the female side, however, although Cainis transcends femininity altogether, the myth still shows an affinity with that of those female virgin huntresses or those warrior women, the Amazons, who mix masculine with feminine traits and express in fullest form some of the most persistent anxieties on both sides about sexuality and the trauma it represents as the initiation into adulthood.

Caineus therefore raises the spectre of this anxiety only to bury (or be buried) by it: we will resurrect it later. For now we will respect the boundaries and see the myth of the centaurs and the Lapiths as a contest between the civilized and the savage that reaches its proper outcome, purified even of any element like Caineus which might contaminate the necessary ideological polarity.

Thus, unlike the indeterminacies we have detected in the gods' amatory pursuits, the battle between centaurs and Lapiths has an immediate and persuasive allegorical value. During the Persian Wars the Greeks were indeed defending their women against the invaders of their territory.

Moreover, their fight to protect the rules for the proper exchange of women assumes a symbolic value as exemplifying their way of life and their image of Greek masculinity. The religio-political significance of the centauromachy is therefore unmistakable in the iconography of the post-war period, represented on four important monuments that span the half century: the Theseion and Parthenon in Athens, the temple of Zeus at Olympia, and the temple of Apollo Epikourios at Bassae.

This battle in turn joins forces with depictions of other emblematic struggles that expand and reinforce the fundamental message (the victory of Greece over Persia, West over East, Hellenism over barbarism, freedom over despotism) by their suggestive relation to one another in the ensemble of their representations. The Parthenon supplies the fullest text, allotting the metopes of each side of the building to a different theme, and uniting the 92 panels by their identical placement on the exterior of the building: the centauromachy on the south, scenes from the fall of Troy on the north, an Amazonomachy on the west, and on the east, above the main entrance, the Gigantomachy, the battle between the Olympian gods and the earth-born monstrous Giants who threatened the sovereignty of heaven and had to be defeated.[17] This last theme, a perennial iconographical favourite, clearly subsumes all the other contests under its ideological banner. It associates the monstrosity of both centaurs and Amazons with that of the Giants, hubristic rivals of the gods, and elevates struggles in which men are the victors to the level of a cosmic confrontation between forces of order and disorder, right and wrong, chaos and civilization.

Each of these symbolic opponents is characterized by traits that mark their polar opposition from the Greeks. The Amazons are more complex, however: they touch upon centaur elements by their close association with horses; they epitomize the extremes of barbarian exoticism by their status as women warriors; and by their identity as females they challenge the cultural conception of a docile femininity contrasted with a naturally dominant masculinity. They are more remote in space; indeed, stories about them shift their locations to conform to the expanding boundaries of the known world. But they are also closer, in that Athenian myth brings them into the very heart of Attica by having Theseus abduct their queen and transfer her to his territory. When he puts her aside in favour of a second wife, Phaedra, her Amazon sisters, in order to avenge her, leave their usual ground to invade Athens itself, meeting defeat finally on the sacred hill of the Areopagus by the Acropolis.

Recent studies have made it clear that the ensemble of myths about Amazons in all their details fill out a coherent and comprehensive picture, which, in addition to its political implications, furnishes an exacting anti-model of Greek marriage in a patriarchal society and faithfully reflects back point for point a negative mirror image of the approved structures of social and sexual relations between male and female. Women may not reject men nor exhibit an independent sexuality. They may not reverse roles by using men for reproductive purposes, discarding sons to keep daughters, and they may not claim equivalent status with men by refusing domestic life in favour of the military exploit. Above all, they may not, in exercising their dominance, subjugate or destroy men.

As anomalies that blur all boundaries between the sexes, the Amazons exercise both a dangerous femininity and masculinity, and in this androgynous confusion, they may exemplify some important Greek ideas about the transition for adolescents of both genders into adult sexuality. The secret of the Amazon's power is that they reside outside and within, exhibiting both a militant virginity and a seductive sexuality. They attract Greek heroes like Achilles with his Penthesilea, Heracles with his quest for Hippolyte's girdle, and Theseus's embrace of Antiope.[18] They may excite men's desire to conquer them in a more equal combat between male and female, and like the ambivalence of the Amazon's girdle, a cross between a warrior's belt and a maiden's cincture, the encounter releases the ambivalence of masculine sexuality that may more safely conjoin the sword with the phallus.[19]

The myths may tell us how the Amazon is finally overcome, but she lives on as one of the most elaborated themes in Greek iconography, whether pictorial or sculptural; she lives on as one of the most persistent psychological elements of the mythic imagination that far outweighs, in my opinion, a certain pallid and complacent reductiveness that accompanies the now canonical explanations of the structures and functions of her myth that end in the message, 'women must marry', or 'the social order must reassert the principle of male dominance on which it is founded'. All this may be true in a formal sense, yet the Amazon continually complicates the issue of male dominance, and her availability for metaphorical use in other contexts also suggests that her forced abduction on to Attic territory may have something more to tell us about the violence inherent in sexuality and marriage and about the nature of feminine response to the violation of its body's boundaries. Caineus and the Amazons are structurally linked in a context of feminine resistance, and to these we may add a third and more provocative myth, that of the Danaids. This story of the 50 maidens who, forced to marry against their will, stabbed their bridegrooms to death on their wedding night, brings the problem right into the bedroom and strikes at the heart of the cultural tensions that lend urgency and vitality to the myth-making impulse.

TRAGEDY

The Danaids

The Danaids are descendants of that important mythic figure, Io, a maiden of Argos, who caught Zeus's eye and who, in attracting his attention, also attracted his spouse's relentless jealousy. To punish Io and to prevent Zeus's access to this new object of desire, Hera appoints Argus, the creature with a thousand eyes who never sleeps, to guard her. Once he is killed by Hermes, the messenger of the gods, Hera transforms the wretched girl into a heifer and sends a gadfly (*oistros/oestrus*) to sting her into flight. In this state she wanders all over the world until her arrival in Egypt when Zeus mates with her by the banks of the Nile through his touch and breath and releases her from her misery. Io's story rearranges the typical patterns of pursuit and flight to give another configuration to the motif of sexual violence, which recurs yet again in a different form in the later history of her family.

A child, Epaphos, was born from that union between Zeus and Io, and this child, in turn, founded a family line that after several generations produced two sons and their progeny: Danaus and his 50 daughters, Egyptus and his 50 sons. Like Io, the Danaids are nubile virgins in flight but they reverse the direction of Io's journey, returning from Egypt, in the first stage of their story, to their ancestral homeland, Argos. Their aim is to seek refuge from their violent suitor cousins who will nevertheless pursue them to those same shores in order to demand their submission. With the arrival of the Danaids on Greek soil, we also arrive at the stage of the tragic theatre, and with this genre we reach the most complex confrontation of fifth century Athens with its mythic tradition.

In the theatre the myth of the Danaids becomes an event re-enacted in present time through which feminine figures, as impersonated by male actors, take on life and movement, and are given a voice they may raise on their own behalf. Moreover, Aeschylus's Danaid trilogy situates the question of *women's* consent (or lack of it) as the cornerstone of his evolutionary perspective on the problems of contemporary society upon which political, social, psychological, and theological questions all converge.[20] The story of the Danaids cannot lend itself easily to the allegorical use of the iconographical variety, in which centaurs and Amazons stand neatly on the other side of the divide and whose defeat can exemplify the Greek victory over Persia. The Danaids may in Aeschylus's version come to marriage eventually through the dissent of that exceptional daughter, Hypermestra, and through certain cultural responses to the emergency the Danaids pose through their view of marriage as rape. But women, not men, decisively win the first round and show how far they are willing to go in defence of their own position.

Second, and more telling, is the fact that the Danaids are peculiar hybrids, stranger in their own way than the cow-maiden, Io. The boundary has slipped between Greek and barbarian. By a certain illogical split, the Egyptians remain the foreign element, characterized by their sexual violence and the general despotic hubris that accompanies it. Their female cousins, however, while nurtured in that same alien environment, are also Greek. Their maternal heritage from Io in fact gives them one of their most compelling claims on the king, Pelasgus, to grant them sanctuary and to accept them as kin, if of a distant sort, into the city. At the same time, they also profess their genealogical tie to Zeus himself, to whom they appeal both as their forefather and as the powerful god who protects suppliants at his altar.

The drama plays it all ways. The Danaids are a unique anomaly and yet a paradigm of the cultural image of virginal femininity. Related to both beast (cow-maiden) and god (Zeus), they are poised between the alien world of a foreign culture (Egypt) and their Greek homeland into which they claim the right of entry. It is not easy to pin down the exact reasons for their passionate revulsion against these marriages. Specifically, they object to the violence of their suitors and yet also claim that cousin marriage is a form of incest. But the terms of their resistance also suggest that they view marriage itself as a form of violent ravishment. Their refusal is abetted by their father's collusion and supported by a fantasy of reliving the asexual finale to the myth of Io and Zeus. Their father's domination suggests the sociological motive that addresses the cruelty of separating the girl from her family, while Io's impregnation by the miraculous touch and breath of the god seems to offer a desirable psychological (and physiological) alternative to the brutal image of the trampled flower of their virginity.

Most important of all is the fierceness of that resistance and the potential for violence the Danaids harbour that might at first seem at odds with their helpless terror. That fierceness is already manifested in the first play when, to convince the king to accept them as suppliants, they add the threat of suicide at the altars. In the next play, they will turn that violence away from themselves, usurping male weapons for their revenge against their bridegrooms. These acts of bloodshed are not just a private familial affair, but finally involve the welfare of the entire city, and require the third play of the trilogy to quiet the shock waves raised by the Amazonian man-slaying brides which go beyond the issue of marriage and the status of women.

Of Aeschylus's Danaid trilogy only the first play, *Suppliants*, remains, apart from a few other significant fragments and evidence of other kinds. Although much can be conjectured, we cannot know precisely, of course, how the second play dramatized the murder of the husbands nor the exact details of the compromise solutions arrived at in the third play. But much can be grasped from the dramaturgy of the surviving play which establishes the general frame of thought and the nature of the issues at stake.

The plot is simple. The Danaids come as suppliants to Argos together with their father. Their demand confronts the king, Pelasgus, with a painful dilemma — grant the rights of these suppliants on the grounds of kinship, respect for the ritual and the moral obligation to support the weak — or protect the welfare of the city against the risk of a foreign invasion (for the Egyptians will surely pursue their quarry) all for the sake of women, and women whose grounds for objection to their suitors are not entirely clear. The reluctant king is finally persuaded by the Danaids; he, in turn, departs to persuade his assembly of citizens, who, in this proto-democratic city, have the right to vote, and they choose finally to admit the suppliants. The king has an immediate opportunity both to confirm his worst fears and to stand true to the city's promise and his own when the Egyptian herald arrives in advance of the suitors and tries to drag the girls forcibly from the altar, violates the territorial sovereignty of Argos and threatens the hostilities to come between Greek and barbarian. The play ends with the king's expulsion of the herald and the introduction of the maidens into the city.

The structures of this first play suggest a certain parallel between the suppliant and the virgin. Both are untouchable, both stand outside the social system on its threshold. Incorporating the suppliant into society by bringing her inside the city operates as a preliminary stage of that other process that will incorporate the virgin into marriage and will bring her inside the house to which the social rules assign her.

Secondly, the issue of eros is closely entwined with all the other elements brought into play. One scholar rightly remarks that the play interrogates

> the true nature of power (*kratos*). What is authority, that of man over women, of husband over wife, of chief of state over his citizens, of the city over the stranger and resident alien, of gods over mortals? Does power (*kratos*) reside in law, mutual accord, sweet persuasion (*peitho*) or does it reside in domination, pure force, brutal violence (*bia*)?[21]

More specifically, the drama shows us that eros and politics are inseparable from one another. The proper model of courtship in a civilized society is one where persuasion takes precedence over force. The suppliant ritual reverses the role of the maidens to the extent that they are now required to court the king so as to persuade him to grant the Danaids' demand. Pelasgus, in turn, must court his citizens to persuade the assembly to support his sponsorship of them. The Danaids, having learned of the process of persuasion themselves, must, it is implied, eventually give up their aversion to males and yield in the end to erotic persuasion.

Although a king, Pelasgus rules in a democratic city where debate and persuasion are the approved means for reaching a decision and taking action. He therefore renounces the notion of absolute monarchical power that would assimilate him, as the Danaids try to do, to the third element of that masculine triad: god, father, king. At the same time, Pelasgus stands at the opposite extreme from the despotic suitors who would exercise their will with violent force. As the paradigm of the Greek political man, the king's comportment already anticipates the paradigm of the proper bridegroom, who by persuasion will win his suit in the erotic domain. Persuasion (*Peitho*) is the cornerstone of Athenian ideology; as an allegorized figure (feminine), she materializes in scenes of marriage on vase paintings and an altar erected to her in public space attests to her presence in the political life of the city.

There are many important elements to be considered, such as the Danaids' relationship to myth (in the story of Io), to theology (in their attachment to Zeus), to family structures (in their domination by their father), and to their own bodies (recognition of their own reproductive powers). But for our purposes, the critical issue is what the myth in its theatrical form is made to tell us about a general fear that relates sexuality to violence and imagines an even more violent retaliation from the woman that requires new cultural adaptations in order to reconcile this disquieting knowledge. Behind the screen that attributes this violence to others, we perceive the problem as internal to psyche and society, and understand why barbarian Egyptian and hybrid Danaid transfer their struggle to Greek territory.

How then to solve the dilemma of the intransigent maidens who are caught between the harsh physical facts represented by the suitors and the fantasy of a miraculous touch and breath the Danaids associate with Io and Zeus? Persuasion, we know, is the key term — that of the political king and later of the bridegroom. But persuasion works too through recourse to the prestige of another mythic paradigm, as the important fragment of the last play, probably spoken by Aphrodite herself, seems to confirm:

Now the pure Heaven desires to pierce or wound the Earth.
Now desire [*eros*] grips the Earth with longing for her marriage.

The rains showering from the mating sky impregnates her, and
for mortals she gives birth to flocks of sheep and to the lifegiving
wheat of Demeter. And from this moist wedding, the season of trees'
blooming comes to fulfilment; of these things I am an immanent cause . . .

(Fragment 44 Nauck 2)

Superseding the myth of Io which, in the Danaid's version, proves a misleading model of sexuality, and that of the Danaids whose story is the dramatic reality enacted on stage, the Sacred Marriage (*Hieros Gamos*) of Heaven and Earth claims an indisputable place of honour. The natural position of Heaven and Earth as the primordial couple is meant to naturalize the relations between the sexes that entail for the male a desire to 'wound' the female, and for her the desire for union. The authority of the argument is difficult to resist, and it has the added advantage of intimating to the female her relation with the larger universe whereby she may imitate the earth, and it compensates her for her grievance by emphasizing her reproductive powers.

This principle of compensation, so central to Greek notions of justice, may well be invoked too for the ritual side, if, as some have argued, it is likely that the Danaids at the end of the trilogy were granted cultic powers that specifically depend on their status as married women. Herodotus mentions in another context that the Danaids brought from Egypt to Argos the festival of the Thesmophoria, a fertility rite reserved for women alone (2.171). It is an appealing hypothesis, as the establishment of the ritual in its details replies to many of the problems posed by the situation of the Danaids.

Aphrodite in her speech refers to the earth as bringing forth the lifegiving wheat of Demeter, and the Thesmophoria is based expressly on the myth of Demeter and Persephone. This myth, beyond any others, provides the cultural archetype of marriage as forcible abduction, as mentioned earlier, and it includes in its scenario a drastic feminine protest in the person of the mother, Demeter, whose grief and anger at the loss of her daughter to Hades, the god of the underworld (in collusion with Zeus) provokes a universal crisis when she withdraws from the earth and the crops cease to grow.

One aspect of the far-reaching compromise to which Zeus must accede grants a periodic reunion of mother and daughter that contravenes in a sense the socially irreversible pattern of matrimony. Yet its terms also admit, at least symbolically, the need to renew consent to that marriage, which involves sanctioning an autonomous power to the woman in connection with the agricultural cycle of the seasons.

The varied uses of this myth extend far beyond what can be discussed here, where our aim is to suggest the logic that may link the Danaids to the founding of the Demetrian festival that, in turn, is commemorated annually by the women of the city. The Danaids' violent protest in response to anterior male violence joins up with Demeter's mode of resistance and releases an active energy that can be channelled back into the ritual sphere for the public welfare, turning to violence again towards men only if these should trespass now on this untouchable feminine domain during the course of the festival. Even more fundamental is the pattern common to both the Danaids and Persephone, the bride of Hades, that associates some form of death with marriage and colours the initiation into sexuality with ideas of abduction and violence. The model of Persephone explicitly imagines marriage as a union with death itself, involving a descent into the underworld and a husband who is the lord of that realm. The Danaids, on the other hand, turn their initiation into death for the bridegrooms, but they have already raised the possibility of their own deaths in their earlier threat to hang themselves from the altars.

In this respect, the Danaids are related to many other girls in Greek myth who kill themselves to avoid being raped or in shame after being raped. The theme of forced seizure attends myths that punish the girl for a premature and irregular union (even if against her will) as well as those, like our examples here, in which abduction leads to marriage and entry into the adult state. A recent study has emphasized the significant differences between these two scenarios; it argues that in the first instance, sexual violence and death/punishment symbolize a preliminary phase that puts an end to childhood but still places the virgin under a taboo that acknowledges her capacity to arouse masculine desire but refuses to sanction it. In the second, however, the motif of abduction symbolizes the end of adolescence and is now the 'positive sign of accession to a new life' and social maturity.[22]

This point is well taken, but it cannot account for the remarkable consistency of this entire repertory that seems incapable of imagining (or allowing) reciprocal desire between the sexes, whether within or without the boundaries of marriage, and shows the female as either succumbing to superior masculine force or actively resisting the desire of the other. The system in fact is based on the paradox that demands sexuality and marriage as the inevitable goal of adulthood but at the same time marks that passage with reluctance, resistance and even violent aversion to the trespass of the body's boundaries. Sociologically, the new relation entails a violent rupture with the old way of life and a harsh separation from the original sources of security. Psychologically, however, sexuality represents a dangerous incursion upon the self and the loss of the virgin's integrity and autonomy. It is a state not to be surrendered willingly, requiring the force of the other's overpowering desire, as we have emphasized here, or calling for other strategies such as ruse, deception and intrigue.

The erotic is to a large extent inseparable from the notion of a coercive power and a certain attendant violence that, in the typical version, tends to polarize masculine and feminine attitudes, arousing the imperious desire of the male and instigating the defensive flight of the female. In my view, such a general scheme finally compromises the clarity of the distinctions made above between the two approaches to the female. Moreover, it insists on a tension between the notion of sexual union (and marriage) as a wedding of opposites in a harmonious ensemble that may symbolize a general cultural harmony, and that darker side, where the mythic imagination cannot keep sexuality in the bedroom and out of the same camp as its antithetical activities such as war, violent struggle, or the animal world where the male tames his horses and the hunter pursues and overtakes his prey. A common metaphorical field shared by the two domains attests to the potential fragility of the lines of demarcation that Greek thought and practice take such pains to establish in official ideology by dividing the two areas of activity in space (inside/outside) and time (before and after adolescence). The result is that the system also implicates one in the other and views them as partaking of a certain identity in difference, even leading, as in the case of the Danaids, to a strong reversal of the social and sexual roles assigned to masculine and feminine.

EROS

A further result of a system that perceives the operation of eros as an irresistible and coercive force and sees its effects as a dangerous encroachment upon the autonomy of the self is to broaden the field of inquiry from its primary focus on the virginal feminine body and its generic susceptibility to violation so as to encompass the ways in which the power attributed to the erotic drive also makes violent assaults upon the male. In presenting the myths of Caineus, the Amazons and the Danaids, my intention has been to steer a course into this wider, more ambiguous territory, which incorporates but does not end with defensive strategies of cultural ideology about sexuality, marriage and the traditional roles of active men and submissive women.

We may recall in this context Aphrodite's message in the fragment from the last play of the Danaid trilogy, which declared that husband Heaven desires to pierce or wound wife Earth and she in turn does not resist but desires her union with him, and how this message was constructed by Aeschylus to solve the dilemma faced by the virginal Danaids. Plutarch, however, in his *Erotikos* (769e.24) suggests the sexual encounter as mutually wounding to both partners. This formulation may sound illogical with respect to the analogy between sword and phallus, so often raised in our texts and made literal in the Danaids' revenge, but it answers to a larger conception of eros and of the nature of intersubjective relations by which both parties are subsumed under the piercing effects of the erotic drive, and it accounts too for the fact that males also refuse and resist the demands of sexuality and marriage. A further curious and significant point is that the figure who personifies the hymeneal, the marriage song, is a male youth named Hymenaeus, who in one version of his myth disappears mysteriously on his wedding day, and in another lost his voice or died at the wedding of Dionysus and Ariadne.[23]

I will return to the general issue of eros in a moment. First, I want to suggest that this idea of eros submits the male to a forcible compulsion of desire in two divergent directions: he may be the desiring subject and he may be the object of another's desire. With respect to the latter, it is time to admit that in presenting the dossier on amorous pursuits by the gods, I made no mention of the fact that these include masculine as well as feminine targets, aimed at by both male and female divinities. Zeus, above all, has his Ganymede, whom he pursues and whom, as the myth tells us, he carries off to Olympus to be the cupbearer of the gods. Poseidon has his male favourites, Apollo too; Pan has his shepherd, and we even find scenes, unattested in our literary sources, in which Dionysus and Hermes follow the bent of pederastic desire. An even more striking parallel obtains between the wind god, Boreas, who takes off the Attic maiden, Oreithyia, and the feminine dawn goddess, Eos, who goes after either the Attic Cephalus or sometimes Tithonus, another male of the Trojan line, who matches Zeus's Ganymede.

The young male, it would seem, suffers under a double handicap in that, unlike his female counterpart, he may attract the unwanted attention of divinities of both sexes. The iconography, it is true, distinguishes for the most part between the two types by depicting the male gods as more menacing towards the maidens they pursue, and with the exception of Eos, the theme of gods showing their desire towards women remains far more popular. But the mythological corpus abounds in narratives in which young men meet an unhappy end in the sexual encounter — with gods and mortals, male and female — and whose fate in some instances, as we shall see, often suggests in symbolic terms the extent and nature of the fundamental fear that afflicts especially the young of both sexes and puts the pleasures of eros into serious jeopardy.

The Greek notion of eros as a wilful and overpowering divinity, granted immortal status by reason of its superior strength and eternal durability, also sees masculine sexuality as motivated by an external force too strong to resist. It is paradoxical that whereas phallic desire represents the aggressive impulse of eros, the individual male is himself overcome by a power difficult or impossible to control. Hence, his submission to eros is simultaneously a sign of both strength and weakness.

Eros is the god who takes away the wits and loosens the limbs. He burns the soul, sweeps over the lover like a mountain storm, lays him low with sickness, even a madness of spirit, and pierces the bone to the marrow. He is an implacable tyrant, and there is none to withstand him except the three virgin goddesses, Athena, Artemis and Hestia, the divinity of the hearth, who have been granted special immunity and are permitted to remain impervious to erotic assault. Zeus wields the thunderbolt and the sceptre as marks of his magisterial sovereignty, and his prodigious sexual appetite supports and naturalizes his symbolic emblems of power. Yet, as the Homeric Hymn to Aphrodite, for example, shows us, the fact that Zeus himself is subject to a power higher than himself impels him to engage in a contest with the erotic which he would vanquish in turn (at least once) by making the goddess of love herself undergo the shameful experience of falling irresistibly in love — with a mortal.

A black-figured vase painting graphically demonstrates the erotic chain of action and reaction: it is one of the earliest representations of Zeus and Ganymede (around 490 BC) and the only surviving example not in red-figure.[24] We see first a full-sized winged figure of Eros pushing a prod against the back of a bearded Zeus. The god is holding his sceptre and pursues the naked Ganymede, whose shoulder he has grasped with his other hand, while the boy in turn seizes the tail of a cock, Zeus's love gift to him.

We know well the banal figure of the impish cherub with his quiver of arrows who adorns our Valentines, but we may not realize how this Eros (or Cupid) was once a mighty cosmogonic god whose game, in spite of its occasionally playful aspects, was more often very serious indeed. Moreover, his arrow of desire is no idle conceit, and its manipulation by another outside the self, whether specifically masculine, as for Eros, or feminine, as for Aphrodite, also expresses a certain cognitive confusion in Greek erotic psychology between subject and object: the 'beloved is at the same time the origin and end of the force that is qualified as desire in the one who loves and draws him irresistibly to the attractive source'.[25] The eye of the other fulfils the same function as a personified Eros, emitting with a glance the arrow of desire that pierces through the self and melts its inward parts with its toxic and magical effects. Indeed, in this representation of the psychology/physiology of desire, a fundamental ambiguity arises as to which element is active or passive, which the aggressor or the victim.

Taken in its ensemble, Eros breaches the defences of the self, whether masculine or feminine, lays it open to an unexpected and overwhelming violence from the outside and, above all, puts it in the power of another. This subjugating force has a physical and social referent in the Greek notion of matrimony that often imagines the virgin girl as an untamed filly, to be domesticated under the yoke of marriage; the male in turn prepares for his role by learning in advance how to tame horses and to exercise control over them as a sign that he has learned mastery over himself.

The system we have described above, however, also compromises masculine autonomy and physical integrity. Thus, it is not surprising to find mythological narratives of young men who also shun the yoke of marriage, preferring to remain with their wholly masculine pursuits and often displaying a hostility to the feminine that leads them into disaster.

What happens to these masculine figures, who flee rather than pursue, may reveal more about the potential dangers of the erotic relation for both sexes than the more straightforward scenario of male violence towards women. Because the male versions are more disguised and hence more symbolic, they can reach a deeper level of psychic imagery. My examples all depict the male as faced with some form of female power, either a divinity or inspired by a divinity, that they are finally unable to resist and through which they meet their end.

The first two examples show the sexual experience as some form of drowning or engulfment, in a woodland pool over which the local nymphs preside. Hylas is a youthful member of Jason's heroic Argonautic expedition, who, on one of the stops during the journey, is suddenly drawn to a watery death by nymphs of the local spring, never to return to his masculine band. The second, probably later, myth, that of Salmacis and Hermaphroditus, elaborates further the import of the more rudimentary myth of Hylas. Ovid tells the story in his *Metamorphoses* (4.285–388) as an inserted tale recounted by the daughters of Minyas, who themselves having refused to join the festival of Dionysus, pass the time at their work with several stories of unhappy passion.

Salmacis was a nymph who fell in love with Hermaphroditus, son of Hermes and Aphrodite, who chanced upon her pool. He rejected her amorous advances, and thinking he was at last alone, plunged into her pool for a swim.

The nymph followed him into the water, where clinging to him in a serpentine embrace, she prayed to the gods never to be separated from him. The gods, says Ovid, heard her prayer, and 'the two merged together with one face and form for both; they were no longer two, nor such as to be called one, woman, and one, man. They seemed neither and yet both'. Hermaphroditus, now a 'half-man', appealed in turn to his own immortal parents that henceforth these waters alone would have the power to enervate any man who entered them, and his wish was granted.

These myths evoke the fear of losing one's identity in the sexual act as a state of permanent fusion with the feminine. The next two examples, however, for the most part, organize their narratives around the fear of injury and fragmentation.

The scene of the first is again a woodland pool, but this time it is the haunt of the virgin goddess, Artemis. The male in question is the hunter Actaeon, who does not enter the pool, but unwittingly comes upon the goddess bathing naked in the spring with her nymphs. The goddess' retaliation is swift and devastating. She turns Actaeon into a stag and his hounds, taking him for an animal prey, fall upon him and tear him apart. The second narrative, involving Pentheus and his ritual dismemberment on the mountain by the women of Thebes (including his mother), who have been possessed by a Dionysiac frenzy, has close affinities with the preceding myth — the two males are in fact cousins — and expands the import of Actaeon's myth. The god Dionysus in Euripides's play the *Bacchae*, exacts from Pentheus, who has scorned the god's worship, his secret desire to go as a voyeur to the mountains in order to witness what he thinks are the women's illicit sexual acts, and the king, now under the spell of the god, agrees to go in feminine disguise and to abandon his former plan for open military violence against the women. The Theban maenads, warned by Dionysus of the presence of a spurious woman, topple him from his lofty viewing perch on a pine tree and his mother, now misrecognizing her son and thinking him a beast (a lion), together with her companions, tear apart their animal victim, bringing his head as a hunting trophy back to the city.

The myths of Pentheus and Actaeon both play off the three terms, beast, human and god, and both shift between literal and symbolic levels. Each young man is a voyeur of feminine secrets; each is a hunter, whether real or metaphorical, and each is treated as an animal to be torn apart by those intimate associates who do not recognize him. Actaeon, metamorphosed into a real animal and turned upon by his hounds, remains wholly in the natural instinctive world. Pentheus's case, however, involves human actors; the women turn into hunters of this more hubristic hunter whose beast identity is rather an illusory effect of Dionysiac madness. In Actaeon's story the remote goddess figure embodies the feminine threat that dictates but does not openly use violence. The story of Pentheus, however, merges an outraged femininity with the direct reversal of the intimate relation between mother and son which works to their mutual disaster. Matters are further complicated by Pentheus's prior donning of female identity which focuses far better than the more fantastic myth of Hermaphroditus the male ambivalence about sexuality and the conflicted desire to merge identity with and yet distinguish it from that of the feminine.

In the *Bacchae*, Pentheus's suspicions about the women's sexual behaviour remain unfounded and his trespass is translated into a religious violation of the Dionysiac mysteries. But the god Dionysus, who liberates the instinctive side of life, and who breaks down the boundaries of the social order — between beast, human and god, and between masculine and feminine — is intimately linked to the erotic in its physical and spiritual dimensions. As a blend himself of masculine and feminine traits and as a god who blends his identity with that of his worshippers, Dionysus transmits a set of responses to the presence of his divinity that may be understood as ritual versions of an untrammelled sexuality that may bring an ecstatic pleasure and release, but may also seriously threaten the stability and uniqueness of the self.

The fact that women are far more closely connected to his rites, his *orgia*, leads me to speculate that these Dionysiac gestures reflect more closely a cultural notion of female orgasmic activity. These symptoms, we might say, diffuse over the entire body as a form of wild kinetic agitation or an intense trance-like state and include the two divergent extremes of feelings of fusion and fragmentation. If the Dionysiac tends in the myths to destroy men more often than women, and if the male approach to the god, as in the case of Pentheus, may be made through feminine disguise, then we might understand better how the other side of male sexual desire may also entail a fear of contamination with the feminine that will transform the male into a maenad. Yet the myths also tell us that both male and female may resist the advent of the god as an unsettling divinity in their midst who, at the furthest limits of his power, can arouse a terrifying mutual violence between the sexes.[26]

My last example is still more explicit. The divinity in question is none other than Aphrodite herself. The male actor is Hippolytus, son of the Amazon, hunter and tamer of horses. He worships only the virginal goddess Artemis, and determined to remain himself a virgin, refuses all contact with Aphrodite and thus incurs her wrath. Her revenge takes a strange twist, as she does not afflict *him* with a terrible passion, as one might expect, but another, a woman who has in no way offended her. This woman, his stepmother Phaedra, in Euripides's play the *Hippolytus*, determines, in fact, to resist this illegal but irresistible love to save her own honour even to the point of death — and eventually his. She does in fact commit suicide, but only after her secret has been betrayed to Hippolytus by another, and having overheard his outraged reaction she decides that her death will also serve as a revenge against him. She leaves a message for her husband, Theseus, accusing the young man of attempted rape, and Theseus invokes the power of his father, the god Poseidon, to punish the malefactor. The god obliges with the monstrous bull sent from the sea. The bull terrifies Hippolytus's horses into a mad stampede and flinging him from the chariot, they drag his body, entangled in their reins, to its broken and bloody doom. Phaedra's motivation, as she says enigmatically before she leaves the scene, is to have him share her disease, and indeed, the state of his suffering body in the description of its symptoms is made to resemble Phaedra's earlier condition, when she lies sick and suffering through the pangs of her erotic affliction.[27]

The effect of Phaedra's message that reverses the roles (he desires me versus I desire him) in fact compels the male to imitate feminine experience in a demonic parody of the effect the erotic has on the body of a woman. The brilliance of the scheme resides in the fact that Phaedra's all too credible fiction relies for its success on the stereotyped image of the lustful young male. Yet at the same time, it exploits the curious status of this virginal male who, by his aversion to sexuality and his exclusive worship of the goddess Artemis, aligns himself with the bride rather than with the bridegroom. Euripides confirms the nature of this failed passage into matrimony and adulthood through the rite to which the play refers at the end, in which Hippolytus is to take his place for all time in the cult of Aphrodite. Henceforth, maidens on the eve of their weddings are to cut their hair as an offering to him. Mourning his violent fate, they are also mourning for themselves.

The tamer of horses who failed to control his horses so that they turned against him, as the hounds against Actaeon, also failed to show the masculine ability required to tame the female in the yoke of marriage. The Amazon's child therefore ends up on the other side, yoked, as the play says, to destruction. As a fugitive figure on the border between the union of masculine and feminine, Hippolytus thus also resembles that other masculine figure, Hymenaeus, who died or disappeared on his wedding night, and who attests in some part to a mysterious boundary zone that we would associate fully with the female body but which in some icons of Greek mythic thought seems to be shared by both male and female.

In mixing the categories of masculine and feminine at the moment that just precedes the 'mixing' of the sexual act, these strange male figures emerge from the shadows of an erotic landscape that highlights more often the typical case of male aggressive desire and the female's struggle to escape from sexual assault. It is important to stress a kind of symmetry here between male and female that refers back to the notion of eros acting upon the self as an external influence, which may be denied only at one's peril: but the fundamental asymmetry remains. In the schematic design of gender categories, which assigns the active role to the male and the passive to the female, the mythic scenario can only envisage the experience of these males as a humiliating exercise in feminization. Projecting this reversal of the power relations and mapping a disguised version of sexual violence on to the male body only intensifies the normative model of female vulnerability to masculine aggression. Thus the ever-present danger the woman faces may turn full circle to ratify the comportment demanded from her that she flee any open sexual advance. This result might lead us then to that flattest level of social explanation, as one scholar has recently put it, that 'pursuit is the role prescribed for the male, flight for the female, and both are judged in accordance with their success in carrying out their respective roles'.[28]

This elision of the primary link between sexuality and aggression as confronted in the mythic imagination leads on to depictions of pursuit and flight such as Keats's 'wild ecstasy', or the thrill of the hunter for whom 'the difficulty of the chase enhances the value of the object, and eventual capture, after fierce competition with rival hunters, is incalculably reassuring to the hunter'.[29] These judgements take for granted what the myths seem also to take for granted — on the surface — but they miss the underlying complexities that reflect male anxiety, not only complacency. They certainly miss the presentation of many of these myths as the 'girl's tragedy',[30] and the fears they raise for the male of feminine resistance and/or retaliation in a system that overtly gives too much power to the one and too little to the other.

CONCLUSIONS

What then does Greek myth have to teach us about the issue of rape? There is no single answer that will suffice nor any secure way to control interpretation from those whose own attitudes are nourished by Greek culture as an underground source, each in his own way. We might close therefore with an allegory too tempting to resist: mythology may be viewed from a male perspective as somewhat like a woman. It/she may be dismissed as lying when confronted with philosophy, history, science, reason, reality and truth, or it/she may be transvalued as the symbolic vector in a cultural system, whether for theological, psychological, aesthetic or allegorical aims. Her charms may seduce and mislead or her appeal may be invoked as testimony to some higher initiation into the secrets of the world. She may be unlawfully appropriated or legitimately married to some worthy and suitable cause, always vulnerable either to abuse or honour. She may vanish as a non-existent object when confronted with the clear light of day, like the cloud phantom Nephele, who replaced Hera in Ixion's myth, or like that phantom, she may abide more truly as a consciously imaginative construct. She is, in many respects, unknowable, mysterious, contradictory, to be pursued as an elusive quarry but finally impossible to grasp in her nature. Man would like to think he can live without her, but he cannot. Who tells the stories? Who passes them on? Who can say what a woman thinks?

Acknowledgement

I owe particular thanks to Professor Jack Winkler of Stanford University, who patiently read several drafts and offered, as always, incisive and generous criticism.

8

Two Narratives of Rape in the Visual Arts: Lucretia and the Sabine Women

NORMAN BRYSON

If we have the feeling that ours is perhaps the first period to pay serious attention to what the tradition of European painting has to say about rape, this is unlikely to be because a superior knowledge of sexual or criminal psychology enables us to decipher what to previous centuries was hidden, but for a reason that is almost the opposite: that contemporary perception of rape is now so conditioned by the specialized discourses of our own period that those of the past are now so alien they can perhaps more easily be brought to light.

A reading of the bibliography available at least in the late 1970s indicates some of the main agencies currently focusing their attention on the subject. Sociology and social psychology, often using elaborate statistical apparatus, categorize societies into those that are comparatively rape-prone and those that are comparatively rape-free; in some studies there are attempts to correlate rape with levels of inter-group and inter-personal violence, with the quality of parent—child bonding, with ideologies of male dominance. The agencies of law find themselves engaged in an analysis comprising many variables: criteria of resistance versus criteria of consent, in the legal definition of rape; the aims of apprehension and conviction versus the aims of retribution, deterrence and rehabilitation, in the management of sentencing; influence over the day-to-day discretionary power of judges, versus wholesale statutory reform, in the debate about changing the rape legislation. In the sphere of psychology, the object of inquiry is subject to fluctuations in which the psychological agencies and their founding assumptions are themselves at stake: in some writings it is the aetiology of rape in the psychic formation of the male that holds the stage; in others it is the impact of rape and its aftermath on the female victim; some analyses

assume the abnormality of the rapist, others his normality, his representative-
ness as male. In practical terms it seems probable that the perception of rape
varies according to which among the complicated array of available discourses
the analyst professionally or intellectually subscribes to. What rape essentially
reveals, in the present context, is the profile of the multiple agencies which
embrace rape as their object of knowledge, a profile whose main feature,
historically considered, is undoubtedly that very multiplicity.[1]

Ours is, remarkably, a culture where rape can no longer be thought of as
unitary, as singular, as an event with appropriate spokesmen. Attacker and
victim are almost the least privileged to speak about rape, and even when
accounts and confessions are forthcoming they are usually elicited and
published by authorities with a stake in the wider *mêlée*. Rape exists for us,
accordingly, in a highly refracted form — there can be few crimes discussed
in such a wide variety of accents and by so many voices, in a hubbub that is
not at all like the classical confrontation between a prosecution and a
defence, nor in the least like a legalistic model of *pros* and *contras*. It is
instead a babel of voices, each empowered by a specialized professional
wisdom, whose difference from the rest of the surrounding field both
guarantees each individual vocal authority, and as a by-product of that,
pushes the general refraction one degree further. Rape is splintered, broken
up, diffracted; it reveals in the proliferation of approaches and arguments a
character less of itself than of those who discuss it and embrace it as theirs. If
the legal code could take pride in granting to the accused the right to conduct
his own defence, however infrequently the right might be exercised, current
methods tend to dispense altogether with such courtesies: that voice, like the
voice of the victim, would in any case be only one more among the many
already charged to speak.

Whence the impossibility of our portraying rape, of rape existing for us as
an image: form one, however privately, and it already belongs to the discourses
of sexual psychopathology. Margaret Harrison portrays the present situation
exactly in her work *Rape*: it shows no actual event, no primary seizure, but
capture of a very different sort, rape as it is engulfed by the secondary
agencies (Plate 1).[2] Part of the power of the work is exactly its recognition of
the impossibility of reclaiming rape for the single representation, of making
rape exist as an image, within a society where the agencies of law,
communication and social management rush in to claim it as variously
theirs. Rape belongs here to the sphere of discourses, not events; even its
physical aspect is mediated by forensic display. The space where rape had
once been something that could receive actual portrayal, where it could be
visualized, no longer exists: the mind is too refractive to have its eye.

Earlier representations of rape had existed in a quite different dispensation, not of refraction but of illustration: instead of disappearing before discourse, they make discourse appear; instead of vanishing into an expanding universe of words, they remain visible, and elicit from that stable visibility an equally stable discursivity — an ideology which in its clarity, unity and didacticism merits the label 'classical'.

POUSSIN AND THE SABINES

Antiquity gave us two great narratives of rape: the rape of the Sabines and of Lucretia. Looking at Poussin's versions of the former (Plates 2 and 3), we are likely to find more to depress than to inspire us.[3] If Poussin is the great formalist, abstractionist before the letter, as the admiration of Cézanne and De Stael might encourage one to believe, then the attraction of the subject must be that a painterly technique based on stasis, on geometric checks and balances, is perversely drawn to triumph over a subject that is the technique's opposite, a subject in which it would be hard to imagine greater movement, dynamism and violence. It is true, moreover, that Poussin seems eager to widen to the greatest extent possible the gap between subject and style. If the whole scene of the rape is one of violent insurgence, then its representation is just the reverse: everything is controlled by a fundamental device, of Arrest. What is taken out of the scene is its duration: every aspect of agitation and turbulence is withdrawn; bodily gestures and postures are frozen into positions from which, leaving an ordinary world of energy and movement, they can enter the immobilized world internal to the representation, and begin to multiply an indefinite number of rhymes and echoes, of arms and hands in parallel, of forms answering each other across space according to the strict logic of Poussin's compositional management.

So simple are Poussin's guiding principles, of parallelism and balance, and yet so intricate in their local execution, that appreciation of the compositional brilliance of both versions — in the Louvre and the Metropolitan — can be safely left to the viewer, who, besides, will have been trained in abstraction, by both the artists and the art historians of our century, to look out for and to value such formalist excellences. When I mentioned that the paintings of the Sabines are likely to depress us, I was referring to exactly that formalist stress: if rape tends to be a double violation of women, first in the act and secondly in what social agencies have so often made of rape in re-presenting it, then Poussin's formalism is about as dehumanizing as the second type of violation can get. That so much compositional intelligence can be deployed in order to eclipse or conquer such a subject is indeed a lowering and depressing business; if the fate of the Sabines is first to be violated by the Romans and then to have their violation reified by Poussin into a game of visual checks and balances, depression is properly one's first reaction, as indignation might be the next.

Such reactions would be understandable, but the situation is in fact more complicated than they allow. Before I can go on, we need to know *exactly* what the story of the Sabine women involves. The story runs thus:

It is only four months since the foundation of Rome. During this period manpower has been a constant problem; Romulus has even declared the city an asylum for those outlawed by neighbouring states. This measure has increased the male population, but Rome needs to reproduce itself, needs new Romans, and to this end Romulus has sent embassies to the neighbouring peoples, inviting them to give their daughters to Romans in marriage. His embassies have met with rebuff. Other measures are now called for. To a specially devised festival of games, the Consuelia, Romulus invites the neighbouring Sabines. They are to be the guests of the city and lodge with Romans during their stay; and they are to bring their families. The games are duly held, in honour of Neptune (to whom, if his darker plans work out, Romulus vows to consecrate an annual thanksgiving ceremony). At a pre-arranged signal — Romulus raises his cloak — the Romans seize the marriageable women of the Sabines and carry them off to various parts of the city, while the male Sabines flee.

As vital to the story of the rape is its sequel. The Sabines watch the other Italian peoples suffer defeat after defeat at Roman hands. They decide not to act in anger but to employ strategy, and to delay their countermeasures until certain of success. Some years pass. At length it is discovered that the daughter of the custodian of the Roman Capitol is willing to betray her city and to admit a Sabine force into the Capitol by stealth at night. The Sabines enter and engage in battle with the Romans, the Sabine king Tatius eventually fighting in solo combat with Romulus. During this final clash the Sabine women, now (and for some time since) Roman matrons, make their fatal intervention. In the words of their spokeswoman Hersilia:

Which shall we call the worse, Roman love-making or Sabine compassion?
If you were making war upon any other occasion, for our sakes you ought
to withhold your hands from those to whom we have made you fathers-in-
law and grandfathers. If it be for our own cause, then take us, and with us
your sons-in-law and your grandchildren. Restore to us our parents and our

kindred, but do not rob us of our children and our husbands. Make us not, we entreat you, twice captives.[4]

The Romans and the Sabines duly make peace. Henceforth the Sabines are to become the equals of the Romans, within Rome itself. The Sabine king, Tatius, is made co-ruler of Rome, together with Romulus. As further commemoration, the Roman ceremony of marriage is marked by various reminders of the Sabine episode, of which the most long-lasting is the custom of carrying the bride over the threshold, in honour of the Sabine women.

The rape of the Sabines is fundamentally different in character from the rape of Lucretia (or of Clarissa). Crucially, the motive for the crime is not sexual, but political: Rome needs Romans. The rape does not consist, therefore, in a cluster of individual acts of sexual violence committed against individual women. First, sexual restraint is the order of the day. Romulus's orders are that no married women be taken, 'which showed that they did not commit this rape wantonly, but with the design of forming alliance with their neighbours by the greatest and surest bonds'.[5] The women are not raped on the spot, like Lucretia by Tarquin. Their captors must in fact sleep apart from the women on the night following the capture, and next day are to assemble together with the women before Romulus, to be assigned a wife at an official ceremony presided over by the king. Notice the word wife: the women are not to be kept in concubinage, for that would indeed go against the whole purpose of the exercise, which is to produce new *and legitimate* Roman citizens. Nor are the Sabine women to be used as slaves. On the contrary, their position within the household is honourable, and later the Romans will promise the Sabines that the women are 'not to carry out any servile work in the house, but only spin' (where spinning will remain the arch-respectable occupation of the Roman matron).[6]

If the rape of the Sabines is not to be understood as a specifically sexual crime, nor is it a crime against individual women in any direct sense. According to Roman law, daughters fall under the sway of the eldest male ascendant in their family, the *pater familias*.[7] In the case of rape, power to prosecute lies with the *pater familias*, not with the woman.[8] The crime committed by the Romans is not, in the modern sense, a crime primarily against the Sabine women, and it is avenged by the *pater familias* in his own name.

When we see, in Poussin's paintings, the abduction of the Sabine women, the crime we are witnessing is not the crime we might think it is, and in a sense it is hardly a crime at all. Sanctioned and indeed devised by the king, it can hardly count as transgression of any of the laws of the Roman state; culminating in marriage and the procreation of legitimate offspring, its sexual aspect is fully within the law regulating sexual conduct. All that is missing is the bestowal of the Sabine daughters on their new husbands by their Sabine fathers, and this seems a vital aspect of the episode.

Roman marriage is of two distinct kinds: with or without *manus*. In marriages without *manus*, the wife remains under the authority of her father or guardian, while her husband has no formal authority over her; her dowry, or in cases of greater wealth her property, remains hers.[9] In marriages with *manus*, the *pater familias* emancipates the daughter or ward to the power of the husband. If the marriage is contracted in this way the bride becomes part of her husband's family, as though she were his daughter (as far as property rights are concerned); she accepts the religion of her husband, and worships at her husband's hearth. There may be an actual ceremony, of *confarreatio* or *coemptio*, conferring *manus*; or the *manus* marriage might result from *usus*, continuous cohabitation for a year. The story of the rape of the Sabines seems so concerned to pronounce the legitimacy of its enforced marriages, and of their offspring, that we see both forms of *manus* validation in action. By ceremony, Romulus declares the marriages binding; by *usus*, the Sabine women become *manus* wives after a year; and finally, after the truce between the Romans and the Sabines, the Sabine fathers recognize the legitimacy of their daughters' situation. If there remained any doubt about whose authority the Sabine women fall under, the conclusion of the story dispels it: the Sabine fathers have recognized the *manus* marriages of their daughters to Romans.

Though the outcome is thus full and honourable matrimony, it is clear from the story that the Sabine women, at any rate, are not fully convinced by Romulus's ceremony, or by the fact of *usus*. They seem not to know to whom they belong, and when they speak of grandfathers killing the fathers of their grandchildren, and of husbands killing their fathers-in-law, they are thinking in kinship categories, and seem entirely unsure of how these should now function, and unsure equally of their own place within them. This appears, indeed, to be their principal complaint: they speak of their injuries by speaking of their juridical status. Blood-ties, it seems, cannot define loyalties or regulate behaviour, since the erstwhile Sabine women are related both to their fathers and to their husbands; only law can decide the issue, not blood, or the shedding of blood. The result of the truce is a legal confirmation of the transfer of authority from father to husband, and at this important level of the story, Hersilia's intervention marks a changeover from rule by force, with attendant confusions within the legal and civic spheres, to rule by law.

The English word 'rape' is an obviously misleading term in this context. The story of the Sabines is placed by Livy and Plutarch at the commencement of their Roman histories, where it functions alongside many other stories as a foundation myth — both a description and a legitimation of the ways in which Rome detached itself from the rest of Italy, to become Rome. It is a fable of law, not of violence, or rather it is a fable of the ways in which law had emerged from violence. If one analyses the whole narrative sequence of which the 'rape' of the Sabines is a part, one can see its function in an overall structure defining relations both between nations and between the sexes.

In the initial state, these are badly dysfunctioning: Rome has no children, and not enough wives; Rome has no neighbours, only hostile surrounding nations. In the final state, Rome has legitimate wives and children, and has absorbed its hostile neighbours into itself. The stages of this transformation are worth tracing.

1   Rome has a founder — Romulus — who is entirely outside the normal reproductive cycle, having been born of the union between a Vestal virgin and a god, and reared in the wilderness by wolves. Genetically, he is a cipher; territorially, he is placeless.

2   Rome grows by offering asylum to extreme outsiders — the criminals of neighbouring states. They cannot reproduce themselves; and, being separated from their birthplace and without households, they, too, are placeless.

3   The rape of the Sabines employs force to convert outsiders into insiders, aliens into wives. Genetically, the women are mixed, belonging half to the inside (their marriages are validated by the king) and half to the outside (they still belong to their fathers). Territorially, the boundary between Rome and not-Rome is unclear; Rome is not yet Rome.

4   The Sabine forces enter the Capitol by stealth at night. The barrier between what is inside the city and what is outside is now undone: the keys of the Capitol are handed over by a Roman traitor (Tarpeia). Nothing prevents the outside from becoming the inside, Sabines from invading Rome, or prevents the inside from becoming the outside, Tarpeia going over to the enemy. The Capitol, the crucial military and symbolic boundary separating Rome from not-Rome, is out of action.

5   At the battle, the women assert that they do not know where or to whom they belong. No authority prevails which can determine what belongs inside Rome and what belongs outside Rome.

6   At the truce, what was outside is legitimated as belonging to the inside.

The Sabine women are recognized as Roman matrons; the people of Rome unite with the Sabine nation, naming the resulting population Romans (after Romulus) and Quirites (after the inhabitants of the Sabine town of Cures). The thirty sectors of Rome are named after thirty Sabine women and a commemorative festival — Matronalia — is instituted.

In context, the episode of the rape of the Sabine women is about law, not seizure, and about the creation of stable relations between the sexes and between states, rather than — what strikes one at first sight in Poussin's paintings — political treachery or sexual transgression. Such contextualization must surely revise one's perception of the nature of Poussin's work. For Pietro da Cortona (Plate 4) the *Rape of the Sabines* is an exercise in baroque movement and agitation; Romulus is not represented, nor the Forum of Rome, nor the 'foundation' aspect of the narrative. Poussin, by contrast, forces one back to one's Livy and Plutarch.[10] Here one re-discovers a narrative of boundaries emergent rather than boundaries transgressed, and what confirms the reading of Poussin in the light of his Roman sources is exactly Poussin's *archaeology*, his inquiry into the origins of Rome, which is also the inquiry of Plutarch and of Livy. Rome is still being built, as we see from the scaffolding on the building to the right in the Louvre version (Plate 2). That scaffolding alone should be enough to make us read the depicted episode as part of the larger narrative. Without it, the architecture is simply a *mise-en-scène*: with it, the image refers us away from the present scene, to its motives and its origins, in Rome and the Roman authors (the absence of anything like the scaffolding equally refers us, in Pietro, *only* to the present scene, to acts of sexual violence disconnected from the grand narrative sequence which Poussin carefully brings into play).

To reinforce the aspect of foundation and origin, Poussin further makes architecture studiously archaic: in the Louvre version (Plate 2), probably the first to be painted, he borrows the open loggia on the right from an archaeological design by Alberti; while the temple to the left is supplied with heavily proportioned Tuscan columns and enormous intercolumniations, which resolutely transport the viewer to ancient Rome, a Rome rebuilt out of what Poussin can discover or conjecture of its past. In Pietro da Cortona the architecture makes no such historical claim. In Poussin's Metropolitan version (Plate 3) he goes further: Romulus is given nobler ceremonial robes; if in the earlier version he seems lightweight, almost an officer, here he is a king, and his action is more clearly considered policy and less like the starter's pistol. In both cases the space is maximally public, the Forum, and it is the official, ceremonial and premeditated character of the rape which is uppermost in the representation. The Pietro again is in complete contrast: the space — half secluded temple, half park — is withdrawn from the civil and political world, into a semi-private scene of spontaneous and individual violations.

The critic, John Berger, says in defence of Poussin that his power to organize did not derive simply from the act of painting, but from his whole attitude towards life itself.[11] Perhaps one can qualify this: the intellectualism of the *Rape of the Sabines* is not simply a matter of composition (and the paintings of that name would repel us if this were all they were concerned with), but of Poussin's wider attitude towards Rome, and Roman history. In fact, his attitude is more complex than his allegiance to Plutarch, and to his other Roman sources, might in itself suggest.

Poussin's Rome is like Dante's Vergil. Poussin immerses himself in the visual and ethical life of antiquity; he is boundless in his admiration for the Roman remains, but he cannot forget his Christian inheritance either, and if Dante's Vergil is Rome's herald of the advent of the Christian era, Poussin's Rome is also haunted from out of its Christian future. Partly his scenes of Roman life find subtle continuities between pre-Christian and post-Christian Rome: his version of the Sacrament of Marriage (Plate 5), for example, forcibly reminds Christian marriage of its debt to the past. Partly his emphasis on such similarities works in just the opposite direction, and presents the Romans as (in the strongest sense) pagans, bounded by Poussin's own archaeological endeavours into a time and ethos which is precisely *not yet* Christian. Much of Poussin's emotional tonality comes from the interplay between these different registers. An extraordinary fidelity to archaeological evidence, literary as well as visual, opens him to a perspective in which Roman events are seen in Roman terms, seen as though (in the words of the English painter Reynolds) 'by a mind thrown back two thousand years, and as it were naturalized in antiquity'.[12] At the same time, Poussin's sense of history also includes the traditions and values of Rome since antiquity, so that accompanying his historicism is a sense of a past in the end irretrievable, unknowable in its own terms; a mystery of the past which casts Poussin's labours as impossible, as alms for oblivion. He commits himself to an erudition so immense that his work seems to lose its place in his own century, and the result is often a melancholy of homelessness that can neither achieve the past, nor shed the present.

Poussin's *Rape of the Sabines* is certainly true to his Roman sources, so that a scene of disorder and violence is rediscovered as premeditated, fashioned by policy, legality, ceremony. Indeed, the more Poussin works on the Sabine subject the more he is able to clarify and dignify his material: in the second version (Plate 3) the aspect of an unruly mob is quite purged away, and the formal elements are reduced in number at the same time as they multiply their internal echoes and links. Yet the subject must also include what the rape of the Sabines is to the Christian era, which of course takes a very different view of rape in general, and that of the Sabine women in particular.

In the Christian era, the Roman law of rape completely alters. Rape becomes, among other things, a far deadlier crime. From the time of Constantine, it is elevated to the status of *crimen publicum* and incurs the death penalty for the man. For the woman, punishment varies according to the degree of sexual guilt. If, in the case of raped virgins, the girl had been willing, her penalty was to be burned to death. If she had been unwilling, she was still punished, though with a lighter sentence, for her cries should have brought neighbours to her assistance. Under Justinian also, the death penalty was waiting both for the man and also for the woman, if she consented.

To the Fathers of the Church, the rape of the Sabines is an outrage which shows only the criminality of pagan Rome, and of the histories which celebrated it. Here is Augustine, who opens sarcastically:[13]

Perhaps the reason why the gods did not impose laws upon the Romans was that, as Sallust says, 'Justice and morality prevailed among them by nature as much by laws'. What could be 'juster', or more 'moral', than to take other men's daughters, not by receiving them from their parents, but by luring them with a fraudulent invitation to a show, and then by carrying them off by force, in a scramble. Even if the Sabines were unfair to refuse to give their daughters on request, it was surely much more unfair to take them by force after this refusal. It would have been more just to have waged war against a people that refused a request for marriage with its daughters than against those who asked for the restoration of daughters who had been carried off . . . I am sick of recalling the many acts of revolting injustice which have disturbed the city's history.[13]

Poussin's representations of the rape falls, and was deliberately chosen so as to fall, between two dispensations which, in their antithetical views of the same event, reveal precisely that sense of brokenness in history which is the other side of Poussin's imaginative empathy, and archaeological erudition. What in the pagan perspective is a story of law and of the emergent harmony between Rome and its conquered neighbours, when seen in the post-pagan perspective is one of crime, infamy and the emergence of a pagan empire unconsecrated by Christian law and Christian revelation. Poussin's versions of the *Rape of the Sabines* are in a sense the opposites of his scene of the *Sacrament of Marriage*. There, we are shown the continuity of customs, so pronounced that Christianity is felt almost as an outside force trying to harness to itself a tradition of ordinary life which existed before Christianity, and which persists rather in parallel with Christianity than within its bounds. The stress is on a sanity of family life that lies deeper than the arrangements of history, and in this it resembles David's version of the *Intervention of the Sabine Women* (Plate 6), where the private roles (wife, husband, parent, child) are recommended as more supportive of civilization than those heroic and anti-familial roles which David had been recommending during the French Revolution (the Horatii, Lucius Junius Brutus, Bara).[14]

Poussin's paintings turn, in the end, on history, and are truly historical paintings in the sense that they show history operating in our deepest moral perceptions as well as in our moral actions. History has made the rape of the Sabines as problematic for the modern world, and for Poussin, as it was straightforward for Plutarch. For Poussin the problem is intense: he is able to recreate Roman history through Roman eyes, and yet the subject he so empathetically depicts is also, in the later world which he inhabits, monstrous. What emerges is a sense of human life made complex and contradictory by the progress of history, pulled about between colliding perspectives within history. This is what his two paintings finally illustrate; and if, in this august meditation of his, the fate of the Sabine women seems to have been subordinated, and a voice of sympathy is still exclaiming 'But what of the women themselves?', his two paintings also spell out some reasons why, in a matter of this kind, compassion cannot be the only, or the final, response.

THE RAPE OF LUCRETIA

This consideration of Poussin will have shown, I hope, the necessity of getting the story right, of re-reading one's Livy or one's Plutarch. It is here one encounters a problem in twentieth century viewing of paintings: as a rule, while even abstruse matters of iconology are widely investigated and understood, and quite arcane aspects of patronage are accorded all due importance, textual sources tend to be undervalued; in the teaching of art history, reading skills are widely ignored. In the case of the second great rape in antiquity, that of Lucretia, it is just as vital to follow the whole of the narrative. What exactly occurred?

We are again in the Rome of the kings.[15] At a nocturnal gathering of friends, Collatinus, a member of the royal family, boasts to his companions that the virtues of his wife, Lucretia, far outshine those of other wives. The company is heated by wine and decides to test the point: they ride off to see how each wife in turn is behaving that very night. The daughters of the king, Tarquinius Superbus, are discovered amusing themselves with various diversions, but at the house of Collatinus they find Lucretia busy (again, arch-respectable occupation of the Roman matron) spinning wool. Lucretia welcomes the company, and is generally awarded the prize. The company departs. But the king's son, Sextus Tarquinius (Tarquin), whether smitten with love (Ovid), or aroused as much by Lucretia's chastity as by her beauty (Livy), or from a black impulse determining to ruin Lucretia's reputation rather than her body (Dio Cassius), decides to return to ask the hospitality of the house for the rest of the night. Later, when all are asleep, he enters Lucretia's bedroom armed with a sword. Lucretia resists his various blandishments and menaces, until Tarquin announces that if she does not let him have his way he will kill not only her but her negro slave, and will place the slave's naked corpse alongside her own, and will tell the world that he found them thus together in adulterous embrace, and killed them on the spot. Before this threat to her reputation, Lucretia yields. Tarquin departs.

The next morning Lucretia summons to the house her father, Lucretius, and husband, Collatinus, telling each to bring a trusted friend. Her father arrives together with Publius Valerius, her husband with the king's kinsman Lucius Junius Brutus. She tells these four of Tarquin's action, saying 'if you are men and care for your children, avenge me, free yourselves, and show the tyrants [the Tarquins] what manner of men you are and what manner of woman of yours they have outraged'.[16] Taking the sword of her ravisher, she announces that she will now kill herself, rather than let the story of Lucretia furnish Roman women with a bad example: 'never shall Lucretia provide a precedent for unchaste women to escape what they deserve' (Livy: *nuc ulla impudica Lucretiae exemplo vivet*). Brutus pulls the bloody weapon from her body and swears by the gods to drive the Tarquins from Rome. The people rally, overthrow the royal house and establish the Republic. Brutus and Collatinus become its first consuls.

In Roman law, a key feature of the story is that Lucretia, albeit under duress, gave her consent to Tarquin; this makes her technically an adulteress, not a victim of rape. As an adulteress her punishment could have been considerable.[17] Livy writes of Lucretia in the reign of Augustus, when Rome is going through one of its periodic fits of public morality: an adulteress could be killed by her *pater familias*; her husband was obliged to divorce her; if convicted of adultery she would lose half her dowry, the adulterer would be subject to a fine and both parties exiled separately. In such circumstances suicide seems an honourable decision. The aspect of consent, important though it will become for Augustine and others, is not, however, what Livy stresses. Lucretia is not committing suicide in order to evade punishment, but from more pressing motives.[18]

The first of these is simply vengeance. As a woman, it is not in her power to avenge her injury; and the revenge she asks for from her men is not personal, revenge on Tarquin, but political, revenge on 'the tyrants'. Her suicide is not in any sense a solitary act, as the death of Clarissa will be solitary; she dies in order to galvanize the men of her household, and to this end she dies before their very eyes.[19] It is not, in other words, a private matter, but an affair of state, and its outcome will be the overthrow of the state.

Her second motive is equally public in character: she will not suffer the name of Lucretia to become a cloak for indecency, a justification for shameless women, for *ulla impudica*. What counts for her is her posthumous status; and not for the first time. She had already put her posthumous reputation first, when yielding to Tarquin's threat of dishonouring her with her negro slave. The sword which finally persuaded her was not the sword which would rob her of life, but of her honour. The sword by which she now dies is not an instrument of private suicide, but a means of arousing her house to vengeance upon another house, and of preserving her name among women.

It is neo-classicism which comes closest to depicting the public character of the rape and its aftermath, and deliberately so. Platitude though it is that neo-classicism in France rises in opposition to rococo, it is nevertheless true, in the deepest sense: the French Academy banishes rococo by creating a new kind of human body, one which belongs in its very tissues to the public domain. The rococo had produced, by equally systematic determination, a body of purely private pleasures. At its most radical, rococo takes the nude out of the public realm of high idealization and formal purgation, and subjects it to a profound desublimation. It rediscovers that body's actual flesh, the temperature of its skin, which is flushed and warm, and the texture of that skin, which is moist from bathing.[20] The bodies of Boucher's women, for example, like those of Natoire and Fragonard, are fresh from a bath that is also a sexual prelude, and the paintings in which they appear are destined not for the salon but the private apartment, and the private patron. To such a connoisseur of beauties rape is beneath contempt, unless it is as the memory of Correggio's *Io*, ravishment by a divine cloud which caresses every single pore of skin, and thus surpasses the limitations of a natural lover (Plate 7: the tinted steam of rococo mythologies is an incarnation of the *caress*). Or rape is contemplated as a superior form of excitement, perhaps not rape at all, as it is in Fragonard's *Le Verrou* (Plate 8).

In the Academy, as rococo fades the body is subject to exactly the severities its painters discover in their Roman authors. The new subjects of the 1770s and 1780s concern not pleasure but virtue, the conduct worthy of a man, a *vir*. The acts celebrated at the Academy are those of extraordinary self-destruction, self-mutilation, self-control: Mucius Scaevola places his hand in the coals to prove to the enemy the indifference of Romans to bodily pain; Regulus returns to the Carthaginians to suffer death in a barrel of spikes; Socrates, accused of turning after strange pleasures, publicly drinks the hemlock; Brutus — the same Brutus who avenges Lucretia — condemns his sons to death; Lucretia sacrifices her body to preserve her honour and to strike at tyranny.

It is Beaufort who most recaptures the severity of the body in the Roman historians (Plate 9), and their conception of the body as belonging first to the *res publica* and to the family, but only remotely to its physical owner, who is accordingly indifferent to its local pleasures or fears.[21] There is a sense in which the entire career of David is anticipated in Beaufort's subject: Lucretia's suicide will become the deaths of Seneca (1773), of Socrates (1777), of Leonidas (1815); her death by the sword will become the deaths of Marat, of Lepelletier, of Camilla; the oath sworn by the Horatian brothers will be transferred to them from Lucius Junius Brutus; Lucretia's indifference to creatural feeling will become the terrible coldness of Brutus sentencing his sons. In fact, David's last sketch, dating from 1825, depicts Lucretia's rape.

If neo-classical painting is especially responsive to the severe, self-mutilating, anti-libidinal body it discovered in the Roman histories, this was not, however, all that could be found there. The focus of Christian interpretation of the story of Lucretia is elsewhere: on Lucretia's rape considered not as a political, but as a spiritual event. There is a single founder of this alternative tradition, Augustine; and for once the historian of ideas does not have to work diagnostically, by reading symptoms the patient cannot himself recognize, since Augustine is quite explicit about the aim of his discussion, which is to discredit the pagan world.

It is impossible not to admire Augustine's dazzling adversarial question: '*if she was adulterous, why is she praised? If chaste, why was she put to death?*'[22] In the earlier Roman authors Lucretia's consent is presented as part of her laudable concern for her reputation: she consents because the alternative is public disgrace, the disgrace of being thought to have been an adulteress whose paramour had been her slave. Her consent is motivated by external ('shame culture') considerations, and is presented as far less important than the key events which follow — the suicide, and above all the revenge. Lucretia earns her place in the histories of Rome, after all, because Brutus's revenge inaugurated the Republic. In Augustine's hands the external and political aspects of the case are conspicuously passed over. He does not consider Lucretia's concern for her reputation, and says nothing of the overthrow of tyranny, or of the Republic. Instead he concentrates, with the energy of a prosecuting attorney, on the question of consent.

Whichever way his question is answered, Lucretia loses. If her honour was indeed without stain, then in killing herself she killed an innocent, and the name for that is murder. But if her consent signalled a faltering in her chastity, although we can now perhaps condone her self-administered punishment, she is guilty of adultery. Technically, in Roman law, this was exactly Lucretia's crime: even in cases where consent was withheld there was still pollution, and if pregnancy resulted not only the child and the mother but the woman's family would thereby be tainted.

It is not with that kind of pollution, however, that the Fathers of the Church are concerned. For Tertullian it was even possible for a virgin to cease to be a virgin because of impure thoughts: purity and impurity are things known to God, and to the conscience appearing before God. In the legal codes of Constantine and Justinian the consenting female is punished by burning precisely because of that internal consent, which in an important sense becomes the crime. Lucretia never wholly lost Tertullian's admiration, since he took it that because Lucretia was chaste in intention, the rape of her body was of little consequence.[23] She was admirable — though of course not as admirable as a Christian nun: 'Easier it is to lay down your life because you have lost a blessing, than to keep by living that for which you would rather die outright.'[24] This formula is interesting: by comparing the case of Lucretia with the fate of a nun, Tertullian focuses on the issue of spiritual chastity, and it is this (not reputation, not the Republic) which also concerns Augustine. In an important passage in the *City of God*, which I quote in full, he considers the violation of women in the religious life:

> In the first place, it must be firmly established that virtue, the condition of right living, holds command over the parts of the body from her throne in the mind; and if that will continues unshaken and steadfast, whatever anyone else does with the body or to the body, provided that it cannot be avoided without committing sin, involves no blame to the sufferer. But there can be committed on another's body not only acts involving pain, but also acts involving lust. And so whenever any act of the latter kind has been committed, although it does not destroy a purity which has been

maintained by the utmost resolution, still it does engender a sense of shame, because it may be believed that an act, which perhaps could not have taken place without some physical pleasure, was accompanied also by a consent of the mind.[25]

Lucretia, for Augustine, is not only a self-murderer, but a woman who, quite unlike a virtuous nun struggling with some villainous Goth during the sack of Rome, actually gave her consent. To this Augustine adds what will become, for Titian and for those working after him, his very disagreeable final twist: 'which perhaps could not have taken place without some physical pleasure [and therefore] was accompanied by a consent of the mind'. There is actual consent, and Lucretia gave it; and there is the 'consent of the mind' which is given automatically whenever there is pleasure. This second consent not even a nun raped by Alaric himself can withhold.

Augustine's aim, in this last turn of the screw, is probably to present the body as unconquerable territory. If a ravished nun is polluted because of the automatic consent which the body yields in taking involuntary pleasure, that damns not the nun but the body itself. Such pleasure is obvious in the case of the man, who cannot conceal it; in the case of the woman, pleasure is hidden, but is none the less unavoidable. The body betrays its pleasures, and thereby betrays the soul. Tarquin's lust cannot be concealed from man, but Lucretia's cannot be concealed from God. Her first consent, the consent she gave to Tarquin, robbed her of heroic status (Augustine maintains); her second consent, the consent her body gave to pleasure, robs her of her true chastity. It is this second consent which will be of much interest to the Renaissance.

LUCRETIA IN ART

Titian's version of Lucretia (Plate 10), on the whole, lacks sensitivity to the political aspect of the case, and to the severe, visibly controlled, self-immolating body which French neo-classicism would evolve from the Roman histories.[26] He chooses to depict not the oath of Brutus, nor even Lucretia's suicide (which is left to Veronese) but the rape itself. No connection is made between Lucretia and her family, as there is in Beaufort; she makes no speeches about her reputation or the overthrow of tyrants. The words Lucretia spoke to Tarquin are not recorded. She has no audience to hear her, and there can be none of the self-absolving rhetoric and drama which will appear next morning before her family. What is shown in the Titian version is exactly what forms the centre of Augustine's discussion: Lucretia's consent.

On the left appears the negro slave: his inclusion confirms that Tarquin has already uttered, or is about to utter, the final threat which will bring Lucretia round; which is to say that Titian's painting represents either the consent itself, or the consent about to be given. 'The Rape of Lucretia' — can a woman who consents be raped? What is a woman who consents called? What is Titian's subject — rape, or adultery?

In Venice certainly in the early Renaissance rape is a crime whose gravity varies according to the status of those involved.[27] If the victim of rape is a *puella*, a girl under 12, the punishment is extremely severe. If the woman is of marriageable age and single, it is less so. If the woman is actually married, it is lighter still. Lucretia would be in the last category were it not for the social sensitivities of the Venetian court. Records for the early Renaissance show that one-fifth of rapes judged by the courts of Venice were committed by the nobility, who represented between 3 and 7 per cent of the population.[28] Of noblemen convicted of rape, only a small fraction were seriously prosecuted. Punishment of nobles for the crime of rape resulted, and was then severe, when the assault had taken place upon a woman of rank. Then the nature of the crime changed: the rape of women of the nobility has been reckoned the most serious crime it was possible for a Venetian nobleman to commit. The sentence involved, typically, a colossal fine, imprisonment for three or more years and banishment for a further three years.

The social-specific nature of Venetian justice during the Renaissance can be illustrated by the following case. Paulus de Canali was accused of raping the wife of a carpenter named Marcus. Witnesses testified that he had broken into her house and raped her there; but the Forty acquitted him. Six months later he was before the Forty, again for breaking and entering and rape, but on this occasion the victim was the wife of a noble, Marcus Corner. Paulus and two others were found guilty, fined 20 ducats each and sentenced to three years' imprisonment, to be followed by three years of banishment from the Venetian Republic.[29]

In so far as it is a painting which expresses something akin to this state of affairs, Titian's *Rape of Lucretia* represents rape committed by a nobleman (far more grave than the Paulus case) upon a woman of noble family. In so far as it is a painting of Tarquin and Lucretia, it represents something else: the giving of consent. Obviously the painting represents both, and what it therefore addresses is, perhaps for the first time in the present discussion, a specifically sexual crime.

There can be no doubt that that painting's sexual nature is heightened by Lucretia's nudity. In Beaufort, Lucretia is fully clothed, a person appearing before others in public and political space. In Titian the image has been purged of every indication not only of public but even of domestic space. It would be wrong to say that the rape occurs in the bedroom of any Roman or Venetian house; it occurs *in bed*, in a bed dislocated both from the household and from its own surrounding space. It is a space altogether cut off from the outside world, and for this to happen in a narrative which is concerned, in its original form, entirely with the public domain (reputations, dynasties, the Republic) is an index of the degree to which in Titian, the focus is on all that is left when the grander narrative and the public motivations and repercussions are taken away: Augustine's domain, of sexuality in its privacy and inward specificity. Nudity serves not only to divest Lucretia of her public self (which was almost Lucretia's only self), but to name what little is left, the private, as the sexual.

The terms have now shifted radically from Livy (or from Beaufort). To him (and to neo-classicism) the rape of Lucretia is the crime of a tyrannical regime, which is avenged by one house or clan attacking another house or clan, and which results in a new political order. In Titian, the rape is the crime of a nobleman against a noblewoman, a crime of *rank*; and a crime that is specifically sexual, where the sexual function is isolated from all other aspects or locations of the self; in which the woman is shown in the moment, or just before the moment, of consent.

If in Beaufort Tarquin's crime is, in the end, tyranny, in Titian the crime is one, more simply, of debauchery or sexual excess. The rapist is not yet subject to those minute categorizations which will constitute, for the modern period, the various typologies of sexual deviation. Tarquin is categorized in the first place by his rank, not by psychopathology. His essence is not that of a rapist but of an aristocrat, and his aristocratic status is not altered by his action; he does not change one identity (civil subject) for another (criminal deviant of type X). Later, the diagnostic category will, as we know, divide into individual branches and will create specific criminal and medical identities: 'to marry a close relative or practice sodomy, to seduce a nun or engage in sadism, to deceive one's wife or violate cadavers, [will] become things that [are] essentially different.'[30]

For the time being, however, although the sexual aspect of the case is named and separated out from its narrative context, it is not yet interrogated, subdivided and appropriated by the multiple and conflicting discourses of the future; not even the discourse of politics seems to trouble it, as republican and revolutionary discourses will trouble and complicate the work of David. Tarquin's act is intelligible in the terms which the painting itself offers, terms which the image is able to supply from its own internal resources directly: an act of force, of creatural violation.

The figure of Lucretia is actually rather harder to read than Tarquin's. The difficulty can be quickly grasped by considering the Wallace Collection's Lucretia, by a Florentine painter of the mid-seventeenth century (Plate 11). Like Titian's image, this too centres on the moment of consent, and on the specifically sexual nature of the scene. Even more than in Titian, Lucretia's body belongs amid the linen and the pillows: the pose is much more clearly one of seduction, and Lucretia's expression is much closer to pleasure. It is not fanciful to see on her lips something of a smile, if not of pleasure in the act (which would push the painting fully into the abyss of kitsch) then of pleasure despite the act, of pleasure, as Augustine describes it, in the second form of consent, the consent that the body gives even though the spirit resolutely holds out; the pleasure which man can never conceal, being as he is, but which woman is able to conceal from all but her conscience, and from God. There is a great deal more at stake in Lucretia's smile than in the Mona Lisa's. If a smile is betrayed, by the consent which involuntary pleasure gives to the act, then woman is after all like man; no more than he, can she hide or prevent her lust.

The image of Tarquin ravishing Lucretia turns, in such a depiction, on the question of sexual difference: the man seems wholly mastered by lust, the woman wholly chaste; yet if there is any trace of a smile, even and particularly Augustine's smile of secondary and involuntary consent, then the issue of difference is resolved, and despite every appearance to the contrary she is after all like him, like *us*. If Lucretia smiles, the fact or possibility of radical (physiological, moral) difference in the constitution of the sexes can be consolingly overcome: Lucretia's smile quickly becomes what we see it is in Cagnacci's representation: a sexual sign, like the dagger, the pillows, the nudity.

Looking again at Titian after Cagnacci, I think we are compelled to find something similar. For Augustine, and for those who, like Titian, followed Augustine's (rather than Livy's or Plutarch's) emphases, it is the consent which is of central importance. To be sure, the Titian has none of Bilivert's vulgarity, his insinuation that perhaps this is a scene of pornography, and nothing like his suggestion of a smile. Nevertheless, in his presentation of Lucretia he stresses themes which belong more to consent or seduction, than to forcible rape: Lucretia's nudity (Titian's northern sources had portrayed her as clothed), the isolation of the bed from domestic and social space, the presence of the linen and pillows; and, of course, her actual consent. The painting is, in fact, a conundrum: we seem to be seeing two separate iconographic subjects superimposed — a man who rapes, and a woman who seduces.

In this sense Titian's image seems strikingly modern. In a scandal both of logic and of sexuality, Titian opens up a paradoxical area in which the modern viewer is free to find his or her own questions: who controls or can control the signs and symptoms of the body; sexual difference; woman's pleasure? The validity of such viewing will depend on critical stance: if classic texts and images are held to change as they travel forwards in time, then classic paintings will rightly yield to different generations different truths. My own view of the Titian in its period is that the work's aspect of conundrum, of confused categories, is a function of the legalistic and debate-like aspect of the discussion which surrounded Lucretia's case once both the Christian, Augustinian interpretation and the interpretation of the Roman historians could be assessed side by side. In Renaissance terms, Lucretia is a *topos* interesting because it brings pagan and Christian frameworks into play simultaneously, and the issue is whether or not she is to be admired, or whether a Christian or a pagan view should be taken of her case. Shakespeare consciously alternates these frameworks; Titian, in his double or super-imposed iconography, seems to me to do the same.

FANTASY AND SURVEILLANCE

The modern questions are unlikely to be Titian's; but they are not out of place when we look at Delacroix. I conclude by invoking *The Death of Sardanapalus* (Plate 12). The painting is not a depiction of rape, yet in its concern with male violence and sexual reification it may be the last coherent and inclusive representation of rape, before the forces of subjectivity represented not least within the work itself are historically captured and fragmented by the proliferating discourses of the *scientia sexualis* of the Western nineteenth and twentieth centuries.

In the guise of an oriental king who commands and then contemplates from his couch the destruction of his harem, Delacroix presents a complete drama from the inner theatre of sexuality. *Sardanapalus* is primarily an assault on the economy of private and public imagery which had regulated the art of the salon. In the *Ancien Régime*, the highest category of painting belonged exclusively to public painting: it was this which united scriptural and mythological subjects, and subjects from national and ancient history, in a domain of art addressed to the individual in his public capacity, to the viewer as citizen. The hierarchy of the genres declines step by step as imagery withdraws from the citizen to the individuated subject (portraiture), to his private and domestic world ('genre') and to his specific, anonymous surroundings (still life). Beaufort is fully within the highest category of public or history painting, as are David and Gros, and even, in his exhibited work, Géricault.

Delacroix appropriates the public space of the salon and of the *tableau d'histoire* for a scene that belongs, spectacularly, to the space of private fantasy. The painting is a manifesto, of a revolutionary kind, of the right to paint not history or the world of the citizen, but subjectivity itself: it proposes and assumes the viewer as one whose experiences include those of the solitary and sexual imagination and its contents, now presented, in an aggressively political gesture, in the full publicity of the annual salon. It is not shocking to encounter the fantasy; what is disruptive is that the fantasy is no longer private, or destined for the private cabinet, but is projected massively, overwhelmingly, into the public arena. Politically, *Sardanapalus* achieves an effect which is the opposite of that sought, for example, by Reynolds. The *Discourses* promote an art which, for the first time in Britain, will create a public, an art whose central forms will, as they shed particularity, address the viewer not as private individual but as citizen; out of disparate individuals, history painting and the grand manner will forge or coerce a national public, a public united in their common visual experience, and by their central interests as members of a united public. *Sardanapalus* reverses this movement, seizes the controls of history painting, and then fragments the unity of its achieved public, returning the citizen to a state of atomic individuality which is nevertheless now under surveillance.

The painting involves, in fact, a double process whose first or familiar aspect is to articulate what had been private into a public space; the mode is confessional, and in this it resembles such familiar models as Rousseau and Sade. The unfamiliar aspect of the process is the opposite of this movement from the inside to the outside: the declaration that public art now moves inside the individual, into the recesses of subjectivity and sexual psychology and psychopathology.

We are used to the first movement, through the oldest myths of the Romanticism. The second is only now becoming clearer to us, as characteristic activity of those agencies which, in the Western nineteenth and twentieth centuries, direct both the techniques of public knowledge and the power of the ascendant social agencies of social management towards the subjectivity of the citizen, as object of that emergent knowledge and power. It is this second movement which, in its current phase, extends towards rape its enormous and still proliferating array of discourses and agencies, which, in the end, so diffract from the object of knowledge that it cannot be coherently represented in the form of the image. It is perhaps to this second movement that we owe the disappearance of rape from coherent and transmissible iconographies.

9

The House that Jack Built: Some Stereotypes of the Rapist in the History of Popular Culture

CHRISTOPHER FRAYLING

'LOOK! THAT WAS JACK THE KNIFE!'

Long before 'video nasties' (or even videos) had hit the headlines,[1] the dramatic and visual 'rules' for the representation of male-sexuality-with-violence had been firmly established in popular Gothick cinema. The visual metaphor was usually the knife, although in the most famous rape fantasy it was the canine teeth. The man doing the stabbing or the penetration tended to be an aristocratic count, such as Dracula; an 'aesthetic' (and therefore strange) young man, such as Conrad Veidt's Cesare; a respected professional man-into-wolf, such as Fredric March's Dr Harry Jekyll or Robert Mitchum's preacher; or, in the B-feature version, a libidinous bug-eyed monster from outer space in a customized diving helmet. The victim tended to be either a pre-lapsarian simpleton — the little peasant girl Maria, Shelley Winters as the wife of the Reverend Harry — or a fallen woman who (we were usually encouraged to believe) was 'looking for it' all along — Lulu, the tart-with-a-heart 'champagne' (Ivy Pearson), Hitchcock's Marion Crane, the lady who was 'dressed to kill' (see plates 14—22).[2]

Some of the victims managed to express themselves just before they died through the most electrifying screams in talking picture history — a celebrated example being Fay Wray in bondage confronted by the hairy paws of a giant gorilla without a penis, in the person of King Kong. The camera tended to tilt at the last moment towards a symbolic icon (such as a shining white reproduction of Canova's *Eros and Psyche* in the 1932 *Dr Jekyll and*

Mr Hyde), or the celluloid image tended discreetly to dissolve seconds before the ghastly act was committed — in the case of James Whale's *Frankenstein*, this *created* the impression that the little girl had been raped — and the audience had to be satisfied with distorted shadows on the opposite wall and the retribution of people like us.

It seems to have been assumed by the producers that the man who paid for the tickets at the local Roxy would identify at some level with the predator — will he or won't he? Do I feel embarrassed by this or don't I? — and that the woman he was taking to the pictures would identify at some level with the victim, and be comforted and protected by the paying customer, perhaps with the aid of popcorn during the interval; perhaps by reclaiming the night together on the way home.

As Brendan Behan once wrote, 'it does take your mind off the cost of living', and at the same time it does reassure you (whichever gender you happen to be) that rapists are part of horror film mythology — frightening, but only in the sense that a nightmare is frightening. Everything is fine when you wake up, like in the closing frames of *The Cabinet of Dr Caligari* (1919) and *Dressed to Kill* (1980), both of which belong to an uninterrupted dramatic and visual tradition dating back to the very origins of cinema.

These cinematic 'rules' evolved during an era, roughly between the 1880s and the early 1930s, when an *aesthetic* of male-sexuality-with-violence was combined by the nascent entertainment industry with the stereotypes of popular melodrama, le Grand-Guignol and throwaway fiction. The aesthetic seems originally to have been developed by some Western European fine artists. In Oskar Kokoschka's expressionist drawing *Murderer, Hope of Women* (1911—12), for example, the image of rape is associated with the knife through both the content and the form: the lines of the drawing look as though they have been stabbed into the paper, just as the man is about to stab the battered and bruised figure of his victim. The overall effect serves to generalize the personal fantasies of earlier 'expressionist' painters such as Edvard Munch — who were sometimes concerned for their own reasons with similar subject matter.[3] The expressionist city-scape of Lyonel Feininger — which, like Kokoschka's drawing, powerfully transforms material objects into emotional ornaments — seems an outward and visible sign of an inner mental torment which could easily express itself in acts of rape:

Perpendicular lines tense towards the diagonal, houses exhibit crooked, angular outlines, planes shift in rhomboid fashion, the lines of force of normal architecture, expressed in perpendiculars and horizontals, are transmogrified into a chaos of broken forms . . . A movement begins, leaves its natural course, is intercepted by another, led on, distorted again, and broken. All this is steeped in a magic play of light . . .[4]

By the year in which *The Cabinet of Dr Caligari* was made, 1919, this evocation of mental states by extreme distortion and stylization of settings had become a visual cliché which could be tried out by a canny producer on a mass audience: diagonals, shadows, jerky movements of the human body preserved for posterity in the performance of Werner Krauss as the devil doctor. The aesthetic of rape had already become the visual equivalent of one of Krafft-Ebing's nastier case studies — in other words, the sign of a psychological rather than a social problem; a case of something called the 'male principle' triumphing over something called the 'female principle'. The addition of more historically specific props — the gaslight, the fog, the winding by-ways of the 'red light district' — which originated in serious drama with Frank Wedekind's *Pandora's Box* (1892—1901),[5] was helped along in the age of silent cinema by the Surrealists. For some of them the man with the knife put the finishing touches to a bizarre collage of Victorian steel-engravings. An issue of the surrealist journal *Minotaure*, for example, with a cover by Dali and colour reproductions of Picasso's work, included a short play by Maurice Heine entitled *Regards sur l'enfer anthropoclasique*, which, with considerable relish, told the story of a meeting between the Marquis de Sade, the Comte de Mesanges and the Reverend Jack the Ripper.

THE COUNT (to JACK): Your work is all over very quickly: butcher's work . . . technically skilful, perhaps, but there's no *art* in that.

JACK: Art is the child of leisure, monseigneur, and necessity encouraged me to get a move on. The essential precaution against all surprise or interruption was to move quickly; that is to say, to give the subject a speedy, silent and neat despatch. That's what this weapon assured me of — wielded with the left hand, but directed towards the point where a right-handed person would have begun, and whence the blood had to spurt far away from me. As for what you style 'art', it was more convenient for me to practise *that* on the bloodless flesh of a docile corpse. I never neglected to devote short periods of time to it — as circumstances permitted me. Would you like to see proof of this? Do grant me that you see here at least a few artistic touches. (He hands the Comte de Mesanges the document reproduced as plate 1).[6]

This encounter between the *grands saigneurs* of history, during a surrealist season in hell, has all the naive exuberance of the Universal horror movies which Hollywood produced, in assembly-line circumstances, from the early 1930s onwards: one of the most celebrated characters in the Universal canon, Dr Praetorius (played by Ernest Thesiger in *The Bride of Frankenstein*, 1935) mirrors the tone of the *Minotaure* play almost exactly. 'Gin?', he says to a rotting cadaver in the cobwebbed crypt, 'it's my *only* weakness!'

Some of these Hollywood Gothick films were made by refugees from a society which had rejected German expressionism (such as Edgar G. Ulmer, who, in *The Black Cat* of 1934, presented the only Bauhaus-style black mass in cinema history), and all of them managed to turn the *angst* of early Weimar pop-culture into a camp celebration of its imagery. Hitchcock's *Psycho*, of 30 years later, manipulates precisely the same imagery — with its 1950s motel next door to the old dark house on the hill — and *that* film has in the last decade become the seminal source for what are now known in the popular press as 'video nasties'. Visitors to Universal Studios today can see, beside a model of the American Gothick house of Norman and Norma Bates, a written message from Brian De Palma, the writer and director of *Dressed To Kill*. The message tells us that nobody can do a knife-attack-in-a-shower-sequence quite like Alfred Hitchcock. At the same time, Clint Eastwood's latest Dirty Harry adventure, *Sudden Impact* (1983), which has a plot about rape and retribution similar to that of the notorious 'nasty' (now banned in Britain) *I Spit On Your Grave* (1980), uses a store-room full of grotesque carnival masks as the setting for its final sequences, turning the story of *The Cabinet of Dr Caligari* back to front.

If this popular visual tradition has gone from strength to strength since the turn of the century — to the extent that it is fairly difficult to recall a commercial cinematic representation of male-sexuality-with-violence that does *not* make some reference to it — the equally popular stereotypes of the man with the knife, the human figure of whom the visual tradition is merely an outward and visible sign, have also gone from strength to strength. Not only in today's tabloid headlines about 'beasts', 'monsters', 'maniacs' and 'psychopaths', which simply reinforce the myth that the rapist is always part of someone else's nightmare, but also in the cultures that give those headlines support and credibility. The stereotypes go back at least as far as the means of mechanical reproduction which helped to spread them around (although successive generations of media pundits and moral guardians have claimed to 'discover' them at regular intervals ever since then). But they do seem to have been *brought into focus*, at precisely the same time as the birth of a visual tradition which ultimately turned them into an encoded channel of communication, by a series of specific historical incidents. These incidents

occurred in Whitechapel, in the East End of London, during the autumn of
1888. They were almost immediately associated with a person unknown who
was rumoured to answer to the name of 'Jack the Ripper'. He himself was not
a rapist, in the modern-day sense of the term — since, for him, the repeated
penetration of his victims with a sharp knife appears to have *been* the sexual
act. He *may* have sodomized his final victim — before or after death —
although we cannot even be sure of that. But the incidents of autumn 1888
have become so deeply confused, over time, with the representation of male-
sexuality-with-violence (to cite the most obvious of today's examples: knife
or razor attacks on women have become the unavoidable metaphor for the
act of rape in countless films, videos and books), that in 'the popular memory'
Jack the Ripper has come to be identified as *the* stereotype (or rather *the*
stereotypes) of the rapist. The Whitechapel murders, and their constant re-
enactment as myth in the mass media, are a key to the understanding of rape
as it has been represented in the popular culture of the twentieth century. So
it is to the events of autumn 1888 that we will turn our close attention.[7]

> SEE THE SHARK, HOW RED HIS FINS ARE
> AS HE SLASHES AT HIS PREY
> JACK THE KNIFE WEARS KID GLOVES WHICH
> GIVE THE MINIMUM AWAY . . .

At 5.30 am on the morning of Saturday 8 September 1888, about five
minutes before she died, Annie Chapman was seen talking to a stranger by
Elizabeth Long, a park keeper's wife. Chapman was, apparently, standing
'against the shutters' of 29 Hanbury Street, Whitechapel. According to this
witness, the man was dark, perhaps a foreigner, aged over 40, about 5 ft 6 in
in height, wearing a brown deerstalker hat and perhaps a dark coat: she did
not manage to get a good look at his face, but later recalled that he had a
'shabby genteel appearance'. Mrs Long overheard him asking Annie Chapman
'will you . . . ?', to which the prostitute replied 'yes'. Just before this, at about
5.25 am, another witness, a carpenter named Albert Cadosh who lived at
27 Hanbury Street, had overheard Chapman sharply saying 'no!', but had not
caught sight of the person to whom this was said. Cadosh returned to the
same place a few minutes later, shortly after Mrs Long, and distinctly heard
'a sort of fall against the fence'. 'I did not look to see what it was', he added at
the inquest, 'and I did not hear any other noise.' Had Albert Cadosh looked
over the fence, he would not have saved Annie Chapman's life, but he might
have interrupted the murderer at his work: for Annie Chapman was strangled,

her throat was cut and she was then savagely mutilated, at approximately 5.30 am.

At just before midnight on Saturday 29 September 1888, about 50 minutes before she died, Elizabeth Stride was seen talking to a stranger by William Marshall, a worker in a nearby indigo warehouse. The two people were standing outside a house in Berner Street. According to this witness, the man was middle-aged, with broad shoulders and a stout build, about 5 ft 6 in in height, probably clean-shaven, wearing a round cap with a small peak on it, a small black cutaway coat and dark trousers. Marshall did not get a good look at the man's face, but later recalled that 'he was decently dressed, and I should say he worked at some light business and had more the appearance of a clerk than anything else'. The witness overheard the man saying to Stride, as he kissed her, 'you would say anything but your prayers'. 'He was mild speaking', Marshall remembered, 'and appeared to be an educated man'.

Half an hour later, on the morning of Sunday 30 September, PC 452H William Smith saw a man 'of respectable appearance' talking to Elizabeth Stride in Berner Street: the man was about 28 years old, 5 ft 7 in in height 'as near as I could say', perhaps with a moustache, wearing a hard felt deerstalker hat of dark colour, an overcoat and dark trousers. PC Smith could not see the man's face, but noticed that 'he had a newspaper parcel in his hand . . . about 18 inches in length and 6 or 8 inches in width'. At 12.45 am, a few minutes before she died, Stride was again seen talking to a man in Berner Street, this time by a boxmaker named James Brown. The prostitute was, apparently, 'standing up against the wall by the Board School', while the man was leaning over her with his arm against the wall: he was wearing 'a long dark coat which reached to his heels'. Brown distinctly heard Stride saying 'not tonight, some other night', but could not see the man's face. Elizabeth Stride had her windpipe severed at about 12.50 am, although this time the murderer does appear to have been interrupted in his work, by Louis Diemschutz, a pedlar of cheap costume jewellery at Westow Hill market and steward of the International Working Men's Club outside which the corpse was found.

Fifty minutes later, a commercial traveller named Joseph Lawende saw a man talking to Catherine Eddowes, just off Duke Street. The prostitute was leaning against the passage to Mitre Square. The man was, according to this witness, young, about 5 ft 7 in in height, with a small, fair moustache, dressed in something like navy serge and wearing either 'a grey cloth cap with a peak' (as Lawende said at the inquest) or 'a deerstalker's cap' (as Lawende later said to the City Police). Since the witness only 'had a short look at him', he could not describe the man's face in detail. But he did see

Eddowes put her hand on the man's chest, not, apparently, in order to push him away. This was at 1.35 am, only a minute or two before the woman was strangled, then savagely mutilated.

At 1.44 am, Police Sergeant 'Steve' White, who was watching near 'a wall lamp' in one of the alleys leading out of Mitre Square, stood aside to let a man pass, a man who was clearly in a hurry. The suspect was, White later recalled

> . . . about five feet ten inches in height, and was dressed rather shabbily, though it was obvious that the material of his clothes was good. Evidently a man who had seen better days, I thought . . . His face was long and thin, nostrils rather delicate, and his hair was jet black. His complexion was inclined to be sallow, and altogether the man was foreign in appearance . . . The man stumbled a few feet away from me, and I made that an excuse for engaging him in conversation. He turned sharply at the sound of my voice, and scowled at me in surly fashion, but he said 'good night' and agreed with me that it was cold. His voice was a surprise to me. It was soft and musical, with just a tinge of melancholy in it, and it was the voice of a man of culture.

One other thing White noticed was that the man seemed to walk 'noiselessly', perhaps because he was wearing rubber shoes, a notable fact since these were 'rather rare'. Only seconds later, the remains of Catherine Eddowes were discovered in Mitre Square by PC 881 Watkins.

At 2 am on the morning of Friday 9 November 1888, an unemployed night watchman named George Hutchinson met Mary Kelly at the intersection of Thrawl Street and Flower and Dean Street. He had known her for about three years, and it seems probable that, during that time, he had been one of her casual clients ('I have been in her company a number of times'). On this occasion, Kelly asked him if he could lend her sixpence, to which he replied 'I can't. I have spent all my money going down to Romford'. She shrugged, then walked off towards Thrawl Street with the words 'I must go and find some money'. According to Hutchinson, she seemed to be feeling 'a little bit spree-ish'. When she reached the corner of Thrawl Street, she encountered a 'respectable' man who touched her on the shoulder and whispered something to her, something which caused them both to 'burst out laughing'. 'My suspicions were instantly aroused', Hutchinson later claimed, 'at seeing so well-dressed a man in this part of London. I felt there was something queer about it. He was wearing a long, dark coat trimmed with astrakhan, with a dark-coloured jacket underneath, light waistcoat, dark trousers, a white linen collar with a black necktie, in which was fixed a horse-shoe pin. He had a pair of dark gaiters with light buttons over button boots

PLATE 1 Margaret Harrison, *Rape*. Arts Council Collection, London.

PLATE 2 Poussin, *The Rape of the Sabines*. Louvre, Paris.

PLATE 3 Poussin, *The Rape of the Sabines.* Metropolitan Museum of Art, New York.

PLATE 4 Pietro da Cortona, *The Rape of the Sabines*. Capitoline Museum, Rome.

PLATE 5 Poussin, *The Sacrament of Marriage*. National Gallery of Scotland, Edinburgh.

PLATE 6 David, *The Intervention of the Sabine Women*. Louvre, Paris.

PLATE 7 Correggio, *Jupiter and Io*. Kunsthistorisches Museum, Vienna.

PLATE 8 Fragonard, *The Bolt*. Louvre, Paris.

PLATE 9 Beaufort, *The Oath of Brutus*. Municipal Museum, Nevers.

PLATE 10 Titian, *Tarquin and Lucretia*. Fitwilliam Museum, Cambridge.

PLATE 11 *The Rape of Lucretia*: Florentine, mid-seventeenth century. Wallace Collection, London.

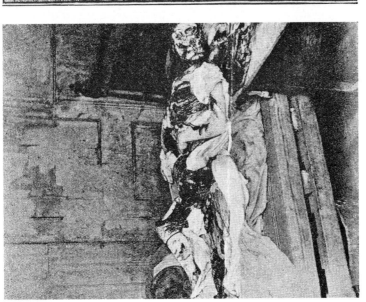

PLATE 12 (*left*) Police photograph of Mary Kelly's corpse, taken on Friday 9 November 1888, and featured in Professor A. Lacassagne's *Vacher l'Eventreur et les crimes sadiques* (Lyons, 1899), as well as providing 'plate 1' for Maurice Heine's playlet in *Minotaure* (Paris, June 1936). PLATE 13 (*right*) The cover of the first instalment of Purkess's penny blood *The Whitechapel Murders* (London, 1888) (Bodleian Library, Oxford).

PLATE 14 The somnambulist Cesare (Conrad Veidt) walks towards the sleeping Jane (Lil Dagover) clutching his white-bladed knife as he will later clutch a white flower in the mad-house. Outside, we can see the angled roofs and tilted chimney-pots of Holstenwall. Will Cesare insert the blade, or will he dare to challenge the hypnotic powers of Dr Caligari? Robert Wiene's *The Cabinet of Dr Caligari*, 1919 (National Film Archive, London).

PLATE 15 The pale-faced young man with the gnawed finger nails and the trilby hat looks down from the mistletoe to the bread knife, as the Salvation Army band plays in the fog outside. 'His hand reaches out, and it is only pleasure that he feels.' What dark inhibitions has Louise Brooks released from her box *this* time? Jack visits Lulu at her Whitechapel garret, in G. W. Pabst's version of *Pandora's Box*, 1928 (National Film Archive, London).

PLATE 16 The portly Count from Transylvania stands amid the armadillos on the widest staircase in the world, licks his lips and says to the wolves outside — 'children of the night — what music they make!' Meanwhile, deep down in the crypt, his brides begin to haunt the dreams of a young solicitor's clerk from the home counties. Dracula (Bela Lugosi) welcomes Renfield (Dwight Frye) to his run-down castle in Tod Browning's *Dracula*, 1931 (National Film Archive, London).

PLATE 17 The creature (Boris Karloff) tries unsuccessfully to communicate with little Maria (Marilyn Harris). His deep-set eyes light up, and he grunts excitedly, as the little peasant girl hands him a daisy and cries, 'Will you play with me?' Later, when the poacher Ludwig carries her limp body down the main street of Goldstadt, the burgomaster will ask, 'Why do you bring her here to me?' The results of Henry Frankenstein's experiment in cybernetic birth have gone seriously wrong . . . James Whale's *Frankenstein*, 1931 (National Film Archive, London).

PLATE 18 (*previous page*) The debonair Dr Harry Jekyll (Fredric March) pays a professional call on 'champagne' Ivy Pearson (Miriam Hopkins) at her Soho apartment, Hollywood-style . . .

PLATE 19 (*previous page*) . . . and later returns as the simian Mr Hyde; at the Variety Music Hall in foggy, gas-lit Soho, chuckling through his protruding teeth and saying to a terrified Ivy, 'Forgive me my dear, you see I hurt you because I love you . . . I grant you I'm no beauty, but under this exterior you'll find the very flower of man.' Rouben Mamoulian's *Dr Jekyll and Mr Hyde*, 1932 (National Film Archive, London).

PLATE 20 (*above*) A preacher with an over-developed sense of sin — the letters L-O-V-E and H-A-T-E tattooed on his fingers — towers over Shelley Winters with an open switch-blade in his raised hand. She seems to be in ecstasy: 'God made me marry you, so you could show me the way, the life, the salvation of my soul — ain't that so, Harry?' As the camera pulls back, the angled roof of the upper room in middle America looks like a tent in the mist-shrouded wilderness. Robert Mitchum prepares to assault his simple-minded wife in their suitably appointed attic bedroom, in Charles Laughton's *Night of the Hunter*, 1955 (National Film Archive, London).

PLATE 21 (*above*) Alfred Hitchcock prepares Janet Leigh (as Marion Crane) for the complex attack-in-the-shower sequence. Just when Marion thinks she is safe from the prying eyes of Norman and the demented chatter of Mom up there at the old dark house on the hill, she turns on the tap, pulls the see-through shower curtains . . . and suddenly a tall, dark, out-of-focus figure appears, brandishing an outsized kitchen knife. 'Mother! Oh God! Mother, mother! Blood, blood!' *Psycho*, 1960 (National Film Archive, London).

PLATE 22 (*following page*) Mrs Kate Miller (Angie Dickinson) fantasizes about being attacked in the shower, during the bizarre opening sequence of Brian De Palma's *Dressed to Kill* (1980). When the elevator finally reaches the seventh floor, the doors slide open, the light turns to red, and a demented psychiatrist in drag slashes at Kate with an open cut-throat razor, as screaming violins on the soundtrack make fashionable reference to *Psycho* . . . 'There's all kinds of ways to get killed in this city', says the cop, 'if you're looking for it.'

and he also wore on his waistcoat a very thick gold watch chain from which hung a seal with a red stone.'

In his left hand the man was carrying a small parcel ('about 8 inches long') wrapped in what looked like 'dark American cloth' (shiny oil-cloth) with a strap around it. The man put his arm around Mary Kelly's shoulders as the couple began walking slowly towards Dorset Street — right past George Hutchinson. As they came closer, Hutchinson, who was already suspicious, took a good, long look at the stranger: he was 'about' 35 years old, 5 ft 6 in in height, with a 'pale complexion', dark eyes, bushy eyebrows, dark hair and 'a slight moustache curled up each end'; he had no side whiskers and his chin was clean-shaven; he had a 'dark felt hat' turned down over the upper part of his face, so Hutchinson actually had to bend down to see him properly, and the man, who may have been a foreigner, turned to make a 'very surley' face at him. As they walked past, Hutchinson heard Kelly say 'all right', and the man reply 'you will be all right for what I have told you'.

The witness followed the couple as they crossed the road into Dorset Street ('the man walked very sharp'), and continued to watch them as they chatted together for about three minutes at the corner of Miller's Court. The man whispered something to Kelly, who replied in a clear voice 'all right, my dear. Come along, you will be comfortable.' He then put his arm around her shoulder, and kissed her. Suddenly she said 'I've lost my handkerchief', at which point the man 'pulled his handkerchief, a red one, out and gave it to her'. 'It caught the lamplight. He waved it around like a bullfighter and made her laugh.' Then they entered 26 Dorset Street, through the Miller's Court entrance. Hutchinson waited a little while before following the couple into the Court, but by the time he reached the window of room 13, where Kelly lived, the candle was out, and all was silent.

He returned to the entrance of the Court, and stayed there for about three-quarters of an hour to 'see if they came down again', but they did not, so Hutchinson went away, to walk the streets for the rest of the night. It was probably Hutchinson who was seen loitering on the pavement outside Miller's Court at 2.30 am by a laundress named Sara Lewis: her description — 'a stout man, not very tall' — was later given in evidence at the inquest on Mary Kelly. At just before 4 am, both Sara Lewis (who was dossing down in the house opposite room 13) and a prostitute named Elizabeth Prater (who rented room 20, directly above Kelly's) heard a young woman's voice faintly crying 'murder!', but since such an occurrence was 'not unusual in the street', neither of them took any notice of it. Mary Ann Cox, a widow who had recently taken to prostitution and who also lived in Miller's Court, heard a man 'go down the court' at 6.15 am (it stuck in her mind because 'it would be too late for market'). These two times, 4 am and 6.15 am, were later confirmed by the medical evidence at the inquest: Kelly was murdered at about 4 am, and it was estimated that the extensive mutilations to her body could have taken the murderer at least two hours to perform; but it proved impossible to discover the exact cause of death, since there was not enough flesh left on her face or neck for the consulting surgeon to be sure whether she had been strangled or stabbed — the evidence of the 'arterial blood which was found on the wall in splashes' did, however, suggest that Mary Kelly's throat had been cut. Her body was found in a condition which has recently led an Italian criminologist to conclude that 'the murderer showed a surrealistic sense of composition, which anticipated some of Dali's inventions . . .'

It is almost certain that one or more of these eye-witnesses had seen, or heard, the man who came to be known by 'the trade name' of Jack the Ripper. On these flimsy foundations, Jack's house has been built and rebuilt. The trouble is, that not only do most of the witnesses resort to unhelpful adjectives ('foreign', 'darkish', 'respectable') in the absence of more substantial evidence, but there are significant differences between the various descriptions as well: he was 'aged over 40', 'middle-aged', 'about 28 years old', young, about 33 at the most, about 35 years old; he was probably clean-shaven, perhaps with a moustache, with a small fair moustache, with a slight moustache which was curled up at the ends but no side whiskers; he had a stout build, he was thin and delicate-looking; he had an educated English voice, he was a foreigner; he was carrying nothing, a small parcel, a larger parcel.

Only five of the witnesses, however, managed to get a really good look at him — Elizabeth Long, PC Smith, Joseph Lawende, Sgt White and George Hutchinson — and their descriptions do have some equally significant characteristics in common; enough, in fact, to build up a modern-day Identikit picture of the murderer. In their descriptions he was about 5 ft 6 in, 5 ft 7 in, about 5 ft 10 in, 5 ft 6 in tall; he wore a brown deerstalker hat and a dark coat, a hard felt deerstalker hat and a dark overcoat, a grey cloth cap with a peak (or a deerstalker's cap) and a navy serge overcoat, an overcoat of good material, a dark felt hat and a long dark coat; he had a shabby genteel appearance, he was respectable in appearance, he was dressed rather shabbily but had evidently seen better days, he was suspiciously well dressed for 'this part of London'; he was perhaps a foreigner, altogether foreign in appearance, may have been a foreigner. These common characteristics could fit any number of suspects (and they were used as the basis for many fruitless arrests at the time), but at least they increase the *likelihood* that the witnesses were all describing the same man, or, perhaps, were sharing the same fantasy.

The *Police Gazette* did not issue a thorough description of the murderer, based on authenticated eye-witnesses accounts, until after the night of Sunday 30 September (before that, the official description ran 'age 37, rather dark beard and moustache, dark jacket and trousers, black felt hat, spoke with a foreign accent' — the description of a music-hall villain if ever there was one, and the excuse for pages of lurid graphics in the illustrated press), so it is improbable that Mrs Long, PC Smith and Joseph Lawende were attempting to jump on any bandwagon. As to the descriptions given by Sgt White and George Hutchinson — which are suspiciously similar, even down to the adjectives — the likelihood of some kind of plagiarism is much greater, particularly since there is evidence that White actually took part in the house-to-house search following *Stride*'s murder (not the Mitre Square event). George Hutchinson came forward with his story, at some considerable risk to himself, immediately after the hurried inquest on Mary Kelly had been officially closed: Sgt White, by contrast, did not publish his account until 30 years later, in an article in the *People's Journal* of 26 September 1919 on the occasion of his retirement from the detective force. So there is always the possibility that the memory of *his* version had become confused over the years with George Hutchinson's more well-known version of the 'facts'.

There is some evidence, however, that Robert Anderson, Assistant Commissioner of the Metropolitan Police in autumn 1888, was convinced that White's description was an accurate one, and that he thought White 'was the only person who ever had a good view of the murderer'. It also seems that, on the basis of White's account, Anderson was persuaded that PC 881 Watkins was not keeping as close a watch on Mitre Square as he might have been — a fact which Watkins later admitted, in part. According to the *People's Journal*, this account was circulated among those concerned with the case, at the time of the murders. Frederick Abberline, the recently promoted Detective Inspector (First Class) in charge of the Ripper investigations, a man who had spent many years pounding the beat with 'H' division, Whitechapel, was much more impressed by Hutchinson's version. After a long interview with Hutchinson, during which he attempted to 'lead' the witness, to trap him into inconsistency, and to fault him on questions of detail, Abberline was convinced by the way in which Hutchinson stuck to his story, and was sure that the witness was acting in good faith. The Chief Detective Inspector went so far as to leave a note in Scotland Yard's files to the effect that Hutchinson's story was both 'important' and reliable: Hutchinson could actually 'identify' the murderer, if the occasion arose.

It may well have been purely because of the resemblance between the man Hutchinson saw and George Chapman, the Borough poisoner, that Abberline came to believe for a time that Chapman was in fact the Ripper: there can have been no other reason, for Chapman's *modus operandi* had nothing at all in common with that of the Whitechapel murderer. Major Henry Smith, the acting Commissioner of the independent City Police, in whose sphere of influence the Eddowes murder was committed, preferred Lawende as a witness: 'I think he spoke the truth', he later wrote, 'because I could not *lead* him in any way. I said to him "You will easily recognize him then?" "Oh no," he said, "I only had a short look at him".' Lawende had provided a 'very fair description' of the murderer.

What this discussion is telling us, in other words, is that each of these senior officers opted for 'their own' witness, the one to whom they had privileged access, whose story they personally could vouch for. Their choices *may* tell us as much about the known rivalries which existed in the Force in 1888 as about the identity of the Ripper. Certainly the thinking of these officers does seem at times to have been highly arbitrary. Sir Charles Warren, the Commissioner of the Metropolitan Police, for example, found particularly congenial the idea that the Ripper might have been 'a renegade Socialist' (and probably Jewish), simply because the Stride murder had occurred outside the International Working Men's Club (the discussion topic that evening had been 'the necessity for socialism amongst Jews') and the body had been found by a Jew. Faced with the same choice of witnesses, the editors of the official *Police Gazette* adopted a different strategy: they issued a whole series of descriptions after the night of Saturday 29 September, which had nothing in common at all. A man had been seen talking to Stride at 12.35 am, a man who was 'aged 28, height 5 feet 8 inches, complexion dark, small dark moustache; respectable appearance, carried a parcel wrapped up in newspaper'; another man had been seen at 12.45 am 'age about 30, height 5 feet 5 inches; complexion fair, hair dark, small brown moustache, full face, broad shoulders'; yet another man had been seen talking to Eddowes at 1.35 am, 'age 30, height 5 feet 7 inches, or 8 inches; complexion fair, moustache fair, medium build; appearance of a sailor . . .'

Yet despite inconsistencies between these various eye-witness accounts, and despite the arbitrary criteria which may have been used to select the best of them, they do constitute the only direct evidence we have of the identity of the Whitechapel murderer. Apart from this evidence, and the medical evidence of the mutilations, including some surviving post-mortem sketches and photographs, all Anderson, Abberline, Smith and Warren had to go on was a few objects that had been left at or near the scenes of the crimes: a small piece of coarse muslin, a brass ring and a pocket comb in a paper case, 'placed in order', or 'arranged' at the feet of Annie Chapman; the fragment of an apron found in Goulston Street shortly after the murder of Catherine Eddowes, stained with blood in such a way as to suggest that a knife had recently been wiped on it; a chalk-written message, perhaps the hasty work of the murderer, scrawled on a wall near where this fragment had been found — 'The Juwes are The men That Will not be Blamed for nothing'; a pile of clothes, which had belonged to Mary Kelly and which were found 'neatly folded' beside her bed; the remains of a fire in Mary Kelly's fireplace, which had blazed so fiercely that it had partially melted a tin kettle — the ashes later revealing some fragments of clothing which proved to belong to a prostitute named Mrs Maria Harvey, a friend of Kelly. Not much on which to build a case in an age when blood tests, semen tests and fingerprint analyses would only have been recognized by readers of science fiction. But enough, it seems, to sustain a legend: or almost enough.

The recent literature about the Whitechapel murders has attempted to fill some of the gaps by inflating the significance of these objects out of all proportion: thus, the list of things 'placed' at Annie Chapman's feet has steadily increased over the years to include some brass rings, a few pennies and two new farthings; the murderer is alleged to have washed his hands at a 'public sink set back from the street' between Mitre Square and Goulston Street (despite the fact that no such 'sink' appears on any contemporary maps); there are seven different published versions of the 'Juwes' message, most of them used to support a different thesis; and speculations about the contents of Mary Kelly's room have long ago reached the stage where it would be impossible to fit all her possessions into room 13, which was less than 12 feet square. If the facts don't fit the legend, then today's sleuths, amateur or professional, tend to print the legend; and readers — used to films which show beautiful young victims (the *average* age of the Ripper's victims was 45, before Mary Kelly broke the pattern) wandering through a thick curtain of expressionist winter fog (in September?) to meet a man in a top hat and opera cloak who is carrying a bulky Gladstone bag, pausing only to chat to Lyceum-style 'locals' on the way — tend to believe it. The 'five little whores' were far from the lovable Cockney 'sparrers' depicted on the screen — only Ingrid Bergman got it almost right in the Spencer Tracey version of Dr Jekyll and Mr Hyde (1941), since Long Liz Stride was born in Gothenberg — but the Ripper game has steadily developed rules all of its own. It is a long way from George Hutchinson's story to expressionist cinema, surrealist collages and the cosy melodrama of Hammer films, but Jack the Ripper has survived the trip unscathed.

Finally, there is evidence of the letters received by the authorities, more than 1,000 a week at the height of the scare in 1888, many of which were allegedly written by the murderer himself, or else kindly supplying his name and address. Eight months after the Kelly murder, the CID was still getting so many letters that a printed form was run off, acknowledging 'with thanks, the receipt of your letter' about the Whitechapel murders. The most recent 'Ripper' letter was received by *Reynolds News* in February 1959: it was written by a retired blacksmith in Worthing, and named his cousin Frank as the murderer! Of the letters sent in the autumn of 1888, three in particular were taken seriously by Scotland Yard — the first addressed to the Central News Office on Friday 28 September, and signed 'Yours truly, Jack the Ripper. Don't mind me giving the trade name'; the second (a postcard) received by the same agency on Monday 1 October, giving details of 'Saucy Jacky's work' and again signed 'Jack the Ripper'; the third sent 'from Hell' to George Lusk of the Whitechapel Vigilance Committee, on Tuesday 16 October, signed 'Catch me when you can Mishter Lusk' and enclosing a portion of what proved to be a human kidney.

The first and second letters — the origin of the name 'Jack the Ripper', a name without which 'in all probability the crimes he committed would long ago have been forgotten' — were thought by Robert Anderson to be 'the creation of an enterprising journalist', while Melville Macnaghten (who became Assistant Chief Constable at the Yard in June 1889) was also convinced he could discern 'the stained forefinger of the journalist' in them. If the author was a reporter actually covering the story (as Macnaghten thought), then this might explain why he seemed to know more about the Eddowes murder than had appeared in the morning papers. Perhaps they were written by someone who had joined the 'dense crowd' which formed to catch a glimpse of the remains of Catherine Eddowes, before they were taken to the mortuary in three separate sacks. The third letter, the one enclosing a piece of human kidney ('tother piece I fried and ate it was very nise') underwent close medical examination — by, among others, Dr Frederick Brown, surgeon to the City Police — to discover whether the kidney could possibly have belonged to Eddowes, but the results were inconclusive: 'on this point no definite opinion can be pronounced, as these organs vary considerably in the same person, and conclusions based on the condition of the right kidney may very well prove misleading'. There was no possibility that the kidney could be matched with the one remaining in Eddowes' body, since the letter had been received over a week after Eddowes was buried in Ilford cemetery, and it scarcely seemed to merit the trouble of a Home Office exhumation order. The kidney despatched to Mr Lusk was thought to be 'in an advanced stage of Bright's disease', but there is no evidence at all, dating from October 1888, to suggest that Eddowes was suffering from the same disease. Yet, in his memoirs written 22 years after the event, Sir Henry Smith claimed that the kidney was *undoubtedly* the one 'found to be missing' from Eddowes' body, and, over the years, by the usual process of embellishment, this hazy memory has gradually hardened into well-supported fact.

In short, apart from the eye-witness accounts, a few objects found near two of the corpses, some letters which are very unlikely to have been written by the murderer, and the medical evidence, the investigators in autumn 1888 — and the sleuths ever since — had, and have, no substantial evidence at all from which to construct a 'solution'. This is one reason why the myths have become so interesting.[8]

ON A BEAUTIFUL BLUE SUNDAY
SEE A CORPSE STRETCHED IN THE STRAND
SEE A MAN DODGE ROUND THE CORNER . . .
JACKY'S FRIENDS WILL UNDERSTAND.

It all started while the murders were actually being committed. The crimes attracted a great deal of publicity at the time — it was, for example, unique for both *The Times* and the *Illustrated Police News* to lead with the same story — and, after the Eddowes murder, this publicity was matched by angry demonstrations on the streets of Whitechapel. Thanks to that nameless journalist who wrote to the Central News Office, the murderer had a name. Thanks to PC Smith and Joseph Lawende, he had a face (or rather, two faces). Thanks to the law and order reporters, the murders of Stride and Eddowes, both on the same night, were linked for the first time with a whole series of previous prostitute murders in Whitechapel: Emma Smith (Monday 2 April 1888), Martha Tabram (Tuesday 7 August 1888), Mary Ann Nichols (Friday 31 August 1888) and Annie Chapman (Saturday 8 September 1888).

At the time of Emma Smith's death in Osborn Street, Whitechapel, (she had been assaulted by a gang of four men, and subsequently died of haemorrhage from stab wounds into her vagina), the London Hospital had not considered the case to be significant enough even to inform the police until four days later, while the newspapers had not bothered to report an event which was clearly thought by some editors to be common enough in the brutal East End of London. Nothing special to interest readers here —

particularly since the East End had come to be associated with an utterly different 'image' during the previous five years: stories about upper-class 'slummers', university settlements, charity organizations, and exposés of appalling housing conditions or the sexual immorality of 'outcast London' made good copy in 1886—8; stories about the brutality of the East End were thought to be either out of date (harking back to tales of Newgate and the Ratcliffe Highway) or dangerous (just over two years after the unemployed dock and building workers had marched to Trafalgar Square). Ten years before, the East End would almost invariably have been described in terms of 'Curses', 'Wilds', 'Deeps', 'Pits' and 'Hell': by 1886—8, a less dramatic image of that economically and socially run-down sector of London was beginning to emerge.[9] Even the popular press had cottoned on to the idea of viewing Whitechapel as less of a slaughterhouse, and more of a deadly dull, sickeningly monotonous place to inhabit. Whether through fear (after the events of February 1886, when, in the words of *The Times*, 'the West End was for a couple of hours in the hands of the mob'), 'a new consciousness of sin' (as Beatrice Webb, among others, supposed) or a simple change in fashion (the 'Corinthians' of the 1820s, who went East to watch the gore, turning into the better-intentioned 'slummers' of the 1880s), the 'men of intellect and property' (newspaper editors among them) no longer thought it wise to view the East End through blood-tinted spectacles by 1886—8. But this 'new consciousness of sin', or whatever it was, quickly evaporated when 'the Ripper' came on the scene. A good story was a good story, whatever damage it did to the image of the East End in the eyes of those up West.

Emma Smith and Martha Tabram had been killed within 300 yards of where Mary Ann Nichols' body was discovered in Buck's Row. Here *was* something special: in retrospect, Stride and Eddowes were reported by the popular press as being the Ripper's *fifth* and *sixth* victims — and detailed information about Smith and Tabram was printed for the first time in September 1888 (with suitably graphic illustrations of Tabram having her throat slit and being punctured with a bayonet, 39 times). After the night of 30 September, a pattern — the Ripper's 'form' — had been created by the press, and extreme reaction was, understandably, not long in following. (Even today, estimates of the number of murders committed by Jack the Ripper range from 20, the highest, to 4, the lowest: the general consensus is that 'Jack' struck five times). A Mrs Mary Burridge, of Blackfriars Road, was so overcome by the *Star*'s lurid account of one of the murders, that she dropped dead on the spot.

Scotland Yard's policy in autumn 1888 seems to have been to release as little information as possible to the press: Abberline, for example, was expressly forbidden from granting publishable interviews about the Ripper. The reporters covering the case for the popular press (who were not the specialized crime correspondents they would be today) constructed a sensational story as best they could from the scant materials at their disposal — a story which had to conform to the (already) well-tried conventions of dramatization, personalization and simplification. In the absence of the staple ingredients for such stories about crime in the 1880s — the dramatic court case, the sentimental letters from the condemned cell, the 'last words' which could be distributed as souvenir brochures at the time of the execution — these reporters tried at first to get as much mileage as they could out of what seemed to be a very saleable feature of this case, the horrible mutilations. Full details of the post-mortem examination of Mary Ann Nichols' corpse were published by many popular newspapers. After that, some pressure seems to have been brought to bear on Dr George Bagster Phillips, the Divisional police surgeon, perhaps by representatives of the Home Office, to prevent him from making such information so readily accessible in the future. At the inquest on Annie Chapman, Dr Phillips referred to 'various mutilations of the body' about which 'I think I had better not go into further detail': a fortnight later, at another hearing, he was pressed by the Coroner, Wynne Baxter, to be more explicit 'in the interests of justice'. Phillips still thought 'it is a very great pity to make this evidence public. These details are fit only for yourself, sir, and the jury', but after the court had been cleared of women and children, and after Phillips had again expressed the view that such publicity would in fact *thwart* 'the ends of justice', he reluctantly agreed to present the results of his post-mortem examination. The coroner then appealed to the 'responsibility of the press' and the popular newspapers responded by printing only a few choice details (a fuller account was later to appear in the *Lancet*, a journal that was actually permitted to mention the word 'uterus').

At the inquest on Mary Jane Kelly, the issue of publication was raised yet again. On this occasion, the body of the victim was moved from the Whitechapel district to Shoreditch mortuary, perhaps in order to prevent Wynne Baxter from having anything to do with the inquest. The Coroner was now to be Dr Roderick Macdonald, who, as an ex-police surgeon, K division, was likely to prove much more cooperative. Two of the jurors complained about this at the opening of the inquest, but to no avail: Macdonald silenced them ('I am not going to discuss the subject'), rushed through the preliminary part of Dr Phillips' evidence, admitted he was suppressing the rest ('there is other evidence which I do not propose to call, for if we at once make public every fact in connection with this terrible murder, the ends of justice might be retarded'), and abruptly terminated the proceedings with the words 'it is for the police authorities to deal with the case'. *The Illustrated Police News*, whose reporter seems to have been present when the police broke into Miller's Court, published a full account of the mutilations (with characteristically gory artists' impressions), but most other newspapers, notably the *Daily Telegraph*, were content to criticize both the Home Office and Dr Phillips for what they considered to be a blatant 'insufficiency of inquiry'. It was a pity, wrote the *Telegraph* correspondent, that Phillips was not a 'free agent' in this matter.

More recent commentators have interpreted Phillips' actions as part of a 'cover up' of one sort or another. There is no need for so elaborate an explanation. Quite simply, the police were not prepared to cooperate with the press.[10] This may have been because they felt their inquiries would be 'thwarted' by publication, because they were concerned that others might copy the Ripper's style, because they were keen to avoid public disorder in the Whitechapel area (Warren, Smith and Anderson all expressed alarm about the spread of 'silly hysterics', which could easily turn into a backlash against the Jews, or worse, another Bloody Sunday), or because they did not like the way the yellow press was exploiting the story. Whatever the reason, Phillips' behaviour was quite consistent with the Yard's view of how reporters should be treated, in autumn 1888.

So it was not surprising that the press, both quality and yellow, should focus its attention on the tensions that already existed between the Metropolitan Police Commissioner, the Home Secretary, the head of the CID, the Metropolitan Police, the City Police and members of the medical profession concerned with the case. Basically, the reporters had very little else to write about, if they wanted to keep the story going, and even the administrative aspects of the 'Ripper' inquiry made good copy. Accounts in *The Times* and the *Telegraph* of the various demarcation disputes which the Commissioner at the Met. (Sir Charles Warren) had brought out into the open seem at times to have become a substitute for in-depth reporting of the actual crimes — and editors of the more popular newspapers were quick to sniff out further scandals, perhaps as a way of getting revenge on Scotland Yard officials for their lack of cooperation. The 'leg men' employed by these editors had not always encountered such hostility in the past, it seems, when the stories they were covering concerned developments *after* the arrest of the criminal. A good example of this 'sniffing out' process concerns the story about two champion bloodhounds which Sir Charles Warren though might be usefully employed in the hunt for the Ripper, in October 1888. The story went around that these bloodhounds had been lost in the fog during a training session on Tooting Common. They had not in fact been lost (one of them was in Scarborough at the time), Sir Charles Warren was not even present, and the whole story was based on a misunderstanding, but this did not stop several newspapers from printing a full account of the bizarre incident, complete with engravings (of Warren as a mindless bloodhound).

Another way in which the popular press could exploit the crimes, at the same time as indirectly criticizing the conduct of the police, was to publish 'suggestions' as to how the Ripper might be captured, suggestions which the Met. could then be attacked for not implementing. W. T. Stead's *Pall Mall Gazette*, an evening newspaper and review, represents the most extreme example of this process: the paper took advantage of London readers' interest by collecting ideas suggested in the morning dailies, and revamping them *all* with trimmings. In between a serialization of Conan Doyle's latest mysteries ('the central figure is a haunted General. Who haunts him and why he is haunted will be wrapped in judicious mystery for seven or eight weeks'), reviews and articles about Mr Richard Mansfield's performance as Dr Jekyll and Mr Hyde, currently packing them in at the Lyceum ('The transformation in Jekyll and Hyde — how it is done by one who knows'), and short stories by Grant Allen (who was soon to create the first super-villain of modern crime literature, with Colonel Clay, the con-man hero of *An African Millionaire*), the *Pall Mall Gazette* gave an exhaustive list of 'suggestions of the public'. These included 'everyone in Whitechapel to report to the police, before going to bed' (which would have had the unfortunate side effect of giving the murderer all sorts of chances as they went home!), issuing rubber shoes to policemen, disguising them as prostitutes, dressing up prize pugilists in drag, and issuing East End prostitutes with lockable steel collars (perhaps attached to a 'powerful storage battery' which could shock).

On 1 October 1888, the *Gazette* used the opportunity of the Ripper's double murder to criticize Lord Salisbury's Irish policy, and for the next month offered a whole range of suggestions about the murderer's identity: he was an army doctor suffering from sunstroke, who had seen *Dr Jekyll and Mr Hyde* once too often; he was a crazy occulist who was seeking to achieve supreme power by these fiendish means; he was an anarchist, perhaps of French, Russian, or Jewish origin; he was an English clergyman; he *may* even have been a member of the detective force. 1887 was the year in which Booth first launched his survey of the London poor in the East End, and on 24 September 1888 the *Gazette* jumped on this bandwagon by suggesting that the 'political moral of the murders' was that they were done by a 'scientific humanitarian', 'capable of taking a scientific survey of the condition of society, and indifferent to the sufferings of the individual, so long as he benefits the community at large' (by drawing attention to shocking conditions in the Whitechapel area).

On 10 September they had cited at length De Quincey's *Essay on Murder Considered as one of the Fine Arts* to the effect that the Ripper might well have 'a benevolent aspect, a gentlemanly bearing, and a peculiarly soft and pleasant voice': 'De Quincey relates how a maniac once asked a girl what she'd think if he appeared by her bedside at midnight with a knife in his hand. If it was anyone else, she replied, I should be terribly frightened, but as soon as I heard *you* speak, I should be reassured.' The *Gazette* continued:

> It is to be hoped that the police and their amateur assistants are not confining their attentions to those who look like 'hard ruffians'. Many of the occupants of the chamber of horrors look like local preachers, Members of Parliament, or . . . nurses. We incline on the whole to the belief . . . that the murderer is a victim of mania which often takes the awful shape of an uncontrollable taste for blood. *Sadism*, as it is termed from the maniac marquis, is happily so strange to the majority of our people that they find it difficult to credit the existence of such powers of mere debauchery. The Marquis de Sade, who died in a lunatic asylum at the age of 74, was an amiable-looking gentleman, and so, possibly enough, may be the Whitechapel murderer.

Since the *Pall Mall Gazette* synthesized all the 'suggestions' made by the morning newspapers, its articles on the Ripper present a broad cross-section of opinion about his possible identity. Other, less broad, cross-sections may be found in the correspondence columns of *The Times* and in the Home Office files (which contain suggestions penned by self-appointed guardians of law and order at the time).[11] *The Times* letters, in particular, were mainly sent in by retired members of the professions, elderly clerics and trigger-happy representatives of the armed forces, who were quick to express their moral outrage on behalf of 'all honest folk', and who sought a cure for all the ills besetting beleaguered Britain by the passage of laws against 'anti-socials' of all descriptions: clearly, they had not had such a good time since the riots of February 1886. Putting all these sources together, we find that the 'suggestions' fall into three main categories.

The Ripper as decadent English Milord[12] Perhaps, like de Quincey's connoisseurs, Wilde's Dorian Gray or the Goncourts' bizarre version of Lord George Selwyn, this gentleman of leisure was seeking after luxurious cruelties which could stimulate his jaded sensibilities. Perhaps, as was suggested by an amateur sleuth who wrote to Scotland Yard, he was one of those 'upper or wealthy sort' who think that the working-class world exists purely 'for their pleasures — that of revenge being included — as a life business; without regard to any law but their own will'. E. W. Hornung's *Raffles* (1899) was also convinced that the Whitechapel murderer fitted this description:

> To follow crime with reasonable impunity you simply must have a parallel ostensible career — the more public the better. The principle is obvious. Mr Charles Peace, of pious memory, disarmed suspicion by acquiring a local reputation for playing the fiddle and taming animals, and its my profound conviction that Jack the Ripper was a really eminent public man, whose speeches were very likely reported alongside his atrocities. Fill the bill in some prominent part, and you'll never be suspected of doubling it with another of equal prominence.

Raffles' naive assumption is, of course, that the 'eminent public man' who murdered whores was practising his art for art's sake: there is no suggestion that 'lower' motives came into it. In other words, the gentleman cracksman is relating the Ripper's motives to his own:

> *Necessity*, my dear Bunny? Does the writer only write when the wolf is at the door? Does the painter paint for bread alone? Must you and I be driven to crime like Tom of Bow or Dick of Whitechapel? You pain me, my dear chap; you needn't laugh, because you do. Art for art's sake is a vile catchword, but I confess it appeals to me. In this case my motives are absolutely pure . . .[13]

W. T. Stead, whose *Pall Mall Gazette* had cited de Quincey's *Essay on Murder Considered as one of the Fine Arts*, was also 'under the impression for more than a year' that 'the veritable Jack the Ripper' was a decadent occultist who called himself Roslyn D'Onston Stephenson, and that the crimes represented the application by a gentleman of leisure of some esoteric art. Stead's deduction is particularly interesting, in that his halfpenny evening newspaper had recently made its name by specializing in exposés of East End child prostitution (complete with two innovations on the newspaper scene, the interview and the cheaply printed illustration). When Stead opted for the 'decadent Milord' explanation, he was, on the face of it, destroying the very image of the East End which his paper had struggled so hard to present, since July 1885: an image of a place where people were exploited for cash rather than butchered for kicks.

But Stead had also been one of the many who campaigned 'with moral indignation' against the publication of Emile Zola's naturalistic novels in England. He had argued that Zola's frank presentation of sex, violence, cruelty and slang were liable to injure public morals, if translations were

made easily available. In October 1888, much to the *Gazette*'s delight, Henry
Vizetelly was summonsed for publishing three 'indecent' novels (including
Nana) in translation, was fined £100 and placed on probation for 12 months.
Stead, and his National Vigilance Association, had temporarily won the day,
ensuring that 'slum novels', dealing among other 'putrid filth' with
drunkenness and prostitution, would not be available to those who could not
read French.[14] So, in a sense, Stead's explanation of the Ripper murders fitted
neatly into the moral position on the role of the artist which his paper had
promoted in the previous year, and which, to judge by sales, may well have
been a popular one. It was simply a case of transposing the arguments against
Vizetelly to the editorials on Whitechapel, and full mileage could still be got
out of the 'modern Babylon' at the same time. *The Lancet* of 27 October
finally made explicit the connection between the two campaigns: in an article
on 'the exploits of Jack the Ripper, as detailed for our delectation at the
breakfast table day after day', the writer noted with suitable disgust 'the same
drift towards sensationalism in the popularity of the realistic novel'. *The
Lancet* continued:

> The realism which M. Zola has popularised in France, and which threatens
> to invade us in England, does not consist in the truthful portraiture of all
> aspects of human life, but in the deliberate and systematic choice of what is
> vile and corrupt for the purposes of fiction. It is as if a painter, determined
> to paint nature and nature only, were to neglect the wood, the stream, the
> ocean and human beauty, and fill his canvas with nothing but sores and
> ulcers and deformities. Such art would be realistic at the expense of
> sacrificing its true ends — namely, the promotion of pleasure by means
> *that elevate and ennoble*.

'A healthy all-round genius, like SHAKSPEARE' *The Lancet* went on,
was 'sure to paint man as a rational, self-controlling being, and not as a
wanton savage': this, in contrast to 'our French neighbours' who tended to
worship people like the author of *The Beast in Man*.

Over the coming years, the novelist George Gissing and the poet Algernon
Swinburne were actually to be named as possible Ripper 'types' — ironically,
in Swinburne's case, since he also had campaigned against the Zola
translations. It was almost as if the Gothick tradition of the penny-dreadfuls
had joined forces with the fin-de-siècle realism of the novel: the *Newgate
Calendar* had met working class fiction and the murderer had as a result to be
presented in the stock role of the 1820s Corinthian, the man of leisure who
visited the Ratcliffe Highway to watch the rat-fighting and the drunken

fights, or to find a torture garden which catered for his particular taste in flesh. La bête humaine in a democratic setting . . .

In Paris, where Stead's 'Maiden Tribute of Modern Babylon' had been something of a *succès de scandale*, the murders were immediately related to another literary phenomenon which was almost equally chauvinistic — the fictional celebration of 'le sadisme anglais': 'Jack' became easily absorbed into a perverted pantheon of English Milords which had recently included George Selwyn, Lord Byron, Algernon Swinburne and the 'Marquis of Mount Edgecumbe'. 'Le vice anglais', if enjoyed to excess outside the confines of public schools could so easily get out of control. Most of the monographs published by Professor Lacassagne's Institute at Lyons had been about French 'vampires', necrophiliacs and sadistic murderers; now at last an Englishman could be added to the list.

The more prosaic I-know-what-I-like context for the *Pall Mall Gazette*'s coverage of the Whitechapel murders to some extent explains both the appeal of the 'decadent artist' or the 'decadent aristocrat' thesis, and the reasons why the paper had an interest in promoting it in 1888.

Less explicable is the recent fascination with 'solutions' that belong to the same category: in the past few years, the names Frank Miles and Walter Sickert have been linked with the Ripper crimes, as have those of the Duke of Clarence, his tutor at Cambridge (James Stephen) and Montague Druitt, an Oxford-educated barrister who was an active member of the MCC and Blackheath Cricket Club — a true heir to the *Raffles* tradition. Apart from the obvious advantage which these candidates share over the man-on-the-Whitechapel-omnibus — there is plenty of archive information about them, so it is not difficult to construct a full-scale biography as part of the 'solution' — the attraction of this category today may well have something to do with revelations about 'the other Victorians'[15] which were first published in the 1960s. Plays about real-life eminents in a fictional setting (such as Graham Greene's *Return of A. J. Raffles*),[16] films about fictional detectives in a real-life setting (such as *A Study in Terror*, and *Murder by Decree*, both featuring Sherlock Holmes and both opting for the Clarence 'solution'), books about the Whitechapel murders (naming Druitt, Clarence, James Stephen, and, most recently, the unlikely trio of Sir William Gull, Walter Sickert and the coachman John Netley as perpetrators of the crimes) have all proved popular in recent years, as have television series about assorted royal scandals of the nineteenth century — perhaps an indication of the power which the idea of 'the other Victorians' has over popular entertainers, and of the fact that the idea is not nearly as subversive as it looks. The only certain thing that can be said about 'the Ripper as other Victorian', is that there is not a shred of hard evidence to link the crimes with *any* of the blue-blooded suspects named. No matter: Stephen Knight's *Jack the Ripper: the Final Solution*, which named three eminent names, sold a lot of copies; Joseph Sickert's admission that the book was based on an elaborate hoax ('it was a whopping fib') was given a few lines in *The Sunday Times*. Readers of *The Final Solution* had all been gulled — perhaps because they wanted to be.[17]

The Ripper as mad doctor In this school of thought he was a crazed medical student who had caught syphilis from a prostitute (possibly even 'had his privy member destroyed'), and sought revenge on the whole pack of them. Or he was an American physician who was collecting as many specimens of the female uterus as he could find, to include as a free handout with a monograph he was writing on diseases of the womb. He was a ship's doctor, or perhaps an amateur whose only practical experience came from filleting fish. If he was not exactly a doctor, then he *might* have acquired his knowledge of anatomy from the slaughterhouse — thus he was a slaughterman, a Jewish ritual slaughterman, or even a woman disguised as a slaughterman. This category seems to have gained legitimation from at least some of the evidence given at the inquests on the Ripper's victims; speaking of the Nichols murder, Dr Rees Ralph Llewellyn suggested that the mutilations were 'fairly skilfully performed'; of the Chapman murder, Dr Phillips opined that 'the mode in which the uterus was extracted showed some anatomical knowledge'; Dr Frederick Brown thought that the murderer of Eddowes showed 'a good deal of knowledge as to the positions of organs in the body cavity and the way of removing them'. But other professional observers were by no means so convinced: Doctors Sequeira and Saunders disagreed with Brown about the Eddowes murder, others reckoned that Kelly had been so severely mutilated that it was impossible to judge the 'skill' of the murderer, while Dr Thomas Bond of the City Police was certain that in each case the mutilations were done 'by a person who has no scientific or anatomical knowledge. In my opinion he does not even possess the technical knowledge of a butcher or horse slaughterman or any person accustomed to cut up dead animals'.

Whether or not the evidence pointed in the direction of 'some anatomical knowledge', this category proved the most popular both in the press, and among commentators from the reading public at large. After all, the dramatization of *Jekyll and Hyde* was very much in the news at the time (one suggestion in the files actually names Richard Mansfield the actor as the murderer, since his 'transformation' was *so* convincing), and the idea that the Ripper might be a doctor who was leading a double life seemed to 'work' in much the same way: the London Hospital in the Whitechapel Road, could provide a secure base for his operations.

Robert Louis Stevenson's *Jekyll and Hyde* metaphor for 'the beast in man' was first published two years before the murders, and had gone through several editions by autumn 1888. The Lyceum adaptation opened in August. In the book, a successful society doctor who mixes in all the right social circles (and some of the wrong ones — there is a suggestion that he knows all about Cleveland Street), unleashes his alter-ego, a brutal counterpart who represents what Jekyll calls the other side of his 'dual nature'. The doctor is tall, pale and thin — of what the Victorians called 'refined features' (features with which the Ripper was associated by several eye-witnesses). The beast is sallow, small and squat, rather like the 'hard ruffian' archetype mentioned in the *Pall Mall Gazette*. Hyde is, in other words, the physical embodiment of Jekyll's great discovery, 'that man is not truly one but truly two'. The doctor's lecture on the subject has been featured in suitably abridged form at the beginning of all the major film versions of the story:

> I say two, because the state of my own knowledge does not pass beyond that point. Others will follow, others will outstrip me on the same lines; and I hazard the guess that man will be ultimately known for a mere polity of multifarious, incongruous and independent denizens. I for my part advanced infallibly in one direction and in one direction only. It was on the moral side, and in my own person, that I learned to recognize the thorough and primitive duality of man . . . It was the curse of mankind that these incongruous faggots were thus bound together — that in the agonized womb of consciousness these polar twins should be continuously struggling.[18]

At a time when neither Freud nor Krafft-Ebing had filtered into popular consciousness, when forensic medicine was still in its infancy (after one of the murders the word went round that an official photograph had been taken of the victim's eyes, since it had been suggested by some European forensic experts that the retina at the moment of death would reflect the face of the murderer),[19] the Jekyll and Hyde model represented the most accessible 'explanation' for newspapers to exploit: an 'explanation' which had as its subtext something about 'the female principle' battling it out with 'the male principle'. Jekyll himself does not interpret the 'dual nature' of man in sexual terms at all: rather, he stresses that it is on the 'moral side' and has something to do with being just and unjust. Whatever the deeper meaning of the metaphor, in 1888 it seemed to newspapermen and their reading public to fit the idea that the Ripper could be an 'amiable-looking gentleman' *and* 'a hard ruffian' both at the same time. He was a bright young doctor who had gone off the rails; he was a soft-spoken gentleman who heard voices in the night; he was Mrs Belloc Lowndes' *Lodger*, Mr Sleuth (1911), Stevenson's Dr Jekyll, the *Pall Mall Gazette*'s version of the Marquis de Sade. This 'either . . . or' explanation might account for the fact that the Ripper was likely to be as normal as thee or me — except when the dreaded beast in man came to the surface: for, apart from anything else, dialectical psychology was, of course, a thing of the future. It appears that Stevenson may have had William Gull, MD, DCL, LLD, FRS, Queen Victoria's Physician Extra-ordinary, in mind, when he created the character of Henry Jekyll, MD, DCL, LLD, FRS: if so, it could explain why Gull, who by 1888 was aged and hemiplegic, has come to be associated with the Ripper murders; plus the fact that he seems to 'fit'.

The Ripper as anarchist, socialist or philanthropist[20] If one literary correlative of our first category is Wilde's *Picture of Dorian Gray* (decadent young thing indulging in murder as one of the fine arts), and of our second is Stevenson's *Dr Jekyll*, this third category has more to do with the image of the East End that had been constructed by the press in the few years before 1888. The 'mad doctor' thesis represented the most accessible 'explanation' at the time, but the Ripper as foreign agitator ran it a close second.

The fact that several of the eye-witness accounts stressed (for whatever reasons) the murderer's 'foreign' appearance, while some of the senior police officers associated with the case were on record as suggesting that the murderer was a 'Jewish Socialist', were used to legitimate this thesis. He was a Jewish agitator, an Irish revolutionary, a 'low class Asiatic', a Thug, a Russian Jew seeking to discredit the English police, an insane Russian doctor, 'a low class Polish Jew', a Polish Jewish shoemaker, King Leopold of the Belgians, and a Portuguese sailor. Anyone who could write 'Mishter Lusk' must be Irish. Anyone who could chalk up the 'Juwes' message must really be Jacob the Ripper. Anyone who could mutilate in the Ripper's fashion must either be Portuguese (according to Napier's *History of the Peninsula War*, it was 'characteristic' of them), or a Malay running amok ('probably primed with opium'). He was certainly not one of us.

This category of explanation relates to the image of the East End in 1888, in two important ways: it fed off the 'anti-alienism' which had paralleled the economic decline of the dockland areas of East London and it mirrored more general fears about the spread of Socialism among members of the 'true working class'. That the economic depression of the East End — and the concomitant rise of overcrowding, sweat-shops, and exploitation — had, by chance, occurred at much the same time as the peak years of immigration from Eastern Europe, was a fact duly noted by those commentators who were concerned about the 'dilution' of good old English stock in the 'outcast' areas of London. There may have been structural reasons for this depression — the shift in patterns of employment around the docks, the competition from regional factories, the changing face of industrial London — but the immigrants provided a ready-made, and simple, explanation of it all which could displace more searching questions about the root causes of economic decline in East London. The 'economy of makeshifts' which was so characteristic of the people of the abyss was thus presented as a *racial* characteristic, in the popular middle-class press. Moreover, the Ripper struck at much the same time as these connections were first being formulated. The *East London Observer* of 15 September 1888 duly noted:

> On Saturday in several quarters of East London the crowds who assembled in the streets began to assume a very threatening attitude towards the Hebrew population of the District. It was repeatedly asserted that no Englishman could have perpetrated such a horrible crime as that of Hanbury Street, and that it must have been done by a JEW — and forthwith the crowds began to threaten and abuse such of the unfortunate Hebrews as they found in the streets . . .

Then, on 30 September, Elizabeth Stride was discovered outside the International Working Men's Educational Club, by a Jew. The result was, in one commentator's words, 'the nearest thing to an East End anti-Jewish pogrom, prior to the advent of Mosley'.

When the *Church Times*, no less, suggested that the Ripper was a Jewish Anarchist, the *Arbeter Fraint* retaliated with the words '. . . such homage to the Holy Spirit!' When *The Times* reported that a Jew named Ritter had been arrested near Cracow for the ritual murder of Christian women, and that 'the evidence touching the superstitions prevailing among some of the ignorant and degraded of his co-religionists remains on record and was never wholly disproved', the Chief Rabbi, Dr Herman Adler, wrote in to 'assert without hesitation that in no Jewish book is such a barbarity even hinted at'. Adler added, 'the tragedies enacted in the East End are sufficiently distressing without the revival of moribund fables and the importation of prejudices abhorrent to the English nation'. But some members of the police force took more convincing than that. Sir Charles Warren thought the murderer might well be a 'Jewish Socialist'; Abberline thought he was George Chapman, a Pole whose real name was Severin Klosowski; Robert Anderson stated as 'a definitely ascertained fact' that the Ripper was 'a low-class Polish Jew'; and

Melville Macnaghten named a certain Kosminski ('a Polish Jew resident in Whitechapel') as one of three key suspects (Kosminski had apparently 'become insane owing to many years' indulgence in solitary vices', and, perhaps as a result, he resembled Sgt Stephen White's eye-witness description).

Official visits were made to kosher abbatoirs, two ritual slaughtermen were arrested, and the special knife used by the shochet was examined by Dr Brown to see whether it could have inflicted wounds of the type found on the victims' bodies. The most highly publicized arrest in the whole case was that of John Pizer, or 'Leather Apron', a Polish Jewish shoemaker, and of the 130 arrests made in the London area alone, a significant proportion were of Jews; following Pizer's arrest, the Ripper became more and more 'foreign in appearance' by the hour. So, when Sir Charles Warren ordered the message about the 'Juwes' to be rubbed off the wall near Goulston Street, he was being far more responsible than many commentators have since suggested. It was strange, however, that he did not agree to let the words be photographed (by City Police photographers, significantly enough), and it may have been an error of judgement that prevented him from simply erasing the word 'Juwes', but the fact remains, that had he allowed the message to stay, he might well have had a riot on his hands (the message was written above a common stairway leading to a tenement block occupied mainly by Jewish immigrants). This was certainly the explanation he gave to the Home Secretary — who was furious — and it seems a reasonable one. (The police file implies that if the writing *was* done by the murderer, it may have had the intention of casting suspicion on three Jews who claimed to have seen him.) Dr Adler immediately wrote to congratulate Warren on his prompt action, reassuring him that the word 'Juwes' did not appear in any Yiddish dialect, and informing him of his conviction that 'the writing emanated from some illiterate Englishman who did not know how to spell the word correctly'. Warren's response was to publish this information in *The Times* of 15 October.

The recent thesis that Warren was 'covering up' for someone when he rubbed out the message, that the message referred to a different form of ritual slaughter based on Masonic mythology, seems not only to ignore the realities of East End history at the time, but also to fall prey to exactly the same mode of argument as led many to accuse the Jews in 1888. In the absence of any 'explanation' of the Ripper's actions, at the time of the murders, harrassed police officers and sharp newspaper editors, as well as correspondents from the reading public, were irresistibly drawn to the 'secret ritual' argument: but there seems little excuse for doing so today.

If the murderer was not Jewish, then he must be Irish (the next worst thing), or Oriental. Failing that, he must be an English Socialist. Warren could not make up his mind whether the Ripper was Jewish, Socialist, or both: he was sure the Socialists had *something* to do with it — even if it meant suggesting that the murders were intended by one wing of the International to 'bring discredit' on another wing — but he could not work out exactly what. We have seen how Stead's *Pall Mall Gazette* put forward 'a scientific humanitarian' as the possible culprit. Others were more specific, implying that the Reverend Samuel Barnett, founder of Toynbee Hall, the signwriter to General Booth of the Salvation Army, and even Dr Barnardo were possible 'types'. John Burns, who was to lead the dock strike of 1889, was detained by the police as he walked home from a late-night workers' meeting.

In a sense, this line of thought represents the other side of the 'alien' thesis. For, if one feature of the East End which was constantly in the news was the peril of unrestricted immigration (and suggestions as to how immigrants might most humanely be deported), another was the danger that pernicious socialist ideas might spread from 'outcast London', the 'residuum of labour', to more respectable or 'true' members of the working class. Once the good old English aristocrat of labour, or the artisan, found socialist ideas attractive, then the Trafalgar Square incident, and its aftermath, would seem just like a side-show. Warren, who had given the orders which resulted in 'Bloody Sunday', was more aware of this than anyone. It was bad enough to watch the emergence of the Independent Labour Party, and the dramatic increase in trade union membership: something had to be done, preferably by non-political action, to seize the initiative from the socialists before their ideas spread *too* far.

In the popular press, the 'non-political actions' of 1884-8 were all treated with a greater or lesser measure of enthusiasm, for they seemed to provide ways of resolving the problem dramatized by Trafalgar Square without actually confronting it. The foundation of Oxford House (in 1884) and Toynbee Hall (a year later); the beginning of Charles Booth's survey of the East End, and the inauguration of the People's Palace in the Mile End Road (both 1887); the announcement of the Salvation Army's new policy of social reform in 1887; the much-publicized increase in the number of 'settlers' (or 'slummers') from the upper rungs of society, all these were easy enough to satirize (Henrietta Barnett's 'all class' East-West tea parties at the Vicarage being an obvious target, almost as obvious, in fact, as the social worker who smugly declared 'charity presents no difficulty to me; I took a First in Moral Philosophy at Cambridge'), but there were urgent reasons why they should be encouraged nevertheless. When the Ripper struck, the 'slummers',

Salvationists, university settlers, social analysts and 'do-gooders' of all descriptions were accused of murderous intentions with equal enthusiasm. Perhaps their work *was* actively dangerous, after all. More importantly, the Whitechapel murders gave editors the opportunity to associate socialism, or just plain philanthropy, with 'outcast' activities — the old-fashioned, sensational image of the East End as a den of vice — and thus to drive a wedge between the 'outcasts' and the 'respectables'. This distinction had been on the hidden agenda ever since Trafalgar Square, and the implied association between ripping and socialism brought it into focus.

If Jack was not a social analyst (like Booth), a settlement man (like Barnett, or, as has been suggested more recently, Druitt), a charity organizer (like Barnardo), a Salvationist (like the other Booth's signwriter), or a revolutionary (probably Jewish — enough said), then there was always the danger that the socialists themselves would seize the initiative by using the crimes for their own propagandistic purposes. Jack, with a fiendish sense of timing, had succeeded in undoing the efforts of many well-intentioned people to publicize a less sensational image of the East End, just at a time when Beatrice Webb (among others) was beginning to realize that these efforts were merely the *first* stage: the East End, as a city within a city, was still little understood and much neglected.

Those who enthused over the 'non-political actions' of 1884-8, suggesting that they represented some kind of *solution* to the problem, were, predictably, shocked when various wings of the Socialist movement *did* use the Ripper crimes as a symbol of the evils of capitalism. *Justice*, the organ of Hyndman's Social Democrats, thundered 'the real criminal is the vicious bourgeois system which, based upon class injustice, condemns thousands to poverty, vice and crime'. Bernard Shaw presented a more whimsical Fabian view, in a letter headed 'Blood Money for Whitechapel', which he sent to the *Star* (a more radical evening paper than the *Gazette*) on 24 September 1888. To him, the identity of the murderer was quite simple — he was a social reformer 'of independent genius'. 'Less than a year ago, the West End press was literally clamouring for the blood of the people, and behaving as the propertied class always does behave when the workers throw it into a frenzy of terror by venturing to show their teeth': but since the beginning to the Whitechapel murders, he said, the West End press had undergone a change of heart:

> Whilst we conventional social democrats were wasting our time on education, agitation and organization, some independent genius has taken the matter in hand, and by simply murdering and disembowelling four

women, converted the proprietary class to an inept sort of communism. The moral is a pretty one, and the Insurrectionists, the Dynamitards, and the Invincibles will not be slow to draw it . . . Every gaol blown up, every window broken, every shop looted, every corpse found disembowelled means another ten pound note for 'ransom' . . .

William Morris' *Commonwealth* made a similar point, with less irony (and, incidentally, with more taste): 'in our age of contradictions and absurdities, a fiend-murderer may become a more effective reformer than all the honest propagandists in the world'. Morris himself had, in fact, been involved in an evening of 'honest propaganda', sponsored by the Socialist League, at the International Club, 40 Berner Street, just eight days before Stride's corpse was discovered there. For these Socialist newspapers, nothing but good could arise from the murders, even if 'four women of the people' had been sacrificed to the cause. It never seemed to occur to them that the image of the East End, as an area where people did not go around murdering one another but where they were dead behind the eyes none the less, had suffered significant damage as a result of the Ripper's experiments in 'slaughterhouse anatomy' (or was it consciousness-raising?). Nor did it occur to them that the 'four women' might not be expendable.[21]

Arthur Morrison, writing an article on 'Whitechapel' for the *People's Palace Journal* of April 1889, was much more concerned than the Social Democrats, the Fabians and the Guild Socialists, about the effects of 'graphically-written descriptions of Whitechapel, by people who have never seen the place'. For Morrison, there were two types of description of the East End — one derived from accounts of Jack the Ripper, the other derived from the literature on 'outcast London' as an abyss into which intrepid missionaries might occasionally leap: both failed to take note of the *variety* of life in that sector of London, of the 'ancient industries' which were in decline, of the ways in which those who did *not* live in 'foul slums' existed day-to-day, above all of the human beings who actually managed somehow to survive, and even establish communities, a network of support, in the East End of London.

The first type of account went as follows:

A horrible black labyrinth . . . reeking from end to end with the vilest exhalations; its streets, mere kennels of horrid putrefaction; its every wall, its every object, slimy with the indigenous ooze of the place; swarming with human vermin, whose trade is robbery, and whose recreation is murder; the catacombs of London — darker, more tortuous, and more dangerous than those of Rome, and supersaturated with foul life.

The second had a firmer basis in reality, but still could not claim in any way to be representative of the place:

> Black and nasty still, a wilderness of crazy dens into which pallid wastrels crawl to die; where several families lie in each fetid room, and fathers, mothers and children watch each other starve; where bony, blear-eyed wretches, with everything beautiful, brave and worthy crushed out of them, and nothing of the glory and nobleness and jollity of this world within the range of their crippled senses, rasp away their puny lives in the sty of the sweater.

Both descriptions, said Morrison, were written by the kind of man who called Whitechapel 'a shocking place where he once went with a curate'. His own rejection of *both* models of the East End put over by the popular press (and popular novels) was to be reinforced by the publication shortly afterwards of the first volume of Charles Booth's *East London*. Booth, also, had had to fight against the public images of 'outcast London':

> East London lay hidden from view behind a curtain on which were painted terrible pictures . . . horrors of drunkenness and vice; monsters and demons of inhumanity . . . Did these pictures truly represent what lay behind, or did they bear to the facts a relation similar to that which the pictures outside a booth at some country fair bear to the performance or show within? This curtain we have tried to lift.

According to Booth's figures only 1.2 per cent of the East End population were in the category of 'loafers and semi-criminals', while well over 60 per cent tried to lead 'decent', respectable lives' ('questions of employment' permitting). The rest were not so much 'debased', as living in conditions of almost perpetual poverty, and even so trying to support one another. Neither Jack, nor the 'do-gooders', had presented a true 'picture'.

These three images of the Whitechapel murderer — Dorian Gray, Dr Jekyll, and a political version of the wandering Jew of the penny-dreadfuls — combined with the 'mental sets' with which they were associated by popular writers — decadence, the beast in man, and socialism or racial pollution — sustained press coverage of the crimes for several months, and enabled editors to slot the Whitechapel events into previously constructed 'angles'. Whichever of the three categories was chosen, it could be linked with a well-defined moral panic, and moral panics were very good for sales. In a sense, the moral panic strategy became a *substitute* for hard copy, since there was so little material available on the actual crimes, and since various steps seem to have been taken to prevent the more exploitable details from getting into print. It also provided three ready-made models of the-sort-of-person-who-might-do-such-things, at a time when the Ripper's motives appeared to go beyond the bounds of a recognizably human nature.

What is surprising, on the face of it, is that these explanations are *still* accepted by self-styled 'Ripperologists' and their readers, when there is so much evidence, social *and* psychological, to contradict them. The Ripper was much more likely to have been the victim himself of the syndrome that leads some deeply depressed, and highly impressionable, men to see a 'fallen woman' as the one last person they can push around than to have been one of the more famous 'other Victorians'; the frustrated victim of (apparent) powerlessness rather than the possessor of real power. We now have the language to describe what 'Jack' was up to, and perhaps why.he was up to it, but the literature has continued to rely on *Gazette*-like solutions, displacing the only usable evidence there is, in favour of the criminal stereotypes of late Victorian England — one philistine, one pre-Freudian, one racialist, all of them deeply misogynistic in character. Moreover the image of the East End as the kind of place where Nancy was regularly murdered by Bill Sikes has also survived into recent books on the Whitechapel murders, although we know better.

In 1888, reporters covering the crimes did not have much else to write about, and in any case were bound to exploit the moral panics of the moment as far as they could: this, to some extent, explains the unprecedented interest shown by newspapers catering for such widely different reading publics. True, these were serial murders, and several newspapers were quick to spot the commercial potential of the serial, often inventing fresh 'episodes' of their own to keep up the readers' interest. True, the name 'Jack the Ripper' seems to have struck a distinct chord — hardly surprising, really, since penny-bloods had for years been chronicling the exploits of Gallant Jack, Left-handed Jack, Roving Jack the Pirate Hunter, Jolly Jack Tar, Arab Jack the London Boy, Blind Jack of Knaresborough, Gentleman Jack, Jack Harkaway, Jack the Giant-Killer, Jack Spry, Jack's the Lad, Jack at Eton, Moonlight Jack King of the Road, Sixteen-String Jack the Hero Highwayman, Spring-Heeled Jack the Terror of London, Three-fingered Jack the Terror of the Antilles, Thrice-Hung Jack, Jack O'Lantern, Jack O'the Cudgel, Jack O'Legs, Jack and Joe the troublesome twins, Slippery Jack, Jack Rann, Jack Junk, Crusoe Jack, and, most famous of them all, Jack Sheppard; while newspaper reports of the 'High Rippers', or 'High Rips' — gangs of youths who like the Hoxton Market and old Nichol Street mobs, went around attacking unaccompanied prostitutes in the East End — filled many column inches in the early 1880s.

True, the internal squabble between various branches of the police force (and the resignations which resulted around the time of the Ripper inquiry — James Monro, head of the CID, in August, Sir Charles Warren in November) were always a stand-by, when material on the Ripper became *too* thin on the ground, or when a newspaper wanted to score points at the expense of those who were hindering inquiries (in the public interest, no doubt) about the more gory aspects of the story. Accepting all this, we are still left with the fact that the image of the East End in the mental landscape of late Victorian newspapermen, and the three moral panics with which the crimes were associated, provided the main support for the process of constructing a recognizable 'Jack the Ripper'.

> BY THE THAMES'S TURBID WATERS
> PEOPLE SUDDENLY TUMBLE DOWN;
> IS IT PLAGUE OR IS IT CHOLERA?
> OR A SIGN THAT JACK'S IN TOWN?

In this sense, Jack was yet another invention of the hard-working Victorian penny-a-liners. Criminologists may write of *Jack L'Eventreur*, or *Giacomo-lo-Squarciatore*, but he only seems to make full sense in an English setting, in the culture which produced the *Mysteries of London*, Sherlock Holmes (who made his first appearance in 1887), and *Dr Jekyll and Mr Hyde*: 'bien sûr, le pays de Sherlock Holmes est plein de malins qui disent "finalement le dernier mot" sur l'Eventreur . . .'

Thomas Purkess certainly had strong ideas about the commercial potential of the myth, right from the time of the murders: in addition to running a successful publishing house at 286 The Strand, which specialized in 'penny awfuls' about famous crimes and criminals, he owned and edited the *Illustrated Police News*, a penny weekly which was still getting full mileage out of the Ripper crimes in 1892, four years and a total of 184 cover pictures after the last murder was committed. In between advertisements for a reissue of numbers 1 and 2 of his own *Charles Peace, or the Adventures of a Notorious Burglar* 'ready on Monday next, with a free coloured plate, entitled "fooled by a woman"', notices of the forthcoming publication of 'The Missing Fanny — a tale of the Divorce Court' and sensational articles on 'Unavenged murders — number 2, the Murder of Emma Jackson in St Giles', Purkess crammed the *Illustrated Police News* with eye-witness accounts, new theories about the Ripper's identity and stories about preventative measures every Saturday for year after year. The murders may have lacked the well-tried ingredients of the sensational Victorian crime story, but Purkess was not about to let this affect his coverage. He also rushed out *The Whitechapel Murders or the Mysteries of the East End*, a bizarre part-work in ten fortnightly episodes, after only two of the murders had been committed.[22] On the cover of this, he showed a bearded villain, straight out of the Paragon or the Old Pavilion music hall in the Whitechapel Road, walking away from a very dead prostitute, lying prostrate beneath a reward poster which claimed that four murders had occurred already.

To compete with this, Simpkin and Marshall, a rather more respectable publishing house, printed *The Curse Upon Mitre Square, AD 1530—1888*, by John Francis Brewer, an enterprising attempt to show that the murder of Catherine Eddowes in Mitre Square occurred on the exact spot where the demon monk, Brother Martin, had desecrated the high altar of Holy Trinity Church, Aldgate, in 1530, by a scene of bloody murder:

> measure this spot as carefully as you will, and you will find that the piece of ground on which Catherine Eddowes lies is the exact spot where the steps of the high altar of Holy Trinity existed . . . Is the ghost of Monk Martin still hovering over the scene of his crime? Or is it the vengeance of the Almighty that has cursed this spot? Who is there so bold as to say that there is no Curse Upon Mitre Square?

Both the *Curse* (Gothick-style) and the *Whitechapel Murders* (Newgate-style) were clearly very hastily compiled — well before the real-life serial had got beyond the first reel. Neither of them showed the remotest interest in the victims.

By the time the third and fourth murders had been committed, some correspondents to the newspapers, and even some reporters and editors were beginning to react against the growth of the Ripper industry, and, specifically, against the more extreme ways in which the events had come to be exploited. There were no complaints about the readiness with which editors jumped at the opportunity to exploit the three main stereotypes of the murderer, of course: these had been around for a long time, and readers would have been surprised if they had occasioned comment. The 'decadent aristocrat' idea had been firmly fixed in the public imagination, and associated with esoteric practices, ever since the Hell Fire Club, and, more recently, the spread of gossip about Lord Byron ('he murdered his mistress, and enjoyed drinking her blood, from a cup made of her cranium . . .'); the 'demon doctor' idea would have come as no surprise to readers who had heard all about the anatomist who employed Burke and Hare, or who had enjoyed *Sweeney Todd* the sadistic barber-surgeon; and the suggestion that the Jews might have been at the bottom of it harked right back to such stand-bys of the penny-a-liners as the Norwich pogrom of 1144 (sparked off by a 'ritualistic' murder) and the King's Road murders of 1771 ('go to Chelsea' being a common slur on passing Jews for many years afterwards), while feeding off common prejudices against the immigrants who were said to be polluting the East End of London. Nor were there any complaints about the profound misogyny which underpinned all three stereotypes of the murderer. So there was no press reaction against the accepted 'explanations' of Jack's behaviour.

Rather, the reaction was alleged to be against those reporters and editors who were hindering the police in their inquiries, who were *enhancing* the Ripper's status as a mythic figure, or who were depraving or corrupting the literate youth (specifically, the literate working-class youth) of England. A correspondent to *The Times* launched into a tirade against the penny crime thrillers which tended to make Dick Turpin, Jack Sheppard or Charley Peace into downmarket versions of Robin Hood: he quoted the case of a youth who had recently been arrested for larceny, and who proceeded to bite the policeman's thumb, shouting 'I am as game as Charley Peace, and I will do as much as him before I die'. On 15 September 1888, *Punch* posed what it considered 'a serious question':

> Is it not within the bounds of probability that to the highly-coloured pictorial advertisements to be seen on almost all the hoardings in London, vividly representing sensational scenes of murder exhibited as 'the great attractions' of certain dramas, the public may be to a certain extent indebted for the horrible crimes in Whitechapel? We say it most seriously — imagine the effect of gigantic pictures of violence and assassination by knife and pistol on the morbid imagination of an unbalanced mind. These hideous picture-posters are a blot on our civilisation and a disgrace to the Drama . . .

And on 13 October *Punch* continued this campaign for censorship of *Police News*-type illustrations by running a cartoon entitled *Horrible London, or the pandemonium of posters* in which a leering, music-hall Ripper was shown sticking up posters advertising crime thrillers and penny-dreadfuls: one of these was clearly based on the cover of Purkess' *Whitechapel Murders*. On 20 October *Punch* printed a mock-operatic playlet entitled *The Detective's Rescue*, in which the 'Goddess of Luke-warm Public Opinion' — conjured up by Sir Charles Warren, no less — disperses a crowd of grim 'sensation-mongers' who are asking a 'dismayed detective' exactly what his methods *are*: Warren's position is that 'a Detective is meant to *detect*', and morbid journalists should leave him alone to do just that.

> Do you think the detective's so green
> As to let you know all that he's traced?

In addition to taking a few side-swipes at a 'defective force' that had only been in existence for ten years, one purpose of this campaign seems to have been to separate the 'responsible' treatment of the crimes in the respectable dailies from the exploitative treatment in the working-class press: penny-dreadfuls, the *Illustrated Police* comics and the East End music hall were all associated with the 'sensation-mongers'. The implication was that, if these media were all cleaned up, in other words taken over by the respectable middle classes ('luke-warm public opinion'), then one major 'blot on our civilisation' would have been removed. People like us (readers of *Punch*) were not, of course, entertained by such things. *Punch* had, in fact, been campaigning against 'this poisonous exotic Sensation' ever since 1861 (when developments from 'across the Atlantic' were blamed), but the campaign of autumn 1888 coincided with the first stirrings of the movement to take over the music-hall of the East, and make it a suitable place for West Enders to spend an amusing night out: songs like the infamous *Sam Hall* ('They've shut me up in quod, For killing of a sod . . . Damn your eyes') were not, apparently, considered amusing enough for such an audience.

Punch moved up the market, however, when it started another campaign, this time against the publication of all the latest developments in the case as they occurred: such journalistic practice, it was suggested, served only to hamper the movements of the police and especially of the 'defective force'. The specific target of this campaign seems to have been the independent *Pall Mall Gazette*, under the Liberal editorship of W. T. Stead. As early as 22 September 1888, *Punch* ran a *Detective's Diary à la Mode*, which attempted to show how dangerous it was for the public to expect an instant arrest, or at least instant results from the detective department: and endless 'suggestions' from the press did not help much either.

Monday — Papers full of the latest tragedy. One of them suggested that the assassin was a man who wore a blue coat. Arrested three blue-coat wearers on suspicion.

Tuesday — The blue-coats proved innocent. Released. Evening journal threw out a hint that deed might have been perpetrated by a soldier. Found a small drummer-boy drunk and incapable. Conveyed him to the Station House.

Wednesday — Drummer-boy released. Letter of anonymous correspondent to daily journal declaring that the outrage could only have been committed by a sailor. Decoyed petty officer of Penny Steamboat on shore, and suddenly arrested him.

Thursday — Petty officer allowed to go. Hint thrown out in the correspondence columns that the crime might be traceable to a lunatic. Noticed an old gentleman purchasing a copy of a Rider Haggard novel. Seized him.

Friday — Lunatic despatched to an asylum. Anonymous letter received, denouncing local clergyman as the criminal. Took the reverend gentleman into custody.

Saturday — Eminent ecclesiastic set at liberty with an apology. Ascertain in a periodical that it is thought just possible that the Police may have committed the crime themselves. At the call of duty, finished the week by arresting myself . . .

This *Detective's Diary* was so full because, as far as the press knew, there was no hard evidence on which to base a charge that would stick, and no available 'explanation' of the Ripper's actions: the suggestions of that 'evening journal' were thus seen to be without foundation — or worse, actively misleading.

The *Lancet* was in a stronger position than *Punch* to judge whether or not the police were in possession of hard evidence: after all, when the Coroner asked the gentlemen of the press at an inquest to take heed of Dr Phillips' remarks about the possible misuse of gory details, the *Lancet* alone felt justified in issuing a full account of the Ripper's style in mutilation. As a journal that was read mainly by members of the medical profession (the prime suspects, according to many a reporter), the *Lancet* was able to stand aside from more commercial considerations of crime reporting and criticize 'the press' in general. On 6 October 1888, the *Lancet* lashed out at 'those manuals of instruction in crime — the penny histories of murder and felony which abound on many bookstalls'.

The ruinous effect of this kind of reading cannot be denied. Tales of silly sentiment, of glaring immorality, of refinement in vice, or romantic passion working out its course in hatred and murder, fill up the pennyworths of garbage which are constantly foisted upon foolish and ignorant purchasers by the gutter purveyors of literature. Youth, untrained in right principle, perhaps overworked, physically and mentally morbid from the want of fresh air and sufficient house room, affords a ground already prepared to receive the tares of this injurious teaching.

This attack on working class literature (youth, characteristically, seems to have been synonymous with working class youth) was followed by assorted letters from outraged clerics and retired physicians, and finally by an editorial entitled 'the Growth of Sensationalism', in which 'the press' was attacked for printing what the *Lancet* alone should have been permitted to print. Evidently only card-carrying members of the profession could handle the full story:

Today, the press takes care to report at inordinate length, and often with objectionable minuteness, the details of the latest murder, divorce or fashionable scandal. The Whitechapel tragedies have afforded a typical case in point — what with gruesome descriptions of the victims, elaborate conjectures as to the precise mode and motive for the crimes, and interminable theories as to the best means of discovering the criminal, one would think that the thoughts of the entire nation were practically absorbed in the contemplation of revolting wickedness.

There followed an elaboration of the thesis that, in the absence of any substantial evidence about the identity of Jack the Ripper, the exploiters were having to work overtime. Towards the end of this editorial, the *Lancet* gave some suggestions about why so much public interest had been aroused in these crimes, and why the culture industry had been so quick to spot their commercial potential:

It may be a question how far this craving for excitement is simply the outcome of the overtension of modern industrial civilisation . . . the modern Englishman lives at such high pressure that simple pleasures may cease to amuse him. If so, the admission is a disquieting one. A return to nature is so much simpler, healthier, and less exhausting — it is important to make this desirable. No benefit can result from a mass exhaustion of emotions.

To reinforce the point, the *Lancet* appended a letter from Lieutenant-Colonel Herbert Everitt of the Church of England Purity Society. (The fact that those who suffered most from 'high pressure' were scarcely in a position to 'return to nature' did not, of course, occur to the editors.)

The *Lancet*'s campaign, however, is an interesting one, coming as it did hot in the heels of an equivalent campaign in the popular press. If the newspapers' treatment of the Whitechapel murders fed off a series of moral panics that were very much in the news already, that same treatment stimulated yet another moral panic of its own, and the cry to censor the crime reporting of the working class press (which might give ignorant people ideas) became louder as the Ripper industry expanded its sphere of operations.[23] *Punch* posed as a middle-of-the-road arbiter of taste — as the spokesperson for what we would now call the silent majority. The *Lancet* posed as the defender of the medical profession's 'right to know', a right which appears to have excluded everyone else. On 3 November, the *Lancet* printed a letter from a Dr G. B. Beale of Tottenham which attributed 'the temporary decline in tone and taste' to 'the Board School system, which has educated to the point of being able to read a vast number who before its institution were unable to do so . . .' The *British Medical Journal* of 22 September claimed to have found the solution, however: 'all civilising influences tend to improve the brain, especially in young people; and in this way the establishment of evening classes, well-conducted clubs, and athletics will tend to lessen ruffianism'. Meanwhile, the *Illustrated Police News* was content to increase its circulation.

Punch's Detective's Diary was not, in fact, original: it was plagiarised from *Fun* magazine of the previous week, as was the new campaign against lurid posters. *Fun* had also printed *The Crime Cauldron*, 'as brewed by certain papers (with sincere apologies to the author of Macbeth)', the most amusing of all the many attacks on the exploitation of the Ripper tragedies:

Enter three Editors:

> Vice seems not to be subdued
> Vice and Crime are on the wind

Round about the cauldron go
In it slips of 'copy' throw.
Headlines of the largest size —
Murderer's letters — all faked lies;
And other spicy bits we've got
To simmer in our charmèd pot.

> Bubble, Bubble! Crime and Trouble
> Make our circulation double.

Here are gory catalogues
Touching murderer — tracking dogs.
Tales of reeking knives and things,
Which the 'service' hourly brings.
There served up with inquest-trouble
Make our crime-broth boil and bubble.

Etc. Etc.

One ironic result of this campaign was the closing of *Dr Jekyll and Mr Hyde* at the Lyceum. Although the play seems to have had some success, Richard Mansfield decided to withdraw it from the repertoire after a short run — and he withdrew it in style, with a benefit performance for the homeless of the East End. The *Daily Telegraph* was quick to show its admiration for the American actor-manager's grand gesture:

Mr Richard Mansfield has determined to abandon the "creepy drama", evidently beloved in America, in favour of wholesome comedy. The murderous Hyde will peer round the drawing-room windows and leap at his victim's throat for the last time . . . Experience has taught this clever young actor that there is no taste in London just now for horrors on the stage. There is quite sufficient to make us shudder out of doors.

Robert Louis Stevenson himself must have been delighted about Mansfield's decision for he had expressed disapproval of the production from the word go, on the grounds that it dared to interpret the conflict between Jekyll and Hyde in *sexual* terms (as Hollywood was later to do, notably in 1932 and 1941, and as Hammer Films were to do from the late 1950s onwards): 'the harm was in Jekyll because he was a hypocrite', wrote Stevenson, 'not because he was fond of women'.[24] If the audience started imagining that *Dr Jekyll and Mr Hyde* was about *sex* . . . whatever next?

JENNY TOWLER TURNED UP LATELY,
WITH A KNIFE STUCK IN HER BREAST,
WHILE JACKKNIFE WALKED THE EMBANKMENT,
NONCHALANTLY UNIMPRESSED

Perhaps because the three powerful Victorian images of the-sort-of-man-who-could-be-the-Whitechapel-murderer have survived into the late twentieth century — in popular culture, and in the history of the idea that rape is always someone else's nightmare — the author at the centre of it all, 'Jack the Ripper', remains the elusive figure he always was: a space in the files, an *absence* which has been given a name by 'an enterprising journalist', and a character by successive writers, reporters and members of the reading public. In terms of historical evidence, he does not exist, so, for all sorts of reasons, he has been constantly re-invented. Ever since the autumn of 1888, this space has been used to accommodate the 'beasts', 'monsters' and 'maniacs' of the moment. Each generation has added embellishments to a genre picture which was first created out of the West End's fear of the outcast East, out of a glimpse into the abyss.

The absence in the fog which is 'Jack the Ripper' has proved a stimulus to more creative imaginations as well. For Wedekind and the Expressionists, he was a suitable Christmas present for Pandora, the girl — or rather the 'female principle' — who released all kinds of dark inhibitions from her box. For Brecht, Jack the Knife was the perfect embodiment of the gangster-as-capitalist, the appropriator of other men's crimes. For the Surrealists, Jack l'Eventreur was one of their satanic majesties, whose activities could be used as material for a collage which set out to amuse and shock. For Hollywood in the golden age, he could mutter things like 'Forgive me, my dear, you see I hurt you because I love you' and *still* remain sympathetic: he could also help to turn the expressionist aesthetic of rape into the set of visual clichés with which he has been associated ever since. For George Orwell, he was one of the last of the English murderers as old masters, whose work threw into relief the activities of modern day suburban hacks who had seen too many Hollywood B movies. More recently, he has been portrayed on the stage as a suitable candidate for a seat in the House of Lords, in films as part of an elaborate cover-up engineered by All Her Majesty's Men, on television as an inter-galactic impulse which feeds off the fear of beautiful women who walk home alone at night, and in music as a singing social worker from Toynbee Hall. The interest generated by those murders of a hundred years ago has been sufficient to support a minor industry — the products of which include books, plays, magazines, television series, advertisements, comics, bubble-gum cards, a board game and, of course, countless 'splatter movies' where 'there's all kinds of ways to get killed . . . if you're looking for it'.

The institutionalized misogyny — shared by police, doctors, journalists, and readers alike — which sustained press coverage of the crimes in autumn 1888, and which treated the 'unfortunate' victims as in some sense expendable, has also helped to sustain outdated 'solutions' to the mystery right up to the present day, 'solutions' which have survived to become deeply embedded in the culture (like Sherlock Holmes, that other great misogynist).

The result is that it has become inconceivable that 'Jack the Ripper' could have been the man next door:

Mr Usher: I wonder if the police have got any sort of line on this necktie murderer.

Doctor: Oh, I shouldn't think so. With psychopaths there's usually no linking motive.

Mr Usher: Well, let's hope he slips up soon.

Doctor: In one way, I rather hope he doesn't. We haven't had a good juicy series of sex murders since Christie, and they're so good for the tourist trade. Foreigners somehow expect the squares of London to be fog wreathed, full of hansom cabs, and littered with ripped whores — don't you think . . . ?[25]

This is the house that Jack built.

Acknowledgements

This article has benefited greatly from discussions, at various stages in its drafting, with Angela Carter, Robert Reiner, Graham Cox and research students in the Department of Cultural History, Royal College of Art. The studies of rape which I have found most useful in preparing it are Hester Eisenstein, *Contemporary Feminist Thought* (London, 1984), pp. 27—35; Elizabeth Wilson, *Violence Against Women* (Harmondsworth, 1983), pp. 59—116; and Beatrice Faust, *Women, Sex and Pornography* (Harmondsworth, 1981), pp. 113—36. Among the articles, Sylvia Walby, Alex Hay and Keith Soothill, 'The Social Construction of Rape', in *Theory, Culture and Society*, 2, (1983), pp. 86—98; Delia Dumaresq, 'Rape — sexuality in the law', in *m/f*, (1981), pp. 41—59; Richard Wright, 'The English rapist', in *New Society*, 17 July 1980, pp. 124—5; and S. Walby, A. Hay and K. Soothill, 'Seducing the public by rape reports', in *New Society*, 31 July 1980, pp. 214—15.

10

Rape — Does it have a Historical Meaning?

ROY PORTER

It seems that rape is too risky, too political a subject to be dealt with comfortably by the present day male historian.[1]

Rape looms small in social histories and in histories of crime and sex written by men.[2] Partly, no doubt, because it is a subject fiendishly difficult to research and interpret. Rape generally leaves its stain on the historical record only if it comes to trial, and the analogy of today's experience suggests that only a fraction (but how small a fraction?) ever reached court in the past; and even in those cases, the evidence that survives is far from the whole story.[3]

But, more importantly, this neglect largely reflects the way rape has so easily been waved aside — by men — as a marginal event, a private catastrophe doubtless, but one of little historical significance, for aren't rapists just a tiny, crazed fringe of sex maniacs?[4] In any case, ingrained misogynistic caricaturing of women (such as the 'no means yes' syndrome) has always allowed men to trivialize rape and render it titillating to the pornographic imagination. These stereotypes in turn infect the way men have written its history.[5]

One major achievement of feminist history has been to end this neglect and challenge this trivialization. Feminists rightly insist that the history of rape cannot be brushed aside as just the psychopathologies of individual perverts; it must be understood in terms of gender relations and sexual politics, stigmatization and scapegoating, violence and crime as a whole. Credit for putting rape back into history must go to the American feminist, Susan Brownmiller; for the key contention of her *Against our Will* is that rape has been a major social force, central to an overall male strategy of domination.[6]

One of Brownmiller's aims is to lay bare the patriarchal attitudes within which rape has been criminalized. From Old Testament Jewish codes up to feudalism, rape was treated primarily as theft, as a property offence, but one perpetrated against *men*. The crime was principally that of stealing or abducting a woman from her rightful proprietors, normally her father or husband.[7] Moreover, in the case of a maiden, rape destroyed her property value on the marriage market, and, because defloration polluted, heaped shame on her family. Hence legal practice routinely compensated patriarchal heads for this loss, usually by financial restitution, and aimed to remove the shame. Violated daughters might be given as offerings to nunneries, and in many societies they were married off to the abductor or rapist. Victims who jibbed at this were often subject to punishment or ostracism; yet certain cases of rape-as-abduction were probably *bona fide* 'elopements', the only course open for couples denied parental permission to marry.[8]

Very gradually the law came round to its more modern form. Statutes and commentators alike reiterated its gravity (in England the offence remained capital till 1840), but opinion gradually came to stress that the true injured party was the woman.[9] Once abduction was made a distinct felony in the sixteenth century, the crime of rape came to be seen essentially as that of sexual ravishment, which in turn was viewed as the theft of chastity and virtue, rather than of body and chattels.[10] Yet since the law still saw wives and children as patriarchal property, court room practice continued to treat rape as a crime to be settled man-to-man. Witness, for instance, this entry in the notebook of a Wiltshire Justice of the Peace, William Hunt:[11]

> 28 June 1745. Granted a warrant against John Newman of the tithing of Marston, yeoman, at the complaint of Jane Biggs, wife of John Biggs of same, for his assaulting her with intent to have carnal knowledge of her body. Upon his appearance, the fact was so clearly proved upon him, upon the oath of the complainant, that I adjudged him to pay unto John Biggs for damages 5 guineas, and at the same time entered into a bond penalty £100 never to molest John Biggs or his wife any more.

Brownmiller convincingly argues that the criminalization of rape in the statute book perpetuated a man's world. More importantly, however, she contends that *committing* rape is actually functionally integral to patriarchy. Patriarchy needs rape; in other words, rape constitutes neither a challenge to, nor the breakdown of, paternalist authority, but its very sanction, its epitome, its 'shock troops'.

Brownmiller is contending for three points. First, male attitudes towards virility ('machismo') and towards women (misogyny) form a 'mass psychology' encouraging rape.[12] Even if few men actually commit acts the law calls rape, all men are potential rapists. Given the opportunity — e.g., as soldiers in an army of occupation — men will indeed rape, and in any case, the sex husbands inflict on their wives would often count as rape, if patriarchal law did not explicitly deny the crime of rape within marriage.[13] Secondly, throughout history rape has been much more prevalent than is generally recognized; for instance, Brownmiller offers abundant harrowing evidence of rape atrocities committed by marauding armies. Thirdly, rape legitimizes patriarchy. As an act, it brutally subordinates women to men's will; as a menace, it constantly polices women's behaviour, limits their freedom and fosters patriarchy's ideology that women need male 'protection' (hence Mae West's quip: 'Funny, every man I meet wants to protect me; I can't figure out what from').

So rape (according to this view) is not the aberration of 'weirdos' but is socially functional and historically charged with meaning; it is not the sickness of perverts, but the sickness of patriarchy. 'From prehistorical times to the present, I believe, rape has played a critical function,' writes Brownmiller; 'it is nothing more or less than a conscious process of intimidation by which *all* men keep *all* women in a state of fear.'[14] As 'man's basic weapon of force against women', rape (a 'male prerogative') is less a sex offence than a protection racket; it is a political crime, men's ultimate way of keeping women subordinated as the second sex.[15]

It is no accident that this view of rape as a political weapon comes out of the United States, for it was there before other nations that rape became a key issue in sexual politics.[16] The incidence of rape in America is not only appallingly high — 75,989 cases were *reported* in 1979 — but continues to escalate (Susan Griffin has claimed that 'forcible rape is the most frequently committed violent crime in America today').[17] It is there that men have themselves politicized rape; Eldridge Cleaver, the Black Panther leader, notoriously urged raping of white women as a tactic in the black struggle.

Brownmiller's history mirrors the current politics of rape in the United States. In fact, past and present must be all of a piece for her, since she views rape as a product of the timeless facts of male biology and psychology. Yet does her reading of rape as a political crime ('a conscious process of intimidation by which *all* men keep *all* women in a state of fear') actually ring true historically? Edward Shorter has argued that it does not, because it wrongly reads the present back into the past.[18]

Shorter does not dispute Brownmiller's assumption that rape was endemic in traditional society;[19] but he does contest her explanation. It was not, he claims, a political crime, but a sex offence, an act of libidinal release, the way men coped with sexual frustration in the highly repressive communities of the pre-industrial past. Traditional village life had to put drastic curbs on legitimate sexual activity. Subsistent economies demanded that peasants married late, and they could not afford bastards. Church courts, community surveillance and misogynistic folk prejudices which saw women as polluting and dangerous, all combined to curb premarital sex between the young. Inevitably, therefore, frustration built up and pent-up energies often found release in rape. Crime statistics show that rape gradually declined during the nineteenth century. This (Shorter suggests) was because as Western societies industrialized and secularized, they could handle population growth better, and came to permit more liberal sexual attitudes, greater indulgence in premarital sex, greater toleration of bastards and, not least, earlier marriage. Also contraception developed. There was thus less frustration, hence less rape.

Shorter's view of rape as a function of the changing economy of sexual repression has its own problems, however. Shorter accuses Brownmiller of back-projecting from the present in interpreting rape as a political crime.[20] Yet he himself seems guilty of anachronism, in assuming that male sexuality is a constant; and he relies on an ultra-mechanistic behavioural model in which repressed sexual drives will find release in one way or another, whether consensually or violently.

Rather than adopting this 'hydraulic' reductionism, it is better to view sexuality as shaped by culture, values and social habit; and elsewhere in this volume the anthropologist Peggy Reeves Sanday draws attention to contemporary societies which seem happily to combine low levels (by our standards) of sexual activity with low rates of rape and other violent offences, and all with little evidence of great 'frustration'.[21] Why should not European males of earlier centuries have been encultured into different sexual expectations from our own, so as to accept — as they certainly did — late marriage with its deferred sexual gratification, without exploding and finding outlets in rape? After all, such conditioning for *men* would only mirror the way young *women* were socialized in the Victorian period into 'passion-lessness'; and historians readily accept that respectable ladies were then trained to get by in life with scant sexual gratification, with only a small minority 'rebelling', as it were, into 'hysteria', 'madness' or 'nymphomania'.

We would do well, I am suggesting, to put into historical perspective today's assumption that sex is sovereign, both as a biological drive and as the key to personality. Through our post-Freudian eyes we all too readily envisage sex as a natural force pitted against civilization, instinct against morality, and so take it for granted that sexual 'restraint' is 'repression', i.e., dammed up energies will break through one way or another. Surely it is dangerous to universalize — as do both Brownmiller and Shorter — from our late twentieth century perspective in which we have sex on the brain and before our eyes as never before? The impact of Freud; the spread of contraception (separating sex from babies and turning it from procreation into recreation);[22] the promotion by late capitalism of its own pleasure principle, consumer sex as part of what Marcuse called 'repressive desublimation'; the cults of youth, 'femininity', and glamour; the coming of affluence, high nutrition, health, cleanliness, leisure, privacy — all these have combined to thrust sex to the forefront of our society. The outcome is more free and legal sexual activity, yet there are also more, not fewer, rapes and other sex offences, such as child molesting.

Sexuality may thus be (as Michel Foucault argued) a modern invention;[23] and we must beware of projecting today's platitudes about needs and gratifications back on to the past. When interpreting sexual patterns, the European 'world we have lost' might better be compared to contemporary Third World societies (e.g., in the Near and Middle East),[24] cultures equally male-dominated, but where different life styles and value systems may not carry the same urgent, rape-centred menace. Envisage a culture enforcing strong sexual taboos, treating women as both pure yet polluting; a community where adults strictly police the young, and enforce gender segregation; an economy dominated by backbreaking toil; a physiology characterized by malnutrition, debility and illness; envisage all this, and the profile of sexual demands and practices may appear very different.

In typical European communities of a few centuries ago there may well have been less lawful sexual activity, both within and outside marriage, but less violent or criminal sex as well.[25] After all, to offer a parallel case, historical demographers believe that epochs of particularly late marriage in the past were times of low rather than high bastardy.[26] Yet all this must remain largely guesswork, because we have absolutely no way of knowing with tolerable accuracy how much sexual violence went on in the Europe of two, four, or six centuries ago. Both Brownmiller (and her followers) and Shorter assume that the rape plateau was high — Brownmiller because rape was the 'nuclear threat' which clinched male domination, Shorter because it was the volcanic eruption of sexual release. Yet, for what they are worth, crime statistics hardly confirm high rape levels in past societies. Recent research by Simpson, Cockburn, Sharpe, Bashar, Macfarlane and others on felony has sparked massive debate as to whether pre-industrial England was more or less violent than industrial society has proved;[27] but their researches show beyond dispute that rapes and other sexual assaults on women made up only a tiny proportion of crimes against the person indicted before the courts. Judges spent infinitely more time hearing cases of male violence against men than of male violence against women. As Bashar found in her study of the Home Counties assizes in the sixteenth and seventeenth centuries, 'the number of rapes appearing in the court records was remarkably small' — less than one per cent of all indictments, in fact.[28]

Now there are scores of good reasons to distrust the value of these figures of prosecutions as indices of social reality. Only a fraction of rapes ever got to court (though presumably also only a fraction of male/male assaults ever did either). A great deal of what we would call rape would have been passed off as *droit de seigneur* or 'seduction' (e.g., the bedding of servant girls by their masters, under conditions in which the maid's 'no' carried no weight); these never resulted in court cases.[29] Moreover, the obstacles hindering women bringing prosecutions would also account for many other rapes never coming before the courts.[30] Yet male chauvinism might cut both ways. If, as Brownmiller rightly stresses, under patriarchy rape was reckoned a crime against men, surely heads of households had strong incentives to prosecute those who violated their mothers, wives or daughters. Court records, thus, do not prove that rape (at least in the 'street-crime' sense of assault upon strangers) was specially prevalent.

To turn from one dubious source of evidence to another, this tentative finding gains some support from contemporary testimony, positive and negative. Susan Griffin writes of her experience of living in America nowadays, 'I have never been free of the fear of rape';[31] but those women in pre-industrial England who put their feelings on paper — middle to upper class women — did not share Griffin's anxiety. I know of no woman who records in her journal that she had suffered rape or attempted rape, or that her friends had been raped. (Men's letters by contrast abound with reports of man-to-man assault.) Despite all the situations when women must have been exposed to sexual assault (being left 'unprotected' with servants or labourers, travelling alone or only in female company, staying in unlocked rooms in inns etc.), there seems little evidence that women such as Celia Fiennes, who rode the length and breadth of England side-saddle for pleasure, went in Griffin-type dread of being raped.[32] Indeed, one of the most revealing comments by a woman I have found suggests the reverse of the Brownmiller/ Griffin argument. At the end of the eighteenth century the actor John Philip Kemble assaulted the actress Miss De Camp; humiliated, he was forced to print an apology in the newspapers. Hester Thrale commented in her journal:

Kemble is forced to make open Apology in the daily papers for a fruitless Attempt at committing a Rape — and to publicly advertise himself as the most infamous of modern scoundrels.[33]

What this case indicates is not the ability of rapists to hold women in fear, but the public ignominy such brutality produced.

Indeed, listening for rape fears in the past, we are surprisingly often met by silence. Early feminists such as Mary Astell, the 'Blue Stockings' or Mary Wollstonecraft, who deplored so many other facets of male tyranny and the wrongs of woman, did not agitate about rape. Nineteenth century women activists campaigned against a multitude of sexual abuses (child prostitution, the Contagious Diseases Acts, etc.) but not, so far as I know, about the ubiquity of rape. The same goes for male reformers. From Thomas More to the Puritans and then to Defoe, Fielding, Colquhoun and beyond, there was a crescendo of complaint about all manner of crime, vice and sexual evils — muggers, drunkards, pickpockets, prostitutes, highwaymen — but no reformer seems to have thought that rape was the scandal of the day.

It is, then, at least conceivable that certain forms of rape were markedly less frequent in earlier communities. Three brief examples may illustrate this interpretation. Nowadays much rape takes place on the road (motorists raping hitch-hikers, or less often, vice versa), but the highwaymen, or even the footpads, of late Stuart and Georgian England do not seem to have anticipated Eldridge Cleaver in avenging themselves on the polite and propertied by raping their victims. If anything the reverse; highwaymen adopted an exaggerated gallantry in their dealings with wayfaring damsels. Secondly, there is little sign that women had recourse to rape allegations in order to exonerate themselves.[34] Take Sharpe's study of bastardy cases in seventeenth century Essex: women offered many excuses for bearing bastards (generally claiming to have been seduced under marriage promises subsequently broken), but Sharpe encountered none who claimed her pregnancy had followed rape.[35] Thirdly, take witchcraft. 'Witches' exercised great power and so were the targets of crude misogyny. One strategy of patriarchy was therefore to silence them. Against witches men used casual violence or prosecuted them in the courts, and above all, from the fifteenth to the seventeenth century, thousands were burnt. At a later stage they tried derision and medicalization (witches were, after all, just pitiable old women, sick and crazed). But there is no sign that men sought to put witches under their thumb by systematic sexual violence against them.[36]

So far I have been suggesting that we have no reason to think that rape was a particularly prominent act in the pre-industrial world. If that is so, it would puncture Brownmiller's assumption that rape has always been crucial in intimidating women and perpetuating male dominion. The reality of male oppression and exploitation of women in Western history is not, of course, in dispute; but was this really routinely accomplished by the terror of rape? Or, to put it another way, was male supremacy so flimsy, so imperfectly rationalized, so tenuously secured by regular, legitimate controls, that men had to fall back upon rape intimidation to maintain their dominance? There is much in Shorter's argument that men did not need rape as a weapon of political control or as a bogey, because their grip was cast-iron in any case:[37]

> Early-modern women were already so completely under male domination that it is hard to imagine what further inroads into their autonomy or independence might have been sliced. Short of falling into slavery, these women could scarcely have been more victimized by the male-controlled social, economic, and political systems in which they found themselves. European village men had no need to play at sexual politics. Their political control of women was already absolute.

Shorter exaggerates women's impotence in traditional societies: within their own spheres, such as the household, their leverage was immense, even if these spheres were subordinate.[38] But traditional society was so securely a man's world that it did not have much need for the 'surplus repression' that endemic rape threats would have conferred. A patriarchal order depending on such crude and violent 'legitimizations' would have forfeited its legitimacy. It would have shown itself to be insecure, which the social regimes of early modern Europe certainly were not. Men no more cherished the threat of the rapist in the wings to maintain their authority over women than property owners encouraged thieves to justify the apparatus of law and order.

This may shed some light on why it is in North America today that rape has become so prominent an arena of political conflict. For rape is distinctive there; heavily politicized precisely because gender relations have become destabilized.[39] In the United States the contradictions in sex roles are uniquely naked, with cults of glamourized women and macho men, with the most strident and successful women's movement and the most vicious male backlash. In these circumstances rape does indeed become male vengeance; but it may be an anachronism to assume that all the world has been America.[40]

RAPE AND THE COMMUNITY

Taking a long-term, wide-angled view, I have been asking so far whether rape has been a significant force in gender relations, playing a 'critical function' in the subjection of women. I have cast doubts on this, though (as I shall argue later) rape has undoubtedly been a key feature of appalling sexual stereotypes and sick male fantasies,[41] whose evils go well beyond the sexual abuse of women, in underwriting militarism, war and environmental 'rape'.[42]

Next, however, I want to scrutinize sexual violence from close up, examining a single case which shows another brutal male and yet another pitiable victim, frozen for a second in the stream of time. But what more does it show? Perhaps another skirmish in the truceless war of the sexes, perpetuating oppression and patriarchal control? Once again, traditional male history fails us; and it is thanks entirely to today's feminism that research is at last interpreting actual cases of rape.

The instance I shall discuss is the alleged rape and murder of Mary Ashford in the English Midlands in 1817, and I shall use it to explore community attitudes and responses to the crime. In doing so, I shall draw heavily on pioneering analysis by Anna Clark.[43] Clark approaches the case through assumptions similar to Brownmiller's, arguing that it demonstrates 'how both patriarchy and class shaped the interpretation and function of sexual violence in the early nineteenth century'.[44] While I agree with much of Clark's reading, I shall also resift the evidence, and suggest some different conclusions.[45]

On 27 May 1817, Mary Ashford, a servant, went with her friend Hannah Cox to a dance at the Tyburn Inn at Erdington. She left around midnight accompanied by a local bricklayer, Abraham Thornton. About 3 am she was seen still with him, sitting on a stile in the fields. Some time later, she returned in good spirits to the house where Hannah Cox was staying, changed clothes and set off to walk home. Her bloodstained corpse was discovered soon afterwards in a water-filled pit at nearby Penn's Mills. Since Thornton had earlier been with her, he was sought out. He admitted having had sex with her, but denied raping or murdering her. He was arrested and tried at Warwick Assizes for her murder, but after a trial lasting 12 hours, the jury found him not guilty.

Strong suspicion naturally fell on Thornton, who had an unsavoury reputation as a ladykiller, and his acquittal came as a shock. Clark assumes that it was obvious that Thornton was indeed guilty of both Ashford's rape and murder. Thus the nub of the problem for her is to explain his *acquittal*, how a 'jury consisting of farmers, artisans, and a tradesman found Thornton innocent of rape and murder, even though he admitted he had had intercourse with Mary Ashford'.[46]

What motives or prejudices, Clark asks, could have led the (all-male) jury to acquit? Clark argues that the judge and jury evidently subscribed to the male chauvinist assumption that, though Thornton may well have used sexual violence on Ashford, such violence did not amount to rape, since in lawful sexual intercourse men might normally 'get physical' to overcome reluctance or simulated resistance ('modesty'), and thereby win the consent which was the dividing line between lawful sex or seduction, and rape. Indeed, in making advances to a respectable maiden, as Mary Ashford had been, men would expect initially to meet resistance. Clark thus argues that in the male circles, 'violence was an acceptable means of seduction', for as she glosses this 'libertine' view:

Those who took the 'libertine' position (so-called by its opponents) saw no basic contradiction in saying women 'consented' to violence. Their argument has two implications: first, that violence was merely one (although not a universal) technique of seduction; and secondly, that a woman's reputation as chaste or unchaste defined others' perceptions of her consent.[47]

Jurymen holding the libertine view that violence might be used to obtain sexual goals without its necessarily constituting rape, could thus accept that Thornton had not raped Ashford: and if he had not raped her, why should he have killed her? His only motive for murder would be to silence her to prevent a rape charge. Hence the circumstantial evidence against Thornton (that he had had sex with her) might be overruled, and the defendant given the benefit of the doubt. Thus (Clark argues), the appalling ability of chauvinist ideology to construe sexual violence as compatible with (even on occasion as integral to) normal sex, and distinct from rape, was crucial in undermining the murder charge against Thornton.

Clark is advancing three main points about 'the interpretation and function of sexual violence', shown by this case.[48] First, the male ideology that 'violence was an acceptable means of seduction' allowed the murderer Thornton to go free and meant, in effect, that a man could rape and even murder with impunity.[49] Secondly, in cases of alleged rape, blame actually got displaced from the rapist to the victim, for 'a victim's failure to resist advances stained her, rather than her attacker, with dishonour'.[50] Hence it was the character and morals of the victim that fell under suspicion: was she one of those girls who 'asked for it' and 'deserved her fate'?[51] Thirdly, Clark argues, the murder and trial were then further exploited by patriarchy to 'control women's behaviour',[52] for the implication of the affair was that the likes of Thornton would always go scot free, a standing threat to female virtue and lives. Therefore women's prophylactic against such men should be to retreat into passive, demure and chaste behaviour, and ensure they had proper patriarchal protection.

I wish to suggest, however, that Clark's interpretation of the proceedings is somewhat misleading, and that this case — while certainly showing the wrongs of woman — does not bear out her conclusions. Two preliminary clarifications need to be made. First, it was not primarily a rape trial but a murder trial. Of course the question of what happened sexually to Mary Ashford was important. Thornton claimed he had had consensual sex with her. The surgeon called in to examine her corpse testified that the lacerations around her genitals were compatible with normal intercourse with a virgin (as Ashford had been),[53] just as the blood coagulated on her clothes and person was consistent with blood loss from defloration, taking into account the fact that Ashford was menstruating. By contrast, contemporary pamphlets and public response make it clear that for popular opinion, the lacerations and blood stains spelled rape. Yet the point is that what exactly transpired sexually between Thornton and Ashford was, quite properly, secondary to the trial. What was really at stake, and what was centre-stage in the court room, was whether there was enough evidence to prove a murder. In other words, despite Clark, Thornton's acquittal does not reveal patriarchal condonement of rape, but the jury's doubts as to whether Thornton was proven a murderer.[54]

Secondly, local opinion was clearly convinced that Thornton had caused Ashford's death by drowning, presumably to prevent a rape indictment. Clark has no doubt that the evidence before the court proved Thornton was guilty: 'She had been raped and drowned', Clark writes, noting that 'Thornton's technique [sic!] of throwing his victim into a pit or pond seemed to be a pattern in such cases'.[55] Yet if one scrutinizes the evidence before the judge and jury, the case is hardly open-and-shut that she had been raped, or (the nub of the trial) feloniously drowned (as distinct from having slipped into the water-filled pit, or even committed suicide). Nor indeed, if one accepts that one or more crimes had in fact been committed, was it certain that the felon was Thornton.

On the one hand, powerful circumstantial evidence incriminated Thornton (he had had sex with her, his shoes fitted footprints found in adjacent fields, etc.). On the other, he had independent witnesses who had given him watertight alibis. Much time was spent and ink spilt hearing and interrogating the testimony of witnesses who had seen Ashford and Thornton, before and after her death, collating times and distances and checking for consistency. At the conclusion of the trial, the evidence against Thornton was weighed up at length (and it seems with considerable even-handedness) by Mr Justice Holroyd in his summing up from the bench.[56]

My aim is not to establish *whodunnit*, but I do wish to suggest that Clark gives a misleading impression. Her discussion implies that the outcome hung upon macho attitudes towards sexual violence ('rape or seduction?'). Rather it seems to have depended on forensic evidence, the credibility of witnesses and alibis, the weight due to circumstantial evidence, and so forth.[57] What was central was not whether rape was to be condoned, but whether the evidence convicted Thornton of murder.[58]

Having entered these caveats, what of Clark's wider conclusions about the case's significance? Clark stresses the 'libertine' ideology which normalized sexual violence and pointed the finger of blame at the victim. No one would deny such rakish attitudes existed, but (though one would not gather this from Clark) such arguments were not in fact aired at the trial or in the surrounding pamphlet literature, except as grotesque Aunt Sallies, to be instantly demolished. The case produced no defences of the position Clark believes swayed the jury. Indeed, far from condoning rape or romanticizing rapists, public opinion (which means male opinion) expressed outrage and mounted a sustained campaign of vilification against the acquitted man. As a contemporary reporter pointed out:[59]

Among the lower classes of people about the neighbourhood, there is a sense of horror against Thornton, that amounts almost to ferocity: and this is accompanied by a most indecorous and general outcry against all the means which led to his dismissal.

Lawyers, judge and pamphleteers alike chorused their horror at violation of women, Mr Justice Holroyd referring repeatedly to the 'heinousness of the crime', a murder 'atrocious and horrid'.[60] Indeed, indignation ran so high that melodramas were staged in the aftermath, Gothicizing the affair and portraying a rapist/murderer (by implication, Thornton) as a crazed monster. As one scene in *The Murdered Maid, or The Clock Struck Four* (relocated in Medieval France) presented the news of the death of the maid:[61]

Enter Peasants, etc. with Torches.

COQUIN: What has happened?

REYNARD: Oh good Heavens! Murder!
LECLERQ: A foul Murder! poor unlucky Marie Ashville, she — the very girl we've just been speaking of, has been found murdered in the pit near Chateau Bromege. [sic!]
COQUIN: Murdered!
REYNARD: Oh Heavens!
LECLERQ: Ev'n so; the hapless victim of some ruffian bearing the outside of a man, but carrying a heart more fierce than the wolves of our forests, — more destructive than even the devouring elements.

In other words, the public response in no way condoned sexual violence; quite the reverse.

Clark's other point is to stress how the trial was exploited 'to control women's behaviour'.[62] Female chastity, claimed the press, was all important, to be prized by women and protected by men. Though her virginity and good character allowed Ashford to be portrayed as an innocent victim, she could nevertheless be posthumously rebuked for her 'imprudence' in going to a dance without male escort, and then spending the night with a man she scarcely knew. The moral drawn time and again, argues Clark, is that women need male 'protection'.[63] There is some truth in Clark's account. For instance, the Reverend Luke Booker published a pamphlet entitled *A Moral Review of the Conduct and Case of Mary Ashford*, making great play of the 'chivalric' view that women should always go under male protection, and hoping that this case would 'furnish an admonitory lesson to young women; deterring them from repairing to scenes of amusement, unsanctioned and untended by proper protection'.[64]

Yet despite Clark's reference to 'many polemicists',[65] it actually appears that Booker was the only contemporary commentator to expand on such themes, and his exaggerated pieties appeared preposterous, drawing catcalls from other pamphleteers. As Clark herself notes, one chid him: 'Really, if the doctor goes on in this manner, his cookmaid will not be able to cross the street with a pie to the baker's without a chaperon.'[66]

In any case, it is one thing to note that a parson penned a patriarchal pamphlet, but quite another to establish that male sexual violence was actually instrumental in policing female conduct. For what the whole case seems to reveal about that particular West Midlands community is the lack of effective male control of female behaviour, and even the absence of fear of male violence.[67] Consider the facts. Mary Ashford, a servant, chose to attend a late-night dance at what seems to have been a disreputable club, without male accompaniment. Her master gave her permission. She then chose to leave at midnight in the company of a man she had only just met. Three hours later she was seen with him, apparently quite contentedly, in the fields. She then parted from him (possibly after having sex) to make her own way home. What sign is there here that rape fears were actually effective in restricting female freedom of movement, or that the morality of the times had created a crushing sense of modesty?[68]

Whatever exactly happened that May night in Erdington, it undoubtedly represents yet another incident in women's exploitation and victimization. What is more dubious, is whether it catches patriarchy red-handed in the act of exonerating rape, on the grounds that, as Griffin puts it, 'the existence of rape in any form is beneficial to the ruling class of white males'.[69] Rather, the Ashford case shows the community uniting in abhorrence of the crime and of the suspected villain, who was so socially ostracized after his acquittal that he soon emigrated to America. The community's desire for good order is more apparent than the war of the sexes.[70]

RAPE AND THE RISE OF THE WEST

This chapter opened with global issues of gender and violence, questions of *The Sexual Dynamics of History: 'Men's power, women's resistance'*, as the London Feminist History Group entitled its recent book.[71] My analysis then led to an individual instance in a specific community. It is all too easy, however, for historians to take refuge in the particular, so the field of vision must be opened up once more, reintegrating particular experiences within a structured interpretation.

Feminists have looked at familiar history through new eyes and drawn fresh conclusions. Sometimes politics and polemics have got the better of analysis. Take for example Shulamith Firestone's conclusion about witchcraft (much quoted since in feminist writings) that 'witches must be seen as women in independent political revolt; within two centuries, eight million were burned at the stake by the Church'.[72] This attempt, common in feminist writings, to depict witches as victimized pioneer freedom fighters may be good as propaganda, but it is preposterous as history. The figure (eight million) is a grotesque exaggeration, and the idea of 'independent political revolt' is difficult to square with what is known of the lives of actual witches (who largely incriminated other women).[73] In surveying the history of rape, however, two formulations arising from the writings of feminists do seem fully justified: (*a*) rape cannot be fully understood in terms of individual rapists, but only in terms of masculine values at large; (*b*) rape is more an expression of misogyny than of pent-up sexual desire.[74]

What seems far more doubtful, however, is the claim that 'the sexual dynamics of history' reveal truths about rape that are trans-historical, facts of nature or biology. Thus Brownmiller justifies her view (that rape is 'a conscious process of intimidation by which *all* men keep *all* women in a state of fear',)[75] ultimately by anatomy. Man's 'biological capacity to rape', is, she contends, 'sufficient to have caused the creation of the male ideology of rape'. Or, put another way, men's oppression of women results from 'anatomical fiat', through 'the inescapable construction of their genital organs'. In the beginning, 'the human male was a natural predator and the human female served as his natural prey': thus do things remain.[76]

Here radical feminism ironically joins in unholy alliance with the socio-biological Right, which would *excuse* or *endorse* machismo as being ordained by biological or territorial imperative.[77] Indeed, Brownmiller's remarks bear an uncanny resemblance to the dictum of the former Solicitor-General for Scotland, the hard-line Tory MP Nicholas Fairbairn, that 'it is part of the business of men and women that they hunt and are hunted, and say "yes" and "no" and mean the opposite'. Radical feminism is right to indict official male theology (which taught that witches possessed people and demons possessed witches), but here threatens to erect a counter-demonology in its place, substituting men for witches as the sources of *maleficium*.[78]

There are dangers in treating history simply as a file of precedents of 'men's power, women's resistance'. To do so would, of course, be particularly bad strategy for those like Brownmiller who look forward to heterosexual relations being radically mended in the future. But it also seems bad history, for most scholars who have examined the diversity of social formations repudiate such psychic universalism. Rather, they show how gender relations and gender politics differ radically from society to society, being determined less by anatomy or 'the selfish gene' than by complex configurations of economic, political, domestic and ideological arrangements. Anthropologists such as Peggy Reeves Sanday[79] have demonstrated that certain societies are highly 'rape-prone', whereas others are notably 'rape-free'; and that these differentials in male sexual aggression correlate with social variables such as the gross violence levels, gender stereotypes and the position of women within the sexual division of labour.

Tribal evidence is of course not easy to evaluate: how much is shown the anthropologist? The indications, however, do point in one direction, to the primacy of 'culture' over biology in setting patterns and levels of sexual violence.[80] What then do we find if we examine the development of Western society in this light?

The West has risen on the backs of women, and man's dominion over women has assuredly been comprehensive. Down the centuries, through law and by custom, women were almost wholly excluded from public life, authority and office, from higher education and the professions, from real estate and business. In the private sphere as well, they were largely debarred from independent control both of property and of their own and their children's personal destinies, being typically under the legal authority of fathers, husbands and guardians. Men monopolized the public domain; the 'second sex' was kept private, domestic, dependent.[81]

In other words, Western society developed along thorough-going patriarchal lines.[82] Permeating politics, power, property and possession, patriarchy came to seem so natural, so inevitable, that it provided the model for religion (the God the Father who instructed wives of their husbands: 'he shall rule over you'), for a cosmos of natural order (the hierarchical Chain of Being) and for a deeply entrenched political theory (kings as fathers to their people).[83] Science itself provided further props to patriarchy. From Aristotle onwards, biology stressed the distinctiveness of male and female, and deemed women inferior, or even monstrous, versions of men. Through Freud, this patriarchalism of the body became sublimated into the patriarchalism of the unconscious mind.[84]

In the institutions producing and reproducing life, from household and kin up to community, a sexual division of labour became deep-rooted.[85] While men doubtless plumed themselves upon their superiority, the vast majority of women acquiesced — how willingly it is hard to say — in their own subordinate status, hidden from history, acting out their own idealizations of womanhood: virgin, wife, mother.[86] In certain spheres, explicit patriarchal dominion came to be challenged and eroded; e.g. from the eighteenth century the daughters of the elite were allowed increasing say in deciding their marriage partners, yet men still informally ruled the roost.

For certain radical feminists, patriarchy and rape are two faces of the same coin: 'patriarchy, the religion of rapism', writes Mary Daly.[87] But is this identification historically true? Certainly one can imagine a patriarchal society that would keep women in place without such 'shock troops' as rapists up its sleeve: for instance, Thomas More's Utopia. But was that the Western reality? The answer must be an emphatic 'no', because the rise of the West — its institutions, attitudes and destiny — has been deeply bound up with sexual violence, threat and reality, at first intertwined with patriarchal (in its literal meaning) government, and later, during the last century and especially in the New World, coexisting, uneasily, unstably, with a polity officially dedicated to equality between the sexes.

Feminists have pinpointed sexual violence in Western society, and exposed its foundations in ideology and power relations. Of all world civilizations, the West is unique in its unrivalled powers of conquest by military might and colonial expansion.[88] Trade follows the flag, and capitalist economics have likewise drawn on quasi-military goals of competition, expansion, struggle, victory, under the leadership of 'captains of industry'. Conquerors both on the battlefield and in the boardroom, men mirrored their conquests (or compensated for their failures) in their encounters with women in 'the war of the sexes'.[89] Endless *double-entendres* and pornographic images link the phallus and weapons of war — even contraceptive sheaths were once called 'armour'.[90] Sex, aggression and invasion became synonymous; women became conquests.

At the same time, however, conquests also became female. For 'rape' perfectly described the objects and effects of Western militarism and imperialism, from Edmund Burke's '*j'accuse*' over the 'rape' of India by the British, through to the 'rape of Belgium' which spurred chivalric fury at the outset of the First World War.[91] What is more, exploration of and lordship over Mother Earth herself, the moving frontier of civilization, also became depicted — by advocates and critics alike — as yet another instance of sexual conquest, of the plough opening up the virgin soil and bringing forth fertility.[92] From the scientific revolution of the seventeenth century, science was presented as the conquest of nature (regarded as female, Mother Nature) by hard-headed male scientists who would rend the veil and probe within.

The Western mind is riddled with, and Western practice moulded by, legitimizations of sexual violence. Sometimes this is idealized — the thrusting executive, the penetrating mind; sometimes it is masked or trivialized — from Gothick horror novels, with their helpless female victims, through to advertising's stylish gender images, whose kitsch transforms violation into desire.[93] Sometimes it becomes intellectual chic, as when versions of Freudianism off-loaded responsibility for rape from men and dumped it on to women; for, in the view of analysts such as Helene Deutsch, rape was eloquent largely in terms of female psychopathology.[94] And, in this mould, the author of our *Social History of Rape* sees the problem of rape as essentially that of explaining away female rape fears, and includes a chapter of rape jokes.[95]

The Western mind thus possesses a vast cultural reservoir of phallocentric aggression directed against women. Being readily masked, it has a high latent use potential, and can become embodied in acceptable forms. Take gynaecology: one need not agree with the radical feminist Mary Daly that men are hell-bent on a 'gynecological crusade to shorten women's lives',[96] but it is worth pondering how a society in which childbirth had traditionally been exclusively in female hands, turned between about 1700 and 1850 into one in which obstetrics was practised almost exclusively by men (in some countries, female deliveries have even at times been outlawed). Occasionally, of course, this gave rise to cases in which male gynaecologists were involved in direct sexual assault against women patients, and also to a pornographic genre featuring the doctor rapist hero. But, more importantly, male gynaecology led in the nineteenth century to a mass medical invasion of the female reproductive system, ending in extreme cases in abuses such as clitoridectomy, but quite standardly in a therapeutics that was over-eager to tamper with women's reproductive system and sexuality. It provides yet another case in which patriarchy's habitual subordination of women was mediated through channels of an overtly sexual nature, uniting rational legitimacy with rape overtones.[97]

The male gynaecologist (sc. rapist) and the male scientist (what the Germans call *Naturforscher*: literally 'nature-poker') provide some of the more innocuous examples of how 'viriculture' consolidates itself. Virility at work and virility in bed, virility in public and in private, were two sides of the same coin whose head was that of a 'real man'. Men must not be effeminate.[98]

One key reason why it has been only rarely that males have opted for 'feminine' ideals, is that Western culture reeks with stigmatizations of women themselves. At best, European thought has regarded women as inferior men, valued for their 'contained' virtues: passivity, chastity, obedience and purity, and idealized as madonnas and maidens. But Western culture is also thoroughly misogynistic.[99] Powerful women stereotypically threaten danger and disorder (the witch); sexually independent women invite contempt as targets of disgust and righteous wrath (the bitch, the whore). And the ultimate source and sanction of misogyny is Judaeo-Christianity, with its foundation myth of Eve, mere spare rib, yet the source of all sexual temptation, shame and sin; the scarlet woman justly scapegoated for the miseries of mankind.[100]

As secularization supplanted religious misogyny with medical and scientific misogyny, the social context motivating woman-hating also changed. In pre-industrial societies, women's subserviency to pregnancy and motherhood made them both visibly polluted yet also (because fertile and the hub of the family) mysteriously, creatively potent — targets of envy, resentment and fear.[101] In recent times, by contrast, glamorized women and the independent lady provide new provocations for male insecurity and retaliation, inviting the figurative (and sometimes literal) chopping up of women into the contrasting images of wife, mother, mistress and whore.[102]

All this, of course, speaks eloquently of ingrained Western awkwardness with sexuality in general, a distrust rationalized and magnified by Christianity. Over the centuries, sex became utterly entangled with religious prohibitions and ecclesiastical regulation; with matrimony, itself increasingly strictly supervised, and, through marriage, with property, family, line and the household economy. Thereby sexual relations became foci of guilt and suspicion, family surveillance and community policing, creating a climate growing up in the West which maladapted the young to their initiation into sexuality or their career as sexual beings.[103] It is perhaps a reflection of failure, that certain radical feminists today condemn all sexual activity 'not initiated by women' as rape,[104] or a further symptom, that child abuse and child rape have been so common, notoriously frequent (as Simpson has shown) in eighteenth century London, prevalent in Freud's Vienna (though Freud perhaps tried to screen it) and increasing today.[105]

The rise of the West thus affords a picture of a patriarchy common throughout the world, but one which more than most fostered beliefs and practices conducive both to concentrated aggression, and especially to male distrust, contempt and hatred for women — which together readily licensed rape. Indeed, rape probably became a way of life in certain sectors of society at certain times — in the anarchic, decentralized feudal kingdoms of the Dark Ages, the vendetta-ridden bandit societies of peasant Sicily, slave plantations, the Wild West, the colonies.

Such 'frontier situations', however, have steadily been superseded by the growth of social institutions and the state. Now rape has been outlawed. This is hardly surprising, for if rape is essentially not sexual release but a crime of violence, can it really lie in the interests of patriarchs or the patriarchal state, to encourage lawlessness? In the hamlets of the *Ancien Régime* or the factory towns of the industrial revolution, women were underdogs, but these communities do not seem to have been the cockpits of rape. Indeed, as I suggested in my analysis of the Ashford case, traditional communities would unite in condemning rape. For its part, the Western state has criminalized rape (contrast the public and ceremonial *legitimization* of rape amongst numerous tribes, such as the Gusii). Nor, as Natalie Davis rightly reminds us, must we underestimate the countervailing power exercised by women themselves, in the village, at the hearth, in the bedroom. History shows women victimized but not powerless;[106] the culture which imagined Clarissa Harlowe also showed Pamela, Roxana and Moll Flanders. English folklore and ballads abound with ruined maidens, generally seduced not raped; but they are at least as full of men outwitted by women.[107]

Within Western history, I have been suggesting, rape has flourished mainly on the margins; at the frontiers, in colonies, in states at war and in states of nature; amongst marauding, invading armies (though sex among soldiers is generally institutionalized in the brothel). Rape has also erupted on the psycho-margins, amongst loners, outsiders, who fail to be encultured into normal patriarchal sex.[108] Above all, rape has marked youth sub-cultures, on the criminal margins. Just as in towns of medieval Europe it was unruly youngsters who raped,[109] so in the United States today Menachim Amir found that some 40 per cent of rapists in Philadelphia were between 15 and 19 years of age, typically single, enmeshed in a subculture of violence, often operating in packs, and engaging in the generalized antisocial hostility of the unassimilated. These young men are not yet absorbed into patriarchy, with its classic roles of husband and father; they lack the permanent erections of mature patriarchy — wealth, property, office, 'standing'.[110]

Patriarchy must cope with the threat to the father. Young men may be dampened down (e.g. as apprentices) or syphoned off (e.g. deflected elsewhere as soldiers); but where such safety valves are not available, adolescents often turn to rape.[111] Rapists are thus the waste of patriarchy, but they are its wayward sons not its shock troops; not its life-blood but a diseased excrescence. It should not be forgotten that Western law and morality have abhorred rape (there is 'no more horrid abuse' according to *The Whole Duty of Man*), and that even if its punishment has indeed been sporadic, it has been severe.[112]

Susan Griffin has written that women 'will not be free until the threat of rape and the atmosphere of violence is ended, and to end that, the nature of male behaviour must be changed'. Amen. But she goes on to claim that rape ('not an isolated act') cannot 'be rooted out from patriarchy without ending patriarchy itself', for 'rape is the quintessential act of our civilization', 'the symbolic expression of the white male hierarchy'.[113] This will not do: it is, not least, insufferably patronizing to women at large, who for their participation in such patriarchal structures as the family get called voluntary slaves by Andrea Dworkin.[114] It is also enormously condescending to the victims of actual rape attacks, who are thereby deemed no worse off than all other women. And, not least, it is simplistic. To speak, as does Mary Daly, of 'the inherent gynocidal intent of patriarchy',[115] substitutes rhetoric for the serious business of understanding the ways hierarchical, gendered societies actually operate, and so it fails to explain the real resilience of patriarchy.

Reducing patriarchy to rape leads Griffin and Daly to misunderstand and underestimate patriarchy. As Marx perceived, capitalists may *resemble* hoodlums, but capitalism is a system possessed of a durability that gangsterdom lacks, not least because (in Gramsci's formulation) capitalism, unlike gangsterdom, is successfully hegemonic. Similarly, patriarchy is not just rape writ large, but has a life of its own independently of rape, and a solidity which no amount of sloganizing will grasp or dissolve. To collapse patriarchy into rape wilfully ignores the subtle play of collusion and participation, power and consent, which have made the fabric of Western history.

Notes

1 INTRODUCTION

1 See also, Ruth E. Hall's *Ask Any Woman: A London inquiry into rape and sexual assault,* Report of the Women's Safety Survey conducted by Women Against Rape (Bristol, 1985) and Carolyn J. Hursch's *The Trouble with Rape* (Chicago, 1977), to cite but two useful sources.

2 The work of Susan Brownmiller and Susan Griffin is especially noteworthy here. For the former, see her very influential *Against Our Will: Men, Women and Rape* (first published New York, 1975, later editions New York, 1976, 1981). For the latter, see her 'The politics of rape' first published in *Ramparts* magazine in 1971, also in her *Rape: The Power of Consciousness* (New York, 1978). It also appears in her *Made From This Earth: Selections from her writings* (London, 1982) and a number of other anthologies.

3 Brownmiller thinks that ancient myths reveal very little. See, *Against Our Will,* p. 313. But she also holds the view that 'Among the ancient Greeks, rape was also socially acceptable behaviour well within the rules of warfare', ibid., p. 25. The *Iliad* seems to provide her evidence.

4 As Norman Bryson points out in chapter 8, rape is not easily accommodated within our symbolic system today.

5 Machiavelli, *The Discourses,* Bernard Crick (ed.), (Harmondsworth, 1970), book III, ch. 26, pp. 477—8.

6 See his *Le Chevalier, La Femme et le Prêtre: Le marriage dans la France féodale* (Paris, 1981).

7 Both Susan Griffin and Susan Brownmiller make this argument, see n. 2. Consider also the London Rape Crisis Centre's *Sexual Violence: The Reality for Women* (London, 1984), pp. 1—7.

8 See also, Ivan Illich's *Gender* (London, 1983), pp. 31—2. He distinguishes between modern and preceding forms of rape, arguing that the former is 'implicitly fostered by the obliteration of gender' (p. 32).

9 In this introduction, rape is presented primarily as an act committed by men on women. This is not to deny the reality of rapes within both sexes. For a discussion of such rapes see Brownmiller, *Against Our Will,* pp.

285—97. Carolyn M. Shafer and Marilyn Frye also consider this issue in 'Rape and respect', in Mary Vetterling-Braggin, Frederick A. Elliston and Jane English (eds), *Feminism and Philosophy* (Totowa, NJ and London, 1977), p. 334. It would seem that rape victims of whatever biological sex are seen by their rapists to have 'feminine' characteristics. This is supported by the evidence contained in Les Sussman and Sally Bordwell's *The Rapist File,* with an introduction by Ellen Frankfort (New York and London, 1981).

10   All political theories have to take the motivation of their potential adherents into consideration. For a relatively recent attempt to generate a political system that would be supported by all its members regardless of their position in it, see John Rawls's *A Theory of Justice* (first published by Harvard University Press, Cambridge, Mass., 1971).

11   The reason why such thinkers as Hincmar may have found writing on rape fairly unproblematic is that within a Christian perspective men are naturally wicked or prone to be so. Hence he had no difficulty in understanding why men rape, since on his view they are, amongst other things, naturally lustful and covetous.

12   This conjectural history must not be confused with what Susan Griffin calls the system of chivalry in her 'The Politics of Rape'. For a more detailed analysis of the Enlightenment's theory of civilization, see Sylvana Tomaselli, 'The Enlightenment debate on women', *History Workshop,* 20 (Autumn 1985), pp. 101—24.

13   See, for instance, Mildred Dickemann, 'Human sociobiology: the first decade', *New Scientist,* 10 October 1985, pp. 38—42.

14   This is a view that can be found in a number of feminist writings, including those of Susan Griffin. For an argument linking man's treatment of women and of nature, see also Carolyn Merchant, *The Death of Nature: Women, Ecology and the Scientific Revolution* (New York, 1980; London, 1982).

15   David P. Barash, 'Sociobiology of rape in mallards (*Anas platyrhynchos*): Responses of the mated males', *Science,* 197, (1977), pp. 788ff.

16   See Jennifer Temkin's illuminating discussion in 'Towards a modern law of rape', *The Modern Law Review,* 45 (1982), pp. 399—419.

17   Susan Rae Peterson, 'Coercion and rape: The state as a male protection racket', in Vetterling-Braggin *et al., Feminism and Philosophy,* pp. 360—1.

18   Brownmiller, *Against Our Will,* p. 350.

19   Ibid., p. 3, and 'The politics of rape', p. 46, are but two examples of this insistence.

2 WOMEN, RAPE, AND LAW REFORM

1 See, e.g., 'Rape — coping with the memories', *Spare Rib,* 109 (August 1981), p. 20; *Guardian,* 24 October, 1983; B. Toner, *The Facts of Rape* (London, 1982), ch. 10.

2 A. W. Burgess and L. L. Holmstrom, *Rape — Crisis and Recovery* (Maryland, 1979), p. 35.

3 W. Young, *Rape Study — A Discussion of Law and Practice,* Department of Justice and Institute of Criminology (Wellington, NZ, 1983), vol. 1, p. 34.

4 See generally on this, *Report of the Advisory Group on the Law of Rape,* Cmnd 6352 (London, 1975); Toner, *Facts of Rape;* London Rape Crisis Centre, *Annual Reports* 1977 onwards.

5 See, e.g., R. Harper and A. McWhinnie, *The Glasgow Rape Case* (London, 1983); G. Chambers and A. Millar, *Investigating Sexual Assault* (Scottish Office Central Research Unit, 1983).

6 See, e.g., J. Scutt (ed.), *Rape Law Reform* (Canberra, 1980); P. R. Wilson, *The Other Side of Rape* (Queensland, 1978).

7 See, e.g., Lorenne Clark and Debra Lewis, *Rape: The Price of Coercive Sexuality* (Toronto, 1977).

8 See A. Snare, 'Sexual violence against women', in *Sexual Behaviour and Attitudes and their Implications for Criminal Law,* Report of 15th Criminological Research Conference (Council of Europe, Strasbourg, 1983), p. 48.

9 See e.g., Young, *Rape Study.*

10 The film was shown on 18 January, 1982 on BBC television in a series called *Police.*

11 A. Firth, 'Interrogation', *Police Review,* 28 November 1975.

12 Chambers and Millar, *Investigating Sexual Assault,* p. 94.

13 Ibid., p. 95.

14 L. L. Holmstrom and A. W. Burgess, *The Victim of Rape: Institutional Reactions* (New York, 1978).

15 D. P. Kelly, 'Victims' reaction to the criminal justice response': Paper presented at 1982 Meeting of the Law and Society Association held in Toronto, Canada.

16 In England, in March 1983, the Home Office issued guidelines to the police for the investigation of rape cases: Home Office Circular 25/1983, 'Investigation of offences of rape'.

17 See Ian Blair, *Investigating Rape: A New Approach for Police* (London, 1985).

18 *Guardian,* 25 January, 1985. On the same occasion it was announced that nine suites with showers and pleasant decorations were being prepared

in police stations around London where victims could be interviewed. Officers have orders to allow women to rest and recover, where possible, before detailed questioning. Specially trained detective inspectors will head rape inquiries, backed up by officers who have been instructed about the 'rape trauma syndrome'.

19 Under the new scheme for dealing with rape victims in London (see n. 18), police officers will act as counsellors to victims, will assist them to move if necessary and will put their welfare first: *The Times*, 25 January 1984. However, they presumably will not be able to provide the long-term assistance which many victims require.

20 See J. Marsh, N. Caplan and A. Geist, *Rape and the Limits of Law Reform* (Boston, 1982), ch. 2.

21 See, for example, M. Carter and R. Harris, 'Women against rape — community care for victims of sexual assault', in Scutt, *Rape Law Reform*, p. 179.

22 According to Blair, *Investigating Rape*, p. 84, by October 1983, 62 victim support schemes registered with the National Association of Victims Support Schemes had either dealt with victims of sexual assault or had agreed a referral policy with the police. However, it is not clear to what extent the volunteers who run these schemes are equipped to deal with sexual assault victims.

23 See, for example, V. Berger, 'Man's trial, woman's tribulation: Rape cases in the courtroom', *Columbia Law Review*, 77 (1977), p. 1.

24 L. Newby, 'Rape victims in court — the Western Australian example', in Scutt, *Rape Law Reform*, p. 117.

25 See, for example, Young, *Rape Study*, vol. I, ch. 7. Out of 64 trials examined in this study, complainants were cross-examined by more than one counsel in 25 per cent of cases because in each there were several defendants who were separately represented.

26 Newby, 'Rape victims in court', p. 119.

27 Ibid., p. 120.

28 See on this P. Pattullo, *Judging Women* (London, 1983).

29 Young, *Rape Study*, vol. I, p. 124: 50 victims were interviewed.

30 Ibid.

31 In Denmark this provision was introduced by way of an amendment to the Civil and Criminal Code of Procedure in June 1980. In Norway it was introduced by Act No.66 of 12 June, 1981 which amended the Criminal Procedure Act 1887.

32 See below, 'The Law', p. xx.

33 See on this, *Sexual Offences — A Report of the Cambridge Department of Criminal Science* (London, 1957), p. 12 and App. 1.

34 *Criminal Statistics for England and Wales, 1983*, Cmnd. 9349 (London, 1984), p. 38.

35   Ibid., Changes in recording practices between 1947 and 1983 cannot account for increases of this dimension. Between 1973 and 1983, the number of recorded rapes rose by 33.7 per cent (ibid.). During the same period, the number of offences of violence rose by approximately 80 per cent (ibid., p. 32). However, in 1984, the number of recorded offences of violence against the person was 3 per cent greater than in 1983, whereas there was a 7 per cent increase in the number of reported rapes *Home Office Statistical Bulletin,* 6/85, 12 March, 1985).

36   *Rape Study,* vol. I, p. 1.

37   Federal Bureau of Investigation, *Uniform Crime Reports* (United States Department of Justice, Washington, DC, 1983). Blair points out that between 1973 and 1982, the *rate* of increase in the occurence of the offence (assessed on the basis of the official statistics of crime) was greater for the Metropolitan Police District than for the United States as a whole: see, Blair, *Investigating Rape,* p. 15.

38   United States Department of Justice, *Criminal Victimization in the United States, 1979* (Washington, DC, 1981).

39   M. Amir, *Patterns in Forcible Rape* (Chicago, 1971).

40   R. L. Dukes and C. L. Mattley, 'Predicting rape victim reportage', *Sociology and Social Research,* 62 (1977), p. 63.

41   Young, *Rape Study,* vol. I, p. 10.

42   *The British Crime Survey: Scotland* (Scottish Office Social Research Study, 1984), p. 15.

43   *The British Crime Survey* (Home Office Research Study No.76, 1983), p. 9.

44   Ibid., p. 4.

45   Ibid., p. 54. The number of sexual assaults revealed in the second British Crime Survey was also extremely low. See *Taking Account of Crime: Key Findings in the 1984 British Crime Survey* (Home Office Research Study 85, 1985).

46   London Rape Crisis Centre, *Annual Report,* 1982, p. 37.

47   R. E. Hall, *Ask Any Woman: A London inquiry into rape and sexual assault* (Bristol, 1985).

48   Ibid., pp. 32—3.

49   Ibid., p. 106.

50   Ibid., pp. 108—13.

51   See Wilson, *The Other Side of Rape,* ch. 6; Lee Henry, 'Hospital care for victims of sexual assault' in Scutt, *Rape Law Reform,* p. 170.

52   Snare, 'Sexual violence against women', p. 66.

53   Hall, *Ask Any Woman,* p. 127.

54   Ibid., p. 108.

55   R. Wright, 'Rape and physical violence' in *Sex Offenders in the Criminal*

Justice System (Cropwood Conference Series No.12) (Cambridge, 1980), p. 101.

56   Chambers and Millar, *Investigating Sexual Assault,* p. 38.
57   Ibid., p. 43.
58   Ibid., p. 10.
59   Ibid.
60   R. Wright, 'A note on the attrition of rape cases', *British Journal of Criminology,* 24 (1984), p. 399.
61   Ibid., p. 400.
62   Young, *Rape Study,* p. 14.
63   *People* v. *Murphy* 145 Michigan Supreme Court Reports 524, 528, 108 North Western Reports 1009, 1011 (1906); *People* v. *Geddes,* 301 Michigan Supreme Court Reports 258, 261, 3 North Western Reports 2d 266, 267 (1942). See also K. A. Cobb and N. R. Schauer, 'Legislative note: Michigan's Criminal Sexual Assault Law', *University of Michigan Journal of Law Reform,* 8 (1974), p. 217.
64   Sexual Offences (Amendment) Act 1976, s. 1.
65   In eight states, the marital rape exemption has been abolished. In Minnesota, Pennsylvania and Colorado the corroboration warning is prohibited. A complete restructuring of the offence of rape has taken place in 25 states. Most states have firm restrictions on sexual history evidence. For further discussion, see C. Backhouse and L. Schoenroth, 'A comparative survey of Canadian and American rape law', *Canada-United States Law Journal,* 6 (1983), 48; D. Russell, *Rape in Marriage* (New York, 1982), App. II; Berger, 'Man's Trial', note 23; H. S. Feild and L. B. Bienen, *Jurors and Rape* (Lexington, Mass., 1980).
66   See below, 'Canada', p. 29.
67   See, e.g., The Crimes (Sexual Assault) Amendment Act 1981 (New South Wales); Law Reform Commission of Tasmania, *Report and Recommendations on Rape and Sexual Offences* (Report No.31, 1982).
68   See Michigan Act No.266 of 1974, Michigan Compiled Laws Annotated: ss.520a—k and s.5201. (Cumulative Supplement 1976—7).
69   At least 25 states in the United States, as well as Canada and New South Wales, Australia, have introduced a ladder of offences instead of rape. This is the hallmark of the Michigan legislation.
70   See An Act to Amend the Criminal Code in relation to Sexual Offences and Other Offences Against the Person, 1980—81—82—83 (Can.), c. 125.
71   This figure was quoted to Ian Blair by an official of the US Law Enforcement Assistance Administration, which is part of the Department of Justice: see Blair, *Investigating Rape,* p. 21.
72   See n. 71.
73   See Blair, *Investigating Rape,* pp. 21—2.

74 See on this J. C. Marsh, A. Geist and N. Caplan, *Rape and the Limits of Law Reform* (1982), ch. 2.

75 See n. 81 and accompanying text.

76 Marsh *et al., Rape and the Limits of Law Reform,* p. 18.

77 See also text at n. 15.

78 See n. 68, s. 520b—520e.

79 Ibid., s. 520i.

80 Ibid., s. 520j.

81 Ibid., s. 5201.

82 Marsh *et al., Rape and the Limits of Law Reform,* p. 27. Police attitudes to rape victims do not appear to have changed markedly either: see ibid., ch. 6. This may in part account for the lack of increase in reported offences. It has been suggested that fear of retaliation and a desire to forget about the rape are overriding concerns for many victims. See Dukes and Mattley, 'Predicting rape victim reportage', pp. 63—84.

83 Marsh *et al., Rape and the Limits of Law Reform,* pp. 28—37.

84 Ibid., pp. 67—73.

85 See on this Paul Rock, *A View from the Shadows: The Ministry of the Solicitor General of Canada and the Making of the Justice for Victims of Crime Initiative* (Oxford, forthcoming).

86 Ibid.

87 By the American writer Diana Russell: see n. 65.

88 Taken from the back cover of Clark and Lewis, *Rape.*

89 Rock, *View from the Shadows.*

90 Ibid.

91 Ibid.

92 Law Reform Commission of Canada, Working Paper No.22, *Sexual Offences* (1978).

93 Criminal Law Revision Committee, Working Paper on Sexual Offences (1980). See also, Criminal Law Revision Committee, Fifteenth Report, *Sexual Offences,* Cmnd 9213 (1984).

94 Compare the Criminal Law Revision Committee Fifteenth Report, paras. 2. 7 and 2.92.

95 Law Reform Commission of Canada, *Sexual Offences,* p. 16.

96 Clark and Lewis, *Rape,* pp. 166—7.

97 Law Reform Commission of Canada, *Sexual Offences,* p. 5.

98 Ibid., p. 14.

99 Ibid., p. 21.

100 See below 'Rape and the Criminal Law Revision Committee', p. xx.

101 Law Reform Commission of Canada, *Sexual Offences,* p. 17.

102 Under the Bill, s. 149 of the Canadian Criminal Code would have read as follows: (1) Every one who indecently assaults another person is guilty of an indictable offence and is liable to imprisonment for fourteen years. (2)

An accused who is charged with an offence under subsection (1) or section 149.1 may be convicted if the evidence establishes that the accused did anything to the other person with his or her consent that, but for such consent, would have been an indecent assault or an aggravated indecent assault, if such consent was obtained by personating the spouse of the other person or by false and fraudulent representations as to the nature and quality of the act, or was extorted by threats or fear of bodily harm.

149.1. Every one who indecently assaults another person is, where the indecent assault results in severe physical or psychological damage to that other person, guilty of an indictable offence and liable to imprisonment for life.

149.2. For the purposes of sections 149 and 149.1 and without restricting the generality of the term 'indecent assault', an indecent assault includes sexual penetration of any bodily orifice.

149.3. No prosecution shall be instituted under section 149 or 149.1 in respect of an offence alleged to have been committed by a person against his or her spouse unless the spouse were living separate and apart at the material time.'

103   See on this Rock, *View from the Shadows.*
104   Ibid.
105   Law Reform Commission of Canada, Report No. 10, *Sexual Offences.*
106   Ibid., p. 14.
107   Ibid., pp. 16—17.
108   Ibid., p. 2.
109   Rock, *View from the Shadows,* See also L. Snider, 'Legal reform and social control: the dangers of abolishing rape', *International Journal of the Sociology of Law* 13(1985), p. 337.
110   Rock, *View from the Shadows.*
111   Ibid.
112   Canadian Criminal Code, s. 246.1.
113   s. 246.2.
114   s. 246.3.
115   s. 246.8.
116   s. 246.6.
117   s. 246.7.
118   s. 246.6.
119   s. 246.4.
120   S. 244(3). But a defendant may presumably argue that although he used force, the complainant did not consent 'by reason of' it.
121   See above 'Michigan', p. xx.
122   For an exposition of subjectivist doctrine, see, e.g., G. Williams, *Textbook of Criminal Law,* 2nd ed. (London, 1983).

123 [1976] Appeal Cases 182.

124 J. Sellars, '*Mens rea* and the judicial approach to "bad excuses" in the criminal law', *Modern Law Review,* 41 (1978), pp. 245, 248.

125 H. C. Deb., vol. 892, col. 1416 (21 May 1975).

126 See, e.g., [1975] Criminal Law Review 718—20.

127 For a recent statement of this opinion, see M. Benn, A. Coote and T. Gill, *The Rape Controversy* (London, 1983).

128 [1976] Appeal Cases 182, 215.

129 Ibid., p. 221.

130 [1975] 1 All England Law Reports 8.

131 Recently, however there has been legal criticism of the case. See, e.g., T. Pickard, 'Culpable mistakes and rape: relating *mens rea* to the crime', *University of Toronto Law Journal,* 30 (1980), p. 75; J. Temkin, 'The limits of reckless rape', [1983] *Criminal Law Review,* p. 5.

132 *Report of the Advisory Group on the Law of Rape* (see n. 4 above), paras. 25—84.

133 s. 1. In the United States, a mistaken belief in consent is a defence only where it is based on reasonable grounds: see, e.g., *U.S.* v. *Short,* 4 Official Reports — United States Court of Military Appeals 437.

134 *Report of the Advisory Group on the Law of Rape,* paras. 85—142.

135 Ibid., p. 37.

136 Sexual Offences (Amendment) Act 1976, ss. 2 and 3. For full discussion of the Parliamentary debate, see J. Temkin, 'Regulating sexual history evidence — the limits of discretionary legislation', *International and Comparative Law Quarterly,* 33 (1984), 942. For research revealing that the Act has not been particularly successful in controlling the use of sexual history evidence, see Z. Adler, 'Rape — the intention of Parliament and the practice of the courts', *Modern Law Review,* 45(1982), p. 664.

137 Sexual Offences (Amendment) Act 1976, ss.4—6. The *Hutchinson* trial, widely reported in the press in September 1984, has been one amongst several cases exposing the weaknesses of the anonymity provisions. For Press Council criticism of media handling of the case, see *Guardian,* 15 November, 1984. In February 1986, the government announced its intention to abolish anonymity for defendants in rape trials. See *The Times* 17 February 1986.

138 CLRC, *Sexual Offences* (see n. 93).

139 See also *Women and Public Appointments: Report of an Investigation into Appointments to Public Bodies* (Equal Opportunities Commission, 1985) which draws attention to the small proportion of women appointed to public office in the United Kingdom. The Policy Advisory Committee on Sexual Offences, consisting mainly of non-lawyers, was appointed to advise the Criminal Law Revision Committee in its work. Eight out of fifteen of its members were female. See CLRC, *Sexual Offences,* App. A. Its advice was not always accepted.

140   CLRC, *Sexual Offences,* para. 2.47.
141   Ibid., para. 2.85.
142   Ibid., para. 2.29.
143   Ibid., paras 2.45, 2.55, 2.87 and 5.12.
144   Ibid., para. 2.87.
145   Ibid., para. 2.88. The Policy Advisory Committee also asked the Chairman
      of the Criminal Bar Association to ask members of the Bar about the
      operation of s.2. He also reported back that all was well. Adler conducted
      a rigorous empirical investigation into the operation of s.2. and reached
      the opposite conclusion: see Adler, 'Rape — the intention of Parliament'.
146   CLRC, *Sexual Offences,* para. 2.90.
147   The same may be said of Australia. See Scutt, *Rape Law Reform,* which
      contains the recommendations and draft Bill of the Women's Electoral
      Lobby, and the proceedings of the National Conference on Rape Law
      Reform held in Hobart in 1980. See also L. Sebba, 'The repeal of the
      requirement of corroboration in sex offences' *Israel Law Review,*
      18(1983), p. 135, in which the efforts of Nitza Shapira-Libai, the Prime
      Minister's Adviser on the Status of Women in Israel, to obtain the
      abolition of the corroboration requirement, are described. In Denmark, it
      is due to the efforts of Mrs Jytte Thorbek that rape victims are now
      legally represented in court and can generally expect to be awarded
      compensation by the court where the defendant is convicted. In Sweden,
      the proposals on rape made by a government-appointed committee in
      1976 were powerfully opposed by women's groups. Snare writes: 'For the
      first time in Swedish history 15 women's organisations representing the
      whole political spectrum managed to work out a joint resolution to
      demand an immediate repeal' of some of its recommendations. The report
      was abandoned as a result and a new committee on sexual offences,
      consisting mainly of women, was set up by the government: see Snare,
      'Sexual violence against women'.
148   For a recent exception, see Women's National Commission, *Violence
      Against Women — Report of an Ad Hoc Working Group* (1985).

4   RAPE, SEDUCTION AND PSYCHOANALYSIS

  1   Susan Brownmiller, *Against Our Will: Men, Women and Rape* (New
      York, 1976) p. 192. On the same page, Brownmiller writes: 'Freud
      himself, remarkable as this may seem, said nothing about rapists . . . His
      confederates were slightly more loquacious, but not by much . . . Even
      among the Freudian criminologists there was a curious reluctance to take

rape head on . . . no Freudian or psychoanalytic authority has ever written a major volume on rape. Articles on rape in psychology journals have been sparse to the point of nonexistence . . .'

2 For a similar discussion of the impact of psychoanalysis on rape trials, see Susan Edwards, *Female Sexuality and the Law* (Oxford, 1981), esp. pp. 100—8. Edwards pinpoints masochism and the rape fantasy as the two areas where psychoanalysis has had the greatest detrimental impact. She argues that a Lacanian psychoanalysis can 'save' rape from these consequences: 'A patriarchal language imposes itself on the individual who acquires a conscious and subconscious sexual identity and at the same time a language by which others are perceived' (p. 107).

3 Brownmiller, *Against Our Will*, p. 350.

4 Ibid., p. 251.

5 Ibid., p. 351.

6 Ibid., p. 346. Capitals in original.

7 David Abrahamsen, *The Psychology of Crime* (New York, 1960), p. 165, quoted in Brownmiller, *Against Our Will*, pp. 194—5. See also D. J. West, C. Roy and Florence L. Nichols, *Understanding Sexual Attacks: A Study Based Upon a Group of Rapists Undergoing Psychotherapy* (London, 1978), pp. 127—8 for a different perspective on Abrahamsen's argument.

8 Brownmiller, *Against Our Will*, p. 195.

9 Ibid., p. 192.

10 Ibid., p. 228.

11 For a defence similar to the one I will propose, see Juliet Mitchell, *Psychoanalysis and Feminism* (London, 1974), esp. p. 353 (*contra* Millett on the reality of rape), p. 342 on the 'common feminist anti-Freudian habit of amalgamating Freud with Helene Deutsch', and p. 354: 'Desire, phantasy, the laws of the unconscious or even unconsciousness are absent from the social realism of the feminist critiques'.

12 Brownmiller, *Against Our Will*, p. 350. 'Lust' is Brownmiller's translation of the German *Lust*, invariably translated in Freud's works as 'pleasure'.

13 Sigmund Freud, 'The economic problem of masochism' (1924c) in: *The Standard Edition of the Complete Psychological Works of Sigmund Freud* (hereafter abbreviated to SE, translated from the German under the general editorship of James Strachey, in collaboration with Anna Freud, assisted by Alix Strachey and Alan Tyson (London, 1953—74), SE XIX, pp. 162, 167.

14 Freud, *The Psychopathology of Everyday Life* (1901b), SE VI, p. 181, n. 1.

15 This feature is well-attested in the literature on rape, and is not regarded as being in need of explanation. Thus Menachem Amir, *Patterns in Forcible Rape* (Chicago, 1971), pp. 166—71, gives 51 per cent of rape

victims as having shown submissive behaviour. Many sources take the fact that rapists are often armed and threaten murder or serious injury as accounting for this response. It should be noted that other studies (e.g. West *et al., Understanding Sexual Attacks*) divide rapists into various categories, some of whom would self-confessedly have been dissuaded from continuing with the assault if they had encountered resistance, while others — the 'sadistic rapists' — would have regarded resistance as an opportunity to escalate the degree of violence already employed, so as to secure the pleasure in the victim's pain that is a part of their aim.

16   Freud, *The Interpretation of Dreams* (1900a), SE V, p. 620.

17   Freud, *Introductory Lectures on Psycho-analysis* (1916—17), SE XVI, p.433, translation modified.

18   Brownmiller, *Against Our Will,* p. 359. Original emphasis retained. Brownmiller follows Deutsch's discussion of rape fantasies, finding it an 'amazing' combination of perception and dogma. She does not, however, quote the following passage, which is commenting on triangular scenes in which the woman is forced by another woman to submit to a man, which is of interest in demonstrating how Deutsch's psychoanalytic method breaks rape fantasies down into other components which are less 'objectionable': 'The superficial elements of these fantasies are easy to grasp: the pain decreases the guilt feeling produced by the pleasure, the rape frees the girl from responsibility, the compulsion exerted by the woman, who represents the mother, is a counterweight to the latter's prohibitions . . . It is no doubt only by sanction of pain and by negation of the object's identity that these fantasies can come before consciousness.' To give a sense of the different focus of Deutsch's interest in these fantasies, we may quote the passage that follows: 'The rape and seduction fantasy, with its primitive sexual content directly relating to the body, is less dangerous than other masochistic fantasies, mostly unconscious, that do not work directly toward the gross sexual goal. If the rape fantasies were directly gratified they would lead to perversion, but this is extremely rare; it is known that the masochistic perversion is less frequently found in women than in men. Where it exists, its content is completely different from that of the rape fantasy: its essence is the wish to be beaten.' Even here, the fantasy is in the service not of direct gratification but is indulged in for the sake of the lover. Deutsch regards the more dangerous fantasies as being those of prostitution. See Helene Deutsch, *The Psychology of Women* (London, 1946), vol. 1, p. 202.

19   Glanville L. Williams, *Criminal Law. The General Part* (London, 1953), pp. 33ff. Quote from p. 33. The second edition of 1961 repeats this section with one slight addition.

20 Ibid., pp. 34—5. The final paragraph of his discussion reads: 'The field of the unconscious is irrelevant to responsibility where it pertains merely to motives, for even conscious motives are ruled out. To illustrate, a man may steal because of an early antagonism to his father, since repressed, which unconsciously leads him to do something of which his father would disapprove. The stealing is deliberate; it is only the motive that belongs to the unconscious. The analysis of neurotic motives is, of course, important in the realm of treatment.'

21 Glanville L. Williams, *Textbook of Criminal Law* (London, 1978) pp. 196—7. My emphasis.

22 Roger Smith, *Trial by Medicine, Insanity and Responsibility in Victorian Trials* (Edinburgh, 1981).

23 See p. 128 of Froma Zeitlin's contribution in this volume (chapter 7).

24 See Thomas W. McCahill, Linda C. Meyer, Arthur M. Fischman, *The Aftermath of Rape* (Lexington, Mass, 1979), p. 106.

25 The price of consent is a theme that emerges from the story of the rape of Lucretia and the many and various commentaries on it, excellently discussed and documented in Ian Donaldson, *The Rape of Lucretia: a Myth and its Transformation* (Oxford, 1983), p. 26.

26 McCahill *et al.*, *The Aftermath of Rape*, p. 104.

27 See Temkin's contribution in this volume (chapter 2) and her important paper, 'Towards a modern law of rape', *The Modern Law Review*, 45 (1982), pp. 399—419.

28 See Florence Rush, 'Freud and the sexual abuse of children', *Chrysalis*, 1 (1977), pp. 31—45, and her *The Best Kept Secret; Sexual Abuse of Children* (Englewood Cliffs, NJ, 1980).

29 Jeffrey M. Masson, *The Assault on Truth: Freud's Suppression of the Seduction Theory* (London, 1984).

30 Alexander Schusdek, 'Freud's seduction theory: a reconstruction', *Journal of the History of the Behavioral Sciences*, 2 (1966), pp. 159—66; Frank J. Sulloway, *Freud. Biologist of the Mind*, (London, 1979), pp. 110ff; and the biographies of Freud by Ernest Jones, Max Schur and Ronald W. Clark.

31 J. M. Masson (ed.), *The Correspondence between Sigmund Freud and Wilhelm Fliess* (Cambridge, Mass., 1985), letter of 30 May, 1893, p. 49, and letter of 2 November 1895, p. 149.

32 Ibid., letter of 3 January 1897, p. 219. See also letter of 11 January 1897, pp. 222—3.

33 Alice Miller, *For Your Own Good. Hidden Cruelty in Child-rearing and the Roots of Violence,* trans. Hildegarde and Hunter Hannum (London, 1983); and *Du Sollst Nicht Merken* (Frankfurt, 1981).

34 See *Abstracts of the scientific writings of Dr. Sigm. Freud (1877—1897),* SE III, p. 253.

35   'The aetiology of hysteria' (1896c), SE III pp. 200—1. This is the single occasion, noted on p. 58, on which Freud uses the term 'rape'.

36   Ibid., SE III p. 202.

37   Ibid.

38   Ibid., SE III, p. 213.

39   Ibid., SE III p. 204.

40   Ibid., SE III p. 207.

41   Ibid.

42   Ibid., SE III, p. 208.

43   Ibid.

44   Ibid., SE III, p. 214. Even here, the tone is one of disgust rather than indignation.

45   Ibid., SE III p. 215. It should be noted that a similar comment holds true of a considerable number of first-hand descriptions of sexual relationships between adults and children, a significant feature that is not discussed by commentators on these descriptions. See, for example, Ellen Bass and Louise Thornton (eds), *I Never Told Anyone. Writings by Women Survivors of Child Sexual Abuse* (New York, 1983).

46   Legally speaking, the child is neither able to consent nor withhold consent — which seems a satisfactory way of avoiding having to discuss the nature of the relationship between adult and child, in favour of the presumption that children have the absolute legal right to be protected from sexual contact with adults.

47   Consciousness is not the criterion, since convictions of rape may follow from rendering a woman unconscious with alcohol or having intercourse with her while she is asleep. Under such circumstances, the presumption of unconsciousness stands in for memory. See J. C. Smith and Brian Hogan, *Criminal Law*, 4th edn (London, 1978), pp. 406 and 409 (on administering drugs to obtain or facilitate intercourse).

48   McCahill *et al., The Aftermath of Rape*, p. 216. See also Susan Griffin, 'Pornography and silence' (1981), in *Made from this Earth. Selections from her Writing 1967—82* (London, 1982), pp. 110—60, p. 134n., and Carol Smart and Barry Smart, 'Accounting for rape. Reality and myth in press reporting', in Carol Smart and Barry Smart (eds), *Women, Sexuality and Social Control* (London, 1978), pp. 89—103, who offer an explanation for this doubt, shame and guilt (p. 93): 'In those cases where there is a lack of congruence between cultural expectations or understandings of rape and the rape itself, there may well follow a reticence on the part of the victim to define the assault as rape, doubts may intrude into the victim's understanding of her ordeal as to whether she unconsciously or unknowingly 'encouraged' or precipitated the assault. Thus the rape victim may begin to engage in a process of self-criticism and blame . . .' See also

Marcia J. Walker and Stanley L. Brodsky (eds.), *Sexual Assault. The Victim and the Rapist* (Lexington, Mass, 1976) and Carolyn J. Hursch, *The Trouble with Rape* (Chicago, 1977), pp. 96—7.

49 Freud, 'Observations on transference-love' (1915a), SE XII, p. 168.

50 Ibid., SE XII, p. 170.

51 Octave Mannoni, 'L'amour de transfert et le réel', *Etudes Freudiennes,* nos. 19—20, Mai 1982, pp. 7—13, esp. p. 13.

52 See Freud, *Introductory Lectures on Psycho-analysis* (1916—17), SE XVI, p. 443: 'It is out of the question for us to yield to the patient's demands deriving from the transference; it would be absurd for us to reject them in an unfriendly, still more in an indignant, manner'.

53 J. Breuer and S. Freud, *Studies on Hysteria* (1895d), SE II, pp. 301—2.

54 Ibid., SE II, pp. 302—3. This wish that the other 'take the initiative', noted by Deutsch as an important feature of rape fantasies (see n. 18 above), has the same paradoxical quality as masochism — a handing over of responsibility (and maybe even of pleasure) to the other. This feature of the erotic lives of women should not be underestimated — it certainly has not been by feminists, who urge women to independence and into taking responsibility for their sexual lives, while indicting male society for depriving women of the opportunity to do so. In a curious fashion, the theme emerges in the passage in Brownmiller's book in which she uses one of her own dreams to 'refute' the Freudian rape symbolism found in dreams: 'Freudian dream interpretation, in which a host of plausible, real-life situations [note the weight of a call upon the real here] are assigned sexual symbolism, can certainly add to one's insecurity. Years ago I once had a dream in which I walked up the stairs to my apartment and was about to open the door when a male figure emerged from the shadows and struck out at me with a hammer. Inundated with popular Freudian psychology, I was distressfully convinced that this dream had to represent a hopeless fear of men and sex — until my Adlerian analyst drew from me the information that I hadn't paid my rent that month and had gotten a dispossess notice from the landlord!' (Brownmiller, *Against Our Will*, p. 256). Noticing in passing the manner in which the 'real-life situation' presses in on this account, pushing aside any deeper or more internally orientated theme, it is curious that the dream-thought the landlord-interpretation expresses is the following: 'If you don't give it to them, then they will dispossess you of it!' It is exactly such a view that, when transposed to the domain of sexual relations, Brownmiller is attacking: the obligation to give, under duress if necessary, or under the weight of utterances of the sort, 'All women want to be raped'.

55 Freud, 'Observations on transference-love', SE XII, p. 165.

56 Freud, *Introductory Lectures,* SE XVI, p. 444. Cf. SE XVI, p. 446: 'in our

technique we have abandoned hypnosis only to rediscover suggestion in the shape of transference'. Or, SE XVI, p. 455: ' . . . we get hold of the whole of the libido [of the patient] which has been withdrawn from the dominance of the ego by attracting a portion of it on to ourselves by means of the transference'.

57 See SE XVI, p. 443: 'The hostile feelings [concerning the analyst] are as much an indication of an emotional tie as the affectionate ones, in the same way as defiance signifies dependence as much as obedience does, though with a 'minus' instead of a 'plus' sign before it'.

58 The 'first' transference-seduction is often taken to be that between Breuer and Anna O., in which Breuer took it 'for real' and ran away. Cf. the 'second' occasion, narrated in Freud, *An Autobiographical Study* (1925d), SE XX, p. 27: 'As [the patient] woke up [from hypnosis] on one occasion, she threw her arms round my neck . . . I was modest enough not to attribute the event to my own irresistible personal attraction, and I felt that I had now grasped the nature of the mysterious element that was at work behind hypnotism'. Note that this modesty determines Freud's position as being 'analytic'; under other circumstances, it might be another emotion (pride, fear) that would characterize it. For further discussion of this episode and the mythical history it inevitably gives rise to, see my 'Who is in analysis with whom? Freud, Lacan, Derrida', *Economy & Society*, 13 (1984), pp. 153–77, and 'The true story of Anna', *Social Issues* (1986), forthcoming.

59 The possibility of rape having a future is found in certain abduction stories, principally those of the rape of the Sabines and the rape of Lucretia, discussed in Norman Bryson's contribution to this volume (chapter 8); the future is in the gradual annulling of the extent of the violation of the property relations through the marriage of the Sabine women, and the having of children by their abductors. Here rape is an origin that gives rise to civil society, altogether different from the moment 'before', when rape was possible (or 'the rule'). On the other hand, the futureless character of rape renders it eminently suitable as the founding myth (or occasion) for blood feuds that never end (as in Sicilian society; see also the original myth of rape in the biographies of bandits such as Pancho Villa). Here rape is repeated endlessly, rather than 'sublimated' into prohibitions and the horror of violation.

60 For a profound discussion of the idiosyncratic dialectics of Freud's concepts, see Jacques Derrida, 'Speculer — sur "Freud"', in his *La Carte Postale* (Paris, 1980), pp. 275–438.

61 See Milan Kundera, *The Book of Laughter and Forgetting* (Harmondsworth, 1983), p. 210.

62 Jean Baudrillard, *De la Séduction* (Paris, 1979). See also two numbers of

the journal *Traverses* (nos. 17 and 18, 1979/80) devoted to Baudrillard's book and the general topic of seduction, in particular the articles by Monique Schneider, Conrad Stein, Vincent Descombes in no. 17; by Mario Perniola, Louis Marin, Alain Arnaud in no. 18.

63   A naturalistic conception of sexuality informs most if not all work in this area orientated around biological concepts, as in the contribution to this volume by Thornhill, Thornhill and Dizinno (chapter 6).

64   The locus classicus for the relation between love and seduction is Plato's *Symposium,* whose 'content' is love (various discourses, including Socrates's on the virtues of loving as opposed to being loved) and whose frame is seduction — the final scene, in which Alcibiades's story of the night he spent with Socrates is interpreted as a seductive manoeuvre designed to tear Agathon away from Socrates. See *Symposium,* 222c-e.

65   On this point, Baudrillard is following, while at the same time questioning, Michel Foucault, *A History of Sexuality,* vol. I (London, 1979). Baudrillard characterizes pornography as a fantasy of a real in which representation does not exist, i.e. a real without seduction. See *De la Séduction,* p. 45.

66   See Susan Edwards, *Female Sexuality,* pp. 144—8. Edwards assimilates rape and seduction as follows: ' . . . it is probable that many [of these breach of promise actions] were not simple cases of broken engagements after lengthy courtships but involved instances where marriage was promised to secure a submission to intercourse. This situation was not rape, but the carefully planned intimidation involved in the seduction does not fall far short. The distinctions depend on the complainant's submission and the defendant's intent' (p. 147). This idea, that seduction is tantamount to rape, is expressed in a number of works, especially those dealing with sexual harrassment. See, for example, Catherine A. Mackinnon, *Sexual Harrassment of Working Women* (New York, 1979). Note that in the early half of the twentieth century, many American states had seduction statutes, expressly designed to penalize cases in which intercourse was achieved by trickery or with promises of marriage.

67   Hubert S. Feild and Leigh B. Beinen, *Jurors and Rape* (Lexington, Mass., 1980), p. 339.

68   Ibid., p. 167.

69   Williams, *Textbook of Criminal Law,* p. 199.

70   Feild and Bienen, *Jurors and Rape,* p. 168.

71   West *et al., Understanding Sexual Attacks,* p. 136, quote Kinsey: 'the difference between a good time and a rape often largely depends upon whether the girl's parents happened to be awake when she returned home'. Kinsey seemingly thought that the reported 'no' depended on the wakefulness of the parents — or maybe even of the super-ego, as in

Glanville Williams' citing of shame as a motive for her believing she had said 'no' (see Williams, *Textbook of Criminal Law*, pp. 196–7). It should also be noted that the distinction between 'against the will' and 'without consent' hinges on the difference between the presence of 'no' and the absence of 'yes'. See Smith and Hogan, *Criminal Law*, pp. 403–4, 407.

72 Kierkegaard, 'Diary of the seducer', in *Either/Or*, vol. I, trans. David F. Swenson and L. M. Swenson (Princeton, 1959), pp. 297–440, esp. p. 337. On champagne, contrast Kierkegaard's description of the champagne aria in *Don Giovanni:* 'He is here, as it were, ideally intoxicated in himself. If every girl in the world surrounded him in this moment, he would not be a source of danger to them, for he is, as it were, too strong to wish to deceive them . . .' ('Immediate stages of the erotic', in *Either/Or*, p. 133).

73 Kierkegaard, 'Immediate stages', p. 100.

74 Forcibly argued by Jacques Lacan, *Le Séminaire Livre II. Le Moi dans la Théorie de Freud et la Technique de la Psychanalyse* (Paris: Seuil, 1978), pp. 260–4, forthcoming as *Seminar II. The Ego in Freud's Theory and in Psychoanalytic Technique*, translated by Sylvana Tomaselli, with notes by John Forrester (Cambridge, 1987).

75 Ross Harrison makes a similar point in his contribution to this volume (chapter 3), when he points out a special feature of rape trials, namely that the identification of the act at the same time entails that the defendant committed the act (in those trials where consent is the principal issue).

5 RAPE AND THE SILENCING OF THE FEMININE

1 This figure does not include statutory rape offences. Susan Brownmiller argues that a conservative estimate of the actual number of rapes is 410,000 (five times the reported figure). See discussion in Bradley A. Te Paske, *Rape and Ritual* (Toronto, 1982).

2 Rape statistics are notoriously unreliable. The relative absence of rape in West Sumatra as compared with the USA is supported by field observations during a period of six months of fieldwork from 1981 to 1984.

3 B. Malinowski, *The Sexual Life of Savages in North-western Melanesia* (London, 1929), p. xxiii.

4 Sherry B. Ortner and Harriet Whitehead (eds), 'Introduction', *Sexual Meanings* (New York, 1981), p. 6.

5 This and the following material is summarized from my article, 'The socio-cultural context of rape', *Journal of Social Issues*, 37 (1981), pp. 5–27.

6 The sociobiologist may argue that maternal nurturance and child-bearing

are biological features and I would agree. However, the point of my argument is that such features are *utilized* by humans as *models of and for behaviour*. For a more extended discussion of the relationship between biological realities and ontological perceptions, see Peggy R. Sanday, *Divine Hunger and Cannibal Monsters: Cannibalism as a Cultural System* (New York, 1986).

7   Susan Griffin, *Pornography and Silence* (New York, 1981), p. 66.
8   Ibid., pp. 42—4.
9   Ibid., p. 96.
10 Ibid., p. 97.
11 See Sanday, 'Socio-cultural context of rape', pp. 13—14. It is not clear from the ethnographies of the Mundurucu whether the myths of former female dominance are held by women or whether there are other tales that contest the prior dominance of women.
12 Leslee Nadelson, 'Pigs, women, and the men's house in Amozonia: an analysis of six Mundurucu myths', in Ortner and Whitehead, *Sexual Meanings*, p. 267.
13 A similar theme is found in Te Paske's Jungian analysis of rape (see n. 1) in which he claims that rape is the means by which the rapist kills the feminine in the other and thereby escapes from entrapment by the feminine in himself.
14 See Nadelson, 'Six Mundurucu myths', p. 270.
15 See Allen Dundes, 'A psychoanalytic study of the bullroarer', *Man* (NS), 11 (1976), pp. 220—38.
16 Ibid., p. 235.
17 Gilbert Herdt, 'Fetish and fantasy in Sambia initiation', in *Rituals of Manhood* (Berkeley, 1982), p. 78.
18 Ibid., p. 80.
19 Ibid., p. 81.
20 Ibid., p. 77.
21 Ibid., p. 89.
22 Ibid., p. 91.
23 Ortner and Whitehead, *Sexual Meanings*, p. 2.
24 Ibid., p. 4.
25 See Sherry B. Ortner, 'Gender and sexuality in hierarchical societies: the case of Polynesia and some comparative implications', Ortner and Whitehead, *Sexual Meanings*, pp. 359—410. See also 'Introduction', ibid., p. 22, and Bradd Shore 'Sexuality and gender in Samoa: conceptions and missed conceptions', ibid., p. 214.
26 Ortner, 'Gender and sexuality', p. 381.
27 Ibid., p. 383.
28 Ibid.
29 Ibid., p. 391.

30   Ibid.
31   Ibid., p. 375.
32   Ibid., p. 377.
33   For a discussion of the meaning of sexual equality and inequality, see Peggy R. Sanday, *Female Power and Male Dominance* (New York, 1981).
34   Formerly, according to the dictates of Islam, Minangkabau men were allowed to marry more than one woman. Presently, however, according to Indonesian law, a man must remain monogamous.
35   See J. J. Bachofen, *Myth, Religion and Mother Right* (Princeton, 1967), p. 81.
36   For a discussion of the codification of Minangkabau ethos and worldview in weaving, see Peggy R. Sanday and Suwati Kartiwa, 'Custom and cloth in West Sumatra', *Expedition*, 26 (1984), pp. 13—29.
37   Quoted by Donald Symons, *The Evolution of Human Sexuality* (New York, 1979), p. 282.
38   From a transcript from a masturbatory satiation session of a sadist presented by Gene G. Abel, Judith V. Becker and Linda J. Skinner at the Fourth National Conference on Sexual Aggression, Denver, Colorado, 1982.
39   In a report entitled 'Hidden rape on a university campus', submitted to the National Institute of Mental Health in 1981, Mary Koss reported that of a sample of 3,862 Kent State students 13 per cent of the female respondents had been raped by acquaintances while another 24 per cent had experienced attempted rape by acquaintances.
40   Quoted by Mark Bowden, 'The incident at Alpha Tau Omega', *The Philadelphia Inquirer Magazine*, 11 September, 1983, p. 21.
41   Nancy Tanner, *On Becoming Human* (Cambridge, 1981).

6   THE BIOLOGY OF RAPE

1   See W. M. Shields and L. M. Shields, 'Forcible rape: an evolutionary perspective', *Ethology and Sociobiology*, 4 (1983), pp. 115—36, and R. Thornhill and N. W. Thornhill, 'Human rape: an evolutionary analysis', *Ethology and Sociobiology*, 4 (1983), pp. 137—73.
2   Thornhill and Thornhill, 'Human rape'.
3   See R. D. Alexander, *Darwinism and Human Affairs* (Seatle, WA 1979), and R. Dawkins, *The Extended Phenotype*, (New York, 1982).
4   The method of recognition of adaptive traits has been fully treated; see both G. C. Williams, *Adaptation and Natural Selection* (Princeton, NJ, 1966) and E. Curio, 'Towards a methodology of teleonomy', *Experientia*, 29 (1973), pp. 1045—58.
5   Thornhill and Thornhill, 'Human rape'.

6   R. C. Lewontin, 'Adaptation', *Scientific American,* 293 (1978), pp. 156—69.
7   Alexander, *Darwinism,* provides a detailed discussion of this effect.
8   The following authors have all commented extensively on this matter: R. D. Alexander, 'The search for a general theory of behavior', *Behavioral Science,* 20 (1975), pp. 77—100; M. Daly and M. Wilson, *Sex, Evolution and Behavior,* 2nd edn. (Boston, MA, 1983); C. G. Hempel, *Philosophy of Natural Science* (Englewood Cliffs, NJ, 1966); T. S. Kuhn, *The Structure of Scientific Revolutions* (Chicago, 1962); P. B. Medawar, *The Art of the Soluble* (London, 1967); K. R. Popper, *The Logic of Scientific Discovery,* English edn (London, 1959).
9   For example, see G. G. Simpson, *This View of Life* (New York, 1964).
10 Application of the hypothetic-deductive model is fully elucidated in R. Thornhill, 'Scientific methodology in entomology', *Florida Entomologist,* 67, (1984), pp. 74—96.
11 S. J. Gould, 'Sociobiology, the art of storytelling', *New Scientist,* 80 (1978), pp. 530—3; and Lewontin, 'Adaptation'.
12 R. H. Peters, 'Tautology in evolution and ecology', *American Naturalist,* 110 (1976), pp. 1—12.
13 Popper, *Scientific Discovery.*
14 A discussion of this point can be found in Alexander, 'General theory of behaviour', and M. T. Ghiselin, *The Triumph of the Darwinian Method* (Berkeley, CA, 1969).
15 Popper, *Scientific Discovery.*
16 C. Darwin, *The Descent of Man and Selection in Relation to Sex,* 2nd edn. (New York, 1874), p. 606.
17 For discussion, see C. L. Harris, *Evolution: Genesis and Revelations* (Albany, NY, 1982).
18 For further discussion, see J. R. Platt, 'Strong inference', *Science,* 146 (1964), pp. 347—53.
19 Shields and Shields, 'Forcible rape'; Thornhill and Thornhill, 'Human rape'.
20 This research is described in detail in the following articles by R. Thornhill: 'Male and female sexual selection and the evolution of mating strategies in insects', in M. S. Blum and N. A. Blum (eds), *Sexual Selection and Reproductive Competition in Insects* (New York, 1979); 'Rape in *Panorpa* scorpionflies and a general rape hypothesis', *Animal Behavior,* 28 (1980), pp. 52—9; *'Panorpa* (Mecoptera: Panorpidae) scorpionflies: systems for understanding resource defense polygyny and alternative male reproductive efforts', *Annual Review of Ecology and Systematics,* 13 (1981), pp. 355—86; 'Alternative hypotheses for traits believed to have evolved by sperm competition', in R. L. Smith (ed.), *Sperm Competition and the Evolution of Animal Mating Systems* (New York, 1984).

21 See references in Shields and Shields, 'Forcible rape', and Thornhill and Thornhill, 'Human rape'; also see R. Thornhill and J. Alcock, *The Evolution of Insect Mating Systems* (Cambridge, Mass., 1983).

22 Thornhill and Alcock, ibid.

23 Alexander, *Darwinism,* and Daly and Wilson, *Sex, Evolution and Behavior,* provide a discussion and illustration of this point.

24 Alexander, *Darwinism*; G. Borgia, 'Human aggression as a biological adaptation', in J. S. Lockard (ed.), *The Evolution of Human Social Behavior* (New York, 1980); Daly and Wilson, *Sex, Evolution and Behavior*; and G. P. Murdock, *Ethnographic Atlas* (Pittsburgh, PA, 1967).

25 N. A. Chagnon, 'Is reproductive success equal in egalitarian societies?', in N. A. Chagnon and W. G. Irons (eds), *Evolutionary Biology and Human Social Behavior: An Anthropological Perspective* (North Scituate, Mass., 1979); also see W. G. Irons, 'Cultural and biological success', in the same volume.

26 This has been suggested by Alexander, 'General theory of behavior'; Chagnon and Irons, *Evolutionary Biology*; Daly and Wilson, *Sex, Evolution and Behavior*; M. Dickemann, 'Female infanticide, reproductive strategies, and social stratification', and B. S. Low, 'Sexual selection and human ornamentation', both in Chagnon and Irons (eds), *Evolutionary Biology.*

27 Mating system theory has been developed and extended by Thornhill and Alcock, *Insect Mating Systems*; G. Borgia, 'Sexual selection and the evolution of mating systems', in Blum and Blum, *Sexual Selection*; J. W. Bradbury and S. L. Vehrencamp, 'Social organization and foraging in emballonurid bats. III. Mating systems', *Behavioral Ecology and Sociobiology,* 2 (1977), pp. 1—17; S. T. Emlen and L. W. Oring, 'Ecology, sexual selection, and the evolution of mating systems', *Science,* 197 (1977), pp. 215—23; and R. L. Trivers, 'Parental investment and sexual selection', in B. Campbell (ed.), *Sexual Selection and the Descent of Man* (Chicago, 1972).

28 See especially Chagnon, 'Reproductive success', and Irons, 'Cultural and biological success'.

29 For discussion see Thornhill and Thornhill, 'Human rape'.

30 For examples see C. Lumsden and E. O. Wilson, *Genes, Mind and Culture: The Coevolutionary Process* (Cambridge, Mass., 1981).

31 W. Cade, 'Alternative male reproductive behaviors', *Florida Entomologist,* 63 (1980), pp. 30—42; R. Dawkins, 'Good strategy or evolutionarily stable strategy', in G. W. Barlow and J. Silverberg, *Sociobiology: Beyond Nature/Nurture?* (Boulder, Co, 1980).

32 For detailed discussion see M. J. West-Eberhard, 'Sexual selection, social

competition and evolution', *Proceedings of the Philosophical Society of America*, 123 (1979), pp. 222—34.

33 J. D. Weinrich, 'Human sociobiology: pairbonding and resource predictability (effects of social class and race)', *Behavioral Ecology and Sociobiology*, 2 (1977), pp. 91—118.

34 In addition to Alexander's *Darwinism*, see also his paper 'The evolution of social behavior', *Annual Review of Ecology and Systematics*, 5 (1974), pp. 325—83; also, Chagnon and Irons, *Evolutionary Biology;* N. Burley and R. Symanski, 'Women without: an evolutionary and cross-cultural perspective on prostitution', in R. Symanski (ed.), *The Immoral Landscape: Female Prostitution in Western Societies* (London, 1981); Dickemann, 'Female infanticide'; M. Dickemann, 'The ecology of mating systems in hypergynous dowry societies', *Biology and Social Life*, 18 (1979), pp. 163—95; M. Dickemann, 'Paternal confidence and dowry competition: a biocultural analysis of Purdah', in R. Alexander and D. Tinkle (eds), *Natural Selection and Social Behavior* (New York, 1981); J. Hartung, 'On natural selection and the inheritance of wealth', *Current Anthropology*, 82 (1980), pp. 799—820.

35 Alexander, 'Evolution of social behavior' and *Darwinism*; M. A. Flinn, 'Uterine vs. agnatic kinship variability and associated cousin marriage preferences; an evolutionary biological analysis', in Alexander and Tinkle, *Natural Selection*; J. Hartung, 'On natural selection'; W. G. Irons, 'Investment and primary social dyads', in Chagnon and Irons, *Evolutionary Biology*; and J. A. Kurland, 'Paternity, mother's brother and human sociality', in Chagnon and Irons, ibid.

36 Thornhill and Thornhill have argued for this possibility: see 'Human rape'.

37 For detailed discussion of evolutionary perspectives on perception and decision-making in humans, see Alexander, *Darwinism*; Lumsden and Wilson, *Genes, Mind and Culture*; D. Symons, *The Evolution of Human Sexuality* (Oxford, 1979).

38 Symons, *Human Sexuality*; Thornhill and Alcock, *Insect Mating Systems*; Trivers, 'Parental investment'; and M. Willson and N. A. Burley, *Female Choice in Plants* (Princeton, NJ, 1983).

39 A discussion of the ways in which sexual conflict may occur in an evolutionary perspective can be found by reviewing G. A. Parker, 'Sexual selection and sexual conflict', in Blum and Blum, *Sexual Selection*; Symons, *Human Sexuality*; Trivers, 'Parental investment'; and S. B. Hrdy, *The Woman that Never Evolved* (Cambridge, Mass., 1981).

40 R. D. Alexander and G. Borgia, 'On the origin and the basis of the male — female phenomenon', in Blum and Blum, *Sexual Selection*; R. Thornhill, 'Cryptic female choice and its implications in the scorpionfly, *Harpobittacus*

nigriceps', *American Naturalist*, 122 (1983), pp. 265—88.

41 Alexander, *Darwinism*; G. Borgia, 'Human aggression as a biological adaptation', in Lockard, *Human Social Behavior.*

42 This has been pointed out by R. D. Alexander, in 'The changing scene in the natural sciences, 1776—1976', *National Academy of Sciences Special Publication*, 12 (1977), pp. 283—337, and in *Darwinism*; as well as by Flinn, 'Kinship variability'; also S. J. C. Gaulin and A. Schlegal, 'Paternal confidence and paternal investment: a cross cultural test of a sociobiological hypothesis', *Ethology and Sociobiology*, 1 (1980), pp. 301—9; also relevant is J. A. Kurland, 'Paternity'; and P. L. van den Berghe, *Human Family Systems* (New York, 1979).

43 See also Shields and Shields, 'Forcible rape'.

44 Thornhill and Thornhill, 'Human rape'.

45 See R. T. Rada (ed.), *Clinical Aspects of the Rapist* (London, 1978) for a review.

46 The leading spokesperson appears to be Susan Brownmiller, as outlined in *Against Our Will: Men, Women, and Rape* (New York, 1975).

47 See Thornhill and Thornhill, 'Human rape', for a test of this.

48 But see L. Ellis and C. Beattie, 'The feminist explanation for rape: an empirical test', *Journal of Sex Research*, 19 (1983), pp. 74—93.

49 Thornhill and Thornhill, 'Human rape'.

50 Ibid.

51 Ibid.

52 Ibid., present data and a detailed discussion of this prediction.

53 As outlined by Williams, *Adaptation and Natural Selection*, and Symons, *Human Sexuality.*

54 Thornhill and Thornhill, 'Human rape'.

55 Thornhill and Thornhill, 'Human rape'; M. Amir, *Patterns in Forcible Rape* (Chicago, 1971) and references therein.

56 Thornhill and Thornhill, 'Human rape'.

57 Ibid.

58 Ibid.

59 N. W. Thornhill, G. Dizinno and R. Thornhill, paper presented at the Annual Meeting of the Animal Behavior Society, Cheney Washington, August 1984.

60 Ibid.

61 Thornhill and Thornhill, 'Human rape'.

62 Ibid.

63 N. W. Thornhill, R. Thornhill and G. Dizinno, paper presented at the Annual Meeting of the American Anthropological Association, Denver, Colorado, November 1984.

64 Sarah B. Hrdy, personal communication.

65 See Thornhill and Thornhill, 'Human rape'.
66 Ibid.
67 Thornhill, Thornhill and Dizinno, see n. 63.
68 Thornhill and Thornhill, 'Human rape'.
69 Ibid; R. Thornhill and N. W. Thornhill, 'Human rape; the strengths of the evolutionary perspective', in C. Crawford, M. F. Smith and D. L. Krebs (eds), *Sociobiology and Psychology: Ideas, Issues and Applications* (New York, 1986).
70 Thornhill and Thornhill, 'Human rape'.
71 See Thornhill and Thornhill, 'Human rape', for an initial evolutionary analysis of rape law and taboos.
72 Also see Shields and Shields, 'Forcible rape'.

7   CONFIGURATIONS OF RAPE IN GREEK MYTH

1   Barbara Herrnstein Smith, 'Contingencies of value', *Critical Inquiry,* 10 (1983), quoting Gadamer, p. 29.
2   William B. Tyrrell, *Amazons: A Study in Athenian Mythmaking* (Baltimore, 1984), p. 5.
3   Ibid., p. 5. For brief introductions to the questions of myth and myth interpretation with special reference to Greek myth, see Jean-Pierre Vernant, 'The Reason of Myth', in Jean-Pierre Vernant, *Myth and Society in Ancient Greece* (Brighton, Sussex, 1980), pp. 186–242, trans. Janet Lloyd from the French, *Mythe et Société en Grèce Ancienne* (Paris, 1974), and Walter Burkert, 'The organization of myth', in *Structure and History in Greek Mythology and Ritual* (Berkeley, Ca, 1979), pp. 1–34.
4   The dossier has been studied in depth by Sophia Kaempf-Dimitriadou, *Die Liebe der Götter in der attischen Kunst der 5 Jahrhunderts v. Chr* (Berne, 1979).
5   Sheila McNally, 'The maenad in early Greek art', *Arethusa,* 11 (1978), pp. 101–35, 126, now in *Women in the Ancient World: the Arethusa Papers*, John Peradotto and J. P. Sullivan (eds) (Albany, NY, 1984), p. 132.
6   H. Sichtermann, 'Zeus and Ganymed in frühklassischer Zeit', *Antike Kunst,* 12 (1959), pp. 23–4.
7   For the various hypotheses see Kaempf-Dimitriadou, *Die Liebe der Götter,* 5, pp. 43–7. See also the discussion of Karl Schefold, *Die Göttersage in der Klassischen und Hellenistischen Kunst* (Munich, 1981), p. 329. Both subscribe to humanistic interpretations of the data.
8   See McNally, 'The maenad'.
9   See the brilliant pioneering study of Otto Brendel, 'The scope and

temperament of erotic art in the Greco-Roman world', in T. Bowie *et al.*, (ed.) *Studies in Erotic Art* (New York and London, 1970), pp. 3—107.

10 On this development, which remains unexplained, see the remarks (and statistics) of T. B. L. Webster, *Potter and Patron in Classical Athens* (London, 1972), pp. 226—43.

11 On the general trends of the second half of the fifth century that prefigure the rise of the fourth and its particular interest in Eros and Aphrodite, see Henri Metzger, *Les Représentations dans la Céramique Attique du IVe Siècle* (Paris, 1951), pp. 13—38.

12 For my understanding of Greek iconography, I am indebted above all to François Lissarrague of the Centre de Recherches Comparées sur les Sociétés Anciennes in Paris, who generously shared with me his encyclopaedic knowledge of Greek vase painting.

13 The standard descriptive work on the iconography of the Amazons is Dietrich von Bothmer, *Amazons in Greek Art* (Oxford, 1957). See also John Boardman, 'Herakles, Theseus, and Amazons', in Donna Kurtz and Brian Sparkes (eds), *The Eye of Greece: Studies in the Art of Athens* (Cambridge, 1982), pp. 1—28. For the centaurs, see Birgitt Schiffler, *Die Typologie des Kentauren in der Antike Kunst* (Frankfurt, 1976).

14 On the myth of Ixion, see especially Marcel Detienne, *The Gardens of Adonis* (Brighton, Sussex, 1977), pp. 83—7, trans. Janet Lloyd from *Les Jardins d'Adonis* (Paris, 1972).

15 On the structuralist values of the centaurs as allied with nature over culture, see G. S. Kirk, *Myth: its Meanings and Functions in Ancient and Other Cultures* (Berkeley, Ca, 1970), pp. 52—62, and the further development in Page DuBois, *Centaurs and Amazons* (Ann Arbor, Mich., 1982), pp. 25—77. Another important myth for the sixth and fifth centuries concerned the centaur Nessus, who attempted to rape Heracles's bride, Deianeira.

16 For the dossier on Cainis/Caineus, see especially Marie Delcourt, *Hermaphroditus: Myths and Rites of the Bisexual Figure in Antiquity* (London, 1961), pp. 33—6, trans. Jennifer Nicholson from the French, *Hermaphroditus* (Paris, 1956). 'Whatever the real etymology of the name Caineus (= Kaineus), the Greeks saw in it at one and the same time *kainis,* the sword; *kaino,* to kill; *kainumai,* to excel; *kainos,* new', p. 36. The motif of centaurs stoning Caineus is prominent in the iconography of vase paintings.

17 See DuBois, *Centaurs and Amazons,* pp. 63—71, for analysis of the pertinent iconography of the Parthenon (and of the temple at Bassae).

18 The names of the Amazons associated with Heracles and Theseus vary from one version to another.

19 On the structures and values of Amazon myths, see Jeannie Carlier-Detienne, 'Les Amazones font la guerre et l'amour', *L'Ethnographie*

(1980—1), pp. 11—33; DuBois, *Centaurs and Amazons*, pp. 25—77, and now the synthesis and expansion of Tyrrell, *Amazons.*

20 What follows is based on my longer piece, 'Eros and politics in the *Suppliants* of Aeschylus' *(forthcoming).*

21 Jean-Pierre Vernant, 'Tensions and ambiguities in Greek tragedy', in J. -P. Vernant and P. Vidal-Naquet, *Tragedy and Myth in Ancient Greece* (Brighton, Sussex, 1981), p. 32, trans. Janet Lloyd from *Mythe et Tragédie en Grèce Ancienne* (Paris, 1972).

22 See Claude Calame, *Les Choeurs de Jeunes Filles en Grèce Archaïque* (Rome, 1977), vol. 1, p. 330. Calame's remarkable study is required reading on the entire subject of feminine rites of passage.

23 There are several variants, as one might expect, for the myth of this curious young man. The most interesting of these makes Hymenaeus a beautiful Argive or Athenian youth, who saved Athenian maidens from Pelasgian pirates, and brought them back safely for marriage in their native land. The terms are reversed but not contradictory. In the first, Hymenaeus is himself abducted (or disappears) at the moment of the wedding; in this version, he restores those who have been abducted and brings them to their marriage rites. Hymenaeus in his two roles therefore personifies the two disparate aspects of the matromonial event: physical act, social institution.

24 This is a black-figured white ground lekythos: Berlin 72032. The names Zeus and Ganymede are inscribed on the vase.

25 Claude Calame, 'Eros inventore e organizzatore della società greca antica', in C. Calame (ed.), *L'Amore in Grecia* (Rome, 1983), p. xxxi. His is an excellent overview of Greek attitudes towards eros and contains valuable bibliography. In addition to Calame's work, I have profited especially from Philippe Borgeaud, *Recherches sur le Dieu Pan* (Geneva, 1979); Laurence Kahn, *Hermès Passe ou les Ambiguïtés de la Communication* (Paris, 1978); Marcel Detienne (in addition to *The Gardens of Adonis),* 'The perfumed panther' in *Dionysos Slain* (Baltimore, 1977), pp. 20—52, trans. M. and L. Muellner from *Dionysos Mis à Mort* (Paris, 1977). Interesting material and observations may be found in E. Pellizer, *Favole d'Identità, Favole di Paura: Storie di caccia e altri racconti della Grecia antica* (Rome, 1982) and in Gundel Koch-Harnack, *Knabenliebe und Tiergeschenke* (Berlin, 1983), pp. 200—8.

26 On male—female antagonism in Greek mythology, see Philip Slater, *The Glory of Hera* (Boston, 1968), whose conclusions, however, should be treated with great caution.

27 I examine this play in depth in 'The power of Aphrodite: eros and the boundaries of the self', in Peter Burian (ed.), *Directions in Euripidean Criticism* (Durham, NC, 1985), pp. 52—111, 189—208.

28 K. J. Dover, *Greek Homosexuality* (Cambridge, Mass., 1978), p. 88.

29 Ibid.
30 Walter Burkert, *Structure and History in Greek Mythology and Ritual* (Berkeley, Ca, 1979), p. 7, and on the ritual relations between sexuality and aggression, especially around maiden sacrifice, see his *Homo Necans: the Anthropology of Ancient Greek Sacrificial Ritual and Myth* (Berkeley, Ca, 1983), trans. Peter Bing from the German *Homo Necans* (Berlin, 1972). See especially his insistence on the biological nature of aggression, pp. 59—71.

8 TWO NARRATIVES OF RAPE IN THE VISUAL ARTS: LUCRETIA AND THE SABINE WOMEN

1 For general bibliography of rape, see D. L. Barnes, *Rape: A Bibliography 1965—1970* (New York, 1977) and H. Schwendinger, 'A review of the rape literature', *Crime and Social Justice*, VI (1976).
2 On the work by Margaret Harrison, see E. Lucie-Smith, *Art in the Seventies* (Oxford, 1980), pp. 92—3.
3 On Poussin's paintings of the Sabine Women, see P. du Colombier, 'Notes sur Nicolas Poussin: L'enlèvement des Sabines et Luca Cambiaso', *Gazette des Beaux-Arts* (1964), I, pp. 81ff; A. Blunt, *The Paintings of Nicolas Poussin* (London, 1966), pp. 128—9; W. Friedländer, *Nicolas Poussin* (London, 1970), pp. 142—5; W. Friedländer and A. Blunt, *The Drawings of Nicolas Poussin* (London, 1974), vol. II, pp. 9—10.
4 Plutarch, *Life of Romulus*, 19. For the story of the Sabine Women, see also Livy, *History of Rome*, I, 9—13; Dionysius of Halicarnassus, *Roman Antiquities*, II, 30.
5 Plutarch, *Life of Romulus*, 14.
6 Ibid., 19.
7 On the position of women in Roman family law, see J. P. V. D. Balsdon, *Roman Women; their History and Habit* (London, 1962); S. Pomeroy, 'Selected Bibliography on Women in Antiquity', *Arethusa*, VI (Spring 1973), pp. 125—57; S. Pomeroy, 'A Classical Scholar's Perspective on Matriarchy', in B. Carroll (ed.), *Liberating Women's History* (Urbana, 1975).
8 See S. Pomeroy, *Goddesses, Whores, Wives, and Slaves: Women in Classical Antiquity* (London, 1975), p. 160.
9 S. Pomeroy, *Goddesses*, pp. 152—5, 215.
10 See W. Friedländer, *Nicolas Poussin*, pp. 31, 144.
11 John Berger, *Permanent Red: Essays in Seeing* (London, 1960), pp. 168—73.
12 Reynolds, *Discourses*, ed. R. Wark (San Marino, Calif., 1959), p. 256.
13 Augustine, *City of God*, ed. D. Knowles (Harmondsworth, 1972), pp. 66—7.

14 On David's *Intervention of the Sabines*, see A. Brookner, *Jacques-Louis David* (London, 1980), pp. 84—95.

15 Livy, *History of Rome*, I, 58; Dio Cassius, *Roman History*, VII, 11; Dionysius of Halicarnassus, *Roman Antiquities*, II, 56—7, 60—1.

16 Dio Cassius, *Roman History*, VII, 11.

17 'Though raped, she was technically an adulteress; therefore she made the honourable decision to commit suicide.' S. Pomeroy, *Goddesses*, p. 161.

18 See I. Donaldson's brilliant *The Rapes of Lucretia: a Myth and its Transformation* (Oxford, 1982).

19 On Richardson's *Clarissa*, see in particular T. Eagleton, *The Rape of Clarissa* (Oxford, 1982).

20 On rococo and the representation of women, see N. Bryson, *Word and Image* (Cambridge, 1981), pp. 91—100.

21 On Beaufort, see A. Brookner, *Jacques-Louis David*, pp. 77—9.

22 Augustine, *City of God*, p. 30.

23 Tertullian, *Writings on Marriage and Remarriage* (London, 1905), p. 95.

24 Tertullian, *Writings* (Edinburgh, 1870), vol. III, p. 20.

25 Augustine, *City of God*, p. 26.

26 See J. Martineau and C. Hope (eds), *The Genius of Venice 1500—1600* (London, 1983), pp. 229—30.

27 See G. Ruggiero, 'Sexual Criminality in the Early Renaissance: Venice 1338—1358', *Journal of Social History* VIII (Summer 1975), 18—37.

28 Ibid., p. 29.

29 Ibid., pp. 30—1.

30 M. Foucault, *The History of Sexuality*, Vol. 2: *An Introduction*, trans R. Hurley (London, 1979), p. 39.

9 THE HOUSE THAT JACK BUILT

1 For interesting studies of the 1970s and 1980s 'splatter movies', 'video nasties' and 'stalk and slash', see Kim Newman, *Nightmare Movies* (London, 1984), esp. pp. 95—141; Martin Barker (ed.), *The Video Nasties* (London, 1984); and John McCarty, *Splatter Movies* (New York, 1981), esp. pp. 134—43.

2 For interesting studies of the 1970s and 1980s variations on the theme, known as 'splatter movies', 'video nasties' and 'stalk and slash', see Kim Newman, *Nightmare Movies* (London, 1984), esp. pp. 95—141; Martin Barker (ed.), *The Video Nasties* (London, 1984); and John McCarty, *Splatter Movies* (New York, 1981), esp. pp. 134—43.

3 For general background to expressionism in the fine arts — early *and* late — see Norbert Lynton, *The Story of Modern Art* (Oxford, 1982), esp. pp. 25—54. Characteristically, the *sex and character* approach to the

question of rape seems to have predominated in theory and in artistic practice.

4 Rudolf Kurtz, *Expressionism and Film* (Berlin, 1926), p. 123. For the iconography of 'Caligarism', see S. S. Prawer, *Caligari's Children* (Oxford, 1980), esp. pp. 164—200.

5 Frank Wedekind, *Pandora's Box,* trans. Stephen Spender (London, 1977), pp. 172—5. In the original production, the part of 'Jack' was played by Wedekind himself, and the part of Lulu (his victim) by Wedekind's wife.

6 Maurice Heine, *Regards sur l'enfer anthropoclasique* (sic), in *Minotaure* (issue number 8, Paris, 15 June 1936). Heine's play, which occupies five double-column pages, pp. 41—5, includes two post-mortem photographs of Jack the Ripper's victims reprinted from Prof. A Lacassagne, *Vacher l'Eventreur et les crimes sadiques* (Lyons, 1899); the author's other contributions to *Minotaure* (as occasional member of the editorial committee, with André Breton and Marcel Duchamp) included a study of 'le roman noir' in issue number 5, especially the work of Horace Walpole, the Marquis de Sade and Monk Lewis, and a study of Lautréamont's *Maldoror* in issue number 12. For general background to *Minotaure*, see Dawn Ades, *Dada and Surrealism Reviewed* (London, 1978), pp. 279—93. Heine may have been reminded of the story of Jack the Ripper by a production of the melodrama *Jack L'Eventreur* (written by André de Lorde and Pierre Chaine) at the Grand-Guignol, which opened on 30 September 1934. Act II of this 'boulevard nasty' set near 'le quartier d'Holborn Square' ends with the murderer disembowelling one of his victims on the stage while screaming, 'Ah! du sang . . . du sang!'

7 This account of the Whitechapel murders has been pieced together from (a) a cross-section of contemporary sources: *The Times* (September 1888 — January 1889); *Daily Telegraph* (September 1888 — January 1889); *Pall Mall Gazette: an evening newspaper and review* (September 1888 — January 1889); *The Star* (September 1888 — January 1889); *Illustrated Police News Law Courts and Weekly Record* (August 1888 — January 1889); *Penny Illustrated Paper and Illustrated Times* (September 1888 — January 1889); *The Lancet* (September 1888 — January 1889); *British Medical Journal* (October 1888 — December 1888); *Punch* (August 1888 — January 1889); and *Fun* (August 1888 — January 1889); and (b) the major secondary sources (in order of appearance): Leonard Matters, *The Mystery of Jack the Ripper* (London, 1929), which opts for an insane 'Dr Stanley' as the culprit; William Stewart, *Jack the Ripper: a new theory* (London, 1939), which opts for an insane woman (probably a midwife) as the culprit; Donald McCormick, *The Identity of Jack the Ripper* (London, 1959), which opts for Alexander Pedachenko, a Czarist doctor *and* secret agent; Robin Odell, *Jack the Ripper in Fact and Fiction* (London, 1965), which opts for an insane schochet, or Jewish slaughterman; Tom Cullen,

Autumn of Terror: Jack the Ripper, his crimes and times (London, 1965), the most scholarly of the secondary sources, which, however, cannot resist opting for Montague Druitt, the cricketing barrister, as the culprit; Michael Harrison, *Clarence* (London, 1972), which opts for the Duke of Clarence and Avondale, KG; Daniel Farson, *Jack the Ripper* (London, 1972), which opts for Montague Druitt, with new 'evidence'; Donald Rumbelow, *The Complete Jack the Ripper* (London, 1975), which sensibly concludes 'I have always had the feeling that on the Day of Judgement, when all things shall be known, when I and other generations of Ripperologists ask for Jack the Ripper to step forward and call out his true name, then we shall turn and look with blank astonishment at one another . . . and say "who?" '; Elwyn Jones and John Lloyd, *The Ripper File* (London, 1975), which opts for Sir William Gull, the Royal Physician, aided by John Netley, a coachman, as the culprits, and suggests that the murders were decreed by 'the 'highest in the land'; Richard Whittington—Egan, *A Casebook on Jack the Ripper* (London, 1975), which sifts through all the available evidence, and comes up with a new suspect, Roslyn D'Onston, an insane occultist who was, however, sane enough to be author of *The Patristic Gospels* (London, 1904); Stephen Knight, *Jack the Ripper — the final solution* (London, 1976), which develops the Gull/Netley thesis and adds the painter Walter Sickert as a *third* culprit; William Vincent, *The Whitechapel Murders* (in *Police Review,* London, weekly from 16 December 1977 to 14 April 1978), which aims to 'inspire some officers of today to delve into the mystery — come on, have a go'; and Frank Spiering, *Prince Jack* (New York, 1978), which re-asserts the 'Clarence' solution. There have been many other (non-book) contributions to the debate, some of which are catalogued in Alexander Kelly, *Jack the Ripper: a bibliography and review of the literature* (London, 1973). The 'Ripper' industry (at least as it concerns the events of autumn 1888) seems to have ground to a halt, in British publications, since the late 1970s, perhaps because of contemporary events in Yorkshire: however, the popular press was not slow in drawing the parallel, and at least four books followed, not to mention an illustrated Sutcliffe souvenir brochure.

8   Most of the printed 'solutions' to this hundred-year-old whodunnit have been turned into films — a clear indication of their strong *resonance* in contemporary popular culture. The 'insane doctor' thesis has appeared, not only in the five major versions of *Dr Jekyll and Mr Hyde* (of which Rouben Mamoulian's of 1932 is still the most impressive), but also in the British film of *Jack the Ripper* (Robert S. Baker, 1958). The 'Jill the Ripper' thesis has appeared in *Dr Jekyll and Sister Hyde* (Roy Ward Baker, 1971), and *Hands of the Ripper* (Peter Sasdy, 1971). The 'decadent aristocratic' thesis has appeared in *A Study in Terror* (James Hill, 1966,

based on Ellery Queen's story which pits Sherlock Holmes against Jack the Ripper, and names 'the Duke of Shires'); and *Murder by Decree* (Bob Clark, 1979, which implicates, but does not name, Gull, Netley and Clarence). Variations on these themes have, of course, appeared in countless 'splatter movies' which ostensibly have nothing to do with the Whitechapel murders: in these, the insane psychiatrist seems to be a favourite contender. An interesting link between the two traditions was made in *Time After Time* (Nicholas Meyer, 1980), which had an 'insane doctor' from Victorian London splattering his way around contemporary Los Angeles, to which he had travelled in H. G. Wells' time machine. All the main 'solutions' have found their way into popular fiction (usually short stories) as well: two representative collections are Allan Barnard (ed.), *The Harlot Killer* (New York, 1953) and Michel Parry (ed.), *Jack the Knife* (Herts, 1975). The most famous short story inspired by Jack the Ripper — Marie Belloc Lowndes' *The Lodger* (1911, later turned into a novel) — has been the source of two classic films, the first directed by Alfred Hitchcock (1926), the second by John Brahm (1944), and two others (1932, 1953). Robert Bloch, the American author of *Psycho* (1960), has written so many versions of the Jack the Ripper story that he has managed to incorporate most of the main 'solutions' at one time or another: his stories include *Yours Truly, Jack the Ripper* (1943, set in contemporary Chicago); *Psycho* (1960); the *Star Trek* episode *Wolf in the Fold* (first screened 22 December 1967, published 1974, concerning an inter-galactic non-corporeal Ripper which feeds on frightened women, and lives in the foggy sector of assorted planets); *A Most Unusual Murder* (1976, concerning the perils of researching the subject); and the novel *Night of the Ripper* (New York, 1984, which manages to include among the cast of characters *all* the recent 'suspects'). In Britain, Richard Gordon added to the 'Ripper industry' of the 1970s with *The Private Life of Jack the Ripper* (London, 1980), a 'medical mystery novel' which names 'Dr Bertram Randolph' as the culprit, and reprints, with professional comment, a lot of nasty material from *The Lancet* of 1888. It is significant that although details of the character of 'the Ripper' may vary from story to story and from film to film, in this bizarre sub-genre, the characters of the *victims* remain much the same as the stereotypical 'five little whores' presented in the popular press of autumn 1888. It is as if the murderer will be interesting to readers, while the victims will not. Perhaps the best comment on this 'Ripper industry' is contained in Marcel Carné's film *Drôle de Drame* (1937): the film treats 'Victorian Limehouse' as the excuse for much surreal satire and the Ripper (Jean-Louis Barrault) is in fact a vegetarian and animal liberationist who kills only meat butchers . . .

9   My account of the 'image' of the East End in the late 1880s owes a great

deal to three works by Peter Keating: *The Working Classes in Victorian Fiction* (New York, 1971), esp. pp. 93—124, 167—198 and 223—45; *Working Class Stories of the 1890s* (London, 1971), and *Into Unknown England, 1866—1913* (London, 1976). Also to Gareth Stedman-Jones, *Outcast London* (Harmondsworth, 1984), esp. pp. 99—151, and 215—314; and Kellow Chesney, *The Victorian Underworld* Harmondsworth, Middlesex, 1974).

10 William Vincent's *The Whitechapel Murders* (in *Police Review,* 16 December 1977 to 14 April 1978) is particularly useful on the attitude of the various branches of the police to the crimes and to the newspapers' coverage of them.

11 Extracts from 'suggestions' in the Home Office files are printed in the books by Donald Rumbelow and Stephen Knight, cited above. One of the more bizarre suggestions in the files is that the Ripper was undoubtedly a renegade cowboy from Buffalo Bill's Wild West.

12 For a more detailed historical study of the tradition in popular culture from which this theme emerged, see my *Vampyre — Lord Ruthven to Count Dracula* (London, 1978), esp. pp. 14—82.

13 E. W. Hornung, *Raffles the Amateur Cracksman* (Nelson Library edition, London, 1909), pp. 34—5 of 'A Costume Piece', and pp. 54—5 of 'Gentlemen and Players'.

14 On 'French naturalism and English working-class fiction', see Keating, *The Working Classes in Victorian Fiction,* pp. 125—38.

15 The fashion, and the phrase, were launched by Steven Marcus, *The Other Victorians: a study of sexuality and pornography in mid-nineteenth century England* (London, 1966), a book which has proved to be of some use in more recent studies of sexual ideology and social structure, but which has too *undifferentiated* an approach to 'Victorian culture' and 'sexual mores'.

16 Graham Greene, *The Return of A. J. Raffles* (London, 1975). For some other examples, see n. 8.

17 On 18 June 1978, *The Sunday Times* reported Sickert's admission under the headline *Jack the Ripper 'solution' was a hoax, man confesses:* Joseph Sickert added 'as an artist I found it easy to paint Jack the Ripper into the story'. Six years later, in 1984, Stephen Knight's *Jack the Ripper — the final solution* was reprinted by the Treasure Press, London, virtually uncorrected. Clearly, this story was *so* good that a little matter of factual inaccuracy could not be allowed to stand in its way. It *had* to be true.

18 Robert Louis Stevenson, *The Strange Case of Dr Jekyll and Mr Hyde,* Corgi edn (London, 1964), pp. 51—2 of 'Henry Jekyll's full statement of the case'.

19 This myth, which is recounted in several of the books listed at n. 6, may have started life in a citation from the *British Journal of Photography* (17

February, 1888), which refers to a story about a French assassin, as recounted by an American journalist. Certainly, the *Journal* makes no mention of such folklore in its coverage of Autumn 1888.

20 For some key sources, see n. 8. Also Gareth Stedman Jones, *Languages of Class: studies in English working class history 1832—1982* (Cambridge, 1983), pp. 204—35, especially useful on the music halls of the period; and Judith R. Walkowitz, *Prostitution and Victorian Society* (Cambridge, 1982), which, although it deals predominantly with the 1860s, provides an important frame of reference.

21 For a very welcome if all too brief analysis of the coverage of the Whitechapel murders from a feminist perspective, see Judith Walkowitz, 'Jack the Ripper and the Myth of Male Violence', *Feminist Studies*, 8 (1982), pp. 543—74. Although Judith Walkowitz and I have been researching independently for several years — and from somewhat difference sources — our conclusions are congruent.

22 Parts 1—5 are in the John Johnson collection of ephemera, at the Bodleian Library. Parts 6—10 do not seem to have survived.

23 For a study of a parallel phenomenon, see Geoffrey Pearson, *Hooligan: A History of Respectable Fears* (London, 1983), and Pearson's 'Falling Standards: a short, sharp history of moral decline', in Martin Baker, *The Video Nasties* (London, 1984), pp. 88—103. The parallels between the recent debate about 'video nasties' in Britain and the moral panic of autumn 1888, allowing for changes in the social structure, are striking, and extremely depressing. Only the elegance of expression appears to have changed.

24 Cited in Prawer, *Caligari's Children*, p. 106.

25 A conversation overheard in the Nell of Old Drury from Anthony Shaffer's script for the film *Frenzy* (Alfred Hitchcock, 1972).

10 RAPE — DOES IT HAVE A HISTORICAL MEANING?

1 N. Bashar, 'Rape in England between 1550 and 1700', in *The Sexual Dynamics of History* (London, 1983), pp. 28—46.

2 Note the absence of rape from discussions in important works such as V. L. Bullough, *Sex, Society and History* (New York, 1976), and J. Weeks, *Sex, Politics and Society* (London, 1981). For history of rape see D. L. Barnes, *Rape: A Bibliography 1965—1975* (New York, 1977); P. Tabori, *The Social History of Rape* (London, 1971); for discussions of women's history see O. Hufton, 'Women in history. 1. Early modern Europe', *Past and Present*, 101 (1983), pp. 125—41; and J. W. Scott, 'Women in history. 2. The modern period', *ibid.*, pp. 141—57.

3   It has been argued that in London today, perhaps only eight per cent of rapes and attempted rapes are even reported to the police, though in a recent survey one in six women claimed to have been the victim of rape or attempted rape. R. Hall, *Ask Any Woman* (London, 1985).

4   For demolition of this myth see, e.g. J. R. and H. Schwendinger, *Rape and Inequality* (Beverly Hills, Ca, 1983).

5   A graphic historical example of trivialization is offered in Richard Steele's *Tatler* (22 October 1709), where Steele's discussion of a trial for rape dissolves into a condemnation of women for getting hysterical over it, arguing that ' it would be much more expedient that the fair were wholly absent [from the court] . . . It is unnecessary pain which the fair ones give themselves on these occasions. I have known a young woman shriek out at some parts of the evidence; and have frequently observed, that when the proof grew particular and strong, there has been such a universal flutter of fans, that one would thing the whole female audience were falling into fits.' For rape conscripted into the pornographic imagination see ' A Ramble in St James' Park', a piece of doggerel by the Earl of Rochester, discussed in A. Goreau, 'Last night's rambles: Restoration literature and the war between the sexes', in A. Bold (ed.), *The Sexual Dimension in Literature* (London, 1983), pp. 49—69, esp. p. 51; for the parallel later genre of 'railway rape' erotic literature, see P. Webb, 'Victorian erotica', in *ibid.,* pp. 90—121.

6   Susan Brownmiller, *Against Our Will: Men, Women and Rape* (New York, 1975). As Heidi Hartmann and E. Ross rightly stress, Brownmiller made 'a major breakthrough in women's history by uncovering the existence of rape as an important element in world history, one which historians have ignored or trivialized': 'Comment on "On Writing the History of Rape"', *Signs*, 3 (1978), pp. 931—5. The feminism of the 1960s hardly mentioned rape.

7   The *Oxford English Dictionary* states the primary meaning and earliest references to 'rape' are in context (as etymology suggests) of seizure rather than ravishment.

8   See J. M. Carter, 'Rape in medieval English society, 1208—1321' (PhD thesis, University of Illinois, 1983); J. B. Post, 'Ravishment of women and the Statutes of Westminster', in J. H. Baker (ed.), *Legal Records and the Historian* (London, 1978), pp. 150—60; J. Thompson, 'Rape: violating the other man's property', *Broadsheet: New Zealand Feminist Magazine,* 33 (1975). As Bashar has emphasized, 'The language of medieval rape statutes defined rape and abduction interchangeably. Both involve the theft of a woman': N. Basher, 'Rape in England between 1550 and 1700', in *The Sexual Dynamics of History* (London, 1983), pp. 28—46, esp. p. 30. See also C. Ruggiero, *The Boundaries of Eros. Sex and Sexuality in*

Renaissance Venice (Oxford, 1985); J. K. Campbell, *Honour, Family and Patronage* (Oxford, 1974), pp. 173, 200—2, 269—71.

9   There is a good discussion of how confused rape law remained in A. Simpson, 'Masculinity and control: the prosecution of sex offences in eighteenth century London' (PhD thesis, New York University, 1984), p. 115ff. See also R. Barber, 'Rape as a capital offence in 19th century Queensland', *Australian Journal of Politics*, 21 (1975), pp. 31—41; Bashar, 'Rape in England', p. 41.

10 See Bashar, 'Rape in England', and Russell Scott, *The Body as Property* (New York, 1981).

11 E. Crittall (ed.), *The Justicing Notebook of William Hunt 1744—1749* (Devizes, 1982), p. 41. Note here that the J. P. offers an informal adjudication; the case did not come to a trial.

12 Brownmiller, *Against Our Will,* heading to chapter 1.

13 For 'rape within marriage', see Jennifer Temkin's chapter in this volume (chapter 2).

14 Brownmiller, *Against Our Will,* p. 15.

15 Ibid., p. 14. For rape as a technique of social control, S. Riger and M. T. Gordon, 'The fear of rape: a study in social control', *The Journal of Social Issues,* 37 (1981), pp. 71—92.

16 The Boston Strangler won a cult following in the United States whereas the Cambridge Rapist in England did not. Rape was not one of the Yorkshire Ripper's typical crimes. For an earlier cult see A. Kelly and C. Wilson, *Jack the Ripper* (London, 1973).

17 Susan Griffin, 'Rape: the all-American crime', *Ramparts,* 10 (1971), pp. 26—35. See also her *Rape: The Power of Consciousness* (New York, 1978), and A. G. Johnson, 'On the prevalence of rape in the United States', *Signs,* 6 (1980), pp. 136—46, who argues that an urban American female today runs a one in three chance of suffering a rape attempt during her life. Illuminating here on the rise of sex crime is C. Wilson, *A Criminal History of Mankind* (London, 1984), pp. 495ff.

18 E. Shorter, 'On writing the history of rape', *Signs,* 3 (1977), pp. 471—82. For a critique, see Hartmann and Ross, 'Comment'.

19 The myth of medieval times as characterized by rape and pillage lives on. See G. Rattray Taylor, *Sex in History* (London, 1953), p. 19: 'Rape and incest characterize the sexual life of the English in the first millenium of our era; homosexuality and hysteria the years that followed.'

20 Shorter endorses the feminist view that rape *is* political in present day America; his claim, however, is that this is a unique situation, partly brought about by a male backlash to feminism.

21 As well as her chapter in this volume (chapter 5), see Peggy Reeves Sanday, 'The socio-cultural context of rape: A cross-cultural study', *The*

Journal of Social Issues, 37 (1981), pp. 5—27; compare G. Rubin, 'The traffic in women: notes on the "Political economy of sex" ', in R. R. Reiter (ed.), *Toward an Anthropology of Women* (New York, 1975).

22 There is lively, if eccentric, discussion in G. Greer, *Sex and Destiny* (London, 1984).

23 M. Foucault, *The History of Sexuality,* vol. 1. *Introduction* (Harmondsworth, 1978).

24 See N. El Saadawi, *The Hidden Faces of Eve: Women in the Arab World* (London, 1980).

25 This view finds some support in B. S. Lindemann, 'To ravish and carnally know: rape in eighteenth century Massachusetts', *Signs,* 10 (1984), pp. 63—82.

26 E. A. Wrigley and R. S. Schofield, *The Population History of England 1541—1871* (London, 1981); P. Laslett *et al., Bastardy and Its Comparative History* (London, 1980).

27 See, for instance, Simpson, 'Masculinity and control'; J. S. Cockburn, 'The nature and incidence of crime in England 1550—1625: a preliminary survey', in J. S. Cockburn (ed.), *Crime in England 1550—1800* (London, 1977); G. Quaife, *Wanton Wenches and Wayward Wives* (London, 1979); K. Sharpe, *Crime in Seventeenth Century England* (Cambridge, 1983); J. S. Cockburn, *Calendar of Assize Records, Essex, Hertfordshire, Kent, Surrey, Sussex: Elizabeth and James I* (London, 1976); A. Macfarlane *The Justice and the Mare's Ale* (Oxford, 1981), pp. 186ff. Macfarlane contends that the common view that pre-industrial English society was lawless, and that civilization and progress have brought law and order, is mythical.

28 Bashar, 'Rape in England'. She concludes: 'either rapes were not reported, or, though reported, some cases did not get to court'. Possible confirmations are provided by the female patients treated for psychiatric disorder by the early seventeenth century doctor Richard Napier. Some one per cent of them complained of trauma following attempted rape. See M. MacDonald, *Mystical Bedlam* (Cambridge, 1981), p. 240.

29 Serious historical study of 'seduction' is needed. Folk sources and popular culture (e.g. ballads) are full of songs of seduction, with its dire consequences for women, but contain very few accounts of rapes. See also Quaife, *Wanton Wenches,* pp. 75f.

30 Simpson, 'Masculinity and control' admirably explains why few reported rapes reached the courts.

31 Griffin, 'Rape'.

32 Fiction too is revealing. In *Pride and Prejudice,* Mrs Bennet is unwilling to have Elizabeth tramp alone across the fields to the next village not because of rape fears but lest her shoes get muddied.

33 K. Balderston (ed.), *Thraleana,* 2 vols (Oxford, 1942), ii, p. 911.

34 Though some women made false rape allegations for blackmail purposes: Simpson, 'Masculinity and control'.

35 Sharpe, *Crime in Seventeenth Century England.* One reason for this may have been the ingrained belief that rape could not lead to pregnancy (i.e. the woman had to take pleasure in sex, and come to orgasm, in order for her to conceive). See Quaife, *Wanton Wenches,* p. 172, and A. Maclaren, *Reproductive Rituals* (London, 1984).

36 For the social context of witchcraft, see Christina Larner, *Enemies of God: the witch-hunt in Scotland* (Oxford, 1981). See also G. Geis, 'Lord Hale, witches and rape', *British Journal of Law and Society,* 5 (1978), pp. 26—44.

37 Shorter, 'On writing the history of rape', p. 475. Some measure of male power over women is given by the grass-roots practice of wife sale. See S. P. Menefee, *Wives for Sale* (Oxford, 1981).

38 See, for example, N. Z. Davis, 'Women on top. Symbolic sexual inversion and political disorder in early modern Europe', in B. A. Babcock (ed.), *The Reversible World* (London, 1978), pp. 147—90; S. C. Rogers, 'Female forms of power and the myth of male dominance: a model of female, male interaction in peasant society', *American Ethnologist,* 2 (1975), pp. 727—56.

39 I. Illich, *Gender* (London, 1983), pp. 32—3.

40 Brownmiller notes how European intellectuals such as Marx have had so little to say about the social functions of rape. This may be because, from a European point of view, its social functions have been negligible.

41 For a sample of stereotypes see M. A. C. Horowitz, 'Aristotle and woman'. *Journal of the History of Biology,* 9 (1976), pp. 183—213, M. Daly, *Gyn/Ecology: The Metaethics of Radical Feminism* (Boston, 1978); I. Donaldson, *The Rape of Lucretia: A Myth and Its Transformation* (Oxford, 1983); S. Marcus, *The Other Victorians* (London, 1971); A. Dworkin, *Pornography: Men Possessing Women* (London, 1981); B. Ehrenreich and D. English, *For Her Own Good* (London, 1979); S. Griffin *Pornography and Silence* (London, 1981).

42 See, for instance, C. Merchant, *The Death of Nature* (Los Angeles, 1982); B. Easlea, *Science and Sexual Oppression. Patriarchy's Confrontation with Woman and Nature* (London, 1981); A. Kolodny, *The Lay of the Land* (Chapel Hill, 1975); G. V. Jacks and R. O. Whyte, *The Rape of the Earth* (London, 1944).

43 Anna K. Clark, 'Rape or seduction? A controversy over sexual violence in the nineteenth century', in *The Sexual Dynamics of History* (London, 1983), pp. 13—27. There is also a full account of this case in Sir J. Hall (ed.), *The Trial of Abraham Thornton* (London, 1926).

44 Clark, 'Rape or seduction?' p. 16.

45 I am very grateful to Dr Dorothy Watkins who has tracked down and assembled the material on the Ashford case and has suggested stimulating interpretations.

46 Clark, 'Rape or seduction?' p. 16.

47 Ibid., p. 13.

48 Ibid., p. 16.

49 Ibid., p. 13.

50 Ibid., p. 19.

51 Ibid., p. 16.

52 Ibid., p. 14.

53 Ibid., p. 16. This view represented contemporary forensic medicine. See for example G. E. Male [sic], *Epitome of Forensic Medicine* (Philadelphia, 1819), p. 229.

54 Recent research has shown that juries were unwilling to convict on capital offences where there was a suspicion of innocence.

55 Clark, 'Rape or seduction?', p. 13.

56 For the judge's summing up, see *The Trial of Abraham Thornton for the Murder of Mary Ashford* (Birmingham, [1867]), p. 32.

57 For intensely detailed discussion of the evidence and alibis see *Full Report of the Trial of Abraham Thornton for the Wilful Murder of Mary Ashford* (Birmingham, ? 1817); E. Holroyd, *Observation upon the Case of Abraham Thornton who was tried at Warwick August 8, 1817, for the Murder of Mary Ashford: Shewing the Danger of Pressing Presumptive Evidence too Far* (London, 1817); [An Attorney at Law], *An Investigation of the Case of Abraham Thornton . . . Being an Answer to a Work upon the Same Subject entitled 'Wager of Battle', Thornton and Mary Ashford, or an Antidote to Prejudice* (London, 1818); John Cooper (ed.), *A Report of the Proceedings against Abraham Thornton* (Warwick, 1818).

58 Was Thornton guilty? By extraordinary good fortune, private testimony — not available at the trial — settles the question of his guilt. Several months after Thornton's trial, Omar Hall, a fellow prisoner who had been in the same cell as Thornton while he had been awaiting trial in Warwick jail, wrote down a 'confession' which records conversations with Thornton. As Hall put it, 'he confessed to have committed the Rape', but denied murdering Ashford. According to Hall, Thornton's story was that after sexual intercourse, Ashford fell into a faint; Thornton tried to revive her with cold water, failed to, concluded she had passed out and died, and tossed her into the pit, leaving her bundle of clothes at the water's edge, to make it appear she had done away with herself. There is no reason why Hall should misrepresent Thornton's conversation with him, though whether Thornton told the truth is another matter. None of this information was public at the time of the trial. These documents are in the Birmingham Reference Library, and I am very grateful to the Head Archivist for

making them available to me. They do not appear to be known to Clark.

59 Quoted in Clark, 'Rape or seduction?', p. 23.

60 See n. 56.

61 *The Murdered Maid, or The Clock Struck Four. A Drama in Three Acts* (Warwick, 1818), 20. The Preface stated: 'This Drama is founded on a Murder which was committed in W . . . . . . .e, in the Spring of 1817, — a crime which excited one universal felling of horror and indignation. Great was the regret of all, that a person, who there was so much reason to believe the perpetrator of this dreadful act, was suffered to escape condign punishment.'

62 Clark, 'Rape or seduction?' p. 21. Clark goes on to stress how popular ballads also show how 'rape could be used as a means of controlling women's behaviour'.

63 As Clark rightly puts it (p. 26), 'Women's resistence to violence in the early nineteenth century was limited to such individual incidents. Although sexual violence was widely publicized, patriarchal assumptions shaped any organized protests against sexual victimization.'

64 The Reverend Luke Booker, *A Moral Review of the Case and Conduct of Mary Ashford* (London, 1818), p.3.

65 Clark, 'Rape or seduction?', p. 13.

66 Ibid., p. 21.

67 Booker himself recognized this dilemma, since he was chivalrous enough to vindicate Mary Ashford's virtue and modesty, yet could hardly ignore the fact that she had behaved in a singularly immodest manner, spending the night with a stranger. Booker's solution was that Ashford's 'imprudent behaviour' was proof not of immodesty but of innocence: *Case and Conduct of Mary Ashford*, p. 19.

68 Clark herself notes the independence and free sexual behaviour of lower class women at the time: 'Rape or seduction?', p. 15. Further contemporary commentary is provided by Jane Austen, who in *Northanger Abbey* presents the young woman anxious about abduction as a figure of fun, and in *Sanditon* shows the would-be Lovelace or Don Juan figure as a joke.

69 Griffin, 'Rape', p. 329.

70 Nowadays rapists are typically ostracized and abused (rather than heroized) in jail. S. Levine, *Why Men Rape* (London, 1982).

71 London Feminist History Group, *The Sexual Dynamics of History* (London, 1983).

72 S. Firestone, *The Dialectic of Sex* (London, 1971), p. 15.

73 See the admirable discussion in J. B. Elshtain, *Public Man, Private Woman* (Oxford, 1981), 219ff.

74 S. R. Peterson, 'Coercion and rape: the state as a male protection racket', in Mary Vetterling-Braggin, Frederick A. Elliston and Jane English (eds),

Feminism and Philosophy (London, 1977), pp. 360—76; S. Schechter, Women and Male Violence (London, 1984).
75 Brownmiller, *Against Our Will,* p. 15.
76 Ibid., p. 16.
77 For the implications of sociobiology for feminist interpretations see S. B. Hrdy, *The Woman that Never Evolved* (Cambridge, Mass., 1981).
78 Fairburn is quoted in B. Toner, *The Facts of Rape* (London, 1982), p. 8; Elshtain, *Public Man,* p. 208; for men as the new demons, see M. Daly, *Pure Lust* (London, 1984).
79 Sanday, 'Socio-cultural context of rape'; *Female Power and Male Dominance* (Cambridge, 1981); 'The social context of rape', *New Society* (30 September 1982), pp. 540—2; see also chapter 5 in this volume.
80 It is important to expose the ideological uses of 'biologism' as the belief that nature is supreme over nurture. But it would be silly to pretend that culturism is any less ideological.
81 S. de Beauvoir, *The Second Sex* (London, 1953); S. Rowbotham, *Hidden from History* (London, 1973).
82 E. Figes, *Patriarchal Attitudes* (London, 1970); A. Rich, 'Compulsory heterosexuality and lesbian existence', in A. Snotiw, C. Stansell and S. Thompson (eds), *Desire* (London, 1984), pp. 212—41, esp. pp. 218—19.
83 G. Schochet, *Patriarchalism and Political Thought* (New York, 1975); Elshtain, *Public Man.*
84 B. Ehrenreich and D. English, *For Her Own Good* (London, 1979); J. Mitchell, *Psychoanalysis and Feminism* (Harmondsworth, 1979).
85 Illich, *Gender*; K. Thomas, 'The double standard', *Journal of the History of Ideas,* 20 (1959), pp. 195—216; E. C. Whitmont, *The Return of the Goddess* (London, 1983).
86 See M. Warner, *Alone of All Her Sex. The myth and the cult of the Virgin Mary* (London, 1970).
87 Daly, *Gyn/Ecology.*
88 W. McNeill, *A World History* (London, 1971).
89 B. Easlea, *Science and Sexual Oppression* (London, 1982); *Fathering the Unthinkable* (London, 1983); R. Folkenflik (ed.), *The English Hero 1660—1800* (Delaware, 1983).
90 For the trivialization of rape in pornography see R. Thompson, *Unfit for Modest Ears* (London, 1981); a good instance in high art is Pope's *The Rape of the Lock,* for which see E. Pollak, 'Rereading *The Rape of the Lock:* Pope and the paradox of female power', *Studies in Eighteenth Century Culture,* 10 (1981), pp. 429—44.
91 I. Kramnick, *The Rage of Edmund Burke* (New York, 1977), pp. 138—9.
92 A. Kolodny, 'The land as woman: literary convention and latent

psychological content', *Woman's Studies*, 1 (1973), pp. 167—82; see also *The Lay of the Land.*

93 C. Merchant, *The Death of Nature* (San Francisco, 1981); Easlea, *Science and Sexual Oppression*; E. Goffman, *Gender Advertisements* (London, 1979).

94 Daly, *Gyn/Ecology*, p. 69; R. S. Albin, 'Psychological studies of rape', *Signs* 3 (1977), pp. 423—35. See also John Forrester's chapter in this volume (chapter 4).

95 Tabori, *Social History of Rape.* Rape fantasies pervade much of Western culture, including its religion (the Virgin Mary has been termed the 'ultimate rape victim'). In one of his Holy Sonnets, John Donne seeks to be raped by God: 'Except you entrall me, never shall be free; Nor ever chast, except you ravish me.'

96 Daly, *Gyn/Ecology*, p. 260; J. Raymond, 'Medicine as patriarchal religion', *Journal of Medicine and Philosophy*, 7 (1982), pp. 197—216.

97 See J. Donnison, *Midwives and Medical Men* (London, 1977); S. Edwards, *Female Sexuality and the Law* (Oxford, 1981); for instance of male doctors sexually assaulting their patients, see J. M. Adair, *Essays on Fashionable Diseases* (London, 1790), p. 257; R. Hall, *Marie Stopes* (London, 1977), p. 260.

98 G. Rattray Taylor, *The Angel Makers* (London, 1958); Simpson, 'Masculinity and control'.

99 B. A. Te Paske, *Rape and Ritual* (Toronto, 1982); K. M. Rogers, *The Troublesome Helpmate. A History of Misogyny in Literature* (Seattle, 1966). The Black Panther leader Stokely Carmichael notoriously claimed that the only place for women in his outfit was 'prone'. Quoted in E. Phillips (ed.), *The Left and the Erotic* (London, 1983), p. 15.

100 M. Daly, *Beyond God the Father* (Boston, 1973).

101 E. Shorter, *The History of Women's Bodies* (London, 1983).

102 S. Brownmiller, *Femininity* (London, 1984); R. T. Lakoff and R. L. Scherr, *Face Value. The Politics of Beauty* (London, 1984).

103 P. Foa, 'What's wrong with rape?', in Vetterling-Braggin *et al.*, *Feminism and Philosophy*, pp. 347—59, esp. p. 347.

104 A. Dworkin, *Right-Wing Women* (London, 1983), p. 60. The denunciation of all male-initiated sex as rape is a nice inverted echo of the male-chauvinist assumption that 'all women want it'.

105 Sharpe, *Crime in Seventeenth Century England*, pp. 63f; Simpson, 'Masculinity and control'; G. M. Masson, *Freud: The Assault on Truth* (London, 1984).

106 For the cotton mill see J. Lambertz, 'Sexual harrassment in the nineteenth century English cotton industry,' *History Workshop Journal*, 19 (1985), pp. 29—61; N. Z. Davis, *Society and Culture in Early Modern Europe*

(London, 1975); M. Springer (ed.), *What Manner of Woman* (New York, 1977).

107   Thompson, *Unfit for Modest Ears*; V. De Sola Pinto (ed.), *The Common Muse* (London, 1957); J. Holloway and J. Black (eds), *Later English Broadside Ballads* (London, 1975).

108   S. Levine and J. Koening (eds), *Why Men Rape* (London, 1982).

109   M. Amir, *Patterns in Forcible Rape* (Chicago, 1971); J. Rossiaud, 'Prostitution, youth and society in the towns of Southeastern France in the fifteenth century', in R. Forster and O. Ranum (eds), *Deviants and the Abandoned in French Society* (Baltimore, 1978), pp. 1—46.

110   Toner, *Facts of Rape,* pp. 104—5.

111   F. Musgrove, *Youth and the Social Order* (London, 1964).

112   See Simpson, 'Masculinity and control'; *The Whole Duty of Man* (London, 1716), p. 110.

113   S. Griffin, 'Rape', p. 332.

114   Dworkin, *Right-Wing Women,* p. 61.

115   Daly, *Gyn/Ecology,* p. 216.

Further Reading

Amir, M. *Patterns in Forcible Rape* (Chicago, 1971).

Barnes, Dorothy L. *Rape: Bibliography 1965—1975* (The Whitson Publishing Company, New York, 1977).

Bashar, Nazife. 'Rape in England between 1550 and 1700', in *The Sexual Dynamics of History* (London, 1983).

Brownmiller, Susan. *Against Our Will: Men, Women and Rape* (New York, 1975, later editions 1976, 1981).

Clark, Lorene and Lewis Debra. *Rape: The Price of Coercive Sexuality* (Toronto, 1977).

Courtivron, Isabelle de. (trans.) 'Rape is an abuse of power', from *Le Quotidien des Femmes*, 3 May 1975, in Elaine Marks and Isabelle de Courtivron (eds), *New French Feminisms: an Anthology* (Amherst, 1980; Brighton, 1981).

Daly, Mary. *Gyn/Ecology: The Metaethics of Radical Feminism* (Boston, 1978, London, 1979).

Donaldson, Ian. *The Rape of Lucretia: a Myth and Its Transformation* (Oxford, 1983).

Dworkin, Andrea. *Pornography: Men Possessing Women* (London, 1981).

Eagleton, Terry. *The Rape of Clarissa* (Oxford, 1982).

Edwards, Allison. *Rape, Racism, and the White Women's Movement: an answer to Susan Brownmiller* (Chicago, 1976).

Frieze, Irene Hanson. 'Causes and consequences of marital rape', *Signs* 8 (1983), pp. 532—3.

Griffin, Susan. 'Rape: the all-American crime', *Ramparts*, 3 (1971), pp. 26—35.

Griffin, Susan. *Rape: The Power of Consciousness* (New York, 1978).

Groth, Nicholas. *Men Who Rape* (New York, 1979).

Hall, Ruth E. *Ask Any Woman: A London inquiry into rape and sexual assault*, Report of the Women's Safety Survey conducted by Women Against Rape (Bristol, 1985).

Hall, Ruth E. *The Rapist who pays the rent* (Bristol, 1982).

Harper, Ross and McWhinnie Arnot. *The Glasgow Rape Case* (London, 1983).

Kemmer, Elizabeth Jane. *Rape and Rape Related Issues: an annotated bibliography* (London, 1977).

Konner, Melvin. *The Tangled Wing: biological constraints on the human spirit* (London, 1983).

London Rape Crisis Centre (ed.), *Sexual Violence: The Reality for Women,* (London, 1984).

Rich, Adrienne. *On Lies, Secrets and Silences: Selected Prose 1966—78* (New York, 1979).

Russell, Diana E. H. *The Politics of Rape* (New York, 1975).

Russell, Diana E. H. *Rape in Marriage* (New York, 1982).

Russell, Diana E. H. *Sexual Exploitation: Rape, Child Sexual Abuse and Workplace Harassment* (London, 1984).

Sanday, Peggy Reeves. *Female Power: Male Dominance: on the origin of sexual inequality* (Cambridge, 1981).

Sanday, Peggy Reeves. 'The socio-cultural context of rape: a cross-cultural study', *The Journal of Social Issues,* 37 (1981), p. 5.

Schwendinger, Julia R. and Schwendinger, Herman, *Rape and Inequality* (London, 1983).

Shorter, Edward. 'On writing the history of rape', *Signs,* 3 (1977), pp. 471—82.

Smart, Carole and Smart, Barry. 'Accounting for rape', in *Women, Sexuality and Social Control* (London, 1978).

Taylor, G. R. *Sex in History* (London, 1953).

Ward, Elizabeth. *Father, Daughter Rape* (London, 1984).

Index

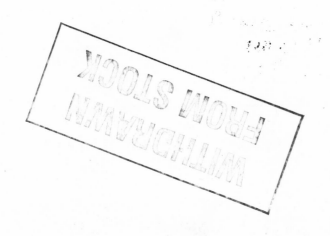